Hands-On Computer Vi
with TensorFlow 2

Leverage deep learning to create powerful image processing apps with TensorFlow 2.0 and Keras

Dr. Benjamin Planche
Eliot Andres

BIRMINGHAM - MUMBAI

Hands-On Computer Vision with TensorFlow 2

Commissioning Editor: Aaron Lazar
Acquisition Editor: Chaitanya Nair
Content Development Editor: Tiksha Sarang
Technical Editor: Riddesh Dawne
Copy Editor: Safis Editing
Project Coordinator: Prajakta Naik
Proofreader: Safis Editing
Indexer: Manju Arasan
Graphics: Jisha Chirayil
Production Coordinator: Nilesh Mohite

First published: May 2019

Production reference: 3310821

Published by Packt Publishing Ltd.
Livery Place
35 Livery Street
Birmingham
B3 2PB, UK.

ISBN 978-1-78883-064-5

www.packt.com

To Varia, for teaching my jumbled neurons what staying true to your vision means.
– Dr. Benjamin Planche

To my mother, Marie.
– Eliot Andres

Packt.com

Subscribe to our online digital library for full access to over 7,000 books and videos, as well as industry leading tools to help you plan your personal development and advance your career. For more information, please visit our website.

Why subscribe?

- Spend less time learning and more time coding with practical eBooks and Videos from over 4,000 industry professionals
- Improve your learning with Skill Plans built especially for you
- Get a free eBook or video every month
- Fully searchable for easy access to vital information
- Copy and paste, print, and bookmark content

Did you know that Packt offers eBook versions of every book published, with PDF and ePub files available? You can upgrade to the eBook version at www.packt.com and as a print book customer, you are entitled to a discount on the eBook copy. Get in touch with us at customercare@packtpub.com for more details.

At www.packt.com, you can also read a collection of free technical articles, sign up for a range of free newsletters, and receive exclusive discounts and offers on Packt books and eBooks.

Contributors

About the authors

Dr. Benjamin Planche is a passionate research scientist in computer vision and machine learning. His main research efforts focus on data scarcity problems and industrial vision systems, leading to numerous patents and publications at international conferences. He worked in various research labs around the world (including in France, Japan, Germany, and the USA).
Benjamin obtained his Ph.D. summa cum laude from the Faculty of Computer Science and Mathematics at the University of Passau, under the supervision of Prof. Dr. Harald Kosch. He also has a double master's degree from INSA-Lyon (France) and the University of Passau (Germany), with first-class honors and a multinational excellence award. He also likes sharing his knowledge and experience on various platforms or applying them to the creation of aesthetic demos.

> *I am grateful to so many people for this chapter of my life. To my friends and family who, I hope, will still recognize me after these long months spent writing. To the editors and reviewers for patiently iterating over this book. To my co-author, for his technical prowess and inspiring lifestyle. And to our readers, for joining the adventure...*

Eliot Andres is a freelance deep learning and computer vision engineer. He has more than 3 years' experience in the field, applying his skills to a variety of industries, such as banking, health, social media, and video streaming. Eliot has a double master's degree from École des Ponts and Télécom, Paris.

His focus is industrialization: delivering value by applying new technologies to business problems. Eliot keeps his knowledge up to date by publishing articles on his blog and by building prototypes using the latest technologies.

> *I would like to thank my friends and family for their unconditional support, especially Emilien Chauvet, who took the time to review all of the chapters. My thanks to the Packt team for their work. I am very grateful to my co-author for his tireless proofreading and for providing incredible advice on style and content.*

About the reviewers

Vijayachandran Mariappan has around 20 years' experience in machine learning/computer vision related to video/audio/multimedia technologies on embedded, mobile, and cloud platforms. He is currently working as a computer vision architect at Cyient, leading various machine learning/deep learning projects, from algorithm development to realization on embedded platforms. He is one of the top 10 experts when it comes to addressing questions related to the deep learning framework TensorFlow on StackOverflow. He is also the co-inventor (main patent holder) of Sling media's Emmy award-winning Slingbox Personal Broadcaster and a CES Best of Innovation winner. He has authored many papers and patents with a Google citation score of 240: h-index: 6.

Narotam Singh has been actively involved with various technical programs and the training of GOI officers in the field of information technology and communication. He did his masters in the field of electronics, having graduated with a degree in physics (Hons). He also holds a diploma in computer engineering and a postgraduate diploma in computer application. Presently, he works in a freelance capacity. He has many research publications to his name and is also a technical reviewer of various books. His present research interests involve AI, machine learning, deep learning, robotics, and spirituality.

Dave Winters is a business and technical consultant. His focus is in the areas of AI/machine learning, analytics, data quality, NoSQL, real-time IoT, and graph databases. Dave is director and chief architect of technology for Cognizant. He runs an innovation group for application modernization engineering BU. Before Cognizant, Dave was partner in a California VC, where his roles included VP professional services, database architect, VP pre-sales, product manager, data warehouse architect, and performance expert. He is retired from the USAF. He was an instructor pilot at USAF Test Pilot School. He has flown many current US and foreign military aircraft. He holds a BS in computer science from Troy, and is also a graduate of USAF SOS management school.

Packt is searching for authors like you

If you're interested in becoming an author for Packt, please visit `authors.packtpub.com` and apply today. We have worked with thousands of developers and tech professionals, just like you, to help them share their insight with the global tech community. You can make a general application, apply for a specific hot topic that we are recruiting an author for, or submit your own idea.

Table of Contents

Preface 1

Section 1: TensorFlow 2 and Deep Learning Applied to Computer Vision

Chapter 1: Computer Vision and Neural Networks 11
Technical requirements 11
Computer vision in the wild 12
Introducing computer vision 12
Main tasks and their applications 13
Content recognition 13
Object classification 13
Object identification 14
Object detection and localization 15
Object and instance segmentation 16
Pose estimation 17
Video analysis 17
Instance tracking 18
Action recognition 18
Motion estimation 19
Content-aware image edition 19
Scene reconstruction 20
A brief history of computer vision 20
First steps to initial successes 20
Underestimating the perception task 21
Hand-crafting local features 21
Adding some machine learning on top 23
Rise of deep learning 24
Early attempts and failures 24
Rise and fall of the perceptron 25
Too heavy to scale 25
Reasons for the comeback 25
The internet – the new El Dorado of data science 26
More power than ever 26
Deep learning or the rebranding of artificial neural networks 27
What makes learning deep? 27
Deep learning era 28
Getting started with neural networks 29
Building a neural network 29
Imitating neurons 29
Biological inspiration 29
Mathematical model 30
Implementation 32
Layering neurons together 33

Mathematical model 34
Implementation 35
Applying our network to classification 36
Setting up the task 37
Implementing the network 38
Training a neural network 40
Learning strategies 40
Supervised learning 40
Unsupervised learning 41
Reinforcement learning 41
Teaching time 42
Evaluating the loss 42
Backpropagating the loss 43
Teaching our network to classify 46
Training considerations – underfitting and overfitting 49
Summary 50
Questions 50
Further reading 50
Chapter 2: TensorFlow Basics and Training a Model 51
Technical requirements 51
Getting started with TensorFlow 2 and Keras 52
Introducing TensorFlow 52
TensorFlow's main architecture 52
Introducing Keras 53
A simple computer vision model using Keras 54
Preparing the data 54
Building the model 55
Training the model 56
Model performance 57
TensorFlow 2 and Keras in detail 58
Core concepts 58
Introducing tensors 58
TensorFlow graphs 59
Comparing lazy execution to eager execution 60
Creating graphs in TensorFlow 2 61
Introducing TensorFlow AutoGraph and tf.function 62
Backpropagating errors using the gradient tape 63
Keras models and layers 64
Sequential and functional APIs 65
Callbacks 65
Advanced concepts 66
How tf.function works 66
Variables in TensorFlow 2 67
Distribution strategies 68
Using the Estimator API 69
Available pre-made Estimators 69
Training a custom Estimator 70
The TensorFlow ecosystem 70
TensorBoard 71

TensorFlow Addons and TensorFlow Extended 72
TensorFlow Lite and TensorFlow.js 73
Where to run your model 73
On a local machine 74
On a remote machine 74
On Google Cloud 75
Summary 75
Questions 76
Chapter 3: Modern Neural Networks 77
Technical requirements 77
Discovering convolutional neural networks 77
Neural networks for multidimensional data 78
Problems with fully connected networks 78
An explosive number of parameters 78
A lack of spatial reasoning 78
Introducing CNNs 79
CNN operations 80
Convolutional layers 80
Concept 80
Properties 82
Hyperparameters 83
TensorFlow/Keras methods 85
Pooling layers 89
Concept and hyperparameters 89
TensorFlow/Keras methods 90
Fully connected layers 92
Usage in CNNs 92
TensorFlow/Keras methods 93
Effective receptive field 93
Definitions 94
Formula 95
CNNs with TensorFlow 95
Implementing our first CNN 96
LeNet-5 architecture 96
TensorFlow and Keras implementations 97
Application to MNIST 99
Refining the training process 99
Modern network optimizers 100
Gradient descent challenges 100
Training velocity and trade-off 100
Suboptimal local minima 101
A single hyperparameter for heterogeneous parameters 102
Advanced optimizers 102
Momentum algorithms 102
The Ada family 104
Regularization methods 105
Early stopping 106
L1 and L2 regularization 106
Principles 106

TensorFlow and Keras implementations 107
Dropout 110
Definition 110
TensorFlow and Keras methods 111
Batch normalization 111
Definition 111
TensorFlow and Keras methods 112
Summary 112
Questions 113
Further reading 113

Section 2: State-of-the-Art Solutions for Classic Recognition Problems

Chapter 4: Influential Classification Tools 117
Technical requirements 117
Understanding advanced CNN architectures 118
VGG – a standard CNN architecture 118
Overview of the VGG architecture 118
Motivation 118
Architecture 119
Contributions – standardizing CNN architectures 120
Replacing large convolutions with multiple smaller ones 120
Increasing the depth of the feature maps 121
Augmenting data with scale jittering 121
Replacing fully connected layers with convolutions 122
Implementations in TensorFlow and Keras 123
The TensorFlow model 123
The Keras model 123
GoogLeNet and the inception module 124
Overview of the GoogLeNet architecture 124
Motivation 124
Architecture 125
Contributions – popularizing larger blocks and bottlenecks 127
Capturing various details with inception modules 127
Using 1 x 1 convolutions as bottlenecks 128
Pooling instead of fully connecting 129
Fighting vanishing gradient with intermediary losses 129
Implementations in TensorFlow and Keras 130
Inception module with the Keras Functional API 130
TensorFlow model and TensorFlow Hub 132
The Keras model 133
ResNet – the residual network 134
Overview of the ResNet architecture 135
Motivation 135
Architecture 136
Contributions – forwarding the information more deeply 137
Estimating a residual function instead of a mapping 137
Going ultra-deep 138
Implementations in TensorFlow and Keras 138
Residual blocks with the Keras Functional API 139

The TensorFlow model and TensorFlow Hub 139
The Keras model 140
Leveraging transfer learning 140
Overview 141
Definition 141
Human inspiration 141
Motivation 142
Transferring CNN knowledge 144
Use cases 144
Similar tasks with limited training data 145
Similar tasks with abundant training data 145
Dissimilar tasks with abundant training data 146
Dissimilar tasks with limited training data 146
Transfer learning with TensorFlow and Keras 146
Model surgery 147
Removing layers 147
Grafting layers 148
Selective training 148
Restoring pretrained parameters 148
Freezing layers 149
Summary 149
Questions 150
Further reading 150

Chapter 5: Object Detection Models 151
Technical requirements 151
Introducing object detection 151
Background 152
Applications 152
Brief history 152
Evaluating the performance of a model 153
Precision and recall 154
Precision-recall curve 154
Average precision and mean average precision 156
Average precision threshold 156
A fast object detection algorithm – YOLO 157
Introducing YOLO 158
Strengths and limitations of YOLO 158
YOLO's main concepts 158
Inferring with YOLO 160
The YOLO backbone 160
YOLO's layers output 161
Introducing anchor boxes 162
How YOLO refines anchor boxes 164
Post-processing the boxes 165
NMS 167
YOLO inference summarized 168
Training YOLO 169
How the YOLO backbone is trained 170
YOLO loss 170

Bounding box loss 171
Object confidence loss 172
Classification loss 173
Full YOLO loss 173
Training techniques 173
Faster R-CNN – a powerful object detection model 174
Faster R-CNN's general architecture 175
Stage 1 – Region proposals 175
Stage 2 – Classification 177
Faster R-CNN architecture 177
RoI pooling 178
Training Faster R-CNN 180
Training the RPN 180
The RPN loss 181
Fast R-CNN loss 182
Training regimen 182
TensorFlow Object Detection API 183
Using a pretrained model 183
Training on a custom dataset 183
Summary 184
Questions 184
Further reading 184
Chapter 6: Enhancing and Segmenting Images 185
Technical requirements 185
Transforming images with encoders-decoders 186
Introduction to encoders-decoders 186
Encoding and decoding 186
Auto-encoding 188
Purpose 189
Basic example – image denoising 191
Simplistic fully connected AE 191
Application to image denoising 191
Convolutional encoders-decoders 192
Unpooling, transposing, and dilating 192
Transposed convolution (deconvolution) 192
Unpooling 195
Upsampling and resizing 196
Dilated/atrous convolution 197
Example architectures – FCN and U-Net 199
Fully convolutional networks 199
U-Net 201
Intermediary example – image super-resolution 202
FCN implementation 202
Application to upscaling images 203
Understanding semantic segmentation 203
Object segmentation with encoders-decoders 204
Overview 204
Decoding as label maps 204
Training with segmentation losses and metrics 206

Post-processing with conditional random fields 208
Advanced example – image segmentation for self-driving cars 209
Task presentation 209
Exemplary solution 210
The more difficult case of instance segmentation 210
From object segmentation to instance segmentation 210
Respecting boundaries 210
Post-processing into instance masks 211
From object detection to instance segmentation – Mask R-CNN 212
Applying semantic segmentation to bounding boxes 212
Building an instance segmentation model with Faster-RCNN 213
Summary 214
Questions 215
Further reading 215

Section 3: Advanced Concepts and New Frontiers of Computer Vision

Chapter 7: Training on Complex and Scarce Datasets 219
Technical requirements 220
Efficient data serving 220
Introducing the TensorFlow Data API 220
Intuition behind the TensorFlow Data API 220
Feeding fast and data-hungry models 220
Inspiration from lazy structures 221
Structure of TensorFlow data pipelines 221
Extract, Transform, Load 222
API interface 223
Setting up input pipelines 224
Extracting (from tensors, text files, TFRecord files, and more) 224
From NumPy and TensorFlow data 224
From files 225
From other inputs (generator, SQL database, range, and others) 225
Transforming the samples (parsing, augmenting, and more) 226
Parsing images and labels 226
Parsing TFRecord files 227
Editing samples 228
Transforming the datasets (shuffling, zipping, parallelizing, and more) 228
Structuring datasets 228
Merging datasets 230
Loading 231
Optimizing and monitoring input pipelines 231
Following best practices for optimization 231
Parallelizing and prefetching 231
Fusing operations 233
Passing options to ensure global properties 234
Monitoring and reusing datasets 235
Aggregating performance statistics 235
Caching and reusing datasets 236
How to deal with data scarcity 237
Augmenting datasets 237

Overview 237
Why augment datasets? 238
Considerations 239
Augmenting images with TensorFlow 241
TensorFlow Image module 241
Example – augmenting images for our autonomous driving application 242
Rendering synthetic datasets 243
Overview 243
Rise of 3D databases 243
Benefits of synthetic data 244
Generating synthetic images from 3D models 245
Rendering from 3D models 246
Post-processing synthetic images 247
Problem – realism gap 248
Leveraging domain adaptation and generative models (VAEs and GANs) 249
Training models to be robust to domain changes 249
Supervised domain adaptation 250
Unsupervised domain adaptation 250
Domain randomization 253
Generating larger or more realistic datasets with VAEs and GANs 254
Discriminative versus generative models 254
VAEs 255
GANs 258
Augmenting datasets with conditional GANs 260
Summary 262
Questions 262
Further reading 262

Chapter 8: Video and Recurrent Neural Networks 263
Technical requirements 263
Introducing RNNs 264
Basic formalism 264
General understanding of RNNs 266
Learning RNN weights 267
Backpropagation through time 268
Truncated backpropagation 269
Long short-term memory cells 270
LSTM general principles 270
LSTM inner workings 271
Classifying videos 273
Applying computer vision to video 273
Classifying videos with an LSTM 274
Extracting features from videos 276
Training the LSTM 281
Defining the model 281
Loading the data 282
Training the model 283
Summary 283
Questions 283
Further reading 284

Chapter 9: Optimizing Models and Deploying on Mobile Devices 285
Technical requirements 285
Optimizing computational and disk footprints 286
Measuring inference speed 286
Measuring latency 287
Using tracing tools to understand computational performance 287
Improving model inference speed 289
Optimizing for hardware 289
Optimizing on CPUs 290
Optimizing on GPUs 290
Optimizing on specialized hardware 290
Optimizing input 291
Optimizing post-processing 291
When the model is still too slow 292
Interpolating and tracking 292
Model distillation 292
Reducing model size 293
Quantization 294
Channel pruning and weight sparsification 294
On-device machine learning 294
Considerations of on-device machine learning 295
Benefits of on-device ML 296
Latency 296
Privacy 296
Cost 296
Limitations of on-device ML 297
Practical on-device computer vision 297
On-device computer vision particularities 297
Generating a SavedModel 298
Generating a frozen graph 298
Importance of preprocessing 299
Example app – recognizing facial expressions 300
Introducing MobileNet 301
Deploying models on-device 301
Running on iOS devices using Core ML 302
Converting from TensorFlow or Keras 302
Loading the model 304
Using the model 304
Running on Android using TensorFlow Lite 305
Converting the model from TensorFlow or Keras 306
Loading the model 306
Using the model 307
Running in the browser using TensorFlow.js 309
Converting the model to the TensorFlow.js format 309
Using the model 310
Running on other devices 311
Summary 312
Questions 312
Migrating from TensorFlow 1 to TensorFlow 2 313

Assessments 329

Other Books You May Enjoy 339

Index 343

Preface

As a result of leveraging deep learning methods such as **convolutional neural networks** (**CNNs**), computer vision is attaining new heights in fields including health, the automotive sector, social media, and robotics. Whether to automate complex tasks, to guide experts in their work, or to help artists in their creative process, more and more companies are integrating computer vision solutions.

In this book, we will explore TensorFlow 2, the brand new version of Google's open source framework for machine learning. Covering its key features, as well as state-of-the-art solutions, we will demonstrate how to efficiently build, train, and deploy CNNs for a variety of real-life tasks.

Who this book is for

This book is intended for anyone with some background in Python programming and image processing (such as knowing how to read and write image files, and how to edit their pixel values). With its gradual learning curve, this book targets not only deep learning novices but also experts who are curious about the new features of TensorFlow 2.

While some theoretical explanations require knowledge of algebra and calculus, concrete examples are provided for learners focused on practical applications. Step by step, you will tackle real-life tasks, such as visual recognition for self-driving cars and smartphone applications.

What this book covers

`Chapter 1`, *Computer Vision and Neural Networks*, introduces you to computer vision and deep learning, providing some theoretical background and teaching you how to implement and train a neural network for visual recognition from scratch.

`Chapter 2`, *TensorFlow Basics and Training a Model*, goes through TensorFlow 2 concepts related to computer vision, as well as some more advanced notions. It introduces Keras—now a submodule of TensorFlow—and describes the training of a simple recognition method implemented with these frameworks.

`Chapter 3`, *Modern Neural Networks*, presents CNNs and explains how they have revolutionized computer vision. This chapter also introduces regularization tools and modern optimization algorithms that can be used to train more robust recognition systems.

`Chapter 4`, *Influential Classification Tools*, provides theoretical details and practical code to expertly apply state-of-the-art solutions—such as Inception and ResNet—to the classification of images. This chapter also explains what makes transfer learning a key concept in machine learning, and how it can be performed with TensorFlow 2.

`Chapter 5`, *Object Detection Models*, covers the architecture of two methods to detect specific objects in images—You Only Look Once, known for its speed, and Faster R-CNN, known for its accuracy.

`Chapter 6`, *Enhancing and Segmenting Images*, introduces autoencoders and how networks such as U-Net and FCN can be applied to image denoising, semantic segmentation, and more.

`Chapter 7`, *Training on Complex and Scarce Datasets*, focuses on solutions to efficiently collect and preprocess datasets for your deep learning applications. TensorFlow tools that build optimized data pipelines are presented, as well as various solutions to compensate for data scarcity (image rendering, domain adaptation, and generative networks such as VAEs and GANs).

`Chapter 8`, *Video and Recurrent Neural Networks*, covers recurrent neural networks, presenting the more advanced version known as the long short-term memory architecture. It provides practical code to apply LSTMs to action recognition in video.

`Chapter 9`, *Optimizing Models and Deploying on Mobile Devices*, details model optimization in terms of speed, disk space, and computational performance. It goes through the deployment of TensorFlow solutions on mobile devices and in the browser, using a practical example.

`Appendix`, *Migrating from TensorFlow 1 to TensorFlow 2*, provides some information about TensorFlow 1, highlighting key changes introduced in TensorFlow 2. A guide to migrate older projects to the latest version is also included. Finally, per-chapter references are listed for those who want to dive deeper.

To get the most out of this book

The following section contains some information and advice to facilitate the reading of this book and to help readers benefit from its supplementary materials.

Download and run the example code files

Practice makes perfect. Therefore, this book not only provides in-depth explanations of TensorFlow 2 and state-of-the-art computer-vision methods, but it also comes with a number of practical examples and complete implementations for each chapter.

Download the code files

You can download the example code files for this book from your account at `www.packt.com`. If you purchased this book elsewhere, you can visit `www.packtpub.com/support` and register to have the files emailed directly to you.

You can download the code files by following these steps:

1. Log in or register at `www.packt.com`.
2. Select the **Support** tab.
3. Click on **Code Downloads**.
4. Enter the name of the book in the **Search** box and follow the onscreen instructions.

Once the file is downloaded, please make sure that you unzip or extract the folder using the latest version of:

- WinRAR/7-Zip for Windows
- Zipeg/iZip/UnRarX for Mac
- 7-Zip/PeaZip for Linux

The code bundle for the book is also hosted on GitHub at `https://github.com/PacktPublishing/Hands-On-Computer-Vision-with-TensorFlow-2`. In case there's an update to the code, it will be updated on the existing GitHub repository.

We also have other code bundles from our rich catalog of books and videos available at `https://github.com/PacktPublishing`. Check them out!

Study and run the experiments

Jupyter Notebook (`https://jupyter.org`) is an open source web application for creating and sharing Python scripts, along with textual information, visual results, equations, and more. We will call *Jupyter notebooks* the documents provided with the book, containing detailed code, expected results, and supplementary explanations. Each Jupyter notebook is dedicated to a concrete computer vision task. For example, one notebook explains how to train a CNN to detect animals in images, while another details all the steps to build a recognition system for self-driving cars, and so on.

As we will see in this section, these documents can either be studied directly, or they can be used as code recipes to run and reproduce the experiments presented in the book.

Study the Jupyter notebooks online

If you simply want to go through the code and results provided, you can directly access them online in the book's *GitHub* repository. Indeed, GitHub is able to render Jupyter notebooks and to display them as static web pages.

However, the GitHub viewer ignores some style formatting and interactive content. For the best online viewing experience, we recommend using instead *Jupyter nbviewer* (`https://nbviewer.jupyter.org`), an official web platform you can use to read Jupyter notebooks uploaded online. This website can be queried to render notebooks stored in GitHub repositories. Therefore, the Jupyter notebooks provided can also be read at the following address: `https://nbviewer.jupyter.org/github/PacktPublishing/Hands-On-Computer-Vision-with-TensorFlow-2`.

Run the Jupyter notebooks on your machine

To read or run these documents on your machine, you should first install Jupyter Notebook. For those who already use *Anaconda* (`https://www.anaconda.com`) to manage and deploy their Python environments (as we will recommend in this book), Jupyter Notebook should be directly available (as it is installed with Anaconda). For those using other Python distributions and those not familiar with Jupyter Notebook, we recommend having a look at the documentation, which provides installation instructions and tutorials (`https://jupyter.org/documentation`).

Once Jupyter Notebook is installed on your machine, navigate to the directory containing the book's code files, open a terminal, and execute the following command:

```
$ jupyter notebook
```

The web interface should open in your default browser. From there, you should be able to navigate the directory and open the Jupyter notebooks provided, either to read, execute, or edit them.

Some documents contain advanced experiments that can be extremely compute-intensive (such as the training of recognition algorithms over large datasets). Without the proper acceleration hardware (that is, without compatible NVIDIA GPUs, as explained in `Chapter 2`, *TensorFlow Basics and Training a Model*), these scripts can take hours or even days (even with compatible GPUs, the most advanced examples can take quite some time).

Run the Jupyter notebooks in Google Colab

For those who wish to run the Jupyter notebooks themselves—or play with new experiments—but do not have access to a powerful enough machine, we recommend using **Google Colab**, also named **Colaboratory** (`https://colab.research.google.com`). It is a cloud-based Jupyter environment, provided by Google, for people to run compute-intensive scripts on powerful machines. You will find more details regarding this service in the GitHub repository.

Download the color images

We also provide a PDF file that has color images of the screenshots/diagrams used in this book. You can download it here: `https://www.packtpub.com/sites/default/files/downloads/9781788830645_ColorImages.pdf`.

Conventions used

There are a number of text conventions used throughout this book.

`CodeInText`: Indicates code words in text, folder names, filenames, file extensions, pathnames, dummy URLs, and user input. Here is an example: "The `.fit()` method of the `Model` object starts the training procedure."

A block of code is set as follows:

```
import tensorflow as tf

x1 = tf.constant([[0, 1], [2, 3]])
x2 = tf.constant(10)
x = x1 * x2
```

When we wish to draw your attention to a particular part of a code block, the relevant lines or items are set in bold:

```
neural_network = tf.keras.Sequential(
    [tf.keras.layers.Dense(64),
     tf.keras.layers.Dense(10, activation="softmax")])
```

Any command-line input or output is written as follows:

```
$ tensorboard --logdir ./logs
```

Bold: Indicates a new term, an important word, or words that you see on screen. For example, words in menus or dialog boxes appear in the text like this. Here is an example: "You can observe the performance of your solution on the **Scalars** page of TensorBoard."

Warnings or important notes appear like this.

Tips and tricks appear like this.

Get in touch

Feedback from our readers is always welcome.

General feedback: If you have questions about any aspect of this book, mention the book title in the subject of your message and email us at `customercare@packtpub.com`.

Errata: Although we have taken every care to ensure the accuracy of our content, mistakes do happen. If you have found a mistake in this book, we would be grateful if you would report this to us. Please visit `www.packtpub.com/support/errata`, selecting your book, clicking on the Errata Submission Form link, and entering the details.

Piracy: If you come across any illegal copies of our works in any form on the Internet, we would be grateful if you would provide us with the location address or website name. Please contact us at `copyright@packt.com` with a link to the material.

If you are interested in becoming an author: If there is a topic that you have expertise in, and you are interested in either writing or contributing to a book, please visit `authors.packtpub.com`.

Reviews

Please leave a review. Once you have read and used this book, why not leave a review on the site that you purchased it from? Potential readers can then see and use your unbiased opinion to make purchase decisions, we at Packt can understand what you think about our products, and our authors can see your feedback on their book. Thank you!

For more information about Packt, please visit `packt.com`.

Section 1: TensorFlow 2 and Deep Learning Applied to Computer Vision

This section covers the fundamentals of computer vision and deep learning, with the help of concrete TensorFlow examples. Starting with a presentation of these technical domains, the first chapter will then walk you through the inner workings of neural networks. This section continues with an introduction to the instrumental features of TensorFlow 2 and Keras, and their key concepts and ecosystems. It ends with a description of machine learning techniques adopted by computer vision experts.

The following chapters will be covered in this section:

- `Chapter 1`, *Computer Vision and Neural Networks*
- `Chapter 2`, *TensorFlow Basics and Training a Model*
- `Chapter 3`, *Modern Neural Networks*

1
Computer Vision and Neural Networks

In recent years, computer vision has grown into a key domain for innovation, with more and more applications reshaping businesses and lifestyles. We will start this book with a brief presentation of this field and its history so that we can get some background information. We will then introduce artificial neural networks and explain how they have revolutionized computer vision. Since we believe in learning through practice, by the end of this first chapter, we will even have implemented our own network from scratch!

The following topics will be covered in this chapter:

- Computer vision and why it is a fascinating contemporary domain
- How we got there—from local hand-crafted descriptors to deep neural networks
- Neural networks, what they actually are, and how to implement our own for a basic recognition task

Technical requirements

Throughout this book, we will be using Python 3.5 (or higher). As a general-purpose programming language, Python has become the main tool for data scientists thanks to its useful built-in features and renowned libraries.

For this introductory chapter, we will only use two cornerstone libraries—NumPy and Matplotlib. They can be found at and installed from `www.numpy.org` and `matplotlib.org`. However, we recommend using Anaconda (`www.anaconda.com`), a free Python distribution that makes package management and deployment easy.

Complete installation instructions—as well as all the code presented alongside this chapter—can be found in the GitHub repository at `github.com/PacktPublishing/Hands-On-Computer-Vision-with-TensorFlow2/tree/master/Chapter01`.

We assume that our readers already have some knowledge of Python and a basic understanding of image representation (pixels, channels, and so on) and matrix manipulation (shapes, products, and so on).

Computer vision in the wild

Computer vision is everywhere nowadays, to the point that its definition can drastically vary from one expert to another. In this introductory section, we will paint a global picture of computer vision, highlighting its domains of application and the challenges it faces.

Introducing computer vision

Computer vision can be hard to define because it sits at the junction of several research and development fields, such as *computer science* (algorithms, data processing, and graphics), *physics* (optics and sensors), *mathematics* (calculus and information theory), and *biology* (visual stimuli and neural processing). At its core, computer vision can be summarized as the *automated extraction of information from digital images*.

Our brain works wonders when it comes to vision. Our ability to decipher the visual stimuli our eyes constantly capture, to instantly tell one object from another, and to recognize the face of someone we have met only once, is just incredible. For computers, images are just blobs of pixels, matrices of red-green-blue values with no further meaning.

The goal of computer vision is to teach computers *how to make sense of these pixels* the way humans (and other creatures) do, or even better. Indeed, computer vision has come a long way and, since the rise of deep learning, it has started achieving *super human* performance in some tasks, such as face verification and handwritten text recognition.

With a hyper active research community fueled by the biggest IT companies, and the ever-increasing availability of data and visual sensors, more and more ambitious problems are being tackled: vision-based navigation for autonomous driving, content-based image and video retrieval, and automated annotation and enhancement, among others. It is truly an exciting time for experts and newcomers alike.

Main tasks and their applications

New computer vision-based products are appearing every day (for instance, control systems for industries, interactive smartphone apps, and surveillance systems) that cover a wide range of tasks. In this section, we will go through the main ones, detailing their applications in relation to real-life problems.

Content recognition

A central goal in computer vision is to *make sense* of images, that is, to extract meaningful, semantic information from pixels (such as the objects present in images, their location, and their number). This generic problem can be divided into several sub-domains. Here is a non-exhaustive list.

Object classification

Object classification (or **image classification**) is the task of assigning proper labels (or classes) to images among a predefined set and is illustrated in the following diagram:

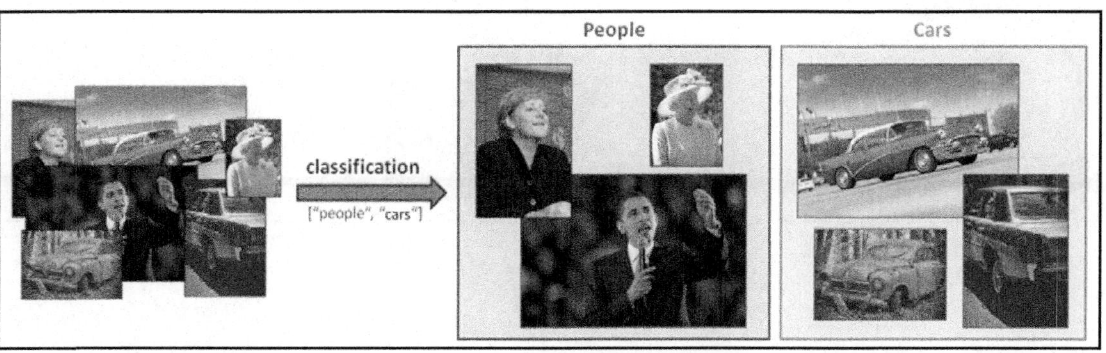

Figure 1.1: Example of a classifier for the labels of people and cars applied to an image set

Object classification became famous for being the first success story of deep convolutional neural networks being applied to computer vision back in 2012 (this will be presented later in this chapter). Progress in this domain has been so fast since then that super human performance is now achieved in various use cases (a well-known example is the classification of dog breeds; deep learning methods have become extremely efficient at spotting the discriminative features of man's best friend).

Common applications are text digitization (using character recognition) and the automatic annotation of image databases.

In `Chapter 4`, *Influential Classification Tools*, we will present advanced classification methods and their impact on computer vision in general.

Object identification

While *object classification* methods assign labels from a predefined set, *object identification* (or *instance classification*) methods learn to *recognize specific instances of a class.*

For example, an *object classification* tool could be configured to return images containing faces, while an *identification* method would focus on the face's features to identify the person and recognize them in other images (*identifying* each face in all of the images, as shown in the following diagram):

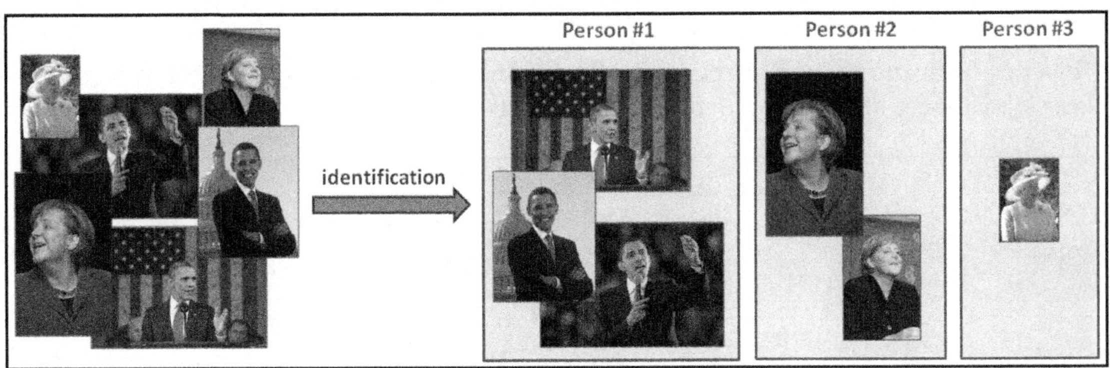

Figure 1.2: Example of an identifier applied to portraits

Therefore, object identification can be seen as a procedure to *cluster* a dataset, often applying some dataset analysis concepts (which will be presented in `Chapter 6`, *Enhancing and Segmenting Images*).

Object detection and localization

Another task is the *detection of specific elements in an image*. It is commonly applied to face detection for surveillance applications or even advanced camera apps, the detection of cancerous cells in medicine, the detection of damaged components in industrial plants, and so on.

Detection is often a preliminary step before further computations, providing smaller patches of the image to be analyzed separately (for instance, cropping someone's face for facial recognition, or providing a bounding box around an object to evaluate its pose for augmented reality applications), as shown in the following diagram:

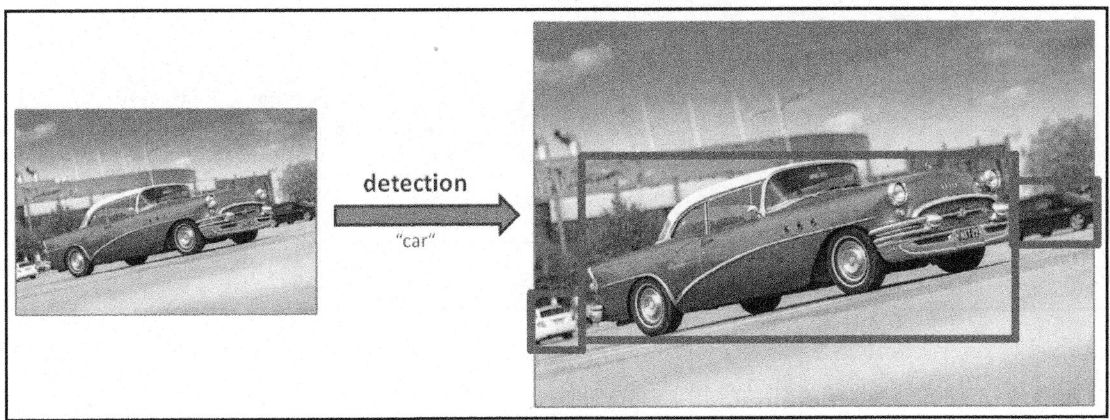

Figure 1.3: Example of a car detector, returning bounding boxes for the candidates

State-of-the-art solutions will be detailed in `Chapter 5`, *Object Detection Models*.

Object and instance segmentation

Segmentation can be seen as a more advanced type of detection. Instead of simply providing bounding boxes for the recognized elements, segmentation methods *return masks labeling all the pixels* belonging to a specific class or to a specific instance of a class (refer to the following *Figure 1.4*). This makes the task much more complex, and actually one of the few in computer vision where deep neural networks are still far from human performance (our brain is indeed remarkably efficient at drawing the precise boundaries/contours of visual elements). Object segmentation and instance segmentation are illustrated in the following diagram:

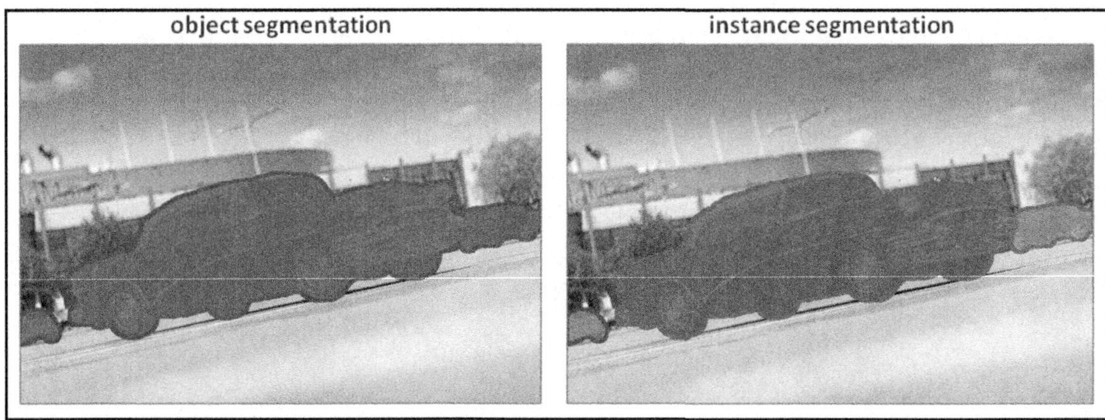

Figure 1.4: Comparing the results of object segmentation methods and instance segmentation methods for cars

In *Figure 1.4,* while the object segmentation algorithm returns a single mask for all pixels belonging to the *car* class, the instance segmentation one returns a different mask for each *car* instance that it recognized. This is a key task for robots and smart cars in order to understand their surroundings (for example, to identify all the elements in front of a vehicle), but it is also used in medical imagery. Precisely segmenting the different tissues in medical scans can enable faster diagnosis and easier visualization (such as coloring each organ differently or removing clutter from the view). This will be demonstrated in `Chapter 6`, *Enhancing and Segmenting Images,* with concrete experiments for autonomous driving applications.

Pose estimation

Pose estimation can have different meanings depending on the targeted tasks. For rigid objects, it usually means *the estimation of the objects' positions and orientations* relative to the camera in the 3D space. This is especially useful for robots so that they can interact with their environment (object picking, collision avoidance, and so on). It is also often used in augmented reality to overlay 3D information on top of objects.

For non-rigid elements, pose estimation can also mean *the estimation of the positions of their sub-parts relative to each other*. More concretely, when considering humans as non-rigid targets, typical applications are the recognition of human poses (standing, sitting, running, and so on) or understanding sign language. These different cases are illustrated in the following diagram:

Figure 1.5: Examples of rigid and non-rigid pose estimation

In both cases—that is, for whole or partial elements—the algorithms are tasked with evaluating their actual position and orientation relative to the camera in the 3D world, based on their 2D representation in an image.

Video analysis

Computer vision not only applies to single images, but also to videos. If video streams are sometimes analyzed frame by frame, some tasks require that you consider an image sequence as a whole in order to take temporal consistency into account (this will be one of the topics of `Chapter 8`, *Video and Recurrent Neural Networks*).

Instance tracking

Some tasks relating video streams could naively be accomplished by studying each frame separately (memory less), but more efficient methods either take into account differences from image to image to guide the process to new frames or take complete image sequences as input for their predictions. *Tracking*, that is, *localizing specific elements in a video stream*, is a good example of such a task.

Tracking could be done frame by frame by applying detection and identification methods to each frame. However, it is much more efficient to use previous results to model the motion of the instances in order to partially predict their locations in future frames. **Motion continuity** is, therefore, a key predicate here, though it does not always hold (such as for fast-moving objects).

Action recognition

On the other hand, **action recognition** belongs to the list of tasks that can only be run with a sequence of images. Similar to how we cannot understand a sentence when we are given the words separately and unordered, we cannot recognize an action without studying a continuous sequence of images (refer to *Figure 1.6*).

Recognizing an action means recognizing a particular motion among a predefined set (for instance, for human actions—dancing, swimming, drawing a square, or drawing a circle). Applications range from surveillance (such as the detection of abnormal or suspicious behavior) to human-machine interactions (such as for gesture-controlled devices):

Figure 1.6: Is Barack Obama in the middle of waving, pointing at someone, swatting a mosquito, or something else? Only the complete sequence of frames could help to label this action

Since object recognition can be split into object classification, detection, segmentation, and so on, so can action recognition (action classification, detection, and so on).

Motion estimation

Instead of trying to recognize moving elements, some methods focus on *estimating the actual velocity/trajectory* that is captured in videos. It is also common to evaluate the motion of the camera itself relative to the represented scene (*egomotion*). This is particularly useful in the entertainment industry, for example, to capture motion in order to apply visual effects or to overlay 3D information in TV streams such as sports broadcasting.

Content-aware image edition

Besides the analysis of their content, computer vision methods can also be applied to *improve the images themselves*. More and more, basic image processing tools (such as low-pass filters for image denoising) are being replaced by *smarter* methods that are able to use prior knowledge of the image content to improve its visual quality. For instance, if a method learns what a bird typically looks like, it can apply this knowledge in order to replace noisy pixels with coherent ones in bird pictures. This concept applies to any type of image restoration, whether it be denoising, deblurring, or resolution enhancing (*super-resolution*, as illustrated in the following diagram):

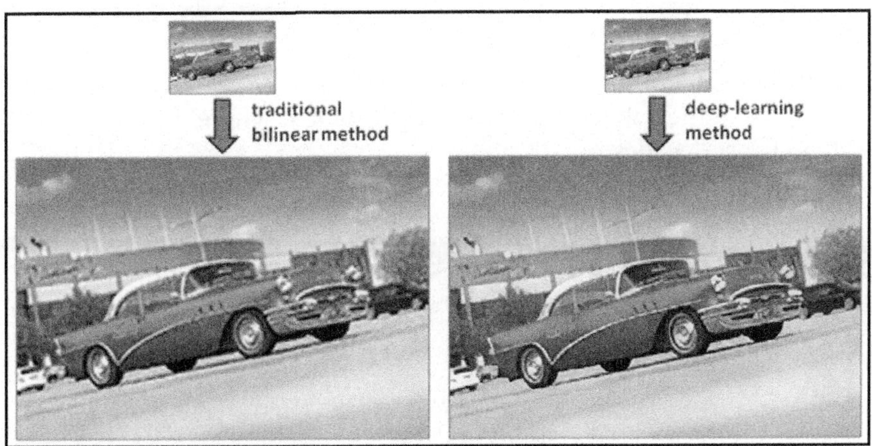

Figure 1.7: Comparison of traditional and deep learning methods for image super-resolution. Notice how the details are sharper in the second image

Content-aware algorithms are also used in some photography or art applications, such as the *smart portrait* or *beauty* modes for smartphones, which aim to enhance some of the models' features, or the *smart removing/editing* tools, which get rid of unwanted elements and replace them with a coherent background.

In `Chapter 6`, *Enhancing and Segmenting Images*, and in `Chapter 7`, *Training on Complex and Scarce Datasets*, we will demonstrate how such *generative* methods can be built and served.

Scene reconstruction

Finally, though we won't tackle it in this book, *scene reconstruction* is the task of *recovering the 3D geometry of a scene*, given one or more images. A simple example, based on human vision, is stereo matching. This is the process of finding correspondences between two images of a scene from different viewpoints in order to derive the distance of each visualized element. More advanced methods take several images and match their content together in order to obtain a 3D model of the target scene. This can be applied to the 3D scanning of objects, people, buildings, and so on.

A brief history of computer vision

> *"Study the past if you would define the future."*
>
> – *Confucius*

In order to better understand the current stand of the heart and current challenges of computer vision, we suggest that we quickly have a look at where it came from and how it has evolved in the past decades.

First steps to initial successes

Scientists have long dreamed of developing artificial intelligence, including *visual intelligence*. The first advances in computer vision were driven by this idea.

Underestimating the perception task

Computer vision as a domain started as early as the 60s, among the **Artificial Intelligence** (**AI**) research community. Still heavily influenced by the *symbolist* philosophy, which considered playing chess and other purely intellectual activities the epitome of human intelligence, these researchers underestimated the complexity of *lower animal functions* such as **perception**. How these researchers believed they could reproduce human perception through a single summer project in 1966 is a famous anecdote in the computer vision community.

Marvin Minsky was one of the first to outline an approach toward building AI systems based on perception (in *Steps toward artificial intelligence*, Proceedings of the IRE, 1961). He argued that with the use of lower functions such as pattern recognition, learning, planning, and induction, it could be possible to build machines capable of solving a broad variety of problems. However, this theory was only properly explored from the 80s onward. In *Locomotion, Vision, and Intelligence* in 1984, Hans Moravec noted that our nervous system, through the process of evolution, has developed to tackle perceptual tasks (more than 30% of our brain is dedicated to vision!).

As he noted, even if computers are pretty good at arithmetic, they cannot compete with our perceptual abilities. In this sense, programming a computer to solve purely intellectual tasks (for example, playing chess) does not necessarily contribute to the development of systems that are intelligent in a general sense or relative to human intelligence.

Hand-crafting local features

Inspired by human perception, the basic mechanisms of computer vision are straightforward and have not evolved much since the early years—the idea is to *first extract meaningful features from the raw pixels*, and *then match these features to known, labeled ones* in order to achieve recognition.

In computer vision, a **feature** is a piece of information (often mathematically represented as a one or two-dimensional vector) that is extracted from data that is relevant to the task at hand. Features include some key points in the images, specific edges, discriminative patches, and so on. They should be easy to obtain from new images and contain the necessary information for further recognition.

Researchers used to come up with more and more complex features. The extraction of edges and lines was first considered for the basic geometrical understanding of scenes or for character recognition; then, texture and lighting information was also taken into account, leading to early object classifiers.

In the 90s, features based on statistical analysis, such as **principal component analysis** (**PCA**), were successfully applied for the first time to complex recognition problems such as face classification. A classic example is the *Eigenface* method introduced by Matthew Turk and Alex Pentland (*Eigenfaces for Recognition*, MIT Press, 1991). Given a database of face images, the mean image and the *eigenvectors/images* (also known as **characteristic vectors/images**) were computed through PCA. This small set of *eigenimages* can theoretically be linearly combined to reconstruct any face in the original dataset, or beyond. In other words, each face picture can be approximated through a weighted sum of the *eigenimages* (refer to *Figure 1.8*). This means that a particular face can simply be defined by the list of reconstruction weights for each *eigenimage*. As a result, classifying a new face is just a matter of decomposing it into *eigenimages* to obtain its weight vector, and then comparing it with the vectors of known faces:

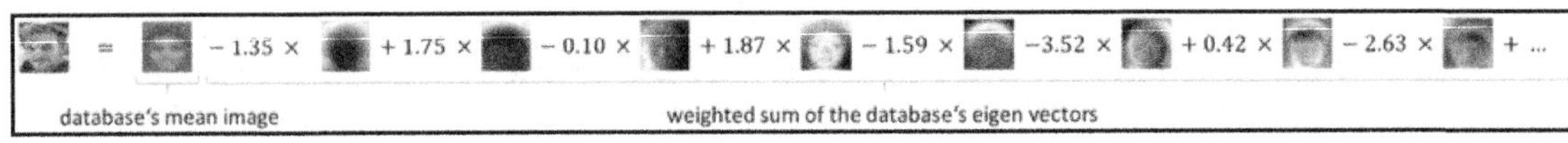

Figure 1.8: Decomposition of a portrait image into the mean image and weighted sum of eigenimages. These mean and eigenimages were computed over a larger face dataset

Another method that appeared in the late 90s and revolutionized the domain is called **Scale Invariant Feature Transform** (**SIFT**). As its name suggests, this method, introduced by David Lowe (in *Distinctive Image Features from Scale-Invariant Keypoints*, Elsevier), represents visual objects by a set of features that are robust to changes in scale and orientation. In the simplest terms, this method looks for some **key points** in images (searching for discontinuities in their *gradient*), extracts a patch around each key point, and computes a feature vector for each (for example, a histogram of the values in the patch or in its gradient). The **local features** of an image, along with their corresponding key points, can then be used to match similar visual elements across other images. In the following image, the SIFT method was applied to a picture using OpenCV (`https://docs.opencv.org/3.1.0/da/df5/tutorial_py_sift_intro.html`). For each localized key point, the radius of the circle represents the size of the patch considered for the feature computation, and the line shows the feature orientation (that is, the main orientation of the neighborhood's gradient):

Figure 1.9: Representation of the SIFT key points extracted from an image (using OpenCV)

More advanced methods were developed over the years—with more robust ways of extracting key points, or computing and combining discriminative features—but they followed the same overall procedure (extracting features from one image, and comparing them to the features of others).

Adding some machine learning on top

It soon appeared clear, however, that extracting robust, discriminative features was only half the job for recognition tasks. For instance, different elements from the same class can look quite different (such as different-looking dogs) and, as a result, share only a small set of common features. Therefore, unlike image-matching tasks, higher-level problems such as semantic classification cannot be solved by simply comparing pixel features from query images with those from labeled pictures (such a procedure can also become sub-optimal in terms of processing time if the comparison has to be done with every image from a large labeled dataset).

This is where *machine learning* come into play. With an increasing number of researchers trying to tackle image classification in the 90s, more statistical ways to discriminate images based on their features started to appear. **Support vector machines** (**SVMs**), which were standardized by Vladimir Vapnik and Corinna Cortes (*Support-vector networks*, Springer, 1995), were, for a long time, the default solution for learning a mapping from complex structures (such as images) to simpler labels (such as classes).

Given a set of image features and their binary labels (for example, *cat* or *not cat,* as illustrated in *Figure 1.10*), an SVM can be optimized to learn the function to separate one class from another, based on extracted features. Once this function is obtained, it is just a matter of applying it to the feature vector of an unknown image so that we can map it to one of the two classes (SVMs that could extend to a larger number of classes were later developed). In the following diagram, an SVM was taught to regress a linear function separating two classes based on features extracted from their images (features as vectors of only two values in this example):

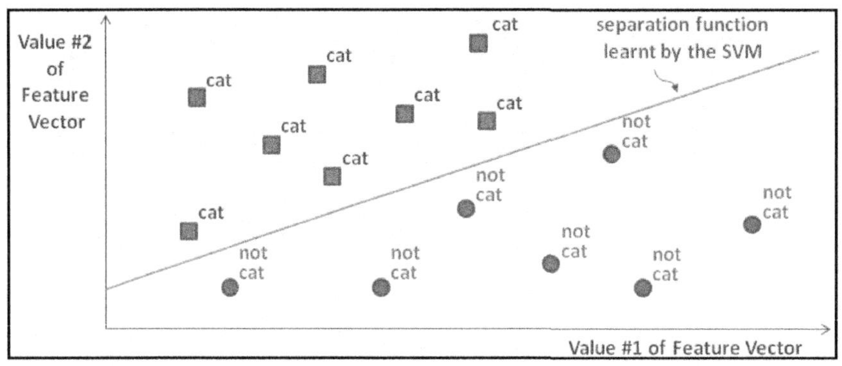

Figure 1.10: An illustration of a linear function regressed by an SVM. Note that using a concept known as the kernel trick, SVMs can also find non-linear solutions to separate classes

Other machine learning algorithms were adapted over the years by the computer vision community, such as *random forests, bags of words, Bayesian models,* and obviously *neural networks.*

Rise of deep learning

So, how did neural networks take over computer vision and become what we nowadays know as **deep learning**? This section offers some answers, detailing the technical development of this powerful tool.

Early attempts and failures

It may be surprising to learn that artificial neural networks appeared even before modern computer vision. Their development is the typical story of an invention too early for its time.

Rise and fall of the perceptron

In the 50s, Frank Rosenblatt came up with the **perceptron**, a machine learning algorithm inspired by neurons and the underlying block of the first neural networks (*The Perceptron: A Probabilistic Model for Information Storage and Organization in the Brain*, American Psychological Association, 1958). With the proper learning procedure, this method was already able to recognize characters. However, the hype was short-lived. Marvin Minsky (one of the fathers of AI) and Seymor Papert quickly demonstrated that the perceptron could not learn a function as simple as `XOR` (exclusive *OR*, the function that, given two binary input values, returns `1` if one, and only one, input is `1`, and returns `0` otherwise). This makes sense to us nowadays—as the perceptron back then was modeled with a linear function while `XOR` is a non-linear one—but, at that time, it simply discouraged any further research for years.

Too heavy to scale

It was only in the late 70s to early 80s that neural networks got some attention put back on them. Several research papers introduced how neural networks, with multiple *layers* of perceptrons put one after the other, could be trained using a rather straightforward scheme—backpropagation. As we will detail in the next section, this training procedure works by computing the network's error and backpropagating it through the layers of perceptrons to update their parameters using *derivatives*. Soon after, the first **convolutional neural network** (**CNN**), the ancestor of current recognition methods, was developed and applied to the recognition of handwritten characters with some success.

Alas, these methods were computationally heavy, and just could not scale to larger problems. Instead, researchers adopted lighter machine learning methods such as SVMs, and the use of neural networks stalled for another decade. So, what brought them back and led to the deep learning era we know of today?

Reasons for the comeback

The reasons for this comeback are twofold and rooted in the explosive evolution of the internet and hardware efficiency.

The internet – the new El Dorado of data science

The internet was not only a revolution in communication; it also deeply transformed data science. It became much easier for scientists to share images and content by uploading them online, leading to the creation of public datasets for experimentation and benchmarking. Moreover, not only researchers but soon everyone, all over the world, started adding new content online, sharing images, videos, and more at an exponential rate. This started *big data* and the *golden age of data science*, with the internet as the new El Dorado.

By simply indexing the content that is constantly published online, image and video datasets reached sizes that were never imagined before, from *Caltech-101* (10,000 images, published in 2003 by Li Fei-Fei et al., Elsevier) to *ImageNet* (14+ million images, published in 2009 by Jia Deng et al., IEEE) or *Youtube-8M* (8+ million videos, published in 2016 by Sami Abu-El-Haija et al., including Google). Even companies and governments soon understood the numerous advantages of gathering and releasing datasets to boost innovation in their specific domains (for example, the i-LIDS datasets for video surveillance released by the British government and the COCO dataset for image captioning sponsored by Facebook and Microsoft, among others).

With so much data available covering so many use cases, new doors were opened (*data-hungry* algorithms, that is, methods requiring a lot of training samples to converge could finally be applied with success), and new challenges were raised (such as how to efficiently process all this information).

More power than ever

Luckily, since the internet was booming, so was computing power. Hardware kept becoming cheaper as well as faster, seemingly following Moore's famous law (which states that processor speeds should double every two years—this has been true for almost four decades, though a deceleration is now being observed). As computers got faster, they also became better designed for computer vision. And for this, we have to thank video games.

The **graphical processing unit** (**GPU**) is a computer component, that is, a chip specifically designed to handle the kind of operations needed to run 3D games. Therefore, a GPU is optimized to generate or manipulate images, parallelizing these heavy matrix operations. Though the first GPUs were conceived in the 80s, they became affordable and popular only with the advent of the new millennium.

In 2007, NVIDIA, one of the main companies designing GPUs, released the first version of **CUDA**, a programming language that allows developers to directly program for compatible GPUs. **OpenCL**, a similar language, appeared soon after. With these new tools, people started to harness the power of GPUs for new tasks, such as machine learning and computer vision.

Deep learning or the rebranding of artificial neural networks

The conditions were finally there for data-hungry, computationally-intensive algorithms to shine. Along with *big data* and *cloud computing*, *deep learning* was suddenly everywhere.

What makes learning deep?

Actually, the term **deep learning** had already been coined back in the 80s, when neural networks first began stacking two or three layers of neurons. As opposed to the early, simpler solutions, *deep learning* regroups *deeper* neural networks, that is, networks with multiple *hidden layers*—additional layers set between their input and output layers. Each layer processes its inputs and passes the results to the next layer, all trained to extract increasingly abstract information. For instance, the first layer of a neural network would learn to react to basic features in the images, such as edges, lines, or color gradients; the next layer would learn to use these cues to extract more advanced features; and so on until the last layer, which infers the desired output (such as predicted class or detection results).

However, *deep learning* only really started being used from 2006, when Geoff Hinton and his colleagues proposed an effective solution to train these deeper models, one layer at a time, until reaching the desired depth (*A Fast Learning Algorithm for Deep Belief Nets*, MIT Press, 2006).

Deep learning era

With research into neural networks once again back on track, deep learning started growing, until a major breakthrough in 2012, which finally gave it its contemporary prominence. Since the publication of ImageNet, a competition (**ImageNet Large Scale Visual Recognition Challenge (ILSVRC)**—`image-net.org/challenges/LSVRC`) has been organized every year for researchers to submit their latest classification algorithms and compare their performance on ImageNet with others. The winning solutions in 2010 and 2011 had classification errors of 28% and 26% respectively, and applied traditional concepts such as SIFT features and SVMs. Then came the 2012 edition, and a new team of researchers reduced the recognition error to a staggering 16%, leaving all the other contestants far behind.

In their paper describing this achievement (*Imagenet Classification with Deep Convolutional Neural Networks*, NIPS, 2012), Alex Krizhevsky, Ilya Sutskever, and Geoff Hinton presented what would become the basis for modern recognition methods. They conceived an 8-layer neural network, later named **AlexNet**, with several *convolutional layers* and other modern components such as **dropout** and **rectified linear activation units** (**ReLUs**), which will all be presented in detail in `Chapter 3`, *Modern Neural Networks*, as they have became central to computer vision. More importantly, they used CUDA to implement their method so that it can be run on GPUs, finally making it possible to train deep neural networks in a reasonable time, iterating over datasets as big as ImageNet.

That same year, Google demonstrated how advances in **cloud computing** could also be applied to computer vision. Using a dataset of 10 million random images extracted from YouTube videos, they taught a neural network to identify images containing cats and parallelized the training process over 16,000 machines to finally double the accuracy compared to previous methods.

And so started the deep learning era we are currently in. Everyone jumped on board, coming up with deeper and deeper models, more advanced training schemes, and lighter solutions for portable devices. It is an exciting period, as the more efficient deep learning solutions become, the more people try to apply them to new applications and domains. With this book, we hope to convey some of this current enthusiasm and provide you with an overview of the modern methods and how to develop solutions.

Getting started with neural networks

By now, we know that neural networks form the core of deep learning and are powerful tools for modern computer vision. But what are they exactly? How do they work? In the following section, not only will we tackle the theoretical explanations behind their efficiency, but we will also directly apply this knowledge to the implementation and application of a simple network to a recognition task.

Building a neural network

Artificial neural networks (**ANNs**), or simply **neural networks** (**NNs**), are powerful machine learning tools that are excellent at processing information, recognizing usual patterns or detecting new ones, and approximating complex processes. They have to thank their structure for this, which we will now explore.

Imitating neurons

It is well-known that neurons are the elemental supports of our thoughts and reactions. What might be less evident is how they actually work and how they can be simulated.

Biological inspiration

ANNs are loosely inspired by how animals' brains work. Our brain is a complex network of neurons, each passing information to each other and processing sensory inputs (as electrical and chemical signals) into thoughts and actions. Each neuron receives its electrical inputs from its *dendrites*, which are cell fibers that propagate the electrical signal from the *synapses* (the junctions with preceding neurons) to the *soma* (the neuron's main body). If the accumulated electrical stimulation exceeds a specific threshold, the cell is *activated* and the electrical impulse is *propagated further* to the next neurons through the cell's *axon* (the neuron's *output cable*, ending with several synapses linking to other neurons). Each neuron can, therefore, be seen as a really *simple signal processing unit*, which—once stacked together—can achieve the thoughts we are having right now, for instance.

Mathematical model

Inspired by its biological counterpart (represented in *Figure 1.11*), the artificial neuron takes several *inputs* (each a number), sums them together, and finally applies an *activation function* to obtain the *output* signal, which can be passed to the following neurons in the network (this can be seen as a directed graph):

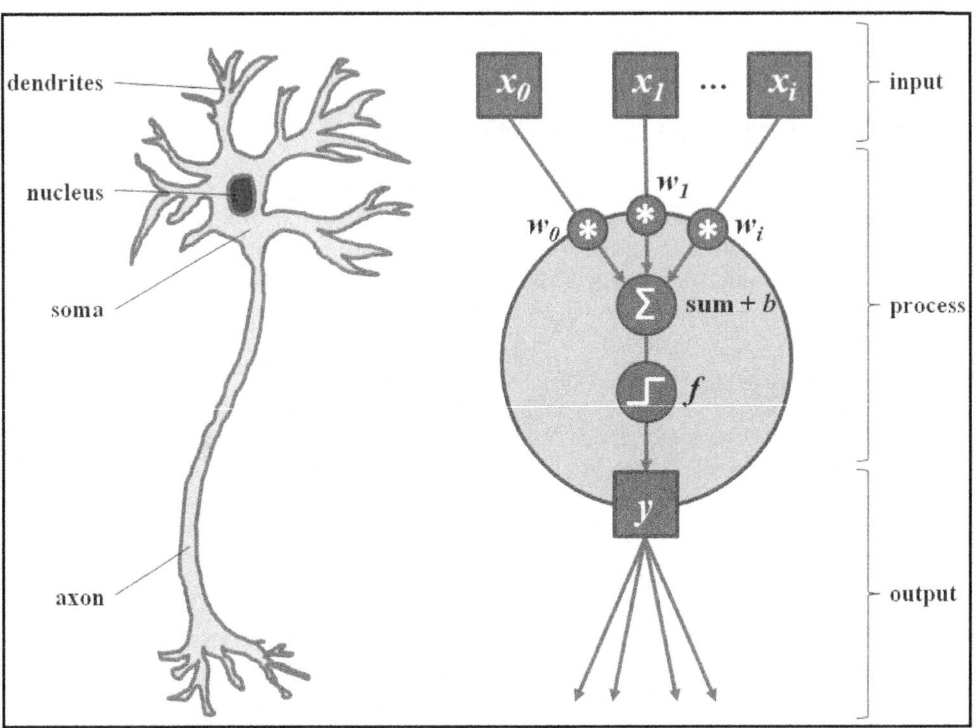

Figure 1.11: On the left, we can see a simplified biological neuron. On the right, we can see its artificial counterpart

The summation of the inputs is usually done in a weighted way. Each **input** is scaled up or down, depending on a weight specific to this particular **input**. These *weights* are the parameters that are adjusted during the training phase of the network in order for the neuron to react to the correct features. Often, another parameter is also trained and used for this summation process—the neuron's *bias*. Its value is simply added to the weighted sum as an *offset*.

Let's quickly formalize this process mathematically. Suppose we have a neuron that takes two input values, x_0 and x_1. Each of these values would be weighted by a factor, w_0 and w_1, respectively, before being summed together, with an optional bias, b. For simplification, we can express the input values as a horizontal vector, x, and the weights as a vertical vector, w:

$$x = \begin{pmatrix} x_0 & x_1 \end{pmatrix}, w = \begin{pmatrix} w_0 \\ w_1 \end{pmatrix}$$

With this formulation, the whole operation can simply be expressed as follows:

$$z = x \cdot w + b$$

This step is straightforward, isn't it? The *dot product* between the two vectors takes care of the weighted summation:

$$x \cdot w = \sum_i x_i w_i = x_1 w_1 + x_2 w_2$$

Now that the inputs have been scaled and summed together into the result, z, we have to apply the *activation function* to it in order to get the neuron's output. If we go back to the analogy with the biological neuron, its activation function would be a binary function such as *if y is above a threshold t, return an electrical impulse that is 1, or else return 0* (with $t = 0$ usually). If we formalize this, the activation function, $y = f(z)$, can be expressed as follows:

$$y = f(z) = \begin{cases} 0 \text{ if } z < t \\ 1 \text{ if } z \geq t \end{cases}$$

The **step function** is a key component of the original perceptron, but more advanced activation functions have been introduced since then with more advantageous properties, such as *non-linearity* (to model more complex behaviors) and *continuous differentiability* (important for the training process, which we will explain later). The most common activation functions are as follows:

- The **sigmoid** function, $\sigma(z) = \dfrac{1}{1 + e^{-z}}$ (with e the exponential function)

- The **hyperbolic tangent**, $\tanh(z) = \frac{e^z - e^{-z}}{e^z + e^{-z}}$
- The **REctified Linear Unit** (**ReLU**), $\text{ReLU}(z) = \max(0, z) = \begin{cases} 0 \text{ if } z < 0 \\ z \text{ if } z \geq 0 \end{cases}$

Plots of the aforementioned common activation functions are shown in the following diagram:

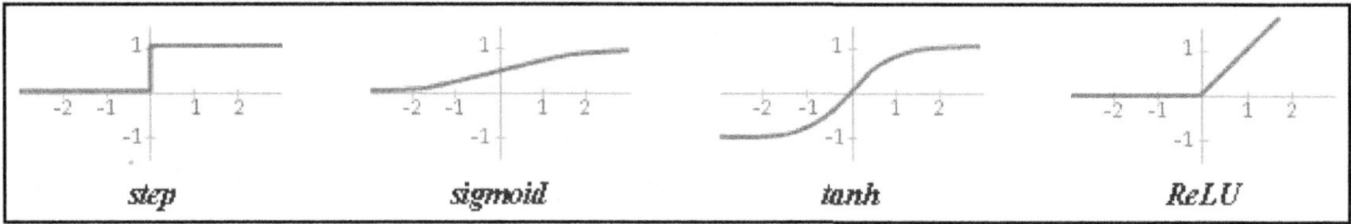

Figure 1.12: Plotting common activation functions

In any case, that's it! We have modeled a simple artificial neuron. It is able to receive a signal, process it, and output a value that can be *forwarded* (a term that is commonly used in machine learning) to other neurons, building a network.

Chaining neurons with no non-linear activation functions would be equivalent to having a single neuron. For instance, if we had a linear neuron with parameters w_A and b_A followed by a linear neuron with parameters w_B and b_B, then $y_B = w_B \cdot y_A + b_B = w_B \cdot (w_A \cdot x + b_A) + b_B = w \cdot x + b$, where $w = w_A w_B$ and $b = b_A + b_B$. Therefore, non-linear activation functions are a necessity if we want to create complex models.

Implementation

Such a model can be implemented really easily in Python (using NumPy for vector and matrix manipulations):

```
import numpy as np

class Neuron(object):
    """A simple feed-forward artificial neuron.
    Args:
        num_inputs (int): The input vector size / number of input values.
        activation_fn (callable): The activation function.
    Attributes:
        W (ndarray): The weight values for each input.
```

```
        b (float): The bias value, added to the weighted sum.
        activation_fn (callable): The activation function.
    """
    def __init__(self, num_inputs, activation_fn):
        super().__init__()
        # Randomly initializing the weight vector and bias value:
        self.W = np.random.rand(num_inputs)
        self.b = np.random.rand(1)
        self.activation_fn = activation_fn

    def forward(self, x):
        """Forward the input signal through the neuron."""
        z = np.dot(x, self.W) + self.b
        return self.activation_function(z)
```

As we can see, this is a direct adaptation of the mathematical model we defined previously. Using this artificial neuron is just as straightforward. Let's instantiate a perceptron (a neuron with the step function for the activation method) and forward a random input through it:

```
# Fixing the random number generator's seed, for reproducible results:
np.random.seed(42)
# Random input column array of 3 values (shape = `(1, 3)`)
x = np.random.rand(3).reshape(1, 3)
# > [[0.37454012 0.95071431 0.73199394]]

# Instantiating a Perceptron (simple neuron with step function):
step_fn = lambda y: 0 if y <= 0 else 1
perceptron = Neuron(num_inputs=x.size, activation_fn=step_fn)
# > perceptron.weights    = [0.59865848 0.15601864 0.15599452]
# > perceptron.bias       = [0.05808361]

out = perceptron.forward(x)
# > 1
```

We suggest that you take some time and experiment with different inputs and neuron parameters before we scale up their dimensions in the next section.

Layering neurons together

Usually, neural networks are organized into *layers,* that is, sets of neurons that typically receive the same input and apply the same operation (for example, by applying the same activation function, though each neuron first sums the inputs with its own specific weights).

Mathematical model

In networks, the information flows from the input layer to the output layer, with one or more *hidden* layers in-between. In *Figure 1.13*, the three neurons **A**, **B**, and **C** belong to the input layer, the neuron **H** belongs to the output or activation layer, and the neurons **D**, **E**, **F**, and **G** belong to the hidden layer. The first layer has an input, x, of size 2, the second (hidden) layer takes the three activation values of the previous layer as input, and so on. Such layers, with each neuron connected to all the values from the previous layer, are classed as being **fully connected** or **dense**:

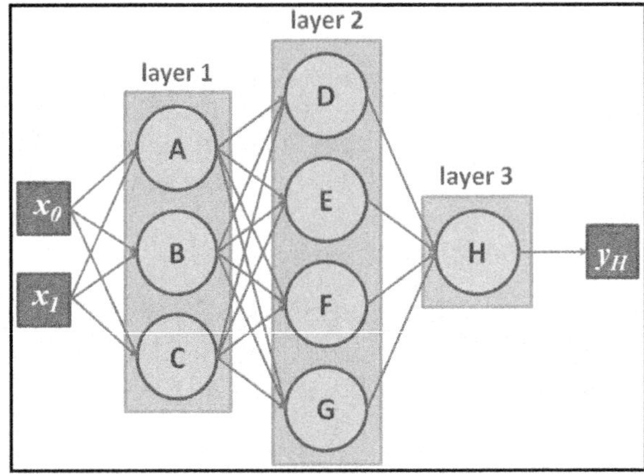

Figure 1.13: A 3-layer neural network, with two input values and one final output

Once again, we can compact the calculations by representing these elements with vectors and matrices. The following operations are done by the first layers:

$$z_A = x \cdot w_A + b_A$$
$$z_B = x \cdot w_B + b_B$$
$$z_C = x \cdot w_C + b_C$$

This can be expressed as follows:

$$z = x \cdot W + b$$

In order to obtain the previous equation, we must define the variables as follows:

$$W = \begin{pmatrix} \vdots & \vdots & \vdots \\ w_A & w_B & w_C \\ \vdots & \vdots & \vdots \end{pmatrix} = \begin{pmatrix} w_{a1} & w_{b1} & w_{c1} \\ w_{a2} & w_{b2} & w_{c2} \end{pmatrix}, \; b = \begin{pmatrix} b_A & b_B & b_C \end{pmatrix}, \; z = \begin{pmatrix} z_A & z_B & z_C \end{pmatrix}.$$

The activation of the first layer can, therefore, be written as a vector, $y = f(z) = \begin{pmatrix} f(z_A) & f(z_B) & f(z_C) \end{pmatrix}$, which can be directly passed as an input vector to the next layer, and so on until the last layer.

Implementation

Like the single neuron, this model can be implemented in Python. Actually, we do not even have to make too many edits compared to our `Neuron` class:

```
import numpy as np

class FullyConnectedLayer(object):
    """A simple fully-connected NN layer.
    Args:
        num_inputs (int): The input vector size/number of input values.
        layer_size (int): The output vector size/number of neurons.
        activation_fn (callable): The activation function for this layer.
    Attributes:
        W (ndarray): The weight values for each input.
        b (ndarray): The bias value, added to the weighted sum.
        size (int): The layer size/number of neurons.
        activation_fn (callable): The neurons' activation function.
    """
    def __init__(self, num_inputs, layer_size, activation_fn):
        super().__init__()
        # Randomly initializing the parameters (using a normal distribution
this time):
        self.W = np.random.standard_normal((num_inputs, layer_size))
        self.b = np.random.standard_normal(layer_size)
        self.size = layer_size
        self.activation_fn = activation_fn

    def forward(self, x):
        """Forward the input signal through the layer."""
        z = np.dot(x, self.W) + self.b
        return self.activation_fn(z)
```

We just have to change the *dimensionality* of some of the variables in order to reflect the multiplicity of neurons inside a layer. With this implementation, our layer can even process several inputs at once! Passing a single column vector x (of shape $1 \times s$ with s number of values in x) or a stack of column vectors (of shape $n \times s$ with n number of samples) does not change anything with regard to our matrix calculations, and our layer will correctly output the stacked results (assuming b is added to each row):

```
np.random.seed(42)
# Random input column-vectors of 2 values (shape = `(1, 2)`):
x1 = np.random.uniform(-1, 1, 2).reshape(1, 2)
# > [[-0.25091976  0.90142861]]
x2 = np.random.uniform(-1, 1, 2).reshape(1, 2)
# > [[0.46398788 0.19731697]]

relu_fn = lambda y: np.maximum(y, 0)    # Defining our activation function
layer = FullyConnectedLayer(2, 3, relu_fn)

# Our layer can process x1 and x2 separately...
out1 = layer.forward(x1)
# > [[0.28712364 0.         0.33478571]]
out2 = layer.forward(x2)
# > [[0.         0.         1.08175419]]
# ... or together:
x12 = np.concatenate((x1, x2))  # stack of input vectors, of shape `(2, 2)`
out12 = layer.forward(x12)
# > [[0.28712364 0.         0.33478571]
#    [0.         0.         1.08175419]]
```

A stack of input data is commonly called a **batch**.

With this implementation, it is now just a matter of chaining fully connected layers together to build simple neural networks.

Applying our network to classification

We know how to define layers, but have yet to initialize and connect them into networks for computer vision. To demonstrate how to do this, we will tackle a famous recognition task.

Setting up the task

Classifying images of handwritten digits (that is, recognizing whether an image contains a `0` or a `1` and so on) is a historical problem in computer vision. The **Modified National Institute of Standards and Technology** (**MNIST**) dataset (`http://yann.lecun.com/exdb/mnist/`), which contains 70,000 grayscale images (*28 × 28* pixels) of such digits, has been used as a reference over the years so that people can test their methods for this recognition task (Yann LeCun and Corinna Cortes hold all copyrights for this dataset, which is shown in the following diagram):

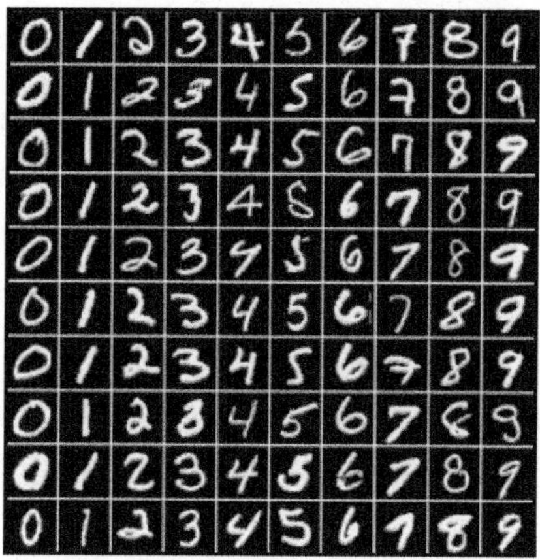

Figure 1.14: Ten samples of each digit from the MNIST dataset

For digit classification, what we want is a network that takes one of these images as input and returns an output vector expressing *how strongly the network believes the image corresponds to each class*. The input vector has *28 × 28 = 784* values, while the output has 10 values (for the 10 different digits, from `0` to `9`). In-between all of this, it is up to us to define the number of hidden layers and their sizes. To predict the class of an image, it is then just a matter of *forwarding the image vector through the network, collecting the output*, and *returning the class with the highest belief score*.

These *belief* scores are commonly transformed into probabilities to simplify further computations or the interpretation. For instance, let's suppose that a classification network gives a score of 9 to the class *dog*, and a score of 1 to the other class, *cat*. This is equivalent to saying that *according to this network, there is a 9/10 probability that the image shows a dog and a 1/10 probability it shows a cat.*

Before we implement a solution, let's prepare the data by loading the MNIST data for training and testing methods. For simplicity, we will use the `mnist` Python module (`https://github.com/datapythonista/mnist`), which was developed by Marc Garcia (under the BSD 3-Clause *New* or *Revised* license, and is already installed in this chapter's source directory):

```
import numpy as np
import mnist
np.random.seed(42)

# Loading the training and testing data:
X_train, y_train = mnist.train_images(), mnist.train_labels()
X_test,  y_test  = mnist.test_images(), mnist.test_labels()
num_classes = 10    # classes are the digits from 0 to 9

# We transform the images into column vectors (as inputs for our NN):
X_train, X_test = X_train.reshape(-1, 28*28), X_test.reshape(-1, 28*28)
# We "one-hot" the labels (as targets for our NN), for instance, transform
label `4` into vector `[0, 0, 0, 0, 1, 0, 0, 0, 0, 0]`:
y_train = np.eye(num_classes)[y_train]
```

More detailed operations for the preprocessing and visualization of the dataset can be found in this chapter's source code.

Implementing the network

For the neural network itself, we have to wrap the layers together and add some methods to forward through the complete network and to predict the class according to the output vector. After the layer's implementation, the following code should be self-explanatory:

```
import numpy as np
from layer import FullyConnectedLayer

def sigmoid(x): # Apply the sigmoid function to the elements of x.
    return 1 / (1 + np.exp(-x)) # y

class SimpleNetwork(object):
    """A simple fully-connected NN.
    Args:
        num_inputs (int): The input vector size / number of input values.
        num_outputs (int): The output vector size.
        hidden_layers_sizes (list): A list of sizes for each hidden layer
to be added to the network
    Attributes:
```

```
        layers (list): The list of layers forming this simple network.
    """

    def __init__(self, num_inputs, num_outputs, hidden_layers_sizes=(64,
32)):
        super().__init__()
        # We build the list of layers composing the network:
        sizes = [num_inputs, *hidden_layers_sizes, num_outputs]
        self.layers = [
            FullyConnectedLayer(sizes[i], sizes[i + 1], sigmoid)
            for i in range(len(sizes) - 1)]

    def forward(self, x):
        """Forward the input vector `x` through the layers."""
        for layer in self.layers: # from the input layer to the output one
            x = layer.forward(x)
        return x

    def predict(self, x):
        """Compute the output corresponding to `x`, and return the index of
the largest output value"""
        estimations = self.forward(x)
        best_class = np.argmax(estimations)
        return best_class

    def evaluate_accuracy(self, X_val, y_val):
        """Evaluate the network's accuracy on a validation dataset."""
        num_corrects = 0
        for i in range(len(X_val)):
            if self.predict(X_val[i]) == y_val[i]:
                num_corrects += 1
        return num_corrects / len(X_val)
```

We just implemented a feed-forward neural network that can be used for classification! It is now time to apply it to our problem:

```
# Network for MNIST images, with 2 hidden layers of size 64 and 32:
mnist_classifier = SimpleNetwork(X_train.shape[1], num_classes, [64, 32])

# ... and we evaluate its accuracy on the MNIST test set:
accuracy = mnist_classifier.evaluate_accuracy(X_test, y_test)
print("accuracy = {:.2f}%".format(accuracy * 100))
# > accuracy = 12.06%
```

We only got an accuracy of ~12.06%. This may look disappointing since it is an accuracy that's barely better than random guessing. But it makes sense—right now, our network is defined by random parameters. We need to train it according to our use case, which is a task that we will tackle in the next section.

Training a neural network

Neural networks are a particular kind of algorithm because they need to be *trained*, that is, their parameters need to be optimized for a specific task by making them learn from available data. Once the networks are optimized to perform well on this *training dataset*, they can be used on new, similar data to provide satisfying results (if the training was done properly).

Before solving the problem of our MNIST task, we will provide some theoretical background, cover different learning strategies, and present how training is actually done. Then, we will directly apply some of these notions to our example so that our simple network finally learns how to solve the recognition task!

Learning strategies

When it comes to teaching neural networks, there are three main paradigms, depending on the task and the availability of training data.

Supervised learning

Supervised learning may be the most common paradigm, and it is certainly the easiest to grasp. It applies when we want to *teach neural networks a mapping between two modalities* (for example, mapping images to their class labels or to their semantic masks). It requires access to a training dataset containing both the *images* and their *ground truth labels* (such as the class information per image or the semantic masks).

With this, the training is then straightforward:

- Give the images to the network and collect its results (that is, predicted labels).
- Evaluate the network's *loss*, that is, how wrong its predictions are when comparing it to the ground truth labels.
- Adjust the network parameters accordingly to reduce this loss.
- Repeat until the network *converges*, that is, until it cannot improve further on this training data.

Therefore, this strategy deserves the adjective *supervised*—an entity (us) supervises the training of the network by providing it with feedback for each prediction (the loss computed from the ground truths) so that the method can learn by repetition (*it was correct/false; try again*).

Unsupervised learning

However, how do we train a network when we do not have any ground truth information available? *Unsupervised learning* is one answer to this. The idea here is to craft a function that *computes the network's loss only based on its input and its corresponding output*.

This strategy applies very well to applications such as clustering (grouping images with similar properties together) or compression (reducing the content size while preserving some properties). For clustering, the loss function could measure how similar images from one cluster are compared to images from other clusters. For compression, the loss function could measure how well preserved the important properties are in the compressed data compared to the original ones.

Unsupervised learning thus requires some *expertise* regarding the use cases so that we can come up with meaningful loss functions.

Reinforcement learning

Reinforcement learning is an **interactive strategy**. An *agent* navigates through an *environment* (for example, a robot moving around a room or a video game character going through a level). The agent has a predefined list of actions it can make (*walk, turn, jump,* and so on) and, after each action, it ends up in a new *state*. Some states can bring *rewards*, which are immediate or delayed, and positive or negative (for instance, a positive reward when the video game character touches a bonus item, and a negative reward when it is hit by an enemy).

At each instant, the neural network is provided only with *observations* from the environment (for example, the robot's visual feed, or the video game screen) and reward feedback (the *carrot and stick*). From this, it has to learn what brings higher rewards and *estimate the best short-term or long-term policy for the agent* accordingly. In other words, it has to estimate the series of actions that would maximize its end reward.

Reinforcement learning is a powerful paradigm, but it is less commonly applied to computer vision use cases. It won't be presented further here, though we encourage machine learning enthusiasts to learn more.

Teaching time

Whatever the learning strategy, the overall training steps are the same. Given some training data, the network makes its predictions and receives some feedback (such as the results of a loss function), which is then used to update the network's parameters. These steps are then repeated until the network cannot be optimized further. In this section, we will detail and implement this process, from loss computation to weights optimization.

Evaluating the loss

The goal of the *loss function* is to evaluate how well the network, with its current weights, is performing. More formally, this function expresses the *quality of the predictions as a function of the network's parameters* (such as its weights and biases). The smaller the loss, the better the parameters are for the chosen task.

Since loss functions represent the goal of networks (*return the correct labels, compress the image while preserving the content*, and so on), there are as many different functions as there are tasks. Still, some loss functions are more commonly used than others. This is the case for the *sum-of-squares* function, also called **L2 loss** (based on the L2 norm), which is omnipresent in supervised learning. This function simply computes the squared difference between each element of the output vector y (the per-class probabilities estimated by our network) and each element of the ground truth vector y^{true} (the target vector with null values for every class but the correct one):

$$L_2(y,\, y^{true}) = \sum_i (y_i^{true} - y_i)^2$$

There are plenty of other losses with different properties, such as **L1 loss**, which computes the *absolute difference* between the vectors, or **binary cross-entropy** (**BCE**) loss, which converts the predicted probabilities into a logarithmic scale before comparing them to the expected values:

$$L_1(y,\, y^{true}) = \sum_i |y_i^{true} - y_i| \quad \text{and} \quad \text{BCE}(y,\, y^{true}) = \sum_i \left[-\, y_i^{true} \log(y_i) + (1 - y_i^{true}) \log(1 - y_i) \right]$$

The logarithmic operation converts the probabilities from [0, 1] into [-∞, 0]. So, by multiplying the results by -1, the loss value moves from +∞ to 0 as the neural network learns to predict properly. Note that the cross-entropy function can also be applied to multi-class problems (not just binary).

It is also common for people to divide the losses by the number of elements in the vectors, that is, computing the mean instead of the sum. The **mean square error** (**MSE**) is the averaged version of the L2 loss, and the **mean absolute error** (**MAE**) is the average version of the L1 loss.

For now, we will stick with the L2 loss as an example. We will use it for the rest of the theoretical explanations, as well as to train our MNIST classifier.

Backpropagating the loss

How can we update the network parameters so that they minimize the loss? For each parameter, what we need to know is how slightly changing its value would affect the loss. If we know which changes would slightly decrease the loss, then it is just a matter of applying these changes and repeating the process until reaching a minimum. This is exactly what the *gradient* of the loss function expresses, and what the *gradient descent* process is.

At each training iteration, the derivatives of the loss with respect to each parameter of the network are computed. These derivatives indicate which small changes to the parameters need to be applied (with a -1 coefficient since the gradient indicates the direction of increase of the function, while we want to minimize it). It can be seen as walking step by step down the *slope* of the loss function with respect to each parameter, hence the name **gradient descent** for this iterative process (refer to the following diagram):

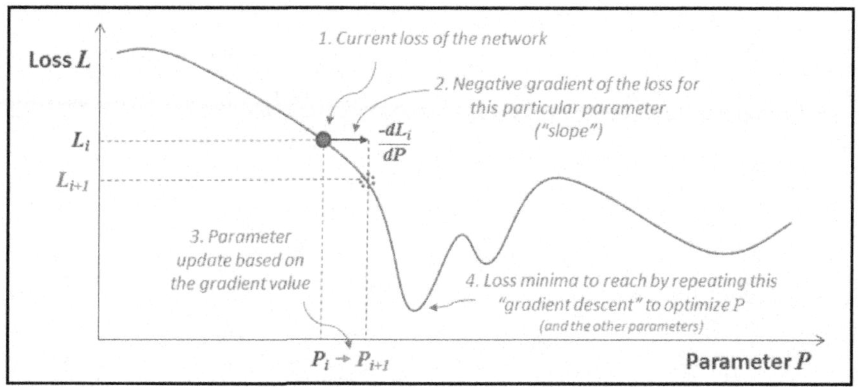

Figure 1.15: Illustrating the gradient descent to optimize a parameter *P* of the neural network

The question now is, how can we compute all of these derivatives (the *slope* values as a function of each parameter)? This is where the **chain rule** comes to our aid. Without going too deep into calculus, the chain rule tells us that the derivatives with respect to the parameters of a layer, k, can be *simply* computed with the input and output values of that layer (x_k, y_k), and the derivatives of the following layer, $k + 1$. More formally, for the layer's weights, W_k, we have the following:

$$\frac{dL}{dW_k} = \frac{dL}{dy_k}\frac{dy_k}{dW_k} = \frac{dL}{dy_k}\frac{dy_k}{dz_k}\frac{dz_k}{dW_k} = \frac{dL}{dx_{k+1}}\frac{dy_k}{dz_k}\frac{d(W_k \cdot x_k + b_k)}{dW_k} = l'_{k+1} \odot f'_k \frac{d(W_k \cdot x_k + b_k)}{dW_k} = x_k^\intercal \cdot (l'_{k+1} \odot f'_k)$$

Here, l'_{k+1} is the derivative that is computed for layer $k + 1$ with respect to its input, $x_{k+1} = y_k$, with f'_k being the derivative of the layer's activation function, and $x^\intercal$ being the *transpose* of x. Note that z_k represents the result of the weighted sum performed by the layer k (that is, before the input of the layer's activation function), as defined in the *Layering neurons together* section. Finally, the $\odot$ symbol represents the *element-wise multiplication* between two vectors/matrices. It is also known as the *Hadamard product*. As shown in the following equation, it basically consists of multiplying the elements pair-wise:

$$\begin{pmatrix} a_0 & a_1 \\ a_2 & a_3 \end{pmatrix} \odot \begin{pmatrix} b_0 & b_1 \\ b_2 & b_3 \end{pmatrix} = \begin{pmatrix} a_0 \times b_0 & a_1 \times b_1 \\ a_2 \times b_2 & a_3 \times b_3 \end{pmatrix}$$

Back to the chain rule, the derivatives with respect to the bias can be computed in a similar fashion, as follows:

$$\frac{dL}{db_k} = \frac{dL}{dy_k}\frac{dy_k}{db_k} = \frac{dL}{dy_k}\frac{dy_k}{dz_k}\frac{dz_k}{db_k} = l'_{k+1} \odot f'_k \frac{d(W_k \cdot x_k + b_k)}{db_k} = l'_{k+1} \odot f'_k$$

Finally, to be exhaustive, we have the following equation:

$$\frac{dL}{dx_k} = \frac{dL}{dy_k}\frac{dy_k}{dx_k} = \frac{dL}{dy_k}\frac{dy_k}{dz_k}\frac{dz_k}{dx_k} = l'_{k+1} \odot f'_k \frac{d(W_k \cdot x_k + b_k)}{dx_k} = W_k^\intercal \cdot (l'_{k+1} \odot f'_k)$$

These calculations may look complex, but we only need to understand what they represent—we can compute how each parameter affects the loss recursively, layer by layer, going backward (using the derivatives for a layer to compute the derivatives for the previous layer). This concept can also be illustrated by representing neural networks as *computational graphs*, that is, as graphs of mathematical operations chained together (the weighted summation of the first layer is performed and its result is passed to the first activation function, then its own output is passed to the operations of the second layer, and so on). Therefore, computing the result of a whole neural network with respect to some inputs consists of *forwarding* the data through this computational graph, while obtaining the derivatives with respect to each of its parameters consists of propagating the resulting loss through the graph backward, hence the term **backpropagation**.

To start this process by the output layer, the derivatives of the loss itself with respect to the output values are needed (refer to the previous equation). Therefore, it is primordial that the loss function can be easily derived. For instance, the derivative of the L2 loss is simply the following:

$$\frac{dL_2(y,\ y_{true})}{dy} = 2(y - y_{true})$$

As we mentioned earlier, once we know the loss derivatives with respect to each parameter, it is just a matter of updating them accordingly:

$$W_k \leftarrow W_k - \epsilon\frac{dL}{dW_k} \quad , \quad b_k \leftarrow b_k - \epsilon\frac{dL}{db_k}$$

As we can see, the derivatives are often multiplied by a factor ϵ (*epsilon*) before being used to update the parameters. This factor is called the **learning rate**. It helps to control how strongly each parameter should be updated at each iteration. A large learning rate may allow the network to learn faster, but with the risk of making steps so big that the network may *miss* the loss minimum. Therefore, its value should be set with care. Let's now summarize the complete training process:

1. Select the n next training images and feed them to the network.
2. Compute and backpropagate the loss, using the chain rule to get the derivatives with respect to the parameters of the layers.
3. Update the parameters with the values of the corresponding derivatives (scaled with the learning rate).
4. Repeat steps 1 to 3 to iterate over the whole training set.
5. Repeat steps 1 to 4 until convergence or until a fixed number of iterations.

One iteration over the whole training set (*steps 1* to *4*) is called an **epoch**. If $n = 1$ and the training sample is randomly selected among the remaining images, this process is called **stochastic gradient descent** (**SGD**), which is easy to implement and visualize, but slower (more updates are done) and *noisier*. People tend to prefer *mini-batch stochastic gradient descent*. It implies using larger n values (limited by the capabilities of the computer) so that the gradient is averaged over each *mini-batch* (or, more simply, named *batch*) of n random training samples (and is thus less noisy).

Nowadays, the term SGD is commonly used, regardless of the value of n.

In this section, we have covered how neural networks are trained. It is now time to put this into practice!

Teaching our network to classify

So far, we have only implemented the feed-forward functionality for our network and its layers. First, let's update our `FullyConnectedLayer` class so that we can add methods for backpropagation and optimization:

```
class FullyConnectedLayer(object):
    # [...] (code unchanged)
    def __init__(self, num_inputs, layer_size, activation_fn,
d_activation_fn):
        # [...] (code unchanged)
        self.d_activation_fn = d_activation_fn # Deriv. activation function
        self.x, self.y, self.dL_dW, self.dL_db = 0, 0, 0, 0 # Storage attr.

    def forward(self, x):
        z = np.dot(x, self.W) + self.b
        self.y = self.activation_fn(z)
        self.x = x  # we store values for back-propagation
        return self.y

    def backward(self, dL_dy):
        """Back-propagate the loss."""
        dy_dz = self.d_activation_fn(self.y)  # = f'
        dL_dz = (dL_dy * dy_dz) # dL/dz = dL/dy * dy/dz = l'_{k+1} * f'
        dz_dw = self.x.T
        dz_dx = self.W.T
        dz_db = np.ones(dL_dy.shape[0]) # dz/db = "ones"-vector
        # Computing and storing dL w.r.t. the layer's parameters:
        self.dL_dW = np.dot(dz_dw, dL_dz)
```

```
        self.dL_db = np.dot(dz_db, dL_dz)
        # Computing the derivative w.r.t. x for the previous layers:
        dL_dx = np.dot(dL_dz, dz_dx)
        return dL_dx

    def optimize(self, epsilon):
        """Optimize the layer's parameters w.r.t. the derivative values."""
        self.W -= epsilon * self.dL_dW
        self.b -= epsilon * self.dL_db
```

The code presented in this section has been simplified and stripped of comments to keep its length reasonable. The complete sources are available in this book's GitHub repository, along with a Jupyter notebook that connects everything together.

Now, we need to update the `SimpleNetwork` class by adding methods to backpropagate and optimize layer by layer, and a final method to cover the complete training:

```
def derivated_sigmoid(y):  # sigmoid derivative function
    return y * (1 - y)

def loss_L2(pred, target): # L2 loss function
    return np.sum(np.square(pred - target)) / pred.shape[0] # opt. for
results not depending on the batch size (pred.shape[0]), we divide the loss
by it

def derivated_loss_L2(pred, target):    # L2 derivative function
    return 2 * (pred - target) # we could add the batch size division here
too, but it wouldn't really affect the training (just scaling down the
derivatives).

class SimpleNetwork(object):
 # [...] (code unchanged)
 def __init__(self, num_inputs, num_outputs, hidden_layers_sizes=(64, 32),
loss_fn=loss_L2, d_loss_fn=derivated_loss_L2):
        # [...] (code unchanged, except for FC layers new params.)
        self.loss_fn, self.d_loss_fn = loss_fn, d_loss_fn

    # [...] (code unchanged)

    def backward(self, dL_dy):
        """Back-propagate the loss derivative from last to 1st layer."""
        for layer in reversed(self.layers):
            dL_dy = layer.backward(dL_dy)
        return dL_dy

 def optimize(self, epsilon):
```

```
        """Optimize the parameters according to the stored gradients."""
        for layer in self.layers:
            layer.optimize(epsilon)

    def train(self, X_train, y_train, X_val, y_val, batch_size=32,
num_epochs=5, learning_rate=5e-3):
        """Train (and evaluate) the network on the provided dataset."""
        num_batches_per_epoch = len(X_train) // batch_size
        loss, accuracy = [], []
        for i in range(num_epochs): # for each training epoch
            epoch_loss = 0
            for b in range(num_batches_per_epoch): # for each batch
                # Get batch:
                b_idx = b * batch_size
                b_idx_e = b_idx + batch_size
                x, y_true = X_train[b_idx:b_idx_e], y_train[b_idx:b_idx_e]
                # Optimize on batch:
                y = self.forward(x) # forward pass
                epoch_loss += self.loss_fn(y, y_true) # loss
                dL_dy = self.d_loss_fn(y, y_true) # loss derivation
                self.backward(dL_dy) # back-propagation pass
                self.optimize(learning_rate) # optimization
            loss.append(epoch_loss / num_batches_per_epoch)
            # After each epoch, we "validate" our network, i.e., we measure
its accuracy over the test/validation set:
            accuracy.append(self.evaluate_accuracy(X_val, y_val))
            print("Epoch {:4d}: training loss = {:.6f} | val accuracy =
{:.2f}%".format(i, loss[i], accuracy[i] * 100))
```

Everything is now ready! We can train our model and see how it performs:

```
losses, accuracies = mnist_classifier.train(
    X_train, y_train, X_test, y_test, batch_size=30, num_epochs=500)
# > Epoch    0: training loss = 1.096978 | val accuracy = 19.10%
# > Epoch    1: training loss = 0.886127 | val accuracy = 32.17%
# > Epoch    2: training loss = 0.785361 | val accuracy = 44.06%
# [...]
# > Epoch  498: training loss = 0.046022 | val accuracy = 94.83%
# > Epoch  499: training loss = 0.045963 | val accuracy = 94.83%
```

Congratulations! If your machine is powerful enough to complete this training (this simple implementation does not take advantage of the GPU), we just obtained our very own neural network that is able to classify handwritten digits with an accuracy of ~94.8%!

Training considerations – underfitting and overfitting

We invite you to play around with the framework we just implemented, trying different *hyperparameters* (layer sizes, learning rate, batch size, and so on). Choosing the proper topography (as well as other *hyperparameters*) can require lots of tweaking and testing. While the sizes of the input and output layers are conditioned by the use case (for example, for classification, the input size would be the number of pixel values in the images, and the output size would be the number of classes to predict from), the hidden layers should be carefully engineered.

For instance, if the network has too few layers, or the layers are too small, the accuracy may stagnate. This means the network is **underfitting**, that is, it does not have enough parameters for the complexity of the task. In this case, the only solution is to adopt a new architecture that is more suited to the application.

On the other hand, if the network is too complex and/or the training dataset is too small, the network may start **overfitting** the training data. This means that the network will learn to fit very well to the training distribution (that is, its particular noise, details, and so on), but won't generalize to new samples (since these new images may have a slightly different noise, for instance). The following diagram highlights the differences between these two problems. The regression method on the extreme left does not have enough parameters to model the data variations, while the method on the extreme right has too many, which means it will struggle to generalize:

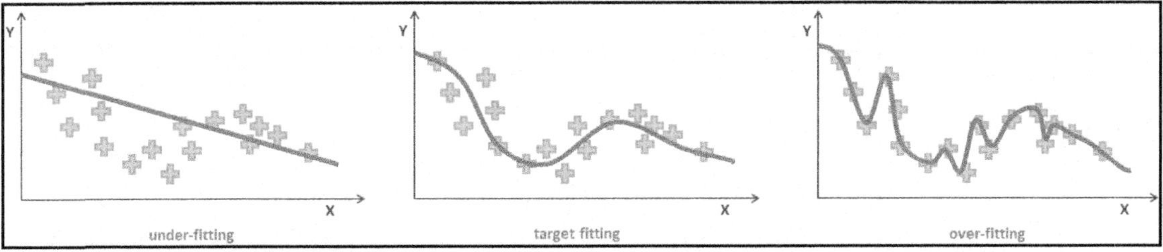

Figure 1.16: A common illustration of underfitting and overfitting

While gathering a larger, more diverse training dataset seems the logical solution to overfitting, it is not always possible in practice (for example, due to limited access to the target objects). Another solution is to adapt the network or its training in order to constrain how much detail the network learns. Such methods will be detailed in `Chapter 3`, *Modern Neural Networks*, among other advanced neural network solutions.

Summary

We covered a lot of ground in this first chapter. We introduced computer vision, the challenges associated with it, and some historical methods, such as SIFT and SVMs. We got familiar with neural networks and saw how they are built, trained, and applied. After implementing our own classifier network from scratch, we can now better understand and appreciate how machine learning frameworks work.

With this knowledge, we are now more than ready to start with TensorFlow in the next chapter.

Questions

1. Which of the following tasks does not belong to computer vision?
    - A web search for images similar to a query
    - A 3D scene reconstruction from image sequences
    - Animation of a video character
2. Which activation function were the original perceptrons using?
3. Suppose we want to train a method to detect whether a handwritten digit is a 4 or not. How should we adapt the network that we implemented in this chapter for this task?

Further reading

- *Hands-On Image Processing with Python* (`https://www.packtpub.com/big-data-and-business-intelligence/hands-image-processing-python`), by Sandipan Dey: A great book to learn more about image processing itself, and how Python can be used to manipulate visual data
- *OpenCV 3.x with Python By Example – Second Edition* (`https://www.packtpub.com/application-development/opencv-3x-python-example-second-edition`), by Gabriel Garrido and Prateek Joshi: Another recent book introducing the famous computer vision library *OpenCV*, which has been around for years (it implements some of the traditional methods we introduced in this chapter, such as edge detectors, SIFT, and SVM)

2
TensorFlow Basics and Training a Model

TensorFlow is a numerical processing library used by researchers and machine learning practitioners. While you can perform any numerical operation with TensorFlow, it is mostly used to train and run deep neural networks. This chapter will introduce you to the core concepts of TensorFlow 2 and walk you through a simple example.

The following topics will be covered in this chapter:

- Getting started with TensorFlow 2 and Keras
- Creating and training a simple computer vision model
- TensorFlow and Keras core concepts
- The TensorFlow ecosystem

Technical requirements

Throughout this book, we will use TensorFlow 2. You can find detailed installation instructions for the different platforms at `https://www.tensorflow.org/install`.

If you plan on using your machine's GPU, make sure you install the corresponding version, `tensorflow-gpu`. It must be installed along with the CUDA Toolkit, a library provided by NVIDIA (`https://developer.nvidia.com/cuda-zone`).

Installation instructions are also available in the README on GitHub at `https://github.com/PacktPublishing/Hands-On-Computer-Vision-with-TensorFlow-2/tree/master/Chapter02`.

Getting started with TensorFlow 2 and Keras

Before detailing the core concepts of TensorFlow, we will start with a brief introduction of the framework and a basic example.

Introducing TensorFlow

TensorFlow was originally developed at Google to allow researchers and developers to conduct machine learning research. It was originally defined as *an interface for expressing machine learning algorithms, and an implementation for executing such algorithms.*

TensorFlow primarily offers to simplify the deployment of machine learning solutions on various platforms—computer CPUs, computer GPUs, mobile devices, and, more recently, in the browser. On top of that, TensorFlow offers many useful functions for creating machine learning models and running them at scale. In 2019, TensorFlow 2 was released with a focus on ease of use while maintaining good performance.

An introduction to TensorFlow 1.0's concepts is available in `Appendix`, *Migrating from TensorFlow 1 to TensorFlow 2* of this book.

The library was open sourced in November 2015. Since then, it has been improved and used by users all around the world. It is considered one of the platforms of choice for research. It is also one of the most active deep learning frameworks in terms of GitHub activity.

TensorFlow can be used by beginners as well as experts. The TensorFlow API has different levels of complexity, allowing newcomers to start with a simple API and experts to create very complex models at the same time. Let's explore those different levels.

TensorFlow's main architecture

TensorFlow's architecture has several levels of abstraction. Let's first introduce the lowest layer and find our way to the uppermost layer:

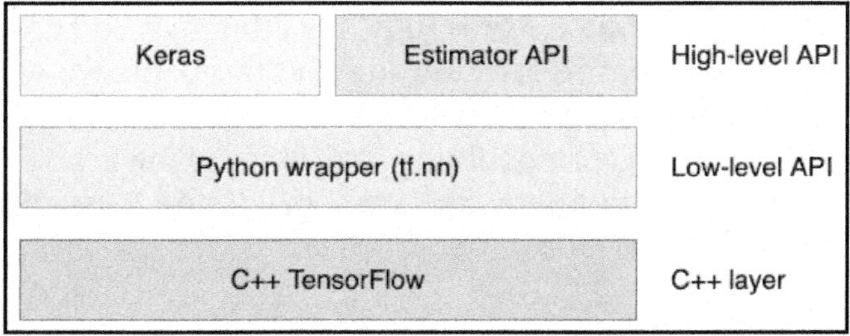

Figure 2.1: Diagram of the TensorFlow architecture

Most deep learning computations are coded in C++. To run operations on the GPU, TensorFlow uses a library developed by NVIDIA called **CUDA**. This is the reason you need to install CUDA if you want to exploit GPU capabilities and why you cannot use GPUs from another hardware manufacturer.

The Python **low-level API** then wraps the C++ sources. When you call a Python method in TensorFlow, it usually invokes C++ code behind the scenes. This wrapper layer allows users to work more quickly because Python is considered easier to use than C++ and does not require compilation. This Python wrapper makes it possible to perform extremely basic operations such as matrix multiplication and addition.

At the top sits the **high-level API**, made of two components—Keras and the Estimator API. **Keras** is a user-friendly, modular, and extensible wrapper for TensorFlow. We will introduce it in the next section. The **Estimator API** contains several pre-made components that allow you to build your machine learning model easily. You can consider them building blocks or templates.

In deep learning, a **model** usually refers to a neural network that was trained on data. A model is composed of an architecture, matrix weights, and parameters.

Introducing Keras

First released in 2015, Keras was designed as an interface to enable fast experimentation with neural networks. As such, it relied on TensorFlow or **Theano** (another deep learning framework, now deprecated) to run deep learning operations. Known for its user-friendliness, it was the library of choice for beginners.

Since 2017, TensorFlow has integrated Keras fully, meaning that you can use it without installing anything other than TensorFlow. Throughout this book, we will rely on `tf.keras` instead of the standalone version of Keras. There are a few minor differences between the two versions, such as compatibility with TensorFlow's other modules and the way models are saved. For this reason, readers must make sure to use the correct version, as follows:

- In your code, import `tf.keras` and not `keras`.
- Go through the `tf.keras` documentation on TensorFlow's website and not the *keras.io* documentation.
- When using external Keras libraries, make sure they are compatible with `tf.keras`.
- Some saved models might not be compatible between different versions of Keras.

The two versions will continue to co-exist for the foreseeable future, and `tf.keras` will become more and more integrated with TensorFlow. To illustrate the power and simplicity of Keras, we will now use it to implement a simple neural network.

A simple computer vision model using Keras

Before we delve into the core concepts of TensorFlow, let's start with a classical example of computer vision—digit recognition with the **Modified National Institute of Standards and Technology** (**MNIST**) dataset. The dataset was introduced in `Chapter 1`, *Computer Vision and Neural Networks*.

Preparing the data

First, we import the data. It is made up of 60,000 images for the training set and 10,000 images for the test set:

```
import tensorflow as tf

num_classes = 10
img_rows, img_cols = 28, 28
num_channels = 1
input_shape = (img_rows, img_cols, num_channels)

(x_train, y_train),(x_test, y_test) = tf.keras.datasets.mnist.load_data()
x_train, x_test = x_train / 255.0, x_test / 255.0
```

It is common practice to import TensorFlow with the alias `tf` for faster reading and typing. It is also common to use `x` to denote input data, and `y` to represent labels.

The `tf.keras.datasets` module provides quick access to download and instantiate a number of classical datasets. After importing the data using `load_data`, notice that we divide the array by `255.0` to get a number in the range *[0, 1]* instead of *[0, 255]*. It is common practice to normalize data, either in the *[0, 1]* range or in the *[-1, 1]* range.

Building the model

We can now move on to building the actual model. We will use a very simple architecture composed of two **fully connected** (also called **dense**) layers. Before we explore the architecture, let's have a look at the code. As you can see, Keras code is very concise:

```
model = tf.keras.models.Sequential()
model.add(tf.keras.layers.Flatten())
model.add(tf.keras.layers.Dense(128, activation='relu'))
model.add(tf.keras.layers.Dense(num_classes, activation='softmax'))
```

Since our model is a linear stack of layers, we start by calling the `Sequential` function. We then add each layer one after the other. Our model is composed of two fully connected layers. We build it layer by layer:

- **Flatten**: This will take the 2D matrix representing the image pixels and turn it into a 1D array. We need to do this before adding a fully connected layer. The *28 × 28* images are turned into a vector of size *784*.
- **Dense** of size *128*: This will turn the *784* pixel values into 128 activations using a weight matrix of size *128 × 784* and a bias matrix of size *128*. In total, this means *100,480* parameters.
- **Dense** of size *10*: This will turn the *128* activations into our final prediction. Notice that because we want probabilities to sum to *1*, we will use the `softmax` activation function.

The `softmax` function takes the output of a layer and returns probabilities that sum up to `1`. It is the activation of choice for the last layer of a classification model.

Note that you can get a description of the model, the outputs, and their weights using `model.summary()`. Here is the output:

```
Model: "sequential"
_________________________________________________________________
Layer (type) Output Shape Param #
=================================================================
flatten_1 (Flatten) (None, 784) 0
_________________________________________________________________
dense_1 (Dense) (None, 128) 100480
_________________________________________________________________
dense_2 (Dense) (None, 10) 1290
=================================================================
Total params: 101,770
Trainable params: 101,770
Non-trainable params: 0
```

With its architecture set and weights initialized, the model is now ready to be trained for the chosen task.

Training the model

Keras makes training extremely simple:

```
model.compile(optimizer='sgd',
 loss='sparse_categorical_crossentropy',
 metrics=['accuracy'])

model.fit(x_train, y_train, epochs=5, verbose=1, validation_data=(x_test,
y_test))
```

Calling `.compile()` on the model we just created is a mandatory step. A few arguments must be specified:

- `optimizer`: This is the component that will perform the gradient descent.
- `loss`: This is the metric we will optimize. In our case, we choose cross-entropy, just like in the previous chapter.
- `metrics`: These are additional metric functions evaluated during training to provide further visibility of the model's performance (unlike `loss`, they are not used in the optimization process).

The Keras `loss` named `sparse_categorical_crossentropy` performs the same cross-entropy operation as `categorical_crossentropy`, but the former directly takes the ground truth labels as inputs, while the latter requires the ground truth labels to be *one-hot* encoded already before hand. Using the `sparse_...` loss thus saves us from manually having to transform the labels.

Passing `'sgd'` to Keras is equivalent to passing `tf.keras.optimizers.SGD()`. The former option is easier to read, while the latter makes it possible to specify parameters such as a custom learning rate. The same goes for the loss, metrics, and most arguments passed to Keras methods.

Then, we call the `.fit()` method. It is very similar to the interface used in **scikit-learn**, another popular machine learning library. We will train for five epochs, meaning that we will iterate over the whole train dataset five times.

Notice that we set `verbose` to `1`. This will allow us to get a progress bar with the metrics we chose earlier, the loss, and the **Estimated Time of Arrival** (**ETA**). The ETA is an estimate of the remaining time before the end of the epoch. Here is what the progress bar looks like:

```
1952/60000 [.............................] - ETA: 6:46 - loss: 0.9248 - acc: 0.6962
```

Figure 2.2: Screenshot of the progress bar displayed by Keras in verbose mode

Model performance

As described in `Chapter 1`, *Computer Vision and Neural Networks*, you will notice that our model is overfitting—training accuracy is greater than test accuracy. If we train the model for five epochs, we end up with an accuracy of 97% on the test set. This is about 2% better than in the previous chapter, where we achieved 95%. State-of-the-art algorithms attain 99.79% accuracy.

We followed three main steps:

1. **Loading the data**: In this case, the dataset was already available. During future projects, you may need additional steps to gather and clean the data.
2. **Creating the model**: This step was made easy by using Keras—we defined the architecture of the model by adding sequential layers. Then, we selected a loss, an optimizer, and a metric to monitor.
3. **Training the model**: Our model worked pretty well the first time. On more complex datasets, you will usually need to fine-tune parameters during training.

The whole process was extremely simple thanks to Keras, the high-level API of TensorFlow. Behind this simple API, the library hides a lot of the complexity.

TensorFlow 2 and Keras in detail

We have introduced the general architecture of TensorFlow and trained our first model using Keras. Let's now walk through the main concepts of TensorFlow 2. We will explain several core concepts of TensorFlow that feature in this book, followed by some advanced notions. While we may not employ all of them in the remainder of the book, you might find it useful to understand some open source models that are available on GitHub or to get a deeper understanding of the library.

Core concepts

Released in spring 2019, the new version of the framework is focused on simplicity and ease of use. In this section, we will introduce the concepts that TensorFlow relies on and cover how they evolved from version 1 to version 2.

Introducing tensors

TensorFlow takes its name from a mathematical object called a **tensor**. You can imagine tensors as N-dimensional arrays. A tensor could be a scalar, a vector, a 3D matrix, or an N-dimensional matrix.

A fundamental component of TensorFlow, the `Tensor` object is used to store mathematical values. It can contain fixed values (created using `tf.constant`) or changing values (created using `tf.Variable`).

In this book, *tensor* denotes the mathematical concept, while *Tensor* (with a capital *T*) corresponds to the TensorFlow object.

Each `Tensor` object has the following:

- **Type**: `string`, `float32`, `float16`, or `int8`, among others.
- **Shape**: The dimensions of the data. For instance, the shape would be `()` for a scalar, `(n)` for a vector of size *n*, and `(n, m)` for a 2D matrix of size *n* × *m*.
- **Rank**: The number of dimensions, *0* for a scalar, `1` for a vector, and *2* for a 2D matrix.

Some tensors can have partially unknown shapes. For instance, a model accepting images of variable sizes could have an input shape of `(None, None, 3)`. Since the height and the width of the images are not known in advance, the first two dimensions are set to `None`. However, the number of channels (`3`, corresponding to red, blue, and green) is known and is therefore set.

TensorFlow graphs

TensorFlow uses tensors as inputs as well as outputs. A component that transforms input into output is called an **operation**. A computer vision model is therefore composed of multiple operations.

TensorFlow represents these operations using a **directed acyclic graph** (**DAC**), also referred to as a **graph**. In TensorFlow 2, graph operations have disappeared under the hood to make the framework easier to use. Nevertheless, the graph concept remains important to understand how TensorFlow really works.

When building the previous example using Keras, TensorFlow actually built a graph:

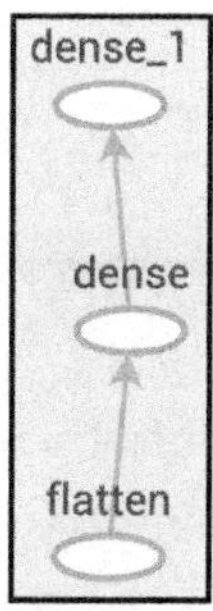

Figure 2.3: A simplified graph corresponding to our model. In practice, each node is composed of smaller operations (such as matrix multiplications and additions)

While very simple, this graph represents the different layers of our model in the form of operations. Relying on graphs has many advantages, allowing TensorFlow to do the following:

- Run part of the operations on the CPU and another part on the GPU
- Run different parts of the graph on different machines in the case of a distributed model
- Optimize the graph to avoid unnecessary operations, leading to better computational performance

Moreover, the graph concept allows TensorFlow models to be portable. A single graph definition can be run on any kind of device.

In TensorFlow 2, graph creation is no longer handled by the user. While managing graphs used to be a complex task in TensorFlow 1, the new version greatly improves usability while still maintaining performance. In the next section, we will peek into the inner workings of TensorFlow and briefly explore how graphs are created.

Comparing lazy execution to eager execution

The main change in TensorFlow 2 is **eager execution**. Historically, TensorFlow 1 always used **lazy execution** by default. It is called *lazy* because operations are not run by the framework until asked specifically to do so.

Let's start with a very simple example to illustrate the difference between lazy and eager execution, summing the values of two vectors:

```
import tensorflow as tf

a = tf.constant([1, 2, 3])
b = tf.constant([0, 0, 1])
c = tf.add(a, b)

print(c)
```

Note that `tf.add(a, b)` could be replaced by `a + b` since TensorFlow overloads many Python operators.

The output of the previous code depends on the TensorFlow version. With TensorFlow 1 (where lazy execution is the default mode), the output would be this:

```
Tensor("Add:0", shape=(3,), dtype=int32)
```

However, with TensorFlow 2 (where eager execution is the default mode), you would get the following output:

```
tf.Tensor([1 2 4], shape=(3,), dtype=int32)
```

In both cases, the output is a Tensor. In the second case, the operation has been run eagerly and we can observe directly that the Tensor contains the result (`[1 2 4]`). In the first case, the Tensor contains information about the addition operation (`Add:0`), but not the result of the operation.

In eager mode, you can access the value of a Tensor by calling the `.numpy()` method. In our example, calling `c.numpy()` returns `[1 2 4]` (as a NumPy array).

In TensorFlow 1, more code would be needed to compute the result, making the development process more complex. Eager execution makes code easier to debug (as developers can peak at the value of a Tensor at any time) and easier to develop. In the next section, we will detail the inner workings of TensorFlow and look at how it builds graphs.

Creating graphs in TensorFlow 2

We'll start with a simple example to illustrate graph creation and optimization:

```
def compute(a, b, c):
    d = a * b + c
    e = a * b * c
    return d, e
```

Assuming `a`, `b`, and `c` are Tensor matrices, this code computes two new values: `d` and `e`. Using eager execution, TensorFlow would compute the value for `d` and then compute the value for `e`.

Using lazy execution, TensorFlow would create a graph of operations. Before running the graph to get the result, a **graph optimizer** would be run. To avoid computing `a * b` twice, the optimizer would **cache** the result and reuse it when necessary. For more complex operations, the optimizer could enable **parallelism** to make computation faster. Both techniques are important when running large and complex models.

As we saw, running in eager mode implies that every operation is run when defined. Therefore, such optimizations cannot be applied. Thankfully, TensorFlow includes a module to work around this—TensorFlow **AutoGraph**.

Introducing TensorFlow AutoGraph and tf.function

The TensorFlow AutoGraph module makes it easy to turn eager code into a graph, allowing automatic optimization. To do so, the easiest way is to add the `tf.function` decorator on top of your function:

```
@tf.function
def compute(a, b, c):
    d = a * b + c
    e = a * b * c
    return d, e
```

A **Python decorator** is a concept that allows functions to be wrapped, adding functionalities or altering them. Decorators start with an `@` (the "at" symbol).

When we call the `compute` function for the first time, TensorFlow will transparently create the following graph:

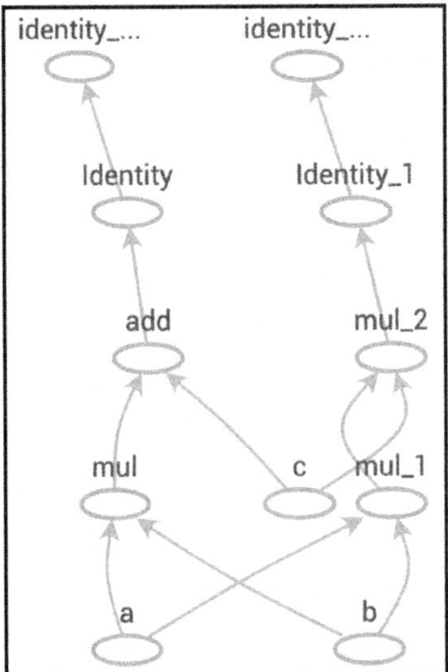

Figure 2.4: The graph automatically generated by TensorFlow when calling the compute function for the first time

TensorFlow AutoGraph can convert most Python statements, such as `for` loops, `while` loops, `if` statements, and iterations. Thanks to graph optimizations, graph execution can sometimes be faster than eager code. More generally, AutoGraph should be used in the following scenarios:

- When the model needs to be exported to other devices
- When performance is paramount and graph optimizations can lead to speed improvements

Another advantage of graphs is their **automatic differentiation**. Knowing the full list of operations, TensorFlow can easily compute the gradient for each variable.

Note that in order to compute the gradient, the operations need to be **differentiable**. Some of them, such as `tf.math.argmax`, are not. Using them in a `loss` function will most likely cause the automatic differentiation to fail. It is up to the user to make sure that the loss is differentiable.

However, since, in eager mode, each operation is independent from one another, automatic differentiation is not possible by default. Thankfully, TensorFlow 2 provides a way to perform automatic differentiation while still using eager mode—the **gradient tape**.

Backpropagating errors using the gradient tape

The gradient tape allows easy backpropagation in eager mode. To illustrate this, we will use a simple example. Let's assume that we want to solve the equation $A \times X = B$, where A and B are constants. We want to find the value of X to solve the equation. To do so, we will try to minimize a simple loss, $abs(A \times X - B)$.

In code, this translates to the following:

```
A, B = tf.constant(3.0), tf.constant(6.0)
X = tf.Variable(20.0) # In practice, we would start with a random value
loss = tf.math.abs(A * X - B)
```

Now, to update the value of X, we would like to compute the gradient of the loss with respect to X. However, when printing the content of the loss, we obtain the following:

```
<tf.Tensor: id=18525, shape=(), dtype=float32, numpy=54.0>
```

In eager mode, TensorFlow computed the result of the operation instead of storing the operation! With no information on the operation and its inputs, it would be impossible to automatically differentiate the `loss` operation.

That is where the gradient tape comes in handy. By running our loss computation in the context of `tf.GradientTape`, TensorFlow will automatically record all operations and allow us to replay them backward afterward:

```
def train_step():
    with tf.GradientTape() as tape:
        loss = tf.math.abs(A * X - B)
    dX = tape.gradient(loss, X)
    print('X = {:.2f}, dX = {:2f}'.format(X.numpy(), dX))
    X.assign(X - dX)

for i in range(7):
    train_step()
```

The previous code defines a single training step. Every time `train_step` is called, the loss is computed in the context of the gradient tape. The context is then used to compute the gradient. The *X* variable is then updated. Indeed, we can see *X* converging toward the value that solves the equation:

```
X = 20.00, dX = 3.000000
X = 17.00, dX = 3.000000
X = 14.00, dX = 3.000000
X = 11.00, dX = 3.000000
X = 8.00, dX = 3.000000
X = 5.00, dX = 3.000000
X = 2.00, dX = 0.000000
```

You will notice that in the very first example of this chapter, we did not make use of the gradient tape. This is because Keras models encapsulate training inside the `.fit()` function—there's no need to update the variables manually. Nevertheless, for innovative models or when experimenting, the gradient tape is a powerful tool that allows automatic differentiation without much effort. Readers can find a more practical use of the gradient tape in the regularization notebook of `Chapter 3`, *Modern Neural Networks.*

Keras models and layers

In the first section of this chapter, we built a simple Keras Sequential model. The resulting `Model` object contains numerous useful methods and properties:

- `.inputs` and `.outputs`: Provide access to the inputs and outputs of the model.
- `.layers`: Lists the model's layers as well as their shape.
- `.summary()`: Prints the architecture of the model.

- `.save()`: Saves the model, its architecture, and the current state of training. It is very useful for resuming training later on. Models can be instantiated from a file using `tf.keras.models.load_model()`.
- `.save_weights()`: Only saves the weights of the model.

While there is only one type of Keras model object, they can be built in a variety of ways.

Sequential and functional APIs

Instead of employing the Sequential API, like at the beginning of this chapter, you can instead use the functional API:

```
model_input = tf.keras.layers.Input(shape=input_shape)
output = tf.keras.layers.Flatten()(model_input)
output = tf.keras.layers.Dense(128, activation='relu')(output)
output = tf.keras.layers.Dense(num_classes, activation='softmax')(output)
model = tf.keras.Model(model_input, output)
```

Notice that the code is slightly longer than it previously was. Nevertheless, the functional API is much more versatile and expressive than the Sequential API. The former allows for branching models (that is, for building architectures with multiple parallel layers for instance), while the latter can only be used for linear models. For even more flexibility, Keras also offers the possibility to subclass the `Model` class, as described in `Chapter 3`, *Modern Neural Networks*.

Regardless of how a `Model` object is built, it is composed of layers. A layer can be seen as a node that accepts one or several inputs and returns one or several outputs, similar to a TensorFlow operation. Its weights can be accessed using `.get_weights()` and set using `.set_weights()`. Keras provides pre-made layers for the most common deep learning operations. For more innovative or complex models, `tf.keras.layers.Layer` can also be subclassed.

Callbacks

Keras callbacks are utility functions that you can pass to a Keras model's `.fit()` method to add functionality to its default behavior. Multiple callbacks can be defined, which will be called by Keras either before or after each batch iteration, each epoch, or the whole training procedure. Predefined Keras callbacks include the following:

- `CSVLogger`: Logs training information in a CSV file.
- `EarlyStopping`: Stops training if the loss or a metric stops improving. It can be useful in avoiding overfitting.

- `LearningRateScheduler`: Changes the learning rate on each epoch according to a schedule.
- `ReduceLROnPlateau`: Automatically reduces the learning rate when the loss or a metric stops improving.

It is also possible to create custom callbacks by subclassing `tf.keras.callbacks.Callback`, as demonstrated in later chapters and their code samples.

Advanced concepts

In summary, the AutoGraph module, the `tf.function` decorator, and the gradient tape context make graph creation and management very simple—if not invisible. However, a lot of the complexity is hidden from the user. In this section, we will explore the inner workings of these modules.

This section presents advanced concepts that are not required throughout the book, but it may be useful for you to understand more complex TensorFlow code. More impatient readers can skip this part and come back to it later.

How tf.function works

As mentioned earlier, when calling a function decorated with `tf.function` for the first time, TensorFlow will create a graph corresponding to the function's operations. TensorFlow will then cache the graph so that the next time the function is called, graph creation will not be necessary.

To illustrate this, let's create a simple `identity` function:

```
@tf.function
def identity(x):
  print('Creating graph !')
  return x
```

This function will print a message every time TensorFlow creates a graph corresponding to its operation. In this case, since TensorFlow is caching the graph, it will print something only the first time it is run:

```
x1 = tf.random.uniform((10, 10))
x2 = tf.random.uniform((10, 10))
```

```
result1 = identity(x1) # Prints 'Creating graph !'
result2 = identity(x2) # Nothing is printed
```

However, note that if we change the input type, TensorFlow will recreate a graph:

```
x3 = tf.random.uniform((10, 10), dtype=tf.float16)
result3 = identity(x3) # Prints 'Creating graph !'
```

This behavior is explained by the fact that TensorFlow graphs are defined by their operations and the shapes and types of the tensors they receive as inputs. Therefore, when the input type changes, a new graph needs to be created. In TensorFlow vocabulary, when a `tf.function` function has defined input types, it becomes a **concrete function**.

To summarize, every time a decorated function is run for the first time, TensorFlow caches the graph corresponding to the input types and input shapes. If the function is run with inputs of a different type, TensorFlow will create a new graph and cache it.

Nevertheless, it might be useful to log information every time a concrete function is run and not just the first time. To do so, use `tf.print`:

```
@tf.function
def identity(x):
  tf.print("Running identity")
  return x
```

Instead of printing information only the first time, this function will print `Running identity` every single time it is run.

Variables in TensorFlow 2

To hold the model weights, TensorFlow uses `Variable` instances. In our Keras example, we can list the content of the model by accessing `model.variables`. It will return the list of all variables contained in our model:

```
print([variable.name for variable in model.variables])
# Prints ['sequential/dense/kernel:0', 'sequential/dense/bias:0',
'sequential/dense_1/kernel:0', 'sequential/dense_1/bias:0']
```

In our example, variable management (including naming) has been entirely handled by Keras. As we saw earlier, it is also possible to create our own variables:

```
a = tf.Variable(3, name='my_var')
print(a) # Prints <tf.Variable 'my_var:0' shape=() dtype=int32, numpy=3>
```

Note that for large projects, it is recommended to name variables to clarify the code and ease debugging. To change the value of a variable, use the `Variable.assign` method:

```
a.assign(a + 1)
print(a.numpy()) # Prints 4
```

Failing to use the `.assign()` method would create a new `Tensor` method:

```
b = a + 1
print(b) # Prints <tf.Tensor: id=21231, shape=(), dtype=int32, numpy=4>
```

Finally, deleting the Python reference to a variable will remove the object itself from the active memory, releasing space for other variables to be created.

Distribution strategies

We trained a simple model on a very small dataset. When using larger models and datasets, more computing power is necessary—this often implies multiple servers.
The `tf.distribute.Strategy` API defines how multiple machines communicate together to train a model efficiently.

Some of the strategies defined by TensorFlow are as follows:

- `MirroredStrategy`: For training on multiple GPUs on a single machine. Model weights are kept in sync between each device.
- `MultiWorkerMirroredStrategy`: Similar to `MirroredStategy`, but for training on multiple machines.
- `ParameterServerStrategy`: For training on multiple machines. Instead of syncing the weights on each device, they are kept on a parameter server.
- `TPUStrategy`: For training on Google's **Tensor Processing Unit** (**TPU**) chip.

The TPU is a custom chip made by Google, similar to a GPU, designed specifically to run neural network computations. It is available through Google Cloud.

To use a distribution strategy, create and compile your model in its scope:

```
mirrored_strategy = tf.distribute.MirroredStrategy()
with mirrored_strategy.scope():
  model = make_model() # create your model here
  model.compile([...])
```

Note that you will probably have to increase the batch size, as each device will now receive a small subset of each batch. Depending on your model, you may also have to change the learning rate.

Using the Estimator API

We saw in the first part of this chapter that the Estimator API is a high-level alternative to the Keras API. Estimators simplify training, evaluation, prediction, and serving.

There are two types of Estimators. Pre-made Estimators are very simple models provided by TensorFlow, allowing you to quickly try out machine learning architectures. The second type is custom Estimators, which can be created using any model architecture.

Estimators handle all the small details of a model's life cycle—data queues, exception handling, recovering from failure, periodic checkpoints, and many more. While using Estimators was considered best practice in TensorFlow 1, in version 2, it is recommended to use the Keras API.

Available pre-made Estimators

At the time of writing, the available pre-made Estimators are `DNNClassifier`, `DNNRegressor`, `LinearClassifier`, and `LinearRegressor`. Here, DNN stands for **deep neural network**. Combined Estimators based on both architectures are also available—`DNNLinearCombinedClassifier` and `DNNLinearCombinedRegressor`.

In machine learning, classification is the process of predicting a discrete category, while regression is the process of predicting a continuous number.

Combined Estimators, also called **deep-n-wide models**, make use of a linear model (for memorization) and a deep model (for generalization). They are mostly used for recommendation or ranking models.

Pre-made Estimators are suitable for some machine learning problems. However, they are not suitable for computer vision problems, as there are no pre-made Estimators with convolutions, a powerful type of layer described in the next chapter.

Training a custom Estimator

The easiest way to create an Estimator is to convert a Keras model. After the model has been compiled, call `tf.keras.estimator.model_to_estimator()`:

```
estimator = tf.keras.estimator.model_to_estimator(model,
model_dir='./estimator_dir')
```

The `model_dir` argument allows you to specify a location where the checkpoints of the model will be saved. As mentioned earlier, Estimators will automatically save checkpoints for our models.

Training an Estimator requires the use of an **input function**—a function that returns data in a specific format. One of the accepted formats is a TensorFlow dataset. The dataset API is described in depth in `Chapter 7`, *Training on Complex and Scarce Datasets*. For now, we'll define the following function, which returns the dataset defined in the first part of this chapter in the correct format, in batches of *32* samples:

```
BATCH_SIZE = 32
def train_input_fn():
    train_dataset = tf.data.Dataset.from_tensor_slices((x_train, y_train))
    train_dataset = train_dataset.batch(BATCH_SIZE).repeat()
    return train_dataset
```

Once this function is defined, we can launch the training with the Estimator:

```
estimator.train(train_input_fn, steps=len(x_train)//BATCH_SIZE)
```

Just like Keras, the training part is very simple, as Estimators handle the heavy lifting.

The TensorFlow ecosystem

In addition to the main library, TensorFlow offers numerous tools that are useful for machine learning. While some of them are shipped with TensorFlow, others are grouped under **TensorFlow Extended (TFX)** and **TensorFlow Addons**. We will now introduce the most commonly used tools.

TensorBoard

While the progress bar we used in the first example of this chapter displayed useful information, we might want to access more detailed graphs. TensorFlow provides a powerful tool for monitoring—**TensorBoard**. Installed by default with TensorFlow, it is also very easy to use when combined with Keras's callbacks:

```
callbacks = [tf.keras.callbacks.TensorBoard('./logs_keras')]
model.fit(x_train, y_train, epochs=5, verbose=1, validation_data=(x_test,
y_test), callbacks=callbacks)
```

In this updated code, we pass the TensorBoard callback to the `model.fit()` method. By default, TensorFlow will automatically write the loss and the metrics to the folder we specified. We can then launch TensorBoard from the command line:

```
$ tensorboard --logdir ./logs_keras
```

This command outputs a URL that we can then open to display the TensorBoard interface. In the **Scalars** tab, we can find graphs displaying the loss and the accuracy:

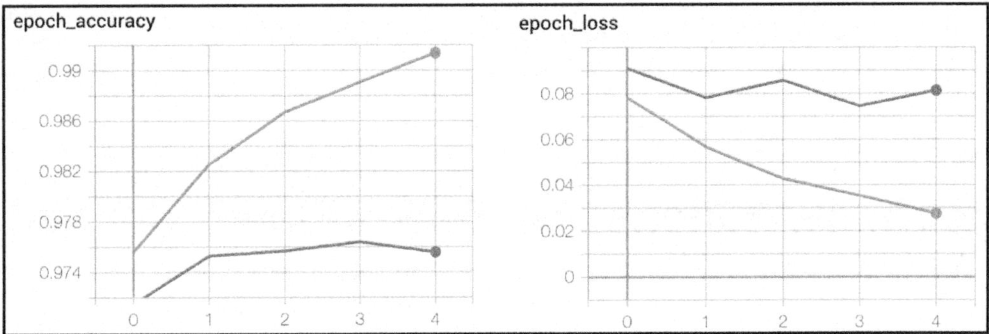

Figure 2.5: Two graphs displayed by TensorBoard during training

As you will see in this book, training a deep learning model requires a lot of fine-tuning. Therefore, it is essential to monitor how your model is performing. TensorBoard allows you to do precisely this. The most common use case is to monitor the evolution of the loss of your model over time. But you can also do the following:

- Plot any metric (such as accuracy)
- Display input and output images
- Display the execution time
- Draw your model's graph representation

TensorBoard is very versatile, and there are many ways to use it. Each piece of information is stored in `tf.summary`—this can be scalars, images, histograms, or text. For instance, to log a scalar you might first create a summary writer and log information using the following:

```
writer = tf.summary.create_file_writer('./model_logs')
with writer.as_default():
  tf.summary.scalar('custom_log', 10, step=3)
```

In the preceding code, we specify the step—it could be the epoch number, the batch number, or custom information. It will correspond to the *x* axis in TensorBoard figures. TensorFlow also provides tools for generating aggregates. To manually log accuracy, you could use the following:

```
accuracy = tf.keras.metrics.Accuracy()
ground_truth, predictions = [1, 0, 1], [1, 0, 0] # in practice this would
come from the model
accuracy.update_state(ground_truth, predictions)
tf.summary.scalar('accuracy', accuracy.result(), step=4)
```

Other metrics are available, such as `Mean`, `Recall`, and `TruePositives`. While setting up the logging of metrics in TensorBoard may seem a bit complicated and time-consuming, it is an essential part of the TensorFlow toolkit. It will save you countless hours of debugging and manual logging.

TensorFlow Addons and TensorFlow Extended

TensorFlow Addons is a collection of extra functionalities gathered into a single repository (`https://github.com/tensorflow/addons`). It hosts some of the newer advancements in deep learning that are too unstable or not used by enough people to justify adding them to the main TensorFlow library. It also acts as a replacement for `tf.contrib`, which was removed from TensorFlow 1.

TensorFlow Extended is an end-to-end machine learning platform for TensorFlow. It offers several useful tools:

- **TensorFlow Data Validation**: A library for exploring and validating machine learning data. You can use it before even building your model.
- **TensorFlow Transform**: A library for preprocessing data. It allows you to make sure training and evaluation data are processed the same way.

- **TensorFlow Model Analysis**: A library for evaluating TensorFlow models.
- **TensorFlow Serving**: A serving system for machine learning models. Serving is the process of delivering predictions from a model, usually through a REST API:

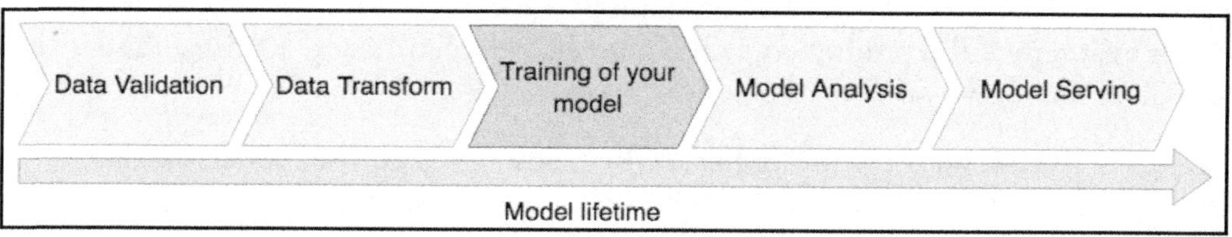

Figure 2.6: End-to-end process of creating and using a deep learning model

As seen in *Figure 2.6*, these tools fulfill the goal of being end to end, covering every step of the process of building and using a deep learning model.

TensorFlow Lite and TensorFlow.js

The main version of TensorFlow is designed for Windows, Linux, and Mac computers. To operate on other devices, a different version of TensorFlow is necessary. **TensorFlow Lite** is designed to run model predictions (inference) on mobile phones and embedded devices. It is composed of a converter transforming TensorFlow models to the required `.tflite` format and an interpreter that can be installed on mobile devices to run inferences.

More recently, **TensorFlow.js** (also referred to as **tfjs**) was developed to empower almost any web browser with deep learning. It does not require any installation from the user and can sometimes make use of the device's GPU acceleration. We detail the use of TensorFlow Lite and TensorFlow.js in `Chapter 9`, *Optimizing Models and Deploying on Mobile Devices*.

Where to run your model

As computer vision models process large amounts of data, they take a long time to train. Because of this, training on your local computer can take a considerable amount of time. You will also notice that creating efficient models requires a lot of iterations. Those two insights will drive your decision regarding where to train and run your models. In this section, we will compare the different options available to train and use your model.

On a local machine

Coding your model on your computer is often the fastest way to get started. As you have access to a familiar environment, you can easily change your code as often as needed. However, personal computers, especially laptops, lack the computing power to train a computer vision model. Training on a GPU may be between 10 and 100 times faster than using a CPU. This is why it is recommended to use a GPU.

Even if your computer has a GPU, only very specific models can run TensorFlow. Your GPU must be compatible with CUDA, NVIDIA's computing library. At the time of writing, the latest version of TensorFlow requires a CUDA compute capability of 3.5 or higher.

Some laptops are compatible with external GPU enclosures, but this defeats the purpose of a portable computer. Instead, a practical way is to run your model on a remote computer that has a GPU.

On a remote machine

Nowadays, you can rent powerful machines with GPUs by the hour. Pricing varies, depending on the GPU power and the provider. It usually costs around $1 per hour for a single GPU machine, with the price going down every day. If you commit to renting the machine for the month, you can get good computing power for around $100 per month. Considering the time you will save waiting for the model to train, it often makes economic sense to rent a remote machine.

Another option is to build your own deep learning server. Note that this requires investment and assembly, and that GPUs consume large amounts of electricity.

Once you have secured access to a remote machine, you have two options:

- Run Jupyter Notebook on the remote server. Jupyter Lab or Jupyter Notebook will then be accessible using your browser, anywhere on the planet. It is a very convenient way of performing deep learning.
- Sync your local development folder and run your code remotely. Most IDEs have a feature to sync your local code with a remote server. This allows you to code in your favorite IDE while still enjoying a powerful machine.

Google Colab, based on Jupyter notebooks, allows you to run notebooks in the cloud for *free*. You can even enable GPU mode. Colab has limited storage space and a limit of 8 hours of consecutive running time. While it is the perfect tool for getting started or experimenting, it is not convenient for larger models.

On Google Cloud

To run TensorFlow on a remote machine, you will need to manage it yourself—installing the correct software, making sure it is up to date, and turning the server on and off. While it is still possible to do so for one machine, and you sometimes need to distribute the training among numerous GPUs, using Google Cloud ML to run TensorFlow allows you to focus on your model and not on operations.

You will find that Google Cloud ML is useful for the following:

- Training your model quickly thanks to elastic resources in the cloud
- Looking for the best model parameters in the shortest amount of time possible using parallelization
- Once your model is ready, serving predictions without having to run your own prediction server

All the details for packaging, sending, and running your model are available in the Google Cloud ML documentation (`https://cloud.google.com/ml-engine/docs/`).

Summary

In this chapter, we started by training a basic computer vision model using the Keras API. We introduced the main concepts behind TensorFlow 2—tensors, graphs, AutoGraph, eager execution, and the gradient tape. We also detailed some of the more advanced concepts of the framework. We went through the main tools surrounding the use of deep learning with the library, from TensorBoard for monitoring, to TFX for preprocessing and model analysis. Finally, we covered where to run your model depending on your needs.

With these powerful tools in hand, you are now ready to discover modern computer vision models in the next chapter.

Questions

1. What is Keras in relation to TensorFlow, and what is its purpose?
2. Why does TensorFlow use graphs, and how do you create them manually?
3. What is the difference between eager execution mode and lazy execution mode?
4. How do you log information in TensorBoard, and how do you display it?
5. What are the main differences between TensorFlow 1 and TensorFlow 2?

3
Modern Neural Networks

In `Chapter 1`, *Computer Vision and Neural Networks*, we presented how recent neural networks, which are more suitable for image processing, surpassed previous computer vision methods of the past decade. However, limited by how much we can reimplement from scratch, we only covered basic architectures. Now, with TensorFlow's powerful APIs at our fingertips, it is time to discover what **convolutional neural networks** (**CNNs**) are, and how these modern methods are trained to further improve their robustness.

The following topics will be covered in this chapter:

- CNNs and their relevance to computer vision
- Implementing these modern networks with TensorFlow and Keras
- Advanced optimizers and how to train CNNs efficiently
- Regularization methods and how to avoid overfitting

Technical requirements

The main resources of this chapter are implemented with TensorFlow. The Matplotlib package (`https://matplotlib.org`) and the scikit-image package (`https://scikit-image.org`) are also used, though only to display some results or to load example images.

As in previous chapters, Jupyter notebooks illustrating the concepts covered in this chapter can be found in the following GitHub folder: `github.com/PacktPublishing/Hands-On-Computer-Vision-with-TensorFlow-2/tree/master/Chapter03`.

Discovering convolutional neural networks

In the first part of this chapter, we will present CNNs, also known as **ConvNets**, and explain why they have become omnipresent in vision tasks.

Neural networks for multidimensional data

CNNs were introduced to solve some of the shortcomings of the original neural networks. In this section, we will address these issues and present how CNNs deal with them.

Problems with fully connected networks

Through our introductory experiment in `Chapter 1`, *Computer Vision and Neural Networks*, and `Chapter 2`, *TensorFlow Basics and Training a Model*, we have already highlighted the following two main drawbacks of basic networks when dealing with images:

- An explosive number of parameters
- A lack of spatial reasoning

Let's discuss each of these here.

An explosive number of parameters

Images are complex structures with a large number of values (that is, $H \times W \times D$ values with H indiacting the image's height, W its width, and D its depth/number of channels, such as $D = 3$ for RGB images). Even the small, single-channel images we used as examples in the first two chapters represent input vectors of size $28 \times 28 \times 1 = 784$ values each. For the first layer of the basic neural network we implemented, this meant a weight matrix of shape (784, 64). This equates to 50,176 (784 × 64) parameter values to optimize, just for this variable!

This number of parameters simply explodes when we consider larger RGB images or deeper networks.

A lack of spatial reasoning

Because their neurons receive all the values from the previous layer without any distinction (they are *fully connected*), these neural networks do not have a notion of *distance/spatiality*. Spatial relations in the data are lost. Multidimensional data, such as images, could also be anything from column vectors to dense layers because their operations do not take into account the data dimensionality nor the positions of input values. More precisely, this means that the notion of proximity between pixels is lost to **fully connected** (**FC**) layers, as all pixel values are combined by the layers with no regard for their original positions.

As it does not change the behavior of dense layers, to simplify their computations and parameter representations, it is common practice to *flatten* multidimensional inputs before passing them to these layers (that is, to reshape them into column vectors).

Intuitively, neural layers would be much smarter if they could take into account **spatial information**; that is, that some input values belong to the same pixel (channel values) or to the same image region (neighbor pixels).

Introducing CNNs

CNNs offer simple solutions to these shortcomings. While they work the same way as the networks we introduced previously (such as feed-forward and backpropagation), some clever changes were brought to their architecture.

First of all, CNNs can handle multidimensional data. For images, a CNN takes as input three-dimensional data (height × width × depth) and has its own neurons arranged in a similar volume (refer to *Figure 3.1*). This leads to the second novelty of CNNs—unlike fully connected networks, where neurons are connected to all elements from the previous layer, each neuron in CNNs only has access to some elements in the neighboring region of the previous layer. This region (usually square and spanning all channels) is called the **receptive field** of the neurons (or the filter size):

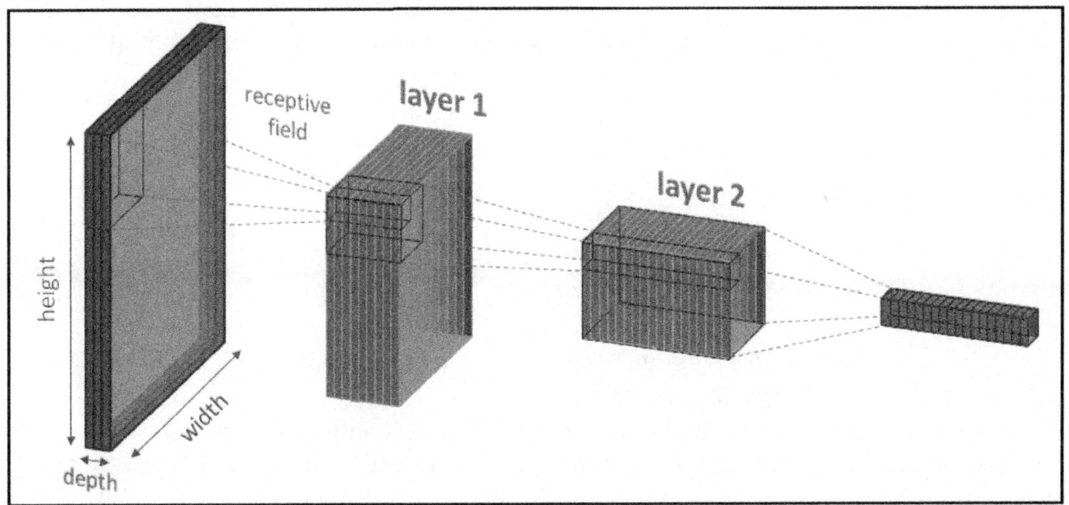

Figure 3.1: CNN representation, showing the *receptive fields* of the top-left neurons from the first layer to the last (further explanations can be found in the following subsections)

By linking neurons only to their neighboring ones in the previous layer, CNNs not only drastically reduce the number of parameters to train, but also preserve the localization of image features.

CNN operations

With this architecture paradigm, several new types of layers were also introduced, efficiently taking advantage of *multidimensionality* and *local connectivity*.

Convolutional layers

CNNs get their name from *convolutional layers*, which are at the core of their architecture. In these layers, the number of parameters is further reduced by sharing the same weights and bias among all neurons connected to the same output channel.

Concept

These specific neurons with shared weights and bias can also be thought of as a single neuron sliding over the whole input matrix with *spatially limited connectivity*. At each step, this neuron is only spatially connected to the local region in the input volume ($H \times W \times D$) it is currently sliding over. Given this limited input of dimensions, $k_H \times k_W \times D$ for a neuron with a filter size (k_H, k_W), the neuron still works like the ones modeled in our first chapter—it linearly combines the input values ($k_H \times k_W \times D$ values) before applying an activation function to the sum (a linear or non-linear function). Mathematically, the response, $z_{i,j}$, of the neuron when presented with the input patch starting at position (i, j) can be expressed as follows:

$$z_{i,j} = \sigma\left(b + \sum_{l=0}^{k_H-1} \sum_{m=0}^{k_W-1} \sum_{n=0}^{D-1} w_{l,m,n} \cdot x_{i+l,j+m,n}\right)$$

$w \in \mathbb{R}^{k_H \times k_W \times D}$ is the neuron's weights (that is, a two-dimensional matrix of shape $k_H \times k_W \times D$), $b \in \mathbb{R}$ is the neuron's bias, and σ is the activation function (for instance, *sigmoid*). Repeating this operation for each position that the neuron can take over the input data, we obtain its complete response matrix, z, of dimensions $H_o \times W_o$, with H_o and W_o being the number of times the neuron can slide vertically and horizontally (respectively) over the input tensor.

In practice, most of the time, square filters are used, meaning that they have a size (k, k) with $k = k_H = k_W$. For the rest of this chapter, we will only consider square filters to simplify the explanations, though it is good to remember that their height and width may vary.

As a convolutional layer can still have N sets of different neurons (that is, N sets of neurons with shared parameters), their response maps are stacked together into an output tensor of shape $H_o \times W_o \times N$.

In the same way that we applied matrix multiplication to fully connected layers, the **convolution operation** can be used here to compute all the response maps at once (hence the name of these layers). Those familiar with this operation may have recognized it as soon as we mentioned *sliding filters over the input matrix*. For those who are unfamiliar with the operation, the results of a convolution are indeed obtained by sliding a filter, w, over the input matrix, x, and computing, at each position, the dot product of the filter and the patch of x starting at the current position. This operation is illustrated in *Figure 3.2* (an input tensor with a single channel is used to keep the diagram easy to understand):

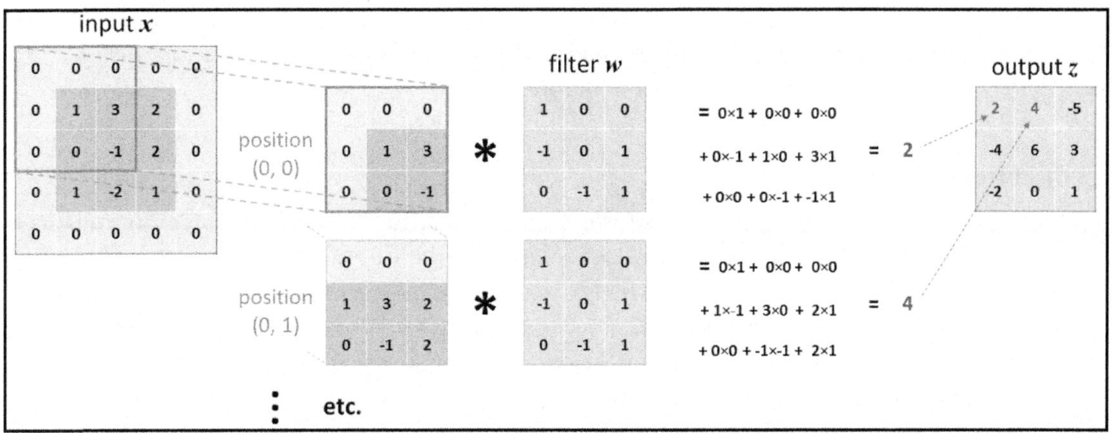

Figure 3.2: A convolution illustrated

In *Figure 3.2*, please note that the input, x, has been *padded* with zeros, which is commonly done in convolutional layers; for instance, when we want the output to be the same size as the original input (a size of 3 × 3 in this example). The notion of padding is further developed later in this chapter.

The proper mathematical term for this operation is actually *cross-correlation*, though *convolution* is commonly used in the machine learning community. The cross-correlation of a matrix, x, with a filter, w, is $\forall i \in [0, H_o - 1]$ and $\forall j \in [0, W_o - 1]$:

$$(w * x)_{i,j} = \sum_{l=0}^{k-1} \sum_{m=0}^{k-1} w_{l,m} \cdot x_{i+l,j+m}$$

Notice the correspondence with our equation for z. On the other hand, the actual mathematical convolution of a matrix, x, with a filter, w, is for all valid positions (i, j):

$$(w \star x)_{i,j} = \sum_{l=0}^{k-1} \sum_{m=0}^{k-1} w_{l,m} \cdot x_{i-l,j-m}$$

As we can see, both operations are quite similar in this setup, and convolution results can be obtained from the cross-correlation operation by simply *flipping* the filters before it.

Properties

A convolutional layer with N sets of different neurons is thus defined by N weight matrices (also called **filters** or **kernels**) of shape $D \times k \times k$ (when the filters are square), and N bias values. Therefore, this layer only has $N \times (Dk^2 + 1)$ values to train. A fully connected layer with similar input and output dimensions would need $(H \times W \times D) \times (H_o \times W_o \times N)$ parameters instead. As we demonstrated previously, the number of parameters for fully connected layers is influenced by the dimensionality of the data, whereas this does not affect the parameter numbers for convolutional layers.

This property makes convolutional layers really powerful tools in computer vision for two reasons. First, as implied in the previous paragraph, it means we can train networks for larger input images without impacting the number of parameters we would need to tune. Second, this also means that convolutional layers can be applied to any images, irrespective of their dimensions! Unlike networks with fully connected layers, purely convolutional ones do not need to be adapted and retrained for inputs of different sizes.

When applying a CNN to images of various sizes, you still need to be careful when sampling the input batches. Indeed, a subset of images can be stacked together into a normal batch tensor only if they all have the same dimensions. Therefore, in practice, you should either sort the images before batching them (mostly done during the training phase) or simply process each image separately (usually during the testing phase). However, both to simplify data processing and the network's task, people usually preprocess their images so they are all the same size (through scaling and/or cropping).

Besides those computational optimizations, convolutional layers also have interesting properties related to image processing. With training, the layer's filters become really good at reacting to specific *local features* (a layer with *N* filters means the possibility to react to *N* different features). Each kernel of the first convolutional layer in a CNN would, for instance, learn to activate for a specific low-level feature, such as a specific line orientation or color gradient. Then, deeper layers would use these results to localize more abstract/advanced features, such as the shape of a face, and the contours of a particular object. Moreover, each filter (that is, each set of shared neurons) would respond to a specific image feature, whatever its location(s) in the image. More formally, convolutional layers are invariant to translation in the image coordinate space.

The response map of a filter over the input image can be described as a map representing the locations where the filter responded to its target feature. For this reason, those intermediary results in CNNs are commonly called **feature maps**. A layer with *N* filters will, therefore, return *N* feature maps, each corresponding to the detection of a particular feature in the input tensors. The stack of *N* feature maps returned by a layer is commonly called a **feature volume** (with a shape of $H_o \times W_o \times N$).

Hyperparameters

A convolutional layer is first defined by its number of filters, *N*, by its input depth, *D* (that is, the number of input channels), and by its filter/kernel size, (k_H, k_W). As square filters are commonly used, the size is usually simply defined by *k* (though, as mentioned earlier, non-square filters are sometimes considered).

However, as mentioned previously, convolutional layers actually differ from the homonym mathematical operation. The operation between the input and their filters can take several additional hyperparameters, affecting the way the filters are *sliding* over the images.

First, we can apply different *strides* with which the filters are sliding. The stride hyperparameter thus defines whether the dot product between the image patches and the filters should be computed at every position when sliding (*stride* = *1*), or every *s* position (*stride* = *s*). The larger the stride, the sparser the resulting feature maps.

Images can also be *zero-padded* before convolution; that is, their sizes can be synthetically increased by adding rows and columns of zeros around their original content. As shown in *Figure 3.2*, this padding increases the number of positions the filters can take over the images. We can thus specify the padding value to be applied (that is, the number of empty rows and columns to be added on each side of the inputs).

The letter *k* is commonly used for the filter/kernel size (*k* for *kernel*). Similarly, *s* is commonly used for the stride, and *p* for the padding. Note that, as with the filter size, the same values are usually used for the horizontal and vertical strides ($s = s_H = s_W$), as well as for the horizontal and vertical padding; though, for some specific use cases, they may have different values.

All these parameters (the number of kernels, *N;* kernel size, *k;* stride, *s;* and padding, *p*) not only affect the layer's operations, but also its output shape. Until now, we defined this shape as (H_o, W_o, *N*), with H_o and W_o the number of times the neuron can slide vertically and horizontally over the inputs. So, what actually are H_o and W_o? Formally, they can be computed as follows:

$$H_o = \frac{H - k + 2p}{s} + 1 \quad , \quad W_o = \frac{W - k + 2p}{s} + 1$$

While we invite you to pick some concrete examples to better grasp these formulas, we can intuitively understand the logic behind them. Filters of size *k* can take a maximum of *H - k + 1* different vertical positions and *W - k + 1* horizontal ones in images of size *H* × *W*. Additionally, this number of positions increases to *H - k + 2p + 1* (with respect to *W - k + 2p + 1*) if these images are padded by *p* on every side. Finally, increasing the stride, *s*, basically means considering only one position out of *s*, explaining the division (note that it is an integer division).

With these hyperparameters, we can easily control the layer's output sizes. This is particularly convenient for applications such as object segmentation; that is, when we want the output segmentation mask to be the same size as the input image.

TensorFlow/Keras methods

Available in the low-level API, `tf.nn.conv2d()` (refer to the documentation at https://www.tensorflow.org/api_docs/python/tf/nn/conv2d) is the default choice for image convolution. Its main parameters are as follows:

- `input`: The batch of input images, of shape *(B, H, W, D)*, with *B* being the batch size.
- `filter`: The *N* filters stacked into a tensor of shape (k_H, k_W, *D*, *N*).
- `strides`: A list of four integers representing the stride for each dimension of the batched input. Typically, you would use [1, s_H, s_W, 1] (that is, applying a custom stride only for the two spatial dimensions of the image).
- `padding`: Either a list of *4 × 2* integers representing the padding before and after each dimension of the batched input, or a string defining which predefined padding case to use; that is, either `VALID` or `SAME` (explanations follow).
- `name`: The name to identify this operation (useful for creating clear, readable graphs).

Note that `tf.nn.conv2d()` accepts some other more advanced parameters, which we will not cover yet (refer to the documentation). *Figures 3.3* and *3.4* illustrate the effects of two convolutional operations with different arguments:

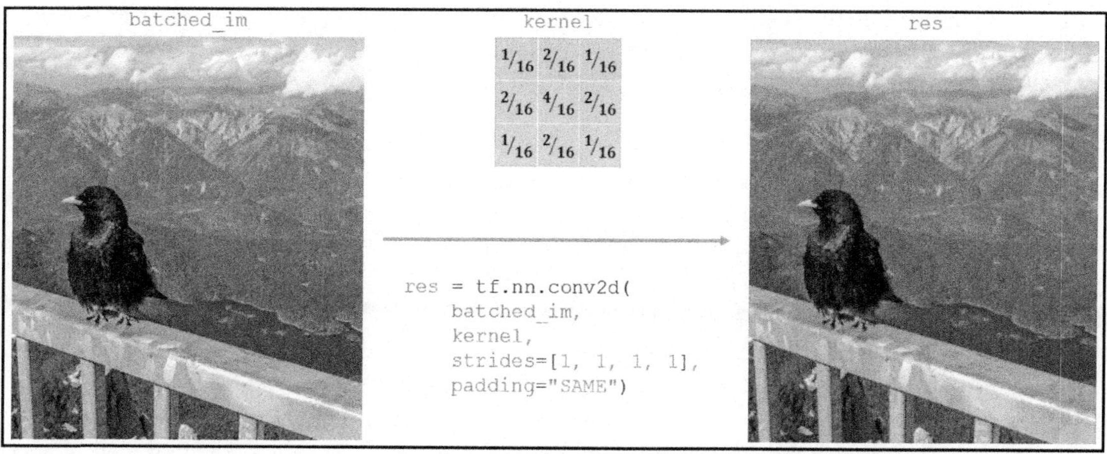

Figure 3.3: Example of a convolution performed on an image with TensorFlow. The kernel here is a well-known one, commonly used to apply *Gaussian blur* to images

In the following screenshot, a kernel that's well known in computer vision is applied:

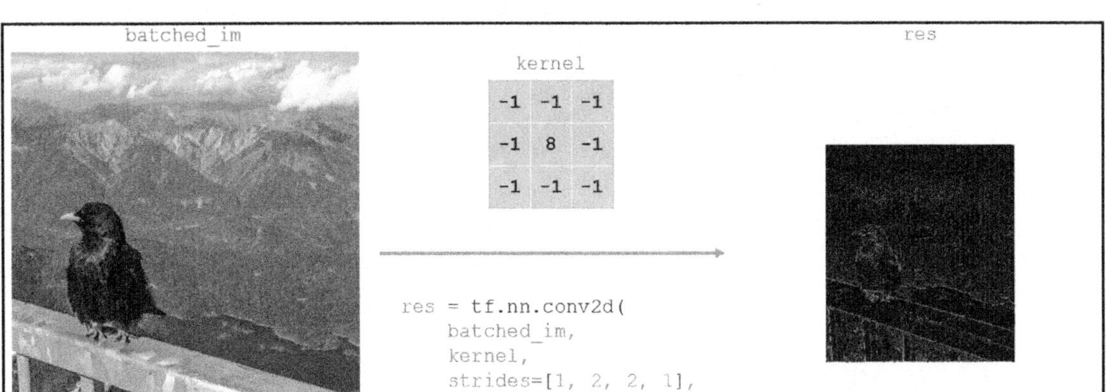

Figure 3.4: Example of another TensorFlow convolution, with a larger stride. This specific kernel is commonly used to extract edges/contours in images

Regarding padding, TensorFlow developers made the choice to provide two different pre-implemented modes so that users do not have to figure out which value, *p*, they need for usual cases. `VALID` means the images won't be padded ($p = 0$), and the filters will slide only over the default *valid* positions. When opting for `SAME`, TensorFlow will calculate the value, *p*, so that the convolution outputs have the *same* height and width as the inputs for a stride of `1` (that is, solving $H_o = H_o$ and $W_o = W$ given the equations presented in the previous section, temporarily setting *s* to 1).

Sometimes, you may want to pad with something more complex than zeros. In those cases, it is recommended to use the `tf.pad()` method (refer to the documentation at `https://www.tensorflow.org/api_docs/python/tf/pad`) instead, and then simply instantiate a convolution operation with `VALID` padding.

TensorFlow also offers several other low-level convolution methods, such as `tf.nn.conv1d()` (refer to the documentation at `https://www.tensorflow.org/api_docs/python/tf/nn/conv1d`) and `tf.nn.conv3d()` (refer to the documentation at `https://www.tensorflow.org/api_docs/python/tf/nn/conv3d`), for one-dimensional and three-dimensional data, respectively, or `tf.nn.depthwise_conv2d()` (refer to the documentation at `https://www.tensorflow.org/api_docs/python/tf/nn/depthwise_conv2d`) to convolve each channel of the images with different filters, and more.

So far, we have only presented convolutions with fixed filters. For CNNs, we have to make the filters trainable. Convolutional layers also apply a learned bias before passing the result to an activation function. This series of operations can, therefore, be implemented as follows:

```
# Initializing the trainable variables (for instance, the filters with
values from a Glorot distribution, and the bias with zeros):
kernels_shape = [k, k, D, N]
glorot_uni_initializer = tf.initializers.GlorotUniform()
# ^ this object is defined to generate values following the Glorot
distribution (note that other famous parameter more or less random
initializers exist, also covered by TensorFlow)
kernels = tf.Variable(glorot_uni_initializer(kernels_shape),
                      trainable=True, name="filters")
bias = tf.Variable(tf.zeros(shape=[N]), trainable=True, name="bias")

# Defining our convolutional layer as a compiled function:
@tf.function
def conv_layer(x, kernels, bias, s):
    z = tf.nn.conv2d(x, kernels, strides=[1,s,s,1], padding='VALID')
    # Finally, applying the bias and activation function (for instance,
ReLU):
    return tf.nn.relu(z + bias)
```

This feed-forward function can further be wrapped into a `Layer` object, similar to how the fully connected layer we implemented in `Chapter 1`, *Computer Vision and Neural Networks,* was built around the matrix operations. Through the Keras API, TensorFlow 2 provides its own `tf.keras.layers.Layer` class, which we can extend (refer to the documentation at `https://www.tensorflow.org/api_docs/python/tf/keras/layers/Layer`). The following code block demonstrates how a simple convolution layer can be built on this:

```
class SimpleConvolutionLayer(tf.keras.layers.Layer):
    def __init__(self, num_kernels=32, kernel_size=(3, 3), stride=1):
        """ Initialize the layer.
        :param num_kernels: Number of kernels for the convolution
        :param kernel_size: Kernel size (H x W)
        :param stride: Vertical/horizontal stride
        """
        super().__init__()
        self.num_kernels = num_kernels
        self.kernel_size = kernel_size
        self.stride = stride

    def build(self, input_shape):
        """ Build the layer, initializing its parameters/variables.
        This will be internally called the 1st time the layer is used.
        :param input_shape: Input shape for the layer (for instance,
```

```
BxHxWxC)
        """
        num_input_ch = input_shape[-1] # assuming shape format BHWC
        # Now we know the shape of the kernel tensor we need:
        kernels_shape = (*self.kernel_size, num_input_ch, self.num_kernels)
        # We initialize the filter values fior instance, from a Glorot
distribution:
        glorot_init = tf.initializers.GlorotUniform()
        self.kernels = self.add_weight( # method to add Variables to layer
            name='kernels', shape=kernels_shape, initializer=glorot_init,
            trainable=True) # and we make it trainable.
        # Same for the bias variable (for instance, from a normal
distribution):
        self.bias = self.add_weight(
            name='bias', shape=(self.num_kernels,),
            initializer='random_normal', trainable=True)

    def call(self, inputs):
        """ Call the layer, apply its operations to the input tensor."""
        return conv_layer(inputs, self.kernels, self.bias, self.stride)
```

Most of TensorFlow's mathematical operations (for example, in `tf.math` and `tf.nn`) already have their derivatives defined by the framework. Therefore, as long as a layer is composed of such operations, we do not have to manually define its backpropagation, saving quite some effort!

While this implementation has the advantage of being explicit, the Keras API also encapsulates the initialization of common layers (as presented in `Chapter 2`, *TensorFlow Basics and Training a Model*), thereby speeding up development. With the `tf.keras.layers` module, we can instantiate a similar convolutional layer in a single call, as follows:

```
conv = tf.keras.layers.Conv2D(filters=N, kernel_size=(k, k), strides=s,
                              padding='valid', activation='relu')
```

`tf.keras.layers.Conv2D()` (refer to the documentation at `https://www.tensorflow.org/api_docs/python/tf/keras/layers/Conv2D`) has a long list of additional parameters, encapsulating several concepts, such as weight regularization (presented later in this chapter). Therefore, it is recommended to use this method when building advanced CNNs, instead of spending time reimplementing such concepts.

Pooling layers

Another commonly used category of layer introduced with CNNs is the *pooling* type.

Concept and hyperparameters

These pooling layers are a bit peculiar because they do not have any trainable parameters. Each neuron simply takes the values in its *window* (the receptive field) and returns a single output, computed from a predefined function. The two most common pooling methods are max-pooling and average-pooling. **Max-pooling** layers return only the maximum value at each depth of the pooled area (refer to *Figure 3.5*), and **average-pooling** layers compute the average at each depth of the pooled area (refer to *Figure 3.6*).

Pooling layers are commonly used with a *stride* value equal to the size of their *window/kernel size,* in order to apply the pooling function over non-overlapping patches. Their purpose is to *reduce the spatial dimensionality of the data,* cutting down the total number of parameters needed in the network, as well as its computation time. For instance, a pooling layer with a 2 × 2 window size and stride of 2 (that is, $k = 2$ and $s = 2$) would take patches of four values at each depth and return a single number. It would thus divide the height and the width of the features by 2; that is, dividing the number of computations for the following layers by 2 × 2 = 4. Finally, note that, as with convolutional layers, you can pad the tensors before applying the operation (as shown in *Figure 3.5*):

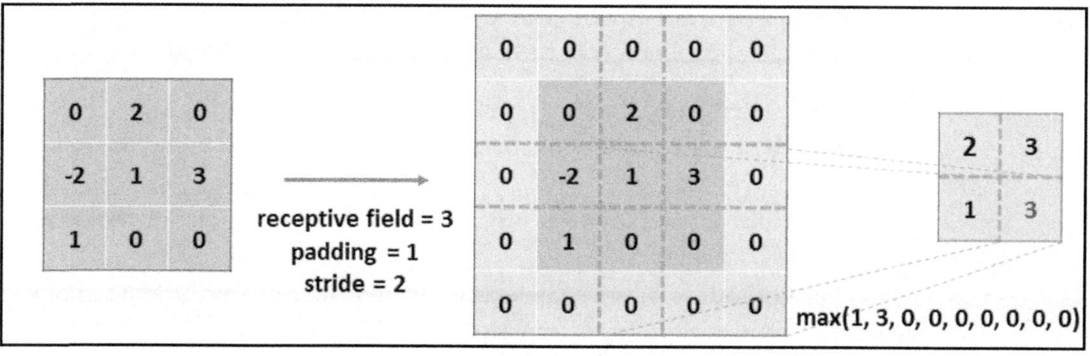

Figure 3.5: Illustration of a max-pooling operation with a window size of 3 × 3, a padding of 1, and a stride of 2 on a single-channel input

Through the padding and stride parameters, it is thus possible to control the dimensions of the resulting tensors. *Figure 3.6* provides another example:

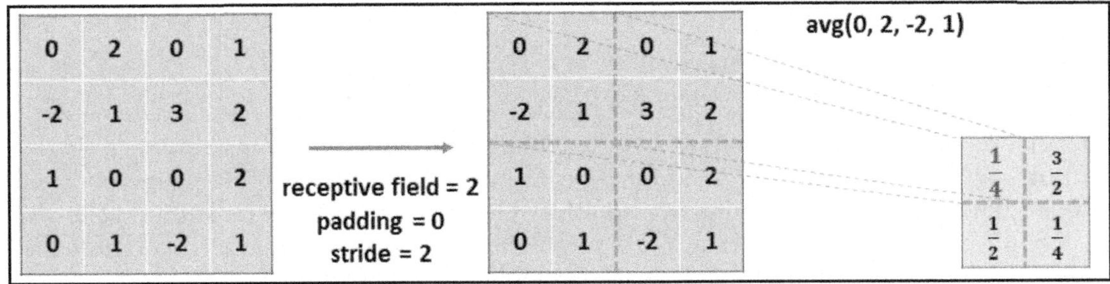

Figure 3.6: Illustration of an average-pooling operation with a window size of 2 × 2, a padding of 0, and a stride of 2 on a single-channel input

With hyperparameters being similar to convolutional layers except for the absence of trainable kernels, pooling layers are, therefore, easy to use and lightweight solutions for controlling data dimensionality.

TensorFlow/Keras methods

Also available from the `tf.nn` package, `tf.nn.max_pool()` (refer to the documentation at `https://www.tensorflow.org/api_docs/python/tf/nn/max_pool`) and `tf.nn.avg_pool()` (refer to the documentation at `https://www.tensorflow.org/api_docs/python/tf/nn/avg_pool`) conveniently have a signature quite similar to `tf.nn.conv2d()`, as follows:

- `value`: The batch of input images of shape (*B*, *H*, *W*, *D*), with *B* being the batch size
- `ksize`: A list of four integers representing the window size in each dimension; commonly, *[1, k, k, 1]* is used
- `strides`: A list of four integers representing the stride for each dimension of the batched input, similar to `tf.nn.conv2d()`
- `padding`: A string defining which padding algorithm to use (`VALID` or `SAME`)
- `name`: The name to identify this operation (useful for creating clear, readable graphs)

Figure 3.7 illustrates an average-pooling operation applied to an image:

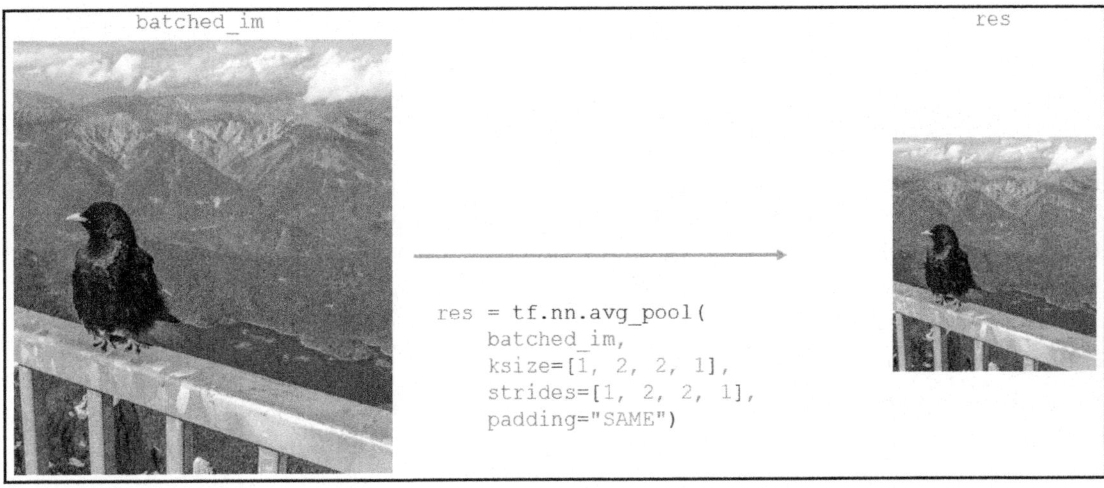

Figure 3.7: Example of average-pooling performed on an image with TensorFlow

In *Figure 3.8,* the max-pooling function is applied to the same image:

Figure 3.8: Example of another max-pooling operation, with an excessively large window size compared to the stride (purely for demonstration purposes)

Here, again, we can still use the higher-level API to make the instantiation slightly more succinct:

```
avg_pool = tf.keras.layers.AvgPool2D(pool_size=k, strides=[s, s],
padding='valid')
max_pool = tf.keras.layers.MaxPool2D(pool_size=k, strides=[s, s],
padding='valid')
```

Since pooling layers do not have trainable weights, there is no real distinction between the pooling operation and the corresponding layer in TensorFlow. This makes these operations not only lightweight, but easy to instantiate.

Fully connected layers

It is worth mentioning that FC layers are also used in CNNs, the same way they are in regular networks. We will present, in the following paragraphs, when they should be considered, and how to include them in CNNs.

Usage in CNNs

While FC layers can be added to CNNs processing multidimensional data, this implies, however, that the input tensors passed to these layers must first be reshaped into a batched column vector—the way we did with the MNIST images for our simple network in `Chapter 1`, *Computer Vision and Neural Networks*, and `Chapter 2`, *TensorFlow Basics and Training a Model* (that is, *flattening* the height, width, and depth dimensions into a single vector).

FC layers are also often called **densely connected**, or simply **dense** (as opposed to other CNN layers that have more limited connectivity).

While it can be advantageous in some cases for neurons to have access to the complete input map (for instance, to combine spatially distant features), fully connected layers have several shortcomings, as mentioned at the beginning of this chapter (for example, the loss of spatial information and the large number of parameters). Moreover, unlike other CNN layers, dense ones are defined by their input and output sizes. A specific dense layer will not work for inputs that have a shape different from the one it was configured for. Therefore, using FC layers in a neural network usually means losing the possibility to apply them to images of heterogeneous sizes.

Despite these shortcomings, these layers are still commonly used in CNNs. They are usually found among the final layers of a network, for instance, to convert the multidimensional features into a 1D classification vector.

TensorFlow/Keras methods

Although we already used TensorFlow's dense layers in the previous chapter, we did not stop to focus on their parameters and properties. Once again, the signature of `tf.keras.layers.Dense()` (refer to the documentation at `https://www.tensorflow.org/api_docs/python/tf/keras/layers/Dense`) is comparable to that of previously introduced layers, with the difference that they do not accept any `strides` or `padding` for parameters, but instead use `units` representing the number of neurons/output size, as follows:

```
fc = tf.keras.layers.Dense(units=output_size, activation='relu')
```

Remember that you should, however, take care of *flattening* the multidimensional tensors before passing them to dense layers. `tf.keras.layers.Flatten()` (refer to the documentation at `https://www.tensorflow.org/api_docs/python/tf/keras/layers/Flatten`) can be used as an intermediate layer for that purpose.

Effective receptive field

As we will detail in this section, the **effective receptive field** (**ERF**) of a neural network is an important notion in deep learning, as it may affect the ability of the network to cross-reference and combine distant elements in the input images.

Definitions

While the receptive field represents the local region of the previous layer that a neuron is connected to, the ERF defines *the region of the input image* (and not just of the previous layer), which affects the activation of a neuron for a given layer, as shown in *Figure 3.9*:

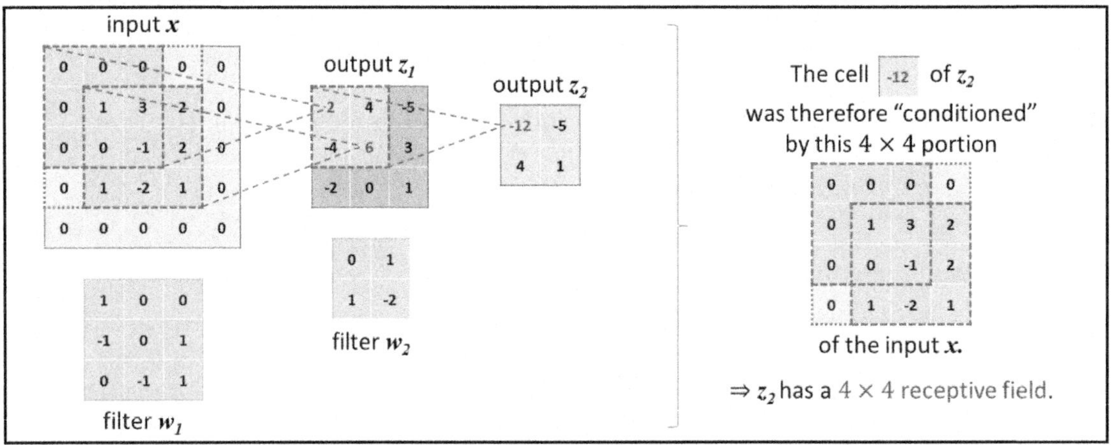

Figure 3.9: Illustration of the receptive field of a layer with a simple network of two convolutional layers

Note that it is common to find the term **receptive field** (**RF**) used in place of ERF, because RF can simply be referred to as the filter size or the window size of a layer. Some people also use RF or ERF to specifically define the input regions affecting each unit of the output layer (and not just any intermediary layer of a network).

Adding to the confusion, some researchers started calling ERF the subset of the input region that is actually affecting a neuron. This was introduced by Wenjie Luo et al. in their paper, *Understanding the Effective Receptive Field in Deep Convolutional Neural Networks,* published in *Advances in Neural Information Processing Systems (2016).* Their idea was that not all pixels *seen* by a neuron contribute *equally* to its response. We can intuitively accept that, for instance, pixels at the center of the RF will have more weight than peripheral ones. The information held by these central pixels can be propagated along multiple paths in the intermediary layers of the network to reach a given neuron, while pixels in the periphery of the receptive field are connected to this neuron through a single path. Therefore, the ERF, as defined by Luo et al., follows a pseudo-Gaussian distribution, unlike the uniform distribution of a traditional ERF.

The authors make an interesting parallel between this representation of the receptive field and the human **central fovea**, the region of the eye responsible for our sharp central vision. This detailed part of the vision is at the basis of many human activities. Half the optical nerves are linked to the fovea (despite its relatively small size), in the same way that central pixels in effective receptive fields are connected to a higher number of artificial neurons.

Formula

No matter what actual role its pixels are playing, the effective receptive field (named R_i here) of the ith layer of a CNN can be recursively computed as follows:

$$R_i = R_{i-1} + (k_i - 1) \prod_{j=1}^{i-1} s_j$$

In this equation, k_i is the filter size of the layer, and s_i is its stride (the last part of the equation thus represents the product of the strides for all the previous layers). As an example, we can apply this formula to the minimalist two-layer CNN presented in *Figure 3.9* to quantitatively evaluate the ERF of the second layer as follows:

$$R_2 = R_1 + (2 - 1) \prod_{j=1}^{1} s_j = 3 + 1 \times 1 = 4$$

This formula confirms that the ERF of a network is directly affected by the number of intermediary layers, their filter sizes, and the strides. Subsampling layers, such as pooling layers or layers with larger strides, greatly increase the ERF at the cost of lower feature resolution.

Because of the local connectivity of CNNs, you should keep in mind how layers and their hyperparameters will affect the flow of visual information across the networks when defining their architecture.

CNNs with TensorFlow

Most state-of-the-art computer vision algorithms are based on CNNs built with the three different types of layers we just introduced (that is, convolutional, pooling, and FC), with some tweaks and tricks that we will present in this book. In this section, we will build our first CNN and apply it to our digit recognition task.

Implementing our first CNN

For our first convolutional neural network, we will implement *LeNet-5*. First introduced by Yann Le Cun in 1995 (in *Learning algorithms for classification: A comparison on handwritten digit recognition, World Scientific Singapore*) and applied to the MNIST dataset, LeNet-5 may not be a recent network, but it is still commonly used to introduce people to CNNs. Indeed, with its seven layers, this network is straightforward to implement, while yielding interesting results.

LeNet-5 architecture

As shown in *Figure 3.10*, LeNet-5 is first composed of two blocks, each containing a convolutional layer (with the kernel size $k = 5$ and stride $s = 1$) followed by a max-pooling layer (with $k = 2$ and $s = 2$). In the first block, the input images are zero-padded by 2 on each side before convolution (that is, $p = 2$, hence an actual input size of 32×32), and the convolution layer has six different filters ($N = 6$). There is no padding before the second convolution ($p = 0$), and its number of filters is set to 16 ($N = 16$). After the two blocks, three fully connected layers merge the features together and lead to the final class estimation (the 10 digit classes). Before the first dense layer, the $5 \times 5 \times 16$ feature volume is flattened into a vector of 400 values. The complete architecture is represented in the following diagram:

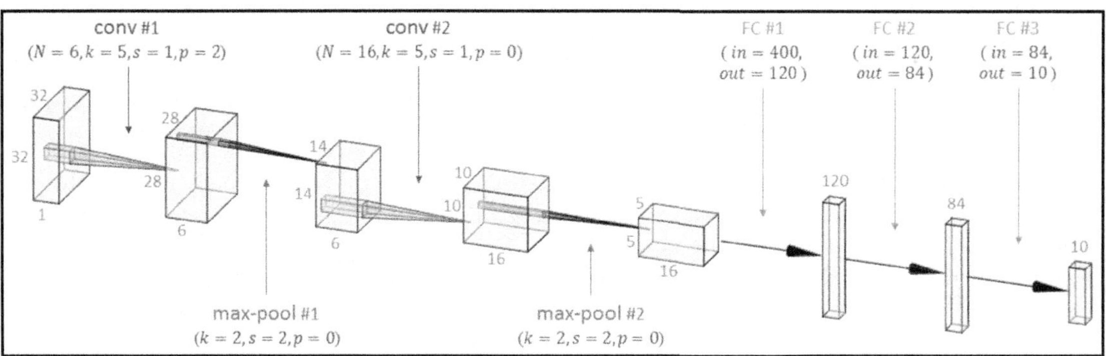

Figure 3.10: LeNet-5 architecture (rendered with the NN-SVG tool by Alexander Lenail—http://alexlenail.me/NN-SVG)

In the original implementation, each convolution layer and dense layer except the last one uses *tanh* as an activation function. However, *ReLU* is nowadays preferred to *tanh*, replacing it in most LeNet-5 implementations. For the last layer, the *softmax* function is applied. This function takes a vector of *N* values and returns a same-size vector, *y*, with its values normalized into a probability distribution. In other words, *softmax* normalizes a vector so that its values are all between 0 and 1, and their sum is exactly equal to 1. Therefore, this function is commonly used at the end of neural networks applied to classification tasks in order to convert the network's predictions into per-class probability, as mentioned in `Chapter 1`, *Computer Vision and Neural Networks* (that is, given an output tensor, $y = [y_0, ..., y_i, ..., y_N]$, y_i represents how likely it is that the sample belongs to class *i* according to the network).

The network's raw predictions (that is, before normalization) are commonly named **logits**. These unbounded values are usually converted into probabilities with the *softmax* function. This normalization process makes the prediction more *readable* (each value represents the confidence of the network for the corresponding class; refer to the belief scores mentioned in `Chapter 1`, *Computer Vision and Neural Networks*) and simplifies the computation of the training loss (that is, the categorical cross-entropy for classification tasks).

TensorFlow and Keras implementations

We have all the tools in hand to implement this network. We suggest that you try them yourself, before checking the TensorFlow and Keras implementations provided. Reusing the notations and variables from `Chapter 2`, *TensorFlow Basics and Training a Model*, a LeNet-5 network using the Keras Sequential API would be as follows:

```
from tensorflow.keras.model import Model, Sequential
from tensorflow.keras.layers import Conv2D, MaxPooling2D, Flatten, Dense

model = Sequential() # `Sequential` inherits from tf.keras.Model
# 1st block:
model.add(Conv2D(6, kernel_size=(5, 5), padding='same', activation='relu',
 input_shape=(img_height, img_width, img_channels))
model.add(MaxPooling2D(pool_size=(2, 2)))
# 2nd block:
model.add(Conv2D(16, kernel_size=(5, 5), activation='relu')
model.add(MaxPooling2D(pool_size=(2, 2)))
# Dense layers:
model.add(Flatten())
model.add(Dense(120, activation='relu'))
model.add(Dense(84, activation='relu'))
model.add(Dense(num_classes, activation='softmax'))
```

The model is created by instantiating and adding the layers one by one, *sequentially*. As mentioned in `Chapter 2`, *TensorFlow Basics and Training a Model*, Keras also provides the **functional API**. This API makes it possible to define models in a more object-oriented approach (as shown in the following code), though it is also possible to directly instantiate `tf.keras.Model` with the layer operations (as illustrated in some of our Jupyter notebooks):

```
from tensorflow.keras import Model
from tensorflow.keras.layers import Conv2D, MaxPooling2D, Flatten, Dense

class LeNet5(Model): # `Model` has the same API as `Layer` + extends it
    def __init__(self, num_classes): # Create the model and its layers
        super(LeNet5, self).__init__()
        self.conv1 = Conv2D(6, kernel_size=(5, 5), padding='same',
                            activation='relu')
        self.conv2 = Conv2D(16, kernel_size=(5, 5), activation='relu')
        self.max_pool = MaxPooling2D(pool_size=(2, 2))
        self.flatten = Flatten()
        self.dense1 = Dense(120, activation='relu')
        self.dense2 = Dense(84, activation='relu')
        self.dense3 = Dense(num_classes, activation='softmax')
    def call(self, x): # Apply the layers in order to process the inputs
        x = self.max_pool(self.conv1(x)) # 1st block
        x = self.max_pool(self.conv2(x)) # 2nd block
        x = self.flatten(x)
        x = self.dense3(self.dense2(self.dense1(x))) # dense layers
        return x
```

Keras layers can indeed behave like functions that can be applied to input data and chained until the desired output is obtained. The functional API allows you to build more complex neural networks; for example, when one specific layer is reused several times inside the networks, or when layers have multiple inputs or outputs.

For those who have already experimented with PyTorch (`https://pytorch.org`), another machine learning framework, this object-oriented approach to building neural networks may seem familiar, as it is favored there.

Application to MNIST

We can now compile and train our model for digit classification. Pursuing this with the Keras API (and reusing the MNIST data variables prepared in the last chapter), we instantiate the optimizer (a simple **stochastic gradient descent** (**SGD**) optimizer) and define the loss (the categorical cross-entropy) before launching the training, as follows:

```
model.compile(optimizer='sgd', loss='sparse_categorical_crossentropy',
              metrics=['accuracy'])
# We also instantiate some Keras callbacks, that is, utility functions
automatically called at some points during training to monitor it:
callbacks = [
    # To interrupt the training if `val_loss` stops improving for over 3
epochs:
    tf.keras.callbacks.EarlyStopping(patience=3, monitor='val_loss'),
    # To log the graph/metrics into TensorBoard (saving files in `./logs`):
    tf.keras.callbacks.TensorBoard(log_dir='./logs', histogram_freq=1)]
# Finally, we launch the training:
model.fit(x_train, y_train, batch_size=32, epochs=80,
          validation_data=(x_test, y_test), callbacks=callbacks)
```

Note the use of `sparse_categorical_crossentropy`, instead of `categorical_crossentropy`, to avoid one-hot encoding the labels. This loss was described in `Chapter 2`, *TensorFlow Basics and Training a Model.*

After ~60 epochs, we observe that our network's accuracy on the validation data reaches above ~98.5%! Compared to our previous attempts with non-convolutional networks, the relative error has been divided by 2 (from a ~3.0% to ~1.5% relative error), which is a significant improvement (given the high accuracy already).

In the following chapters, we will fully appreciate the analytical power of CNNs, applying them to increasingly complex visual tasks.

Refining the training process

Network architectures are not the only things to have improved over the years. The way that networks are trained has also evolved, improving how reliably and quickly they can converge. In this section, we will tackle some of the shortcomings of the gradient descent algorithm we covered in `Chapter 1`, *Computer Vision and Neural Networks,* as well as some ways to avoid overfitting.

Modern network optimizers

Optimizing multidimensional functions, such as neural networks, is a complex task. The gradient descent solution we presented in the first chapter is an elegant solution, though it has some limitations that we will highlight in the following section. Thankfully, researchers have been developing new generations of optimization algorithms, which we will also discuss.

Gradient descent challenges

We previously presented how the parameters, *P*, of a neural network (that is, all the weight and bias parameters of its layers) can be iteratively updated during training to minimize the loss, *L*, backpropagating its gradient. If this gradient descent process could be summarized in a single equation, it would be the following:

$$P_{i+1} \leftarrow P_i - v_i \quad \text{with } v_i = \epsilon \frac{dL_i}{dP_i}$$

ϵ is the learning rate hyperparameter, which accentuates or attenuates how the network's parameters are updated with regard to the gradient of the loss at every training iteration. While we mentioned that the learning rate value should be set with care, we did not explain how and why. The reasons for caution in this setup are threefold.

Training velocity and trade-off

We partially covered this point earlier. While setting a high learning rate may allow the trained network to converge faster (that is, in fewer iterations, as the parameters undergo larger updates each iteration), it also may prevent the network from finding a proper loss minimum. *Figure 3.11* is a famous illustration representing this trade-off between optimization over-cautiousness and haste:

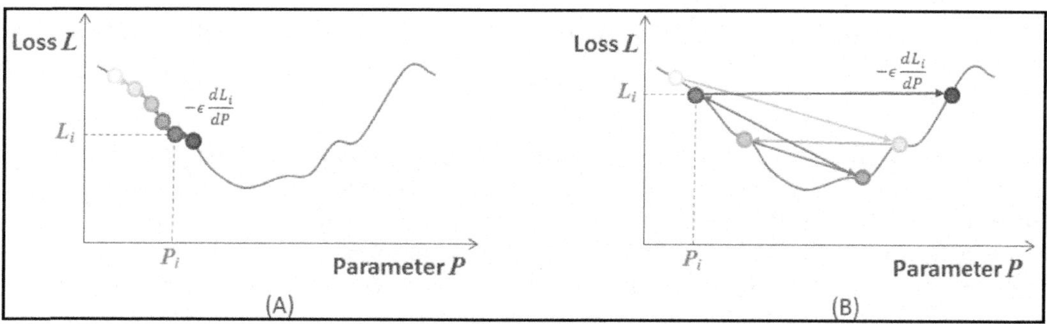

Figure 3.11: Illustration of the learning rate trade-off

From *Figure 3.11*, we can observe that an excessively low learning rate will slow down convergence (diagram A on the left), while an excessively high learning rate may cause it to overshoot the local minima (diagram B on the right).

Intuitively, there should be a better solution than trial and error to find the proper learning rate. For instance, a popular solution is to dynamically adjust the learning rate during training, starting with a larger value (for faster exploration of the loss domain at first) and decreasing it after every epoch (for more careful updating when getting closer to the minimum). This process is named **learning rate decay**. Manual decaying can still be found in many implementations, though, nowadays, TensorFlow offers more advanced learning rate schedulers and optimizers with adaptive learning rates.

Suboptimal local minima

A common problem when optimizing complex (that is, *non-convex*) methods is getting stuck in **suboptimal local minima**. Indeed, gradient descent may lead us to a local minimum it cannot escape, even though a *better* minimum lies close by, as shown in *Figure 3.12*:

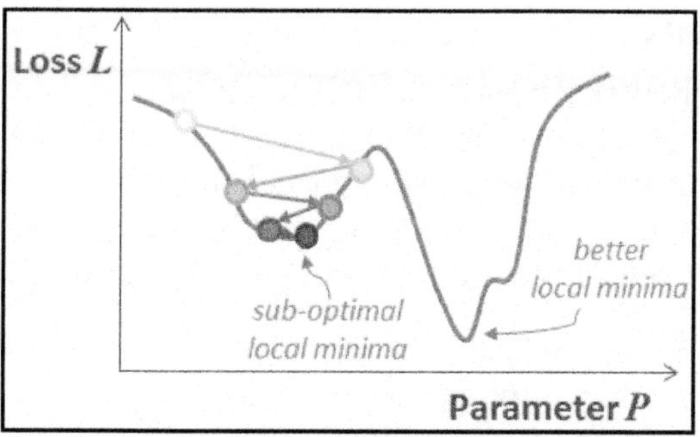

Figure 3.12: Example of gradient descent ending up in a sub-optimal local minimum

Because of the random sampling of training samples (causing the gradients to often differ from one mini-batch to another), the SGD presented in `Chapter 1`, *Computer Vision and Neural Networks*, is already able to *jump out* of shallow local minima.

Note that the gradient descent process cannot ensure the convergence to a **global minimum** (that is, the convergence to the best set of parameters among all possible combinations). This would imply scanning the complete loss domain, to make sure that a given minimum is indeed the *best* (this would mean, for instance, computing the loss for all possible combinations of the parameters). Given the complexity of visual tasks and the large number of parameters needed to tackle them, data scientists are usually glad to just find a satisfying local minimum.

A single hyperparameter for heterogeneous parameters

Finally, in traditional gradient descent, the same learning rate is used to update all the parameters of the network. However, not all these variables have the same sensitivity to changes, nor do they all impact the loss at every iteration.

It may seem beneficial to have different learning rates (for instance, per subset of parameters) to update crucial parameters more carefully, and to more boldly update parameters that are not contributing often enough to the network's predictions.

Advanced optimizers

Some of the intuitions we presented in the previous paragraphs have been properly studied and formalized by researchers, leading to new optimization algorithms based on SGD. We will now list the most common of these optimizers, detailing their contributions and how to use them with TensorFlow.

Momentum algorithms

First suggested by Boris Polyak (in *Some methods of speeding up the convergence of iteration methods*, Elsevier, 1964), the momentum algorithm is based on SGD and inspired by the physics notion of **momentum**—as long as an object is moving downhill, its speed will increase with each step. Applied to gradient descent, the idea is to take previous parameter updates, v_{i-1}, into account, adding them to the new update terms, v_i, as follows:

$$v_i = \epsilon \frac{dL_i}{dP_i} + \mu v_{i-1}$$

Here, μ (*mu*) is the momentum weighing (the value between 0 and 1), defining the fraction of the previous updates to apply. If the current and previous steps have the same direction, their magnitudes will add up, accelerating the SGD in this relevant direction. If they have different directions, the momentum will dampen these oscillations.

In `tf.optimizers` (also accessible as `tf.keras.optimizers`), momentum is defined as an optional parameter of SGD (refer to the documentation at `https://www.tensorflow.org/api_docs/python/tf/keras/optimizers/SGD`) as follows:

```
optimizer = tf.optimizers.SGD(lr=0.01, momentum=0.9, # `momentum` = "mu"
                              decay=0.0, nesterov=False)
```

This optimizer accepts a `decay` parameter, fixing the learning rate decay over each update (refer to the previous paragraphs).

This optimizer instance can then be directly passed as a parameter to `model.fit()` when launching the training through the Keras API. For more complex training scenarios (for instance, when training interdependent networks), the optimizer can also be called, providing it with the loss gradients and the model's trainable parameters. The following is an example of a simple training step implemented manually:

```
@tf.function
def train_step(batch_images, batch_gts): # typical training step
    with tf.GradientTape() as grad_tape: # Tell TF to tape the gradients
        batch_preds = model(batch_images, training=True) # forward
        loss = tf.losses.MSE(batch_gts, batch_preds)     # compute loss
    # Get the loss gradients w.r.t trainable parameters and back-propagate:
    grads = grad_tape.gradient(loss, model.trainable_variables)
    optimizer.apply_gradients(zip(grads, model.trainable_variables))
```

`tf.optimizers.SGD` has one interesting Boolean parameter—to switch from the common momentum method to Nesterov's algorithm. Indeed, a major problem of the former method is that by the time the network gets really close to its loss minimum, the accumulated momentum will usually be quite high, which may cause the method to miss or oscillate around the target minimum.

The **Nesterov accelerated gradient** (**NAG** or **Nesterov momentum**) offers a solution to this problem (a related course is *Introductory Lectures on Convex Programming Volume I: Basic course,* by Yurii Nesterov, *Springer Science and Business Media*). Back in the 1980s, Yurii Nesterov's idea was to give the optimizer the possibility to have a look at the slope ahead so that it *knows* it should slow down if the slope starts going up. More formally, Nesterov suggested directly reusing the past term v_{i-1} to estimate which values, P_{i+1}, the parameters would take if we keep following this direction. The gradient is then evaluated with respect to those approximate future parameters, and it is used to finally compute the actual update as follows:

$$P_{i+1} \leftarrow P_i - v_i \quad \text{with} \;\; v_i = \epsilon \frac{dL_i}{d(P_i - \mu v_{i-1})} + \mu v_{i-1}$$

This version of the momentum optimizer (where the loss is derived with respect to the parameters' values updated according to the previous steps) is more adaptable to gradient changes, and can significantly speed up the gradient descent process.

The Ada family

Adagrad, **Adadelta**, and **Adam** are several iterations and variations around the idea of adapting the learning rate depending on the sensitivity and/or activation frequency of each neuron.

Developed first by John Duchi et al. (in *Adaptive Subgradient Methods for Online Learning and Stochastic Optimization,* Journal of Machine Learning Research, 2011), the *Adagrad* optimizer (for *adaptive gradients*) uses a neat formula (which we won't expand on here, though we invite you to search for it) to automatically decrease the learning rate more quickly for parameters linked to commonly found features, and more slowly for infrequent ones. In other words, as presented in the Keras documentation, *the more updates a parameter receives, the smaller the updates* (refer to the documentation at `https://keras.io/optimizers/`). This optimization algorithm not only removes the need to manually adapt/decay the learning rate, but it also makes the SGD process more stable, especially for datasets with sparse representations.

Introducing *Adadelta* in 2013, Matthew D. Zeiler et al. (in *ADADELTA: An Adaptive Learning Rate Method, arXiv preprint*) offered a solution to one problem inherent to *Adagrad.* As it keeps decaying the learning rate every iteration, at some point, the learning rate becomes too small and the network just cannot learn anymore (except maybe for infrequent parameters). *Adadelta* avoids this problem by keeping in check the factors used to divide the learning rate for each parameter.

RMSprop by Geoffrey Hinton is another well-known optimizer (introduced in his Coursera course, *Lecture 6.5-rmsprop: Divide the gradient by a running average of its recent magnitude*). Associated with, and quite similar to *Adadelta*, *RMSprop* was also developed to correct *Adagrad*'s flaw.

Adam (for **adaptive moment estimation**) is another iteration by Diederik P. Kingma et al. (in *Adam: A method for stochastic optimization*, ICLR, 2015). In addition to storing previous update terms, v_i, to adapt the learning rate for each parameter, *Adam* also keeps track of the past momentum values. It is, therefore, often identified as a mix between *Adadelta* and *momentum*. Similarly, **Nadam** is an optimizer inheriting from *Adadelta* and *NAG*.

All these various optimizers are available in the `tf.optimizers` package (refer to the documentation at `https://www.tensorflow.org/api_docs/python/tf/train/`). Note that there is no consensus regarding which of these optimizers may be the best. *Adam* is, however, preferred by many computer vision professionals for its effectiveness on scarce data. *RMSprop* is also often considered a good choice for recurrent neural networks (introduced in `Chapter 8`, *Video and Recurrent Neural Networks*).

A Jupyter notebook demonstrating how to use these various optimizers is provided in the Git repository. Each optimizer is also applied to the training of our *LeNet-5* for MNIST classification, in order to compare their convergence.

Regularization methods

Efficiently teaching neural networks so that they minimize the loss over training data is, however, not enough. We also want these networks to perform well once applied to new images. We do not want them to *overfit* the training set (as mentioned in `Chapter 1`, *Computer Vision and Neural Networks*). For our networks to generalize well, we mentioned that rich training sets (with enough variability to cover possible testing scenarios) and well-defined architectures (neither too shallow to avoid underfitting, nor too complex to prevent overfitting) are key. However, other methods have been developed over the years for **regularization**; for example, the process of refining the optimization phase to avoid overfitting.

Early stopping

Neural networks start overfitting when they iterate too many times over the same small set of training samples. Therefore, a straightforward solution to prevent this problem is to figure out the number of training epochs a model needs. The number should be low enough to stop before the network starts overfitting, but still high enough for the network to learn all it can from this training set.

Cross-validation is the key here to evaluate when training should be stopped. Providing a validation dataset to our optimizer, the latter can measure the performance of the model on images the network has not been directly optimized for. By *validating* the network, for instance, after each epoch, we can measure whether the training should continue (that is, when the validation accuracy appears to be still increasing) or be stopped (that is, when the validation accuracy stagnates or drops). The latter is called **early stopping**.

In practice, we usually monitor and plot the validation loss and metrics as a function of the training iterations, and we restore the saved weights at the optima (hence the importance of regularly saving the network during training). This monitoring, early stopping, and restoration of optimum weights can be automatically covered by one of the optional Keras callbacks (`tf.keras.callbacks.EarlyStopping`), as already showcased in our previous training.

L1 and L2 regularization

Another way to prevent overfitting is to modify the loss in order to include regularization as one of the training objectives. The L1 and L2 regularizers are prime examples of this.

Principles

In machine learning, a **regularization term**, *R(P)*, computed over the parameters, *P*, of the method, *f*, to optimize (for instance, a neural network) can be added to the loss function, *L*, before training, as follows:

$$L(y, y^{true}) + \lambda R(P) \quad \text{with} \;\; y = f(x, P)$$

Here, λ is a factor controlling the strength of the regularization (typically, to scale down the amplitude of the regularization term compared to the main loss), and $y = f(x, P)$ is the output of the method, *f*, parametrized by *P* for the input data, *x*. By adding this term, *R(P)*, to the loss, we force the network not only to optimize its task, but to optimize it while *constraining* the values its parameters can take.

For L1 and L2 regularization, the respective terms are as follows:

$$R_{L1}(P) = \|P\|_1 = \sum_k |P_k| \quad , \quad R_{L2}(P) = \frac{1}{2}\|P\|_2^2 = \frac{1}{2}\sum_k P_k^2$$

L2 regularization (also called **ridge regularization**) thus compels the network to minimize the sum of its squared parameter values. While this regularization leads to the decay of all parameter values over the optimization process, it more strongly punishes large parameters due to the squared term. Therefore, L2 regularization encourages the network *to keep its parameter values low and thus more homogeneously distributed*. It prevents the network from developing a small set of parameters with large values influencing its predictions (as it may prevent the network from generalizing).

On the other hand, the **L1 regularizer** (also called the **LASSO (least absolute shrinkage and selection operator) regularizer**, first introduced in *Linear Inversion of Band-Limited Reflection Seismograms,* by *Fadil Santosa and William Symes, SIAM, 1986*) compels the network to minimize the sum of its absolute parameter values. The difference between this and L2 regularization may seem symbolic at first glance, but their properties are actually quite different. As larger weights are not penalized by squaring, L1 regularization instead makes the network shrink the parameters linked to less important features toward zero. Therefore, it prevents overfitting by forcing the network to ignore less meaningful features (for instance, tied to dataset noise). In other words, L1 regularization forces the network to adopt sparse parameters; that is, to rely on a smaller set of non-null parameters. This can be advantageous if the footprint of the network should be minimized (for mobile applications, for example).

TensorFlow and Keras implementations

To implement those techniques, we should define the regularization loss and attach this function to every target layer. At each training iteration, these additional losses should be computed over the layers' parameters, and summed with the main task-specific loss (for instance, the cross-entropy over the network's predictions) so that they can all be backpropagated together by the optimizer. Thankfully, TensorFlow 2 provides several tools to simplify this process.

Additional losses can be attached to `tf.keras.layers.Layer` and `tf.keras.Model` instances through their `.add_loss(losses, ...)` method, with the `losses` tensors or zero-argument callables returning the loss values. Once properly added to a layer (see the following code), these losses will be computed every time the layer/model is called. All the losses attached to a `Layer` or `Model` instance, as well as the losses attached to its sublayers, will be computed, and the list of loss values will be returned when calling the `.losses` property. To better understand this concept, we'll extend the simple convolution layer implemented previously to add optional regularization to its parameters:

```
from functools import partial

def l2_reg(coef=1e-2): # reimplementation of tf.keras.regularizers.l2()
    return lambda x: tf.reduce_sum(x ** 2) * coef

class ConvWithRegularizers(SimpleConvolutionLayer):
    def __init__(self, num_kernels=32, kernel_size=(3, 3), stride=1,
                 kernel_regularizer=l2_reg(), bias_regularizer=None):
        super().__init__(num_kernels, kernel_size, stride)
        self.kernel_regularizer = kernel_regularizer
        self.bias_regularizer = bias_regularizer

    def build(self, input_shape):
        super().build(input_shape)
        # Attaching the regularization losses to the variables.
        if self.kernel_regularizer is not None:
            # for instance, we tell TF to compute and save
            # `tf.nn.l1_loss(self.kernels)` at each call (that is
iteration):
            self.add_loss(partial(self.kernel_regularizer, self.kernels))
        if self.bias_regularizer is not None:
            self.add_loss(partial(self.bias_regularizer, self.bias))
```

Regularization losses should guide the models toward learning more robust features. They should not take precedence over the main training loss, which is preparing the model for its task. Therefore, we should be careful not to put too much weight on the regularization losses. Their values are usually dampened by a coefficient between 0 and 1 (refer to `coef` in our `l2_reg()` loss function). This weighing is especially important, for instance, when the main loss is averaged (for example, MSE and MAE). So that the regularization losses do not outweigh it, we should either make sure that they are also averaged over the parameters' dimensions, or we should decrease their coefficient further.

At each training iteration of a network composed of such layers, the regularization losses can be computed, listed, and added to the main loss as follows:

```
# We create a NN containing layers with regularization/additional losses:
model = Sequential()
model.add(ConvWithRegularizers(6, (5, 5), kernel_regularizer=l2_reg())
model.add(...) # adding more layers
model.add(Dense(num_classes, activation='softmax'))

# We train it (c.f. function `training_step()` defined before):
for epoch in range(epochs):
    for (batch_images, batch_gts) in dataset:
        with tf.GradientTape() as grad_tape:
            loss = tf.losses.sparse_categorical_crossentropy(
                batch_gts, model(batch_images)) # main loss
            loss += sum(model.losses)          # list of addit. losses
        # Get the gradients of combined losses and back-propagate:
        grads = grad_tape.gradient(loss, model.trainable_variables)
        optimizer.apply_gradients(zip(grads, model.trainable_variables))
```

We introduced `.add_loss()`, as this method can greatly simplify the process of adding layer-specific losses to custom networks. However, when it comes to adding regularization losses, TensorFlow provides a more straightforward solution. We can simply pass the regularization loss function as a parameter of the `.add_weight()` method (also named `.add_variable()`) used to create and attach variables to a `Layer` instance. For example, the kernels' variable could be directly created with the regularization loss as follows: `self.kernels = self.add_weight(..., regularizer=self.kernel_regularizer)`. At each training iteration, the resulting regularization loss values can still be obtained through the layer or model's `.losses` property.

When using predefined Keras layers, we do not need to bother extending the classes to add regularization terms. These layers can receive regularizers for their variables as parameters. Keras even explicitly defines some regularizer callables in its `tf.keras.regularizers` module. Finally, when using Keras training operations (such as `model.fit(...)`), Keras automatically takes into account additional `model.losses` (that is, the regularization terms and other possible layer-specific losses), as follows:

```
# We instantiate a regularizer (L1 for example):
l1_reg = tf.keras.regularizers.l1(0.01)
# We can then pass it as a parameter to the target model's layers:
model = Sequential()
model.add(Conv2D(6, kernel_size=(5, 5), padding='same', activation='relu',
                 input_shape=input_shape, kernel_regularizer=l1_reg))
```

```
model.add(...) # adding more layers
model.fit(...) # training automatically taking into account the reg. terms.
```

Dropout

So far, the regularization methods we have covered are affecting the way networks are trained. Other solutions are affecting their architecture. **Dropout** is one such method and one of the most popular regularization tricks.

Definition

Introduced in *Dropout: A Simple Way to Prevent Neural Networks from Overfitting* (*JMLR, 2014*) by Hinton and his team (who made numerous contributions to deep learning), *dropout* consists of randomly disconnecting (*dropping out*) some neurons of target layers at every training iteration. This method thus takes a hyperparameter ratio, ρ, which represents the probability that neurons are being turned off at each training step (usually set between 0.1 and 0.5). The concept is illustrated in *Figure 3.13*:

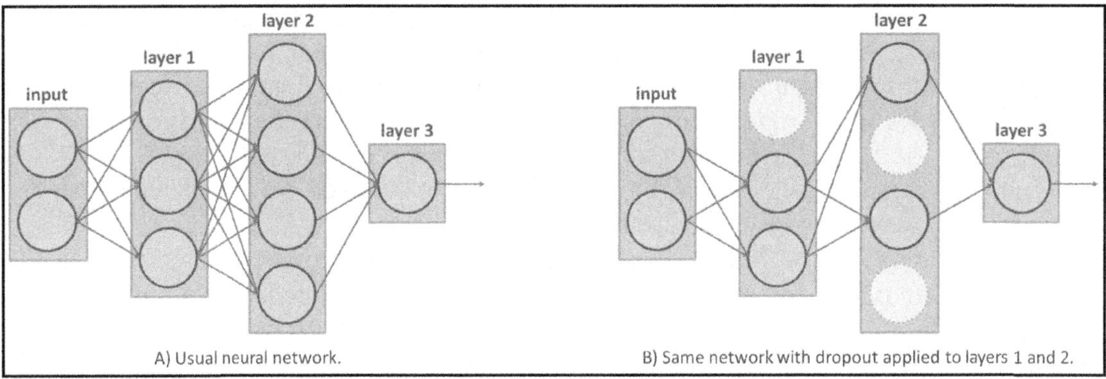

Figure 3.13: Dropout represented on a simple neural network (note that dropped-out neurons of layers are randomly chosen in each iteration)

By artificially and randomly impairing the network, this method forces the learning of robust and concurrent features. For instance, as dropout may deactivate the neurons responsible for a key feature, the network has to figure out other significant features in order to reach the same prediction. This has the effect of developing redundant representations of data for prediction.

Dropout is also often explained as a cheap solution to simultaneously train a *multitude* of models (the randomly impaired versions of the original network). During the testing phase, dropout is not applied to the network, so the network's predictions can be seen as the combination of the results that the partial models would have provided. Therefore, this information averaging prevents the network from overfitting.

TensorFlow and Keras methods

Dropout can be called as a function through `tf.nn.dropout(x, rate, ...)` (refer to the documentation at `https://www.tensorflow.org/api_docs/python/tf/nn/dropout`) to directly obtain a tensor with values randomly dropped, or as a layer through `tf.keras.layers.Dropout()` (refer to the documentation at `https://www.tensorflow.org/api_docs/python/tf/layers/dropout`), which can be added to neural models. By default, `tf.keras.layers.Dropout()` is only applied during training (when the layer/model is called with the `training=True` parameter) and is deactivated otherwise (forwarding the values without any alteration).

Dropout layers should be added directly after layers we want to prevent from overfitting (as dropout layers will randomly drop values returned by their preceding layers, forcing them to adapt). For instance, you can apply dropout (for example, with a ratio, $\rho = 0.2$) to a fully connected layer in Keras, as shown in the following code block:

```
model = Sequential([ # ...
    Dense(120, activation='relu'),
    Dropout(0.2),     # ...
])
```

Batch normalization

Though our list is not exhaustive, we will introduce a final common regularization method, which is also directly integrated into the networks' architectures.

Definition

Like dropout, **batch normalization** (proposed by Sergey Ioffe and Christian Szegedy in *Batch Normalization: Accelerating Deep Network Training by Reducing Internal Covariate Shift, JMLR, 2015*) is an operation that can be inserted into neural networks and affects their training. This operation takes the batched results of the preceding layers and *normalizes* them; that is, it subtracts the batch mean and divides it by the batch standard deviation.

Since batches are randomly sampled in SGD (and thus are rarely the same twice), this means that the data will almost never be normalized the same way. Therefore, the network has to learn how to deal with these data fluctuations, making it more robust and generic. Furthermore, this normalization step concomitantly improves the way the gradients flow through the network, facilitating the SGD process.

The behavior of batch normalization layers is actually a bit more complex than what we have succinctly presented. These layers have a couple of trainable parameters that are used in denormalization operations, so that the next layer does not just try to learn how to undo the batch normalization.

TensorFlow and Keras methods

Similar to dropout, batch normalization is available in TensorFlow both as a function, `tf.nn.batch_normalization()` (refer to the documentation at `https://www.tensorflow.org/api_docs/python/tf/nn/batch_normalization`) and as a layer, `tf.keras.layers.BatchNormalization()` (refer to the documentation at `https://www.tensorflow.org/api_docs/python/tf/keras/layers/BatchNormalization`), making it straightforward to include this regularization tool inside networks.

All these various optimization techniques are precious tools for deep learning, especially when training CNNs on imbalanced or scarce datasets, which is often the case for custom applications (as elaborated on in `Chapter 7`, *Training on Complex and Scarce Datasets*).

Similar to the Jupyter notebook for the optimizers study, we provide another notebook demonstrating how these regularization methods can be applied, and how they affect the performance of our simple CNN.

Summary

With the help of TensorFlow and Keras, we caught up with years of research in deep learning. As CNNs have become central to modern computer vision (and machine learning in general), it is essential to understand how they perform, and what kinds of layers they are composed of. As presented in this chapter, TensorFlow and Keras provide clear interfaces to efficiently build such networks. They are also implementing several advanced optimization and regularization techniques (such as various optimizers, L1/L2 regularization, dropout, and batch normalization) to improve the performance and robustness of trained models, which is important to keep in mind for any application.

We now have the tools to finally tackle more challenging computer vision tasks.

In the next chapter, we will therefore present several CNN architectures applied to the task of classifying large picture datasets.

Questions

1. Why does the output of a convolutional layer have a smaller width and height than the input, unless it is padded?
2. What would be the output of a max-pooling layer with a receptive field of (2, 2) and stride of 2 on the input matrix in *Figure 3.6*?
3. How could LeNet-5 be implemented using the Keras functional API in a non-object-oriented manner?
4. How does L1/L2 regularization affect networks?

Further reading

- *On the importance of initialization and momentum in deep learning* (`http://proceedings.mlr.press/v28/sutskever13.pdf`), by Ilya Sutskever et al. This often-referenced conference paper, published in 2013, presents and compares the momentum and NAG algorithms.
- *Dropout: A Simple Way to Prevent Neural Networks from Overfitting* (`http://www.jmlr.org/papers/volume15/srivastava14a/srivastava14a.pdf`), by Nitish Srivastava et al. This other conference paper, published in 2014, introduced dropout. It is a great read for those who want to know more about this method and see it applied to several famous computer vision datasets.

Section 2: State-of-the-Art Solutions for Classic Recognition Problems

In this section, you will discover and apply modern methods to solve a variety of problems. Classification, a canonical machine learning task, will serve as a great example to introduce up-to-date neural network architectures (such as **Inception** and **ResNet**) and transfer learning. Object detection, useful for self-driving cars and other robots, will serve to illustrate the trade-off between speed and accuracy through the comparison of two widely used algorithms—**YOLO** and **Faster R-CNN**. Finally, building upon the two previous chapters, the final chapter in this section ends with an in-depth presentation of encoder-decoder networks applied to image denoising and semantic segmentation.

The following chapters will be covered in this section:

- `Chapter 4`, *Influential Classification Tools*
- `Chapter 5`, *Object Detection Models*
- `Chapter 6`, *Enhancing and Segmenting Images*

4
Influential Classification Tools

After the deep learning breakthrough in 2012, research toward more refined classification systems based on **convolutional neural networks** (**CNNs**) gained momentum. Innovation is moving at a frantic pace nowadays, as more and more companies are developing smart products. Among the numerous solutions developed over the years for object classification, some have became famous for their contributions to computer vision. They have been derived and adapted for so many different applications that they have achieved must-know status, and so deserve their own chapter.

In parallel with the advanced network architectures introduced by these solutions, other methods have been explored to better prepare CNNs for their specific tasks. So, in the second part of this chapter, we will look at how the knowledge acquired by networks on specific use cases can be transferred to new applications for enhanced performance.

The following topics will be covered in this chapter:

- What instrumental architectures such as VGG, inception, and ResNet have brought to computer vision
- How these solutions can be reimplemented or directly reused for classification tasks
- What transfer learning is, and how to efficiently repurpose trained networks

Technical requirements

Jupyter notebooks illustrating the concepts presented in this chapter can be found in the GitHub folder at `github.com/PacktPublishing/Hands-On-Computer-Vision-with-TensorFlow-2/tree/master/Chapter04`.

The only new package introduced in this chapter is `tensorflow-hub`. Installation instructions can be found at `https://www.tensorflow.org/hub/installation` (though it is a single-line command with `pip`: `pip install tensorflow-hub`).

Understanding advanced CNN architectures

Research in computer vision has been moving forward both through incremental contributions and large innovative leaps. Challenges organized by researchers and companies, inviting experts to submit new solutions in order to best solve a predefined task, have been playing a key role in triggering such instrumental contributions. The ImageNet classification contest (**ImageNet Large Scale Visual Recognition Challenge** (**ILSVRC**); see `Chapter 1`, *Computer Vision and Neural Networks*) is a perfect example. With its millions of images split into 1,000 fine-grained classes, it still represents a great challenge for daring researchers, even after the significant and symbolic victory of AlexNet in 2012.

In this section, we will present some of the classic deep learning methods that followed AlexNet in tackling ILSVRC, covering the reasons leading to their development and the contributions they made.

VGG – a standard CNN architecture

The first network architecture we will present is **VGG** (or *VGGNet*), developed by the *Visual Geometry Group* from Oxford University. Though the group only achieved second place in the ILSVRC classification task in 2014, their method influenced many later architectures.

Overview of the VGG architecture

Looking at the motivation of the VGG authors, and then their contributions, we will present how the VGG architecture achieved higher accuracy with fewer parameters.

Motivation

AlexNet was a game changer, being the first CNN successfully trained for such a complex recognition task and making several contributions that are still valid nowadays, such as the following:

- The use of a **rectified linear unit** (*ReLU*) as an activation function, which prevents the vanishing gradient problem (explained later in this chapter), and thus improving training (compared to using sigmoid or tanh)
- The application of **dropout** to CNNs (with all the benefits covered in `Chapter 3`, *Modern Neural Networks*)
- The typical CNN architecture combining blocks of convolution and pooling layers, with dense layers afterward for the final prediction

- The application of random transformations (image translation, horizontal flipping, and more) to synthetically augment the dataset (that is, augmenting the number of different training images by randomly editing the original samples—see `Chapter 7`, *Training on Complex and Scarce Datasets,* for more details)

Still, even back then, it was clear that this prototype architecture had room for improvement. The main motivation of many researchers was to try going deeper (that is, building a network composed of a larger number of stacked layers), despite the challenges arising from this. Indeed, more layers typically means more parameters to train, making the learning process more complex. As we will describe in the next paragraph, however, Karen Simonyan and Andrew Zisserman from Oxford's VGG group tackled this challenge with success. The method they submitted to ILSVRC 2014 reached a top-5 error of 7.3%, dividing the 16.4% error of AlexNet by more than two!

Top-5 accuracy is one of the main classification metrics of ILSVRC. It considers that a method has predicted properly if the correct class is among its five first guesses. Indeed, for many applications, it is fine to have a method that's able to reduce a large number of class candidates to a lower number (for instance, to leave the final choice between the remaining candidates to an expert user). The top-5 metrics are a specific case of the more generic top-k metrics.

Architecture

In their paper (*Very Deep Convolutional Networks for Large-Scale Image Recognition, ArXiv, 2014*), Simonyan and Zisserman presented how they developed their network to be deeper than most previous ones. They actually introduced six different CNN architectures, from 11 to 25 layers deep. Each network is composed of five blocks of several consecutive convolutions followed by a max-pooling layer and three final dense layers (with dropout for training). All the convolutional and max-pooling layers have `SAME` for padding. The convolutions have $s = 1$ for stride, and are using the *ReLU* function for activation. All in all, a typical VGG network is represented in the following diagram:

Figure 4.1: VGG-16 architecture

The two most performant architectures, still commonly used nowadays, are called **VGG-16** and **VGG-19**. The numbers (16 and 19) represent the *depth* of these CNN architectures; that is, the number of *trainable* layers stacked together. For example, as shown in *Figure 4.1*, VGG-16 contains 13 convolutional layers and 3 dense ones, hence a depth of 16 (excluding the non-trainable operations; that is, the 5 max-pooling and 2 dropout layers). The same goes for VGG-19, which is composed of three additional convolutions. VGG-16 has approximately 138 million parameters, and VGG-19 has 144 million. Those numbers are quite high, although, as we will demonstrate in the following section, the VGG researchers took a new approach to keep these values in check despite the depth of their architecture.

Contributions – standardizing CNN architectures

In the following paragraphs, we will summarize the most significant contributions introduced by these researchers while further detailing their architecture.

Replacing large convolutions with multiple smaller ones

The authors began with a simple observation—a stack of two convolutions with 3×3 kernels has the same receptive field as a convolution with 5×5 kernels (refer to `Chapter 3`, *Modern Neural Networks*, for the **effective receptive field** (**ERF**) formula).

Similarly, three consecutive 3×3 convolutions result in a 7×7 receptive field, and five 3×3 operations result in an 11×11 receptive field. Therefore, while AlexNet has large filters (up to 11×11), the VGG network contains more numerous but smaller convolutions for a larger ERF. The benefits of this change are twofold:

- **It decreases the number of parameters**: Indeed, the N filters of an 11×11 convolution layer imply $11 \times 11 \times D \times N = 121DN$ values to train just for their kernels (for an input of depth D), while five 3×3 convolutions have a total of $1 \times (3 \times 3 \times D \times N) + 4 \times (3 \times 3 \times N \times N) = 9DN + 36N^2$ weights for their kernels. As long as $N < 3.6D$, this means fewer parameters. For instance, for $N = 2D$, the number of parameters drops from $242D^2$ to $153D^2$ (refer to the previous equations). This makes the network easier to optimize, as well as much lighter (we invite you to look at the decrease for the replacements of the 7×7 and 5×5 convolutions).

- **It increases the non-linearity**: Having a larger number of convolution layers—each followed by a *non-linear* activation function such as *ReLU*—increases the networks' capacity to learn complex features (that is, by combining more non-linear operations).

Overall, replacing larger convolutions with small, consecutive ones allowed the VGG authors to effectively go deeper.

Increasing the depth of the feature maps

Based on another intuition, the VGG authors doubled the depth of the feature maps for each block of convolutions (from 64 after the first convolution to 512). As each set is followed by a max-pooling layer with a 2 × 2 window size and a stride of 2, the depth doubles while the spatial dimensions are halved.

This allows the encoding of spatial information into more and more complex and discriminative features for classification.

Augmenting data with scale jittering

Simonyan and Zisserman also introduced a **data augmentation** mechanism that they named **scale jittering**. At each training iteration, they randomly scale the batched images (from 256 pixels to 512 pixels for their smaller side) before cropping them to the proper input size (*224 × 224* for their ILSVRC submission). With this random transformation, the network will be confronted with samples with different scales and will learn to properly classify them despite this scale jittering (refer to *Figure 4.2*). The network becomes more robust as a result, as it is trained on images covering a larger range of realistic transformations.

Data augmentation is the procedure of synthetically increasing the size of training datasets by applying random transformations to their images in order to create different versions. Details and concrete examples are provided in `Chapter 7`, *Training on Complex and Scarce Datasets*.

The authors also suggested applying random scaling and cropping at test time. The idea is to generate several versions of the query image this way and to feed them all to the network, with the intuition that it increases the chance of feeding content on a scale the network is particularly used to. The final prediction is obtained by averaging the results for each version.

In their paper, they demonstrate how this process tends to also improve accuracy:

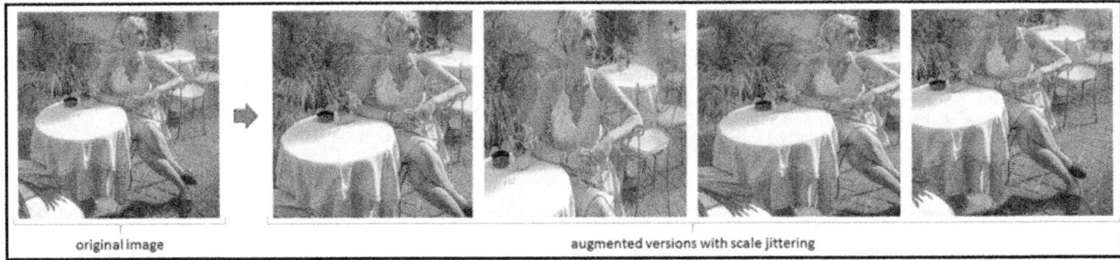

Figure 4.2: Example of scale jittering. Notice that it is common to not preserve the aspect ratio of the content to further transform the images

The same principle was previously used by the AlexNet authors. During both training and testing, they were generating several versions of each image with different combinations of cropping and flipping transformations.

Replacing fully connected layers with convolutions

While the classic VGG architecture ends with several **fully connected** (**FC**) layers (such as AlexNet), the authors suggest an alternative version. In this version, the dense layers are replaced by convolutional ones.

The first set of convolutions with larger kernels (7×7 and 3×3) reduces the spatial size of the feature maps to 1×1 (with no padding applied beforehand) and increases their depth to 4,096. Finally, a 1×1 convolution is used with as many filters as classes to predict from (that is, $N = 1{,}000$ for ImageNet). The resulting $1 \times 1 \times N$ vector is normalized with the `softmax` function, and then flattened into the final class predictions (with each value of the vector representing the predicted class probability).

1×1 convolutions are commonly used to change the depth of the input volume without affecting its spatial structure. For each spatial position, the new values are interpolated from all the depth values at that position.

Such a network without any dense layers is called a **fully convolutional network** (**FCN**). As mentioned in `Chapter 3`, *Modern Neural Networks*, and as has been highlighted by the VGG authors, FCNs can be applied to images of different sizes, with no need for cropping beforehand.

Interestingly, to achieve the best accuracy for ILSVRC, the authors trained and used both versions (normal and FCN), once again averaging their results to obtain the final predictions. This technique is named **model averaging** and is frequently used in production.

Implementations in TensorFlow and Keras

Thanks to the efforts that the authors put into creating a clear architecture, VGG-16 and VGG-19 are among the simplest classifiers to reimplement. Example code can be found in the GitHub folder for this chapter, for educational purposes. However, in computer vision, as in many domains, it is always preferable not to reinvent the wheel and to instead reuse existing tools that are available. The following paragraphs present different preimplemented VGG solutions that you can directly adapt and reuse.

The TensorFlow model

While TensorFlow itself does not offer any official implementation of the VGG architectures, neatly implemented VGG-16 and VGG-19 networks are available in the `tensorflow/models` GitHub repository (`https://github.com/tensorflow/models`). This repository, maintained by TensorFlow contributors, contains numerous well-curated state-of-the-art or experimental models. It is often recommended that you should search this repository when looking for a specific network.

We invite our readers to have a look at the VGG code there (currently available at `https://github.com/tensorflow/tensorflow/blob/master/tensorflow/contrib/slim/python/slim/nets/vgg.py`), as it reimplements the FCN version we described earlier.

The Keras model

The Keras API has an official implementation of these architectures, accessible via its `tf.keras.applications` package (refer to the documentation at `https://www.tensorflow.org/api_docs/python/tf/keras/applications`). This package contains several other well-known models and provides *pre trained* parameters for each (that is, parameters saved from prior training on a specific dataset). For instance, you can instantiate a VGG network with the following command:

```
vgg_net = tf.keras.applications.VGG16(
    include_top=True, weights='imagenet', input_tensor=None,
    input_shape=None, pooling=None, classes=1000)
```

With these default arguments, Keras instantiates the VGG-16 network and loads the persisted parameter values obtained after a complete training cycle on ImageNet. With this single command, we have a network ready to classify images into the 1,000 ImageNet categories. If we would like to retrain the network from scratch instead, we should fix `weights=None` and Keras will randomly set the weights.

In Keras terminology, the *top* layers correspond to the final consecutive dense layers. Therefore, if we set `include_top=False`, the VGG dense layers will be excluded, and the network's outputs will be the feature maps of the last convolution/max-pooling block. This can be useful if we want to reuse the pre trained VGG network to extract meaningful features (which can be applied to more advanced tasks), and not just for classification. The `pooling` function parameter can be used in those cases (that is, when `include_top=False`) to specify an optional operation to be applied to the feature maps before returning them (`pooling='avg'` or `pooling='max'` to apply a global average- or max- pooling).

GoogLeNet and the inception module

Developed by researchers at Google, the architecture we will now present was also applied to ILSVRC 2014 and won first place for the classification task ahead of VGGNet. **GoogLeNet** (for *Google* and *LeNet*, as an homage to this pioneering network) is structurally very different from its linear challenger, introducing the notion of *inception blocks* (the network is also commonly called an **inception network**).

Overview of the GoogLeNet architecture

As we will see in the following section, the GoogLeNet authors, Christian Szegedy and others, approached the conception of a more efficient CNN from a very different angle than the VGG researchers (*Going Deeper with Convolutions*, Proceedings of the CVPR IEEE conference, 2014).

Motivation

While VGG's authors took AlexNet and worked on standardizing and optimizing its structure in order to obtain a clearer and deeper architecture, researchers at Google took a different approach. Their first consideration, as mentioned in the paper, was the optimization of the CNN computational footprint.

Indeed, in spite of careful engineering (refer to VGG), the deeper CNNs are, the larger their number of trainable parameters and their number of computations per prediction become (it is costly with respect to memory and time). For instance, VGG-16 weighs approximately 93 MB (in terms of parameter storage), and the VGG submission for ILSVRC took two to three weeks to train on four GPUs. With approximately 5 million parameters, GoogLeNet is 12 times lighter than AlexNet and 21 times lighter than VGG-16, and the network was trained within a week. As a result, GoogLeNet—and more recent inception networks—can even run on more modest machines (such as smartphones), which contributed to their lasting popularity.

We have to keep in mind that, despite this impressive reduction in the numbers of parameters and operations, GoogLeNet did win the classification challenge in 2014 with a top-5 error of 6.7% (against 7.3% with VGG). This performance is the result of the second target of Szegedy and others—the conception of a network that was not only deeper but also larger, with blocks of parallel layers for *multiscale processing*. While we will detail this solution later in this chapter, the intuition behind it is simple. Building a CNN is a complex, iterative task. How do we know which layer (such as convolutional or pooling) should be added to the stack in order to improve the accuracy? How do we know which kernel size would work best for a given layer? After all, kernels of different sizes will not react to features of the same scale. How can we avoid such a trade-off? A solution, according to the authors, is to use the *inception modules* they developed, composed of several different layers working in parallel.

Architecture

As shown in *Figure 4.3*, GoogLeNet architecture is not as straightforward as the previous architectures we studied, although it can be analyzed region by region. The input images are first processed by a classic series of convolutional and max-pooling layers. Then, the information goes through a stack of nine inception modules. These modules (often called **subnetworks**; further detailed in *Figure 4.4*), are blocks of layers stacked vertically and horizontally. For each module, the input feature maps are passed to four parallel sub-blocks composed of one or two different layers (convolutions with different kernel sizes and max-pooling).

The results of these four parallel operations are then concatenated together along the depth dimension and into a single feature volume:

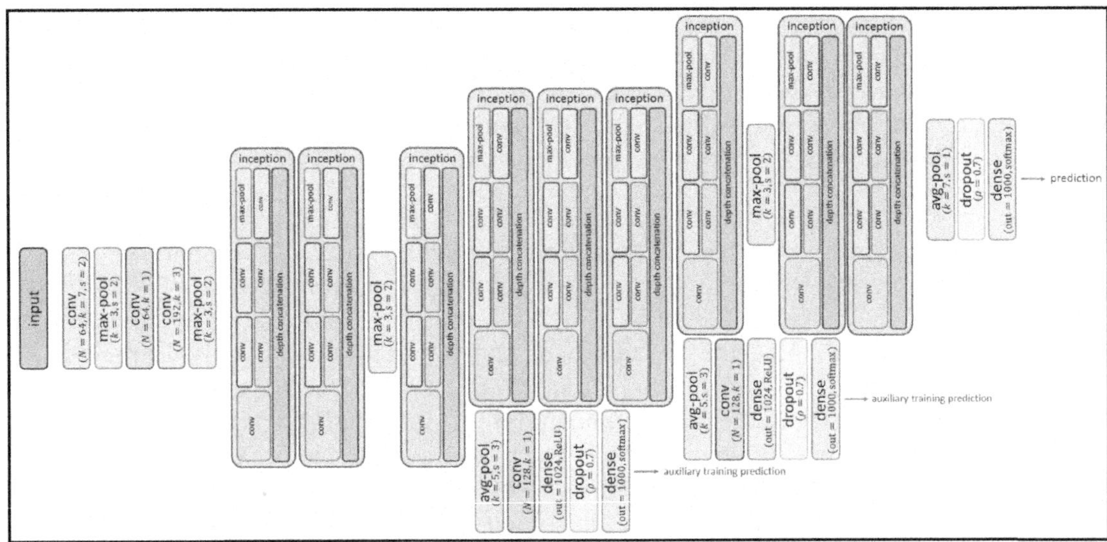

Figure 4.3: GoogLeNet architecture. The inception modules are detailed in *Figure 4.4*

In the preceding figure, all the convolutional and max-pooling layers have `SAME` for padding. The convolutions have $s = 1$ for stride if unspecified and are using the *ReLU* function for activation.

This network is composed of several layer blocks sharing a similar structure with parallel layers—the inception modules. For instance, the first inception module, represented in *Figure 4.3*, receives a feature volume of size $28 \times 28 \times 192$ for input. Its first parallel sub-block, composed of a single 1×1 convolution output ($N = 64$ and $s = 1$), thus generates a $28 \times 28 \times 64$ tensor. Similarly, the second sub-module, composed of two convolutions, outputs a $28 \times 28 \times 128$ tensor; and the two remaining ones output a $28 \times 28 \times 32$ and a $28 \times 28 \times 32$ feature volume, respectively. Therefore, by stacking these four results together along the last dimension, the first inception module outputs a $28 \times 28 \times 256$ tensor, which is then passed to the second module, and so on. In the following diagram, the naive solution is represented on the left, and the module used in GoogLeNet (that is, the inception module v1) is shown on the right (note that in GoogLeNet, the number of filters N increases the deeper the module is):

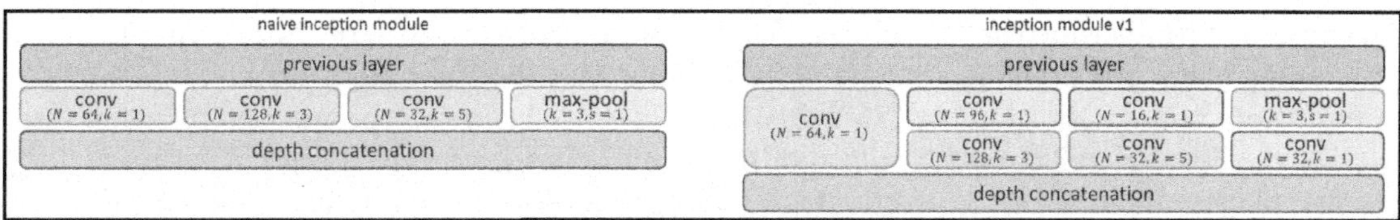

Figure 4.4: Inception modules: naive versus actual

The features of the last module are average, pooled from *7 × 7 × 1,024* to *1 × 1 × 1,024*, and are finally densely converted into the prediction vector. As shown in *Figure 4.3*, the network is further composed of two auxiliary branches, also leading to predictions. Their purpose will be detailed in the next section.

In total, GoogLeNet is a 22-layer deep architecture (counting the trainable layers only), with a total of more than 60 convolutional and FC layers. And yet, this much larger network has 12 times fewer parameters than AlexNet.

Contributions – popularizing larger blocks and bottlenecks

The low number of parameters, as well as the network's performance, are the results of several concepts implemented by the GoogLeNet authors. We will cover the main ones in this section.

In this section, we will present only the key concepts differentiating the inception networks from the ones we introduced previously. Note that the GoogLeNet authors reapplied several other techniques that we have already covered, such as the prediction of multiple crops for each input image and the use of other image transformations during training.

Capturing various details with inception modules

Introduced by Min Lin and others in their influential **Network in Network** (**NIN**) paper in 2013, the idea of having a CNN composed of sub-network modules was adapted and fully exploited by the Google team. As previously mentioned and shown in *Figure 4.4*, the basic inception modules they developed are composed of four parallel layers—three convolutions with filters of size *1 × 1*, *3 × 3*, and *5 × 5*, respectively, and one max-pooling layer with stride `1`. The advantages of this parallel processing, with the results concatenated together after, are numerous.

As explained in the Motivation sub-section, this architecture allows for the multiscale processing of the data. The results of each inception module combine features of different scales, capturing a wider range of information. We do not have to choose which kernel size may be the best (such a choice would require several iterations of training and testing cycles), that is, the network learns by itself which convolutions to rely on more for each module.

Additionally, while we presented how vertically stacking layers with non-linear activation functions positively affects a network's performance, this is also true for horizontal combinations. The concatenation of features mapped from different layers further adds to the non-linearity of the CNN.

Using 1 x 1 convolutions as bottlenecks

Though not a contribution *per se*, Szegedy et al. made the following technique notorious by efficiently applying it to their network.

As previously mentioned in the *Replacing fully connected layers with convolutions* section, 1×1 convolutional layers (with a stride of 1) are often used to change the overall depth of input volumes without affecting their spatial structures. Such a layer with N filters would take an input of shape $H \times W \times D$ and return an interpolated $H \times W \times N$ tensor. For each pixel in the input image, its D channel values will be interpolated by the layer (according to its filter weights) into N channel values.

This property can be applied to reduce the number of parameters required for larger convolutions by compressing the features' depth beforehand (using $N < D$). This technique basically uses 1×1 convolutions as **bottlenecks** (that is, as intermediary layers reducing the dimensionality and, thus, the number of parameters). Since activations in neural networks are often redundant or left unused, such bottlenecks usually barely affect the performance (as long as they do not drastically reduce the depth). Moreover, GoogLeNet has its parallel layers to compensate for the depth reduction. Indeed, in inception networks, bottlenecks are present in every module, before all larger convolutions and after max-pooling operations, as illustrated in *Figure 4.4*.

Given the *5 × 5* convolution in the first inception module (taking as input a *28 × 28 × 192* volume) for example, the tensor containing its filters would be of the dimension *5 × 5 × 192 × 32* in the naive version. This represents 153,600 parameters just for this convolution. In the first version of the inception module (that is, with bottlenecks), a *1 × 1* convolution is introduced before the 5 × 5 one, with *N* = 16. As a result, the two convolutions require a total of *1 × 1 × 192 × 16 + 5 × 5 × 16 × 32 = 15,872* trainable values for their kernels. This is 10 times fewer parameters than the previous version (just for this single *5 × 5* layer), for the same output size! Furthermore, as mentioned already, the addition of layers with a non-linear activation function (*ReLU*) further improves the networks' ability to grasp complex concepts.

We are presenting GoogLeNet as submitted to ILSVRC 2014 in this chapter. More commonly named **Inception V1**, this architecture has been refined by its authors since then. **Inception V2** and **Inception V3** contain several improvements, such as replacing the *5 × 5* and *7 × 7* convolutions by smaller ones (as done in VGG), improving the bottlenecks' hyperparameters to reduce the information loss, and adding *BatchNorm* layers.

Pooling instead of fully connecting

Another solution used by the inception authors to reduce the number of parameters was to use an average-pooling layer instead of a fully connected one after the last convolutional block. With a *7 × 7* window size and stride of 1, this layer reduces the feature volume from *7 × 7 × 1,024* to *1 × 1 × 1,024* without any parameter to train. A dense layer would have added (*7 × 7 × 1,024*) × 1,024 = *51,380,224* parameters. Though the network loses a bit in expressiveness with this replacement, the computational gain is enormous (and the network already contains enough non-linear operations to capture the information it needs for the final prediction).

The last and only FC layer in GoogLeNet has *1,024 × 1,000 = 1,024,000* parameters, a fifth of the total number the network has!

Fighting vanishing gradient with intermediary losses

As briefly mentioned when introducing the architecture, GoogLeNet has two auxiliary branches at training time (removed after), also leading to predictions.

Their purpose is to improve the propagation of the loss through the network during training. Indeed, deeper CNNs are often plagued with **vanishing gradient**. Many CNN operations (for instance, *sigmoid*) have derivatives with small amplitudes (below one). Therefore, the higher the number of layers, the smaller the product of the derivatives becomes when backpropagating (as more values below one are multiplied together, the closer to zero the result will become). Often, the gradient simply vanishes/shrinks to zero when reaching the first layers. Since the gradient values are directly used to update the parameters, these layers won't effectively learn if the gradient is too small.

The opposite phenomenon—the **exploding gradient** problem—can also happen with deeper networks. When operations whose derivatives can take on larger magnitudes are used, their product during backpropagation can become so big that it makes the training unstable (with huge, erratic weight updates) or it can even sometimes overflow (`NaN` values).

The down-to-earth, yet effective, solution to this problem implemented here is to reduce the distance between the first layers and predictions, by introducing additional classification losses at various network depths. If the gradient from the final loss cannot flow properly to the first layers, these will still be trained to help with classification thanks to the closer intermediary losses. Incidentally, this solution also slightly improves the robustness of the layers affected by multiple losses, as they must learn to extract discriminative features that are not only useful to the main network, but also to the shorter branches.

Implementations in TensorFlow and Keras

While the inception architecture may look complex to implement at first glance, we already have most of the tools to do so. Moreover, several pretrained versions are also made available by TensorFlow and Keras.

Inception module with the Keras Functional API

The networks we have implemented so far were purely sequential, with a single path from inputs to predictions. The inception model differs from those, with its multiple parallel layers and branches. This gives us the opportunity to demonstrate that such operational graphs are not much more difficult to instantiate with the available APIs. In the following section, we will write an inception module using the Keras Functional API (refer to the documentation at `https://keras.io/getting-started/sequential-model-guide/`).

So far, we have mostly been using the Keras Sequential API, which is not well-adapted for multipath architectures (as its name implies). The Keras Functional API is closer to the TensorFlow paradigm, with Python variables for the layers being passed as parameters to the next ones to build a graph. The following code presents a simplistic model implemented with both APIs:

```
from keras.models import Sequential, Model
from keras.layers import Dense, Conv2D, MaxPooling2D, Flatten, Input

# Sequential version:
model = Sequential()
model.add(Conv2D(32, kernel_size=(5, 5), input_shape=input_shape))
model.add(MaxPooling2D(pool_size=(2, 2)))
model.add(Flatten())
model.add(Dense(10, activation='softmax'))

# Functional version:
inputs = Input(shape=input_shape)
conv1 = Conv2D(32, kernel_size=(5, 5))(inputs)
maxpool1 = MaxPooling2D(pool_size=(2, 2))(conv1)
predictions = Dense(10, activation='softmax')(Flatten()(maxpool1))
model = Model(inputs=inputs, outputs=predictions)
```

With the functional API, a layer can easily be passed to multiple others, which is what we need for the parallel blocks of the inception modules. Their results can then be merged together using a `concatenate` layer (refer to the documentation at `https://keras.io/layers/merge/#concatenate_1`). Therefore, the naive inception block presented in *Figure 4.4* can be implemented as follows:

```
from keras.layers import Conv2D, MaxPooling2D, concatenate

def naive_inception_block(previous_layer, filters=[64, 128, 32]):
    conv1x1 = Conv2D(filters[0], kernel_size=(1, 1), padding='same',
                     activation='relu')(previous_layer)
    conv3x3 = Conv2D(filters[1], kernel_size=(3, 3), padding='same',
                     activation='relu')(previous_layer)
    conv5x5 = Conv2D(filters[2], kernel_size=(5, 5), padding='same',
                     activation='relu')(previous_layer)
    max_pool = MaxPooling2D((3, 3), strides=(1, 1),
                            padding='same')(previous_layer)
    return concatenate([conv1x1, conv3x3, conv5x5, max_pool], axis=-1)
```

We will leave it to you to adapt this code to implement the proper modules for Inception V1 by adding the bottleneck layers.

TensorFlow model and TensorFlow Hub

Google offers several scripts and tutorials explaining how to directly use its inception networks, or how to retrain them for new applications. The directory dedicated to this architecture in the `tensorflow/models` Git repository (`https://github.com/tensorflow/models/tree/master/research/inception`) is also rich and well-documented. Moreover, a pretrained version of Inception V3 is available on **TensorFlow Hub**, which gives us the opportunity to introduce this platform.

TensorFlow Hub is a repository of pretrained models. In a similar way to how Docker allows people to easily share and reuse software packages, removing the need to reconfigure distributions, TensorFlow Hub gives access to pretrained models so that people do not have to spend time and resources reimplementing and retraining. It combines a website (`https://tfhub.dev`) where people can search for specific models (depending, for example, on the target recognition task), and a Python package to easily download and start using these models. For instance, we can fetch and set up an Inception V3 network as follows:

```
import tensorflow as tf
import tensorflow_hub as hub

url = "https://tfhub.dev/google/tf2-preview/inception_v3/feature_vector/2"
hub_feature_extractor = hub.KerasLayer( # TF-Hub model as Layer
    url, # URL of the TF-Hub model (here, an InceptionV3 extractor)
    trainable=False, # Flag to set the layers as trainable or not
    input_shape=(299, 299, 3), # Expected input shape (found on tfhub.dev)
    output_shape=(2048,), # Output shape (same, found on the model's page)
    dtype=tf.float32) # Expected dtype

inception_model = Sequential(
    [hub_feature_extractor, Dense(num_classes, activation='softmax')],
    name="inception_tf_hub")
```

Though this code is quite succinct, a lot is happening. A preliminary step was to browse the `tfhub.dev` website and decide on a model there. On the page presenting the selected model (`https://tfhub.dev/google/tf2-preview/inception_v3/feature_vector/2`; stored in `model_url`), we can read that the inception model we chose is defined as an **image feature vector** that expects *299* x *299* x *3* inputs, among other details. To use a TensorFlow Hub model, we need to know how to interface with it.

The *image feature vector* type tells us that this network returns extracted features; that is, the results of the last convolutional block before the dense operations. With such a model, it is up to us to add the final layers (for instance, so that the output size corresponds to the number of considered classes).

The latest versions of the TensorFlow Hub interface seamlessly with Keras, and a complete pretrained TensorFlow Hub model can be fetched and instantiated as a Keras layer thanks to `tensorflow_hub.KerasLayer(model_url, trainable, ...)`. Like any Keras layer, it can then be used inside larger Keras models or TensorFlow estimators.

Though this may not seem as straightforward as using the Keras Applications API, TensorFlow Hub has an exotic catalog of models, which is destined to increase over time.

One of the Jupyter notebooks available in the Git repository is dedicated to TensorFlow Hub and its usage.

The Keras model

As with VGG, Keras provides an implementation of Inception V3, optionally, with weights pretrained on ImageNet. `tf.keras.applications.InceptionV3()` (refer to the documentation at `https://keras.io/applications/#inceptionv3`) has the same signature as the one presented for VGG.

We have mentioned AlexNet, the winning solution of ILSVRC 2012, as well as VGGNet and GoogLeNet, which prevailed during the 2014 edition. You might be wondering who won in 2013. The challenge that year was dominated by the **ZFNet** architecture (named after its creators, Matthew Zeiler and Rob Fergus from New York University). If ZFNet is not covered in this chapter, it is because its architecture was not particularly innovative, and has not really been reused afterward.

However, Zeiler and Fergus' significant contribution lay somewhere else—they developed and applied several operations to the visualization of CNNs (such as **unpooling** and **transposed convolution**, also known as **deconvolution**, which are both detailed in `Chapter 6`, *Enhancing and Segmenting Images*). Indeed, a common criticism of neural networks was that they behave like *black boxes*, and that no one can really grasp why and how they work so well. Zeiler and Fergus' work was an important first step toward opening up CNNs to reveal their inner processes (such as how they end up reacting to particular features and how they learn more abstract concepts as they go deeper.) Visualizing how each layer of their network reacted to specific images and contributed to the final prediction, the authors were able to optimize its hyperparameters and thus improve its performance (*Visualizing and Understanding Convolutional Networks*, Springer, 2014).

Research toward understanding neural networks is still ongoing (for instance, with a multitude of recent work capturing and analyzing the *attention* of networks toward specific elements) and has already greatly helped to improve current systems.

ResNet – the residual network

The last architecture we will address in this chapter won the 2015 edition of ILSVRC. Composed of a new kind of module, the residual module, **ResNet** (**residual network**) provides an efficient approach to creating very deep networks, beating larger models such as Inception in terms of performance.

Overview of the ResNet architecture

Developed by Kaiming He et al., researchers at Microsoft, the ResNet architecture is an interesting solution to learning problems affecting CNNs. Following the structure of previous sections, we will first clarify the author's targets and introduce their novel architecture (refer to *Deep Residual Learning for Image Recognition*, Proceedings of the CVPR IEEE conference, 2016).

Motivation

Inception networks demonstrated that going larger is a valid strategy in image classification, as well as other recognition tasks. Nevertheless, experts still kept trying to increase networks in order to solve more and more complex tasks. However, the question *Is learning better networks as easy as stacking more layers?*, asked in the preamble of the paper written by He et al., is justified.

We know already that the deeper a network goes, the harder it becomes to train it. But besides the *vanishing/exploding gradient* problems (covered by other solutions already), He et al. pointed out another problem that deeper CNNs face—*performance degradation*. It all started with a simple observation—the accuracy of CNNs does not linearly increase with the addition of new layers. A degradation problem appears as the networks' depth increases. Accuracy starts saturating and even degrading. Even the training loss starts decreasing when negligently stacking too many layers, proving that the problem is not caused by overfitting. For instance, the authors compared the accuracy of an 18-layer-deep CNN with a 34-layer one, showing that the latter performs worse than the shallower version during and after training. In their paper, He et al. proposed a solution to build very deep and performant networks.

With *model averaging* (applying ResNet models of various depths) and *prediction averaging* (over multiple crops of each input image), the ResNet authors reached a historically low 3.6% top-5 error rate for the ILSVRC challenge. This was the first time an algorithm beat humans on that dataset. Human performance had been measured by the challenge organizers, with the best human candidate reaching a 5.1% error rate (refer to *ImageNet Large-Scale Visual Recognition Challenge*, Springer, 2015). Achieving super-human performance on such a task was a huge milestone for deep learning. We should, however, keep in mind that, while algorithms can expertly solve a specific task, they still do not have the human ability to extend that knowledge to others, or to grasp the context of the data they are to deal with.

Architecture

Like Inception, ResNet has known several iterative improvements to its architecture, for instance, with the addition of bottleneck convolutions or the use of smaller kernels. Like VGG, ResNet also has several pseudo-standardized versions characterized by their depth: ResNet-18, ResNet-50, ResNet-101, ResNet-152, and others. Indeed, the winning ResNet network for ILSVRC 2015 vertically stacked 152 trainable layers (with a total of 60 million parameters), which was an impressive feat at that time:

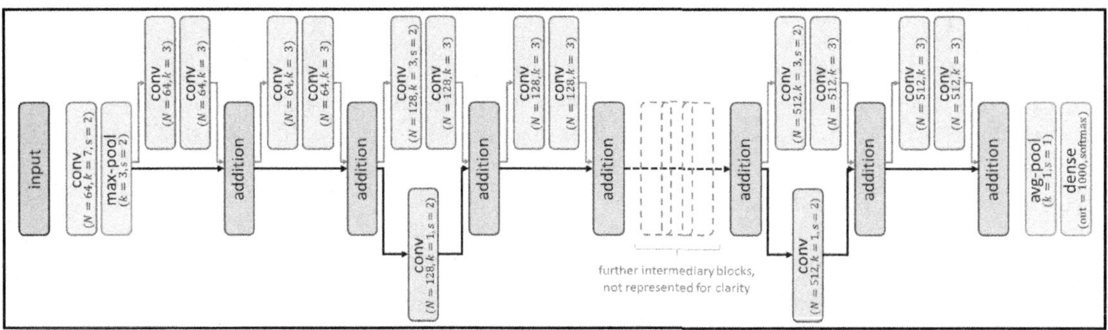

Figure 4.5: Exemplary ResNet architecture

In the preceding diagram, all the convolutional and max-pooling layers have `SAME` for padding, and for stride $s = 1$ if unspecified. Batch normalization is applied after each 3×3 convolution (on the residual path, in gray), and 1×1 convolutions (on the mapping path in black) have no activation function (identity).

As we can see in *Figure 4.5*, the ResNet architecture is slimmer than the Inception architecture, though it is similarly composed of layer blocks with parallel operations. Unlike Inception, where each parallel layer non-linearly processes the input information, ResNet blocks are composed of one non-linear path, and one identity path. The former (represented by the thinner gray arrows in *Figure 4.5*) applies a couple of convolutions with batch normalization and *ReLU* activation to the input feature maps. The latter (represented by the thicker black arrows) simply forward the features without applying any transformation.

The last statement is not always true. As shown in *Figure 4.5*, 1×1 convolutions are applied in order to adapt the depth of the features, when the depth is increased in parallel by the non-linear branches. On those occasions, to avoid a large increase in the number of parameters, the spatial dimensionality is also reduced on both sides using a stride of $s = 2$.

As in inception modules, the feature maps from each branch (that is, the transformed features and the original ones) are merged together before being passed to the next block. Unlike inception modules, however, this merging is not performed through depth concatenation, but through element-wise addition (a simple operation that does not require any additional parameters). We will cover, in the following section, the benefits of these residual blocks.

Note that, in most implementations, the last 3×3 convolution of each residual block is not followed directly by *ReLU* activation. Instead, the non-linear function is applied after merging with the identity branch is done.

Finally, the features from the last block are average-pooled and densely converted into predictions, as in GoogLeNet.

Contributions – forwarding the information more deeply

Residual blocks have been a significant contribution to machine learning and computer vision. In the following section, we will cover the reasons for this.

Estimating a residual function instead of a mapping

As the ResNet authors pointed out, the degradation phenomenon would not happen if layers could easily learn **identity mapping** (that is, if a set of layers could learn weights so that their series of operations finally return the same tensors as the input layers).

Indeed, the authors argue that, when adding some layers on top of a CNN, we should at least obtain the same training/validation errors if these additional layers were able to converge to the identity function. They would learn to at least pass the result of the original network without degrading it. Since that is not the case—as we can often observe a degradation—it means that identity mapping is not easy to learn for CNN layers.

This led to the idea of introducing residual blocks, with two paths:

- One path further processes the data with some additional convolutional layers
- One path performs the identity mapping (that is, forwarding the data with no changes)

We may intuitively grasp how this can solve the degradation problem. When adding a residual block on top of a CNN, its original performance can at least be preserved by setting the weights of the processing branch to zero, leaving only the predefined identity mapping. The processing path will only be considered if it benefits loss minimization.

The data forwarding path is usually called **skip** or **shortcut**. The processing one is commonly called **residual path**, since the output of its operations is then added to the original input, with the magnitude of the processed tensor being much smaller than the input one when the identity mapping is close to optimal (hence, the term *residual*). Overall, this residual path only introduces small changes to the input data, making it possible to forward patterns to deeper layers.

In their paper, He et al. demonstrate that their architecture not only tackles the degradation problem, but their ResNet models achieve better accuracy than traditional ones for the same number of layers.

Going ultra-deep

It is also worth noting that residual blocks do not contain more parameters than traditional ones, as the skip and addition operations do not require any. They can, therefore, be efficiently used as building blocks for *ultra-deep* networks.

Besides the 152-layer network applied to the ImageNet challenge, the authors illustrated their contributions by training an impressive 1,202-layer one. They reported no difficulty training such a massive CNN (although its validation accuracy was slightly lower than for the 152-layer network, allegedly because of overfitting).

More recent works have been exploring the use of residual computations to build deeper and more efficient networks, such as **Highway** networks (with a trainable switch value to decide which path should be used for each residual block) or **DenseNet** models (adding further skip connections between blocks).

Implementations in TensorFlow and Keras

As with previous architectures, we already have the tools needed to reimplement ResNet ourselves, while also having direct access to preimplemented/pretrained versions.

Residual blocks with the Keras Functional API

As practice, let's implement a basic residual block ourselves. As shown in *Figure 4.5*, the residual path consists of two convolutional layers, each one followed by batch normalization. The *ReLU* activation function is applied directly after the first convolution. For the second, the function is only applied after merging with the other path. Using the Keras Functional API, the residual path can thus be implemented in a matter of five or six lines, as demonstrated in the following code.

The shortcut path is even simpler. It contains either no layer at all, or a single 1×1 convolution to reshape the input tensor when the residual path is altering its dimensions (for instance, when a larger stride is used).

Finally, the results of the two paths are added together, and the *ReLU* function is applied to the sum. All in all, a basic residual block can be implemented as follows:

```
from tf.keras.layers import Activation, Conv2D, BatchNormalization, add

def residual_block_basic(x, filters, kernel_size=3, strides=1):
    # Residual Path:
    conv_1 = Conv2D(filters=filters, kernel_size=kernel_size,
                    padding='same', strides=strides)(x)
    bn_1 = BatchNormalization(axis=-1)(conv_1)
    act_1 = Activation('relu')(bn_1)
    conv_2 = Conv2D(filters=filters, kernel_size=kernel_size,
                    padding='same', strides=strides)(act_1)
    residual = BatchNormalization(axis=-1)(conv_2)
    # Shortcut Path:
    shortcut = x if strides == 1 else Conv2D(
        filters, kernel_size=1, padding='valid', strides=strides)(x)
    # Merge and return :
    return Activation('relu')(add([shortcut, residual]))
```

A more elegant function is presented in one of the Jupyter notebooks. This notebook also contains a complete implementation of the ResNet architecture and a brief demonstration of a classification problem.

The TensorFlow model and TensorFlow Hub

Like the Inception networks, ResNet ones have their own official implementation provided in the `tensorflow/models` Git repository, as well as their own pretrained TensorFlow Hub modules.

We invite you to check out the official `tensorflow/models` implementation, as it offers several types of residual blocks from more recent research efforts.

The Keras model

Finally, Keras once again provides its own ResNet implementations—for instance, `tf.keras.applications.ResNet50()` (refer to the documentation at `https://keras.io/applications/#resnet50`)—with the option to load parameters pretrained on ImageNet. These methods have the same signature as previously covered Keras applications.

The complete code for the usage of this Keras application is also provided in the Git repository.

The list of CNN architectures presented in this chapter does not pretend to be exhaustive. It has been curated to cover solutions both instrumental to the computer vision domain and of pedagogical value.

As research in visual recognition keeps moving forward at a fast pace, more advanced architectures are being proposed, building upon previous solutions (as Highway and DenseNet methods do for ResNet, for instance), merging them (as with the Inception-ResNet solution), or optimizing them for particular use cases (such as the lighter MobileNet, which was made to run on smartphones). It is, therefore, always a good idea to check what the state of the art has to offer (for example, on official repositories or research journals) before trying to reinvent the wheel.

Leveraging transfer learning

This idea of reusing knowledge provided by others is not only important in computer science. The development of human technology over the millennia is the result of our ability to transfer knowledge from one generation to another, and from one domain to another. Many researchers believe that applying this guidance to machine learning could be one of the keys to developing more proficient systems that will be able to solve new tasks without having to relearn everything from scratch.

Therefore, this section will present what **transfer learning** means for artificial neural networks, and how it can be applied to our models.

Overview

We will first introduce what transfer learning is and how it is performed in deep learning, depending on the use cases.

Definition

In the first part of this chapter, we presented several well-known CNNs, developed for the ImageNet classification challenge. We mentioned that these models are commonly repurposed for a broader range of applications. In the following pages, we will finally elaborate on the reasons behind this reconditioning and how it is performed.

Human inspiration

Like many developments in machine learning, transfer learning is inspired by our own human way of tackling complex tasks and gathering knowledge.

As mentioned in the introduction of this section, the first inspiration is our ability as a species to transfer knowledge from one individual to another. Experts can efficiently transfer the precious knowledge they have gathered over the years to a large number of students through oral or written teaching. By harnessing the knowledge that has been accumulated and distilled generation after generation, human civilizations have been able to continuously refine and extend their technical abilities. Phenomena that took millennia for our ancestors to understand— such as human biology, the solar system, and more—became common knowledge.

Furthermore, as individuals, we also have the ability to transfer some expertise from one task to another. For example, people mastering one foreign language have an easier time learning similar ones. Similarly, people who have been driving a car for some time already have knowledge of the rules of the road and some related reflexes, which are useful if they want to learn how to drive other vehicles.

These abilities to master complex tasks by building upon available knowledge, and to repurpose acquired skills to similar activities, are central to human intelligence. Researchers in machine learning dream of reproducing them.

Motivation

Unlike humans, most machine learning systems have been designed, so far, for single, specific tasks. Directly applying a trained model to a different dataset would yield poor results, especially if the data samples do not share the same semantic content (for instance, MNIST digit images versus ImageNet photographs) or the same image quality/distribution (for instance, a dataset of smartphone pictures versus a dataset of high-quality pictures). As CNNs are trained to extract and interpret specific features, their performance will be compromised if the feature distribution changes. Therefore, some transformations are necessary to apply networks to new tasks.

Solutions have been investigated for decades. In 1998, Sebastian Thrun and Lorien Pratt edited *Learning to Learn*, a book compiling the prevalent research stands on the topic. More recently, in their *Deep Learning* book (`http://www.deeplearningbook.org/contents/representation.html` on page 534, MIT Press), Ian Goodfellow, Yoshua Bengio, and Aaron Courville defined transfer learning as follows:

> *[...] the situation where what has been learned in one setting (for example, distribution p_1) is exploited to improve generalization in another setting (say, distribution p_2).*

It makes sense for researchers to suppose that, for example, some of the features a CNN is extracting to classify hand-written digits could be partially reused for the classification of hand-written texts. Similarly, a network that learned to detect human faces could be partially repurposed for the evaluation of facial expressions. Indeed, even though the inputs (full images for face detection versus cropped ones for the new task) and outputs (detection results versus classification values) are different, some of the network's layers are already trained to extract facial features, which is useful for both tasks.

In machine learning, a **task** is defined by the inputs provided (for example, pictures from smartphones) and the expected outputs (for example, prediction results for a specific set of classes). For instance, classification and detection on ImageNet are two different tasks with the same input images but different outputs.

In some cases, algorithms can target similar tasks (for example, pedestrian detection) but have access to different sets of data (for example, CCTV images from different locations, or from cameras of different quality). These methods are thus trained on different **domains** (that is, data distributions).

It is the goal of transfer learning to apply the knowledge either from one task to another or from one domain to another. The latter type of transfer learning is called **domain adaptation** and will be more specifically covered in `Chapter 7`, *Training on Complex and Scarce Datasets*.

Transfer learning is especially interesting when not enough data is available to properly learn the new task (that is, there are not enough image samples to estimate the distribution). Indeed, deep learning methods are data hungry; they require large datasets for their training. Such datasets—especially labeled ones for supervised learning—are often tedious, if not impossible, to gather. For example, experts building recognition systems to automate industries cannot go to every plant to take hundreds of pictures of every new manufactured product and its components. They often have to deal with much smaller datasets, which are not large enough for the CNNs to satisfactorily converge. Such limitations explain the efforts to reuse knowledge acquired on well-documented visual tasks for those other cases.

With their millions of annotated images from a large number of categories, ImageNet—and, more recently, COCO—are particularly rich datasets. It is assumed that CNNs trained on those have acquired quite an expertise in visual recognition, hence the availability in Keras and TensorFlow Hub of standard models (Inception, ResNet-50, and others) already trained on these datasets. People looking for models to transfer knowledge from commonly use these.

Transferring CNN knowledge

So, how can you transfer some knowledge from one model to another? Artificial neural networks have one advantage over human brains that facilitates this operation: they can be easily stored and duplicated. The expertise of a CNN is nothing but the values taken by its parameters after training—values that can easily be restored and transferred to similar networks.

Transfer learning for CNNs mostly consists of reusing the complete or partial architecture and weights of a performant network trained on a rich dataset to instantiate a new model for a different task. From this conditioned instantiation, the new model can then be *fine-tuned*; that is, it can be further trained on the available data for the new task/domain.

As we highlighted in the previous chapters, the first layers of a network tend to extract low-level features (such as lines, edges, or color gradients), whereas final convolutional layers react to more complex notions (such as specific shapes and patterns). For classification tasks, the final pooling and/or fully connected layers then process these high-level feature maps (often called **bottleneck features**) to make their class predictions.

This typical setup and related observations led to various transfer learning strategies. Pretrained CNNs, with their final prediction layers removed, started being used as efficient *feature extractors*. When the new task is similar enough to the ones these extractors were trained for, they can directly be used to output pertinent features (the *image feature vector* models on TensorFlow Hub are available for that exact purpose). These features can then be processed by one or two new dense layers, which are trained to output the task-related predictions. To preserve the quality of the extracted features, the layers of the feature extractors are often *frozen* during this training phase; that is, their parameters are not updated during the gradient descent. In other cases, when the tasks/domains are less similar, some of the last layers of the feature extractors—or all of them—are *fine-tuned*; that is, trained along with the new prediction layers on the task data. These different strategies are further explained in the next paragraphs.

Use cases

In practice, which pretrained model should we reuse? Which layers should be frozen or fine-tuned? The answers to these questions depend on the similarity between the target task and the tasks that models have already been trained on, as well as the abundance of training samples for the new application.

Similar tasks with limited training data

Transfer learning is especially useful when you want to solve a particular task and do not have enough training samples to properly train a performant model, but do have access to a larger and similar training dataset.

The model can be pretrained on this larger dataset until convergence (or, if available and pertinent, we can fetch an available pretrained model). Then, its final layers should be removed (when the target task is different, that is, its output differs from the pretraining task) and replaced with layers adapted to the target task. For example, imagine that we want to train a model to distinguish between pictures of bees and pictures of wasps. ImageNet contains images for these two classes, which could be used as a training dataset, but their number is not high enough for an efficient CNN to learn without overfitting. However, we could first train this network on the full ImageNet dataset to classify from the 1,000 categories to develop broader expertise. After this pretraining, its final dense layers can be removed and replaced by layers configured to output predictions for our two target classes.

As we mentioned earlier, the new model can finally be prepared for its task by freezing the pretrained layers and by training only the dense ones on top. Indeed, since the target training dataset is too small, the model would end up overfitting if we do not freeze its feature extractor component. By fixing these parameters, we make sure that the network keeps the expressiveness it developed on the richer dataset.

Similar tasks with abundant training data

The bigger the training dataset available for the target task, the smaller the chances of the network overfitting if we completely retrain it. Therefore, in such cases, people commonly unfreeze the latest layers of the feature extractor. In other words, the bigger the target dataset is, the more layers there are that can be safely fine-tuned. This allows the network to extract features that are more relevant to the new task, and thus to better learn how to perform it.

The model has already been through a first training phase on a similar dataset and is probably close to convergence already. Therefore, it is common practice to use a smaller learning rate for the fine-tuning phase.

Dissimilar tasks with abundant training data

If we have access to a rich enough training set for our application, does it even make sense to use a pretrained model? This question is legitimate if the similarity between the original and target tasks is too low. Pretraining a model, or even downloading pretrained weights, can be costly. However, researchers demonstrated through various experiments that, in most cases, it is better to initialize a network with pretrained weights (even from a dissimilar use case) than with random ones.

Transfer learning makes sense when the tasks or their domains share at least some basic similarities. For instance, images and audio files can both be stored as two-dimensional tensors, and CNNs (such as ResNet ones) are commonly applied to both. However, the models are relying on completely different features for visual and audio recognition. It would typically not benefit a model for visual recognition to receive the weights from a network trained for an audio-related task.

Dissimilar tasks with limited training data

Finally, what if the target task is so specific that training samples are barely available and using pretrained weights does not make much sense? First, it would be necessary to reconsider applying or repurposing a deep model. Training such a model on a small dataset would lead to overfitting, and a deep pretrained extractor would return features that are too irrelevant for the specific task. However, we can still benefit from transfer learning if we keep in mind that the first layers of CNNs react to low-level features. Instead of only removing the final prediction layers of a pretrained model, we can also remove some of the last convolutional blocks, which are too task-specific. A shallow classifier can then be added on top of the remaining layers, and the new model can finally be fine-tuned.

Transfer learning with TensorFlow and Keras

To conclude this chapter, we will briefly cover how transfer learning can be performed with TensorFlow and Keras. We invite our readers to go through the related Jupyter notebook in parallel, to have transfer learning illustrated on classification tasks.

Model surgery

Indirectly, we have already presented how standard pretrained models provided through TensorFlow Hub and Keras applications can be fetched and easily transformed into feature extractors for new tasks. However, it is also common to reuse non-standard networks; for example, more specific state-of-the-art CNNs provided by experts, or custom models already trained for some previous tasks. We will demonstrate how any models can be edited for transfer learning.

Removing layers

The first task is to remove the final layers of the pretrained model to transform it into a feature extractor. As usual, Keras makes this operation quite easy. For `Sequential` models, the list of layers is accessible through the `model.layers` attribute. This structure has a `pop()` method, which removes the last layer of the model. Therefore, if we know the number of final layers we need to remove to transform a network into a specific feature extractor (for instance, two layers for a standard ResNet model), this can be done as follows:

```
for i in range(num_layers_to_remove):
    model.layers.pop()
```

In pure TensorFlow, editing an operational graph supporting a model is neither simple nor recommended. However, we have to keep in mind that unused graph operations are not executed at runtime. So, still having the old layers present in the compiled graph will not affect the computational performance of the new model, as long as they are not called anymore. Therefore, instead of removing layers, we simply need to pinpoint the last layer/operation of the previous model we want to keep. If we somehow lost track of its corresponding Python object, but know its name (for instance, by checking the graph in Tensorboard), its representative tensor can be recovered by looping over the layers of the model and checking their names:

```
for layer in model.layers:
    if layer.name == name_of_last_layer_to_keep:
        bottleneck_feats = layer.output
        break
```

However, Keras provides additional methods to simplify this process. Knowing the name of the last layer to keep (for instance, after printing the names with `model.summary()`), a feature extractor model can be built in a couple of lines:

```
bottleneck_feats = model.get_layer(last_layer_name).output
feature_extractor = Model(inputs=model.input, outputs=bottleneck_feats)
```

Sharing its weights with the original model, this feature-extraction model is ready for use.

Grafting layers

Adding new prediction layers on top of a feature extractor is straightforward (compared with previous examples with TensorFlow Hub), as it is just a matter of adding new layers on top of the corresponding model. For example, this can be done as follows, using the Keras API:

```
dense1 = Dense(...)(feature_extractor.output) # ...
new_model = Model(model.input, dense1)
```

As we can see, through Keras, TensorFlow 2 makes it straightforward to shorten, extend, or combine models!

Selective training

Transfer learning makes the training phase a bit more complex because we should first restore the pretrained layers and define which ones should be frozen. Thankfully, several tools are available that simplify these operations.

Restoring pretrained parameters

TensorFlow has some utility functions to warm-start estimators; that is, to initialize some of their layers with pretrained weights. The following snippet tells TensorFlow to use the saved parameters of a pretrained estimator for the new one for the layers sharing the same name:

```
def model_function():
    # ... define new model, reusing pretrained one as feature extractor.

ckpt_path = '/path/to/pretrained/estimator/model.ckpt'
ws = tf.estimator.WarmStartSettings(ckpt_path)
estimator = tf.estimator.Estimator(model_fn, warm_start_from=ws)
```

The `WarmStartSettings` initializer takes an optional `vars_to_warm_start` parameter, which can also be used to provide the names of the specific variables (as a list or a regex) that you want to restore from the checkpoint files (refer to the documentation for more details at `https://www.tensorflow.org/api_docs/python/tf/estimator/WarmStartSettings`).

With Keras, we can simply restore the pretrained model before its transformation for the new task:

```
# Assuming the pretrained model was saved with `model.save()`:
model = tf.keras.models.load_model('/path/to/pretrained/model.h5')
# ... then pop/add layers to obtain the new model.
```

Although it is not exactly optimal to restore the complete model before removing some of its layers, this solution has the advantage of being concise.

Freezing layers

In TensorFlow, the most versatile method for freezing layers consists of removing their `tf.Variable` attributes from the list of variables passed to the optimizer:

```
# For instance, we want to freeze the model's layers with "conv" in their
name:
vars_to_train = model.trainable_variables
vars_to_train = [v for v in vars_to_train if "conv" in v.name]

# Applying the optimizer to the remaining model's variables:
optimizer.apply_gradients(zip(gradient, vars_to_train))
```

In Keras, layers have a `.trainable` attribute, which can simply be set to `False` in order to freeze them:

```
for layer in feature_extractor_model.layers:
    layer.trainable = False  # freezing the complete extractor
```

Again, for complete transfer learning examples, we invite you to go through the Jupyter notebooks.

Summary

Classification challenges, such as ILSVRC, are great playgrounds for researchers, leading to the development of more advanced deep learning solutions. In their own way, each of the architectures we detailed in this chapter became instrumental in computer vision and are still applied to increasingly complex applications. As we will see in the following chapters, their technical contributions inspired other methods for a wide range of visual tasks.

Moreover, not only did we learn to reuse state-of-the-art solutions, but we also discovered how algorithms themselves can benefit from the knowledge acquired from previous tasks. With transfer learning, the performance of CNNs can be greatly improved for specific applications. This is especially true for tasks such as object detection, which will be the topic of our next chapter. Annotating datasets for object detection is more tedious than for image-level recognition, so methods usually have access to smaller training datasets. It is, therefore, important to keep transfer learning in mind as a solution to obtain efficient models.

Questions

1. Which TensorFlow Hub module can be used to instantiate an inception classifier for ImageNet?
2. How can you freeze the first three residual macro-blocks of a ResNet-50 model from Keras applications?
3. When is transfer learning not recommended?

Further reading

- *Hands-On Transfer Learning with Python* (`https://www.packtpub.com/big-data-and-business-intelligence/hands-transfer-learning-python`), by Dipanjan Sarkar, Raghav Bali, and Tamoghna Ghosh: This book covers transfer learning in more detail, while applying deep learning to domains other than computer vision.

5
Object Detection Models

From self-driving cars to content moderation, detecting objects and their position in an image is a canonical task in computer vision. In this chapter, we will introduce techniques used for **object detection**. We will detail the architecture of two of the most prevalent models among the current state of the art—**You Only Look Once** (**YOLO**) and **Regions with Convolutional Neural Networks** (**R-CNN**).

The following topics will be covered in this chapter:

- The history of object detection techniques
- The main object detection approaches
- Implementing fast object detection using YOLO architecture
- Improving object detection using Faster R-CNN architecture
- Using Faster R-CNN with the TensorFlow Object Detection API

Technical requirements

The code for this chapter is available in the form of notebooks at `https://github.com/PacktPublishing/Hands-On-Computer-Vision-with-TensorFlow-2/tree/master/Chapter05`.

Introducing object detection

Object detection was briefly introduced in `Chapter 1`, *Computer Vision and Neural Networks*. In this section, we will cover its history, as well as the core technical concepts.

Background

Object detection, also called **object localization**, is the process of detecting objects and their **bounding boxes** in an image. A bounding box is the smallest rectangle of an image that fully contains an object.

A common input for an object detection algorithm is an image. A common output is a list of bounding boxes and object classes. For each bounding box, the model outputs the corresponding predicted class and its confidence.

Applications

The applications of object detection are numerous and cover many industries. For instance, object detection can be used for the following purposes:

- In self-driving cars, to locate other vehicles and pedestrians
- For content moderation, to locate forbidden objects and their respective size
- In health, to locate tumors or dangerous tissue using radiographs
- In manufacturing, for assembly robots to put together or repair products
- In the security industry, to detect threats or count people
- In wildlife conservation, to monitor an animal population

These are just a few examples—more and more applications are being discovered every day as object localization becomes more powerful.

Brief history

Historically, object detection relied on a classical computer vision technique: **image descriptors**. To detect an object, for instance, a bike, you would start with several pictures of this object. Descriptors corresponding to the bike would be extracted from the image. Those descriptors would represent specific parts of the bike. When looking for this object, the algorithm would attempt to find the descriptors again in the target images.

To locate the bike in the image, the most commonly used technique was the **floating window**. Small rectangular areas of the images are examined, one after the other. The part with the most matching descriptors would be considered to be the one containing the object. Over time, many variations were used.

This technique presented a few advantages: it was robust to rotation and color changes, it did not require a lot of training data, and it worked with most objects. However, the level of accuracy was not satisfactory.

While neural networks were already in use in the early 1990s (for detecting faces, hands, or text in images), they started outperforming the descriptor technique on the ImageNet challenge by a very large margin in the early 2010s.

Since then, performance has been improving steadily. Performance refers to how good the algorithm is at the following things:

- **Bounding box precision**: Providing the correct bounding box (not too large or too narrow)
- **Recall**: Finding all the objects (not missing any objects)
- **Class precision**: Outputting the correct class for each object (not mistaking a cat for a dog)

Performance improvement also means that the models are getting faster and faster at computing results (for a specific input image size and at a specific computing power). While early models took considerable time (more than a few seconds) to detect objects, they can now be used in real time. In the context of computer vision, real time usually means more than five detections per second.

Evaluating the performance of a model

To compare different object detection models, we need common evaluation metrics. For a given test set, we run each model and gather its predictions. We use the predictions and the ground truth to compute an evaluation metric. In this section, we will have a look at the metrics used to evaluate object detection models.

Precision and recall

While they are usually not used to evaluate object detection models, **precision** and **recall** serve as a basis to compute other metrics. A good understanding of precision and recall is, therefore, essential.

To measure precision and recall, we first need to compute the following for each image:

- **The number of true positives**: **True positives** (**TP**) determine how many predictions match with a ground truth box of the same class.
- **The number of false positives**: **False positives** (**FP**) determine how many predictions do not match with a ground truth box of the same class.
- **The number of false negatives**: **False negatives** (**FN**) determine how many ground truths do not have a matching prediction.

Then, precision and recall are defined as follows:

$$precision = \frac{TP}{TP + FP}$$
$$recall = \frac{TP}{TP + FN}$$

Notice that if the predictions exactly match all the ground truths, there will not be any false positives or false negatives. Therefore, precision and recall will be equal to 1, a perfect score. If a model too often predicts the presence of an object based on non-robust features, precision will deteriorate because there will be many false positives. On the contrary, if a model is too strict and considers an object detected only when precise conditions are met, recall will suffer because there will be many false negatives.

Precision-recall curve

Precision-recall curve is used in many machine learning problems. The general idea is to visualize the precision and the recall of the model at each **threshold of confidence**. With every bounding box, our model will output a confidence—a number between 0 and 1 characterizing how confident the model is that a prediction is correct.

Because we do not want to keep the less confident predictions, we usually remove those below a certain threshold, T. For instance, if $T = 0.4$, we will not consider any prediction with a confidence below this number.

Moving the threshold has an impact on precision and on recall:

- **If T is close to 1**: Precision will be high, but the recall will be low. As we filter out many objects, we miss a lot of them—recall shrinks. As we only keep confident predictions, we do not have many false positives—precision rises.
- **If T is close to 0**: Precision will be low, but the recall will be high. As we keep most predictions, we will not have any false negatives—recall rises. As our model is less confident in its predictions, we will have many false positives—precision shrinks.

By computing the precision and the recall at each threshold value between 0 and 1, we can obtain a precision-recall curve, as shown here:

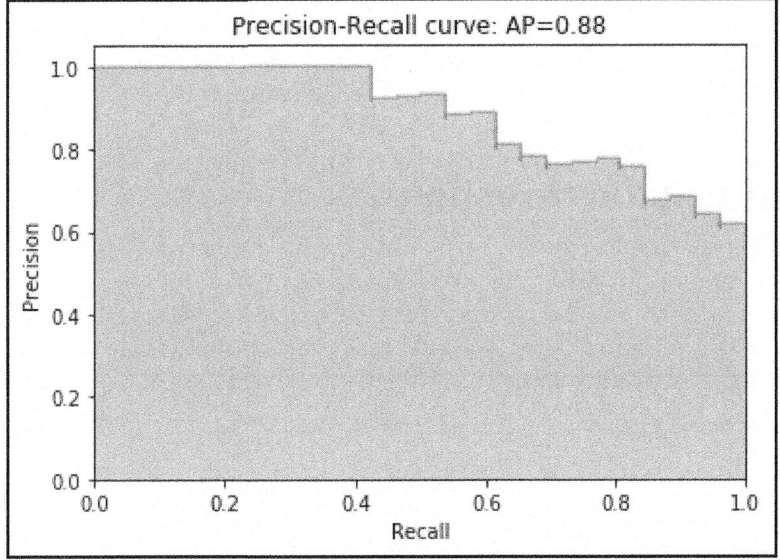

Figure 5.1: Precision-Recall curve

Choosing a threshold is a trade-off between accuracy and recall. If a model is detecting pedestrians, we will pick a high recall in order not to miss any passers-by, even if it means stopping the car for no valid reason from time to time. If a model is detecting investment opportunities, we will pick a high precision to avoid choosing the wrong opportunities, even if it means missing some.

Average precision and mean average precision

While the precision-recall curve can tell us a lot about the model, it is often more convenient to have a single number. **Average precision** (**AP**) corresponds to the area under the curve. Since it is always contained in a one-by-one rectangle, AP is always between 0 and 1.

Average precision gives information about the performance of a model for a single class. To get a global score, we use **mean Average Precision** (**mAP**). This corresponds to the mean of the average precision for each class. If the dataset has 10 classes, we will compute the average precision for each class and take the average of those numbers.

Mean average precision is used in at least two object detection challenges—**PASCAL Visual Object Classes** (usually referred to as **Pascal VOC**), and **Common Objects in Context** (usually referred to as **COCO**). The latter is larger and contains more classes; therefore, the scores obtained are usually lower than for the former.

Average precision threshold

We mentioned earlier that true and false positives were defined by the number of predictions matching or not matching the ground truth boxes. However, how do you decide when a prediction and the ground truth are matching? A common metric is the **Jaccard index**, which measures how well two sets overlap (in our case, the sets of pixels represented by the boxes). Also known as **Intersection over Union** (**IoU**), it is defined as follows:

$$\mathrm{IoU}(A, B) = \frac{|A \cap B|}{|A \cup B|} = \frac{|A \cap B|}{|A| + |B| - |A \cap B|}$$

$|A|$ and $|B|$ are the **cardinality** of each set; that is, the number of elements they each contain. $A \cap B$ is the intersection of the two sets, and therefore the numerator $|A \cap B|$ represents the number of elements they have in common. Similarly, $A \cup B$ is the union of the sets (as seen in the following diagram), and therefore the denominator $|A \cup B|$ represents the total number of elements the two sets cover together:

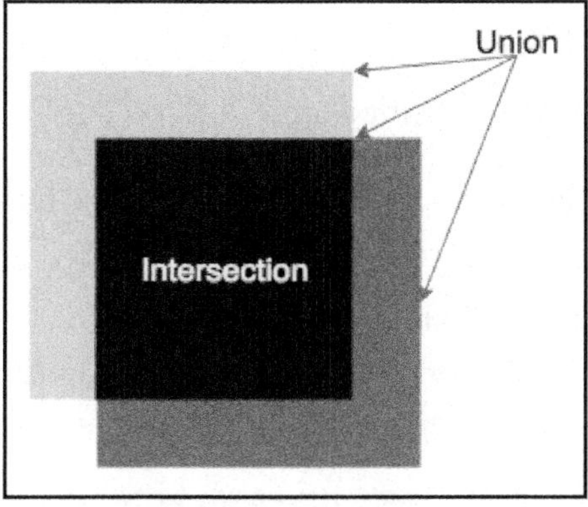

Figure 5.2: Intersection and union of boxes illustrated

Why compute such a fraction and not just use the intersection? While the intersection would provide a good indicator of how much two sets/boxes overlap, this value is absolute and not relative. Therefore, two big boxes would probably overlap by many more pixels than two small boxes. This is why this ratio is used—it will always be between 0 (if the two boxes do not overlap) and 1 (if two boxes overlap completely).

When computing the average precision, we say that two boxes overlap if their IoU is above a certain threshold. The threshold usually chosen is *0.5*.

For the Pascal VOC challenge, 0.5 is also used—we say that we use mAP@0.5 (pronounced *mAP at 0.5*). For the COCO challenge, a slightly different metric is used—mAP@[0.5:0.95]. This means that we compute mAP@0.5, mAP@0.55, ..., *mAP*@0.95, and take the average. Averaging over IoUs rewards models with better localization.

A fast object detection algorithm – YOLO

While the acronym may make you smile, YOLO is one of the fastest object detection algorithms available. The latest version, YOLOv3, can run at more than 170 **frames per second** (**FPS**) on a modern GPU for an image size of *256* × *256*. In this section, we will introduce the theoretical concept behind its architecture.

Introducing YOLO

First released in 2015, YOLO outperformed almost all other object detection architectures, both in terms of speed and accuracy. Since then, the architecture has been improved several times. In this chapter, we will draw our knowledge from the following three papers:

- *You Only Look Once: Unified, real-time object detection (2015)*, Joseph Redmon, Santosh Divvala, Ross Girshick, and Ali Farhadi
- *YOLO9000: Better, Faster, Stronger (2016)*, Joseph Redmon and Ali Farhadi
- *YOLOv3: An Incremental Improvement (2018)*, Joseph Redmon and Ali Farhadi

For the sake of clarity and simplicity, we will not describe all the small details that allow YOLO to reach its maximum performance. Instead, we will focus on the general architecture of the network. We'll provide an implementation of YOLO so that you can compare our architecture with code. It is available in the chapter's repository.

This implementation has been designed to be easy to read and understand. We invite those readers who wish to acquire a deep understanding of the architecture to first read this chapter and then refer to the original papers and the implementation.

The main author of the YOLO paper maintains a deep learning framework called **Darknet** (`https://github.com/pjreddie/darknet`). This hosts the official implementation of YOLO and can be used to reproduce the paper's results. It is coded in C++ and is not based on TensorFlow.

Strengths and limitations of YOLO

YOLO is known for its speed. However, it has been recently outperformed in terms of accuracy by **Faster R-CNN** (covered later in this chapter). Moreover, due to the way it detects objects, YOLO struggles with smaller objects. For instance, it would have trouble detecting single birds from a flock. As with most deep learning models, it also struggles to properly detect objects that deviate too much from the training set (unusual aspect ratios or appearance). Nevertheless, the architecture is constantly evolving, and those issues are being worked on.

YOLO's main concepts

The core idea of YOLO is this: **reframing object detection as a single regression problem**. What does this mean? Instead of using a sliding window or another complex technique, we will divide the input into a $w \times h$ grid, as represented in this diagram:

Figure 5.3: An example involving a plane taking off. Here, w = 5, h = 5, and B = 2, meaning, in total, 5 × 5 × 2 = 50 potential boxes, but only 2 are shown in the image

For each part of the grid, we will define *B* bounding boxes. Then, our only task will be to predict the following for each bounding box:

- The center of the box
- The width and height of the box
- The probability that this box contains an object
- The class of said object

Since all those predictions are numbers, we have therefore transformed the object detection problem into a regression problem.

It is important to make a distinction between the grid cells that divide the pictures into equal parts ($w \times h$ parts to be precise) and the bounding boxes that will locate the objects. Each grid cell contains *B* bounding boxes. Therefore, there will be $w \times h \times B$ possible bounding boxes in the end.

In practice, the concepts used by YOLO are a bit more complex than this. What if there are several objects in one part of the grid? What if an object overlaps several parts of the grid? More importantly, how do we choose a loss to train our model? We will now have a deeper look at YOLO architecture.

Inferring with YOLO

Because the architecture of the model can be quite hard to understand in one go, we will split the model into two parts—inference and training. **Inference** is the process of taking an image input and computing results. **Training** is the process of learning the weights of the model. When implementing a model from scratch, inference cannot be used before the model is trained. But, for the sake of simplicity, we are going to start with inference.

The YOLO backbone

Like most image detection models, YOLO is based on a **backbone model**. The role of this model is to extract meaningful features from the image that will be used by the final layers. This is why the backbone is also called the **feature extractor**, a concept introduced in `Chapter 4`, *Influential Classification Tools*. The general YOLO architecture is depicted here:

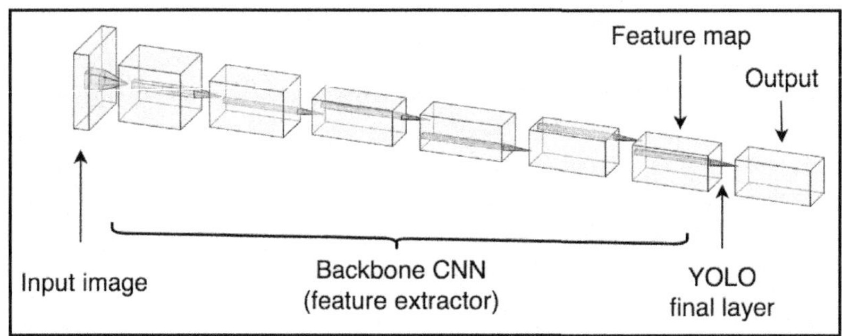

Figure 5.4: YOLO architecture summarized. Note that the backbone is exchangeable and that its architecture may vary

While any architecture can be chosen as a feature extractor, the YOLO paper employs a custom architecture. The performance of the final model depends heavily on the choice of the feature extractor's architecture.

The final layer of the backbone outputs a feature volume of size $w \times h \times D$, where $w \times h$ is the size of the grid and D is the depth of the feature volume. For instance, for VGG-16, $D = 512$.

The size of the grid, $w \times h$, depends on two factors:

- **The stride of the complete feature extractor**: For VGG-16, the stride is 16, meaning that the feature volume output will be 16 times smaller than the input image.
- **The size of the input image:** Since the feature volume's size is proportional to the size of the image, the smaller the input, the smaller the grid.

YOLO's final layer accepts the feature volume as an input. It is composed of convolutional filters of size 1×1. As seen in `Chapter 4`, *Influential Classification Tools*, a convolutional layer of size 1×1 can be used to change the depth of the feature volume without affecting its spatial structure.

YOLO's layers output

YOLO's final output is a $w \times h \times M$ matrix, where $w \times h$ is the size of the grid, and M corresponds to the formula $B \times (C + 5)$, where the following applies:

- B is the number of bounding boxes per grid cell.
- C is the number of classes (in our example, we will use 20 classes).

Notice that we add 5 to the number of classes. This is because, for each bounding box, we need to predict $(C + 5)$ numbers:

- t_x and t_y will be used to compute the coordinates of the center of the bounding box.
- t_w and t_h will be used to compute the width and height of the bounding box.
- c is the confidence that an object is in the bounding box.
- $p1, p2, ...,$ and pC are the probability that the bounding box contains an object of class $1, 2, ..., C$ (where $C = 20$ in our example).

This diagram summarizes how the output matrix appears:

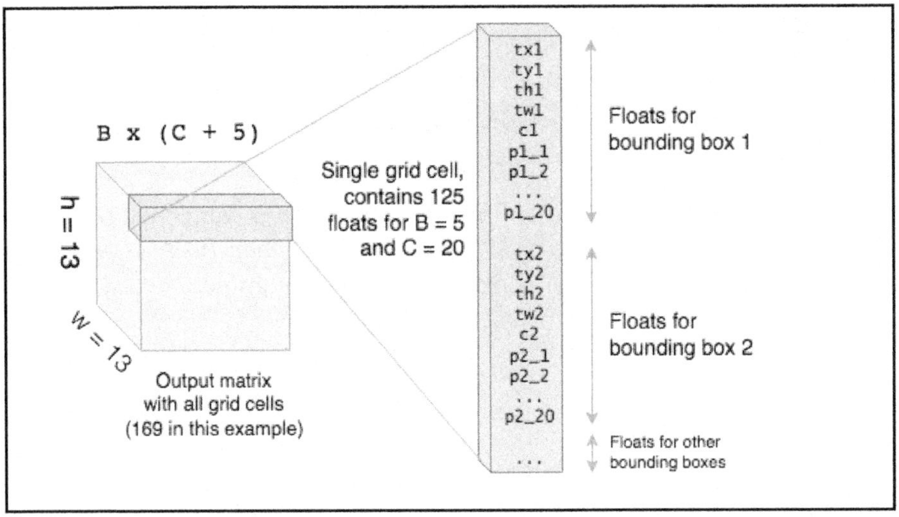

Figure 5.5: Final matrix output of YOLO. In this example, $B = 5$, $C = 20$, $w = 13$, and $h = 13$. The size is 13 × 13 × 125

Before we explain how to use this matrix to compute the final bounding boxes, we need to introduce an important concept—**anchor boxes**.

Introducing anchor boxes

We mentioned that t_x, t_y, t_w, and t_h are used to compute the bounding box coordinates. Why not ask the network to output the coordinates directly (x, y, w, and h)? In fact, that is how it was done in YOLO v1. Unfortunately, this resulted in a lot of errors because objects vary in size.

Indeed, if most of the objects in the train dataset are big, the network will tend to predict w and h as being very large. And when using the trained model on small objects, it will often fail. To fix this problem, YOLO v2 introduced **anchor boxes**.

Anchor boxes (also called **priors**) are a set of bounding box sizes that are decided upon before training the network. For instance, when training a neural network to detect pedestrians, tall and narrow anchor boxes would be picked. An example is shown here:

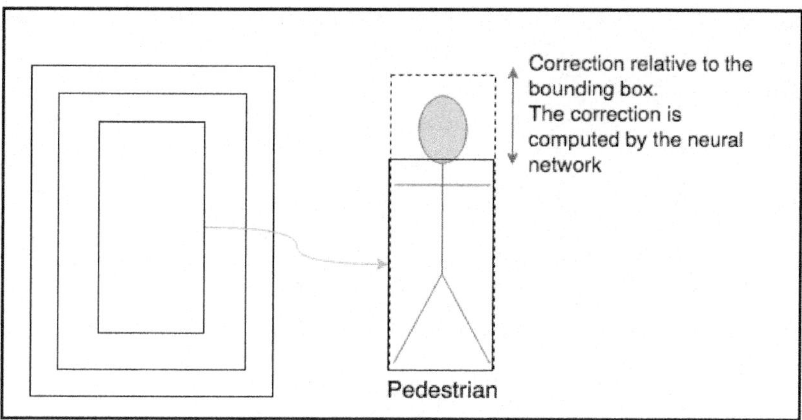

Figure 5.6: On the left are the three bounding box sizes picked to detect pedestrians. On the right is how we adapt one of the bounding boxes to match a pedestrian

A set of anchor boxes is usually small—from 3 to 25 different sizes in practice. As those boxes cannot exactly match all the objects, the network is used to refine the closest anchor box. In our example, we fit the pedestrian in the image with the closest anchor box and use the neural network to correct the height of the anchor box. This is what t_x, t_y, t_w, and t_h correspond to—**corrections to the anchor box**.

When they were first introduced in the literature, anchor boxes were picked manually. Usually, nine box sizes were used:

- Three squares (small, medium, and large)
- Three horizontal rectangles (small, medium, and large)
- Three vertical rectangles (small, medium, and large)

However, in the YOLOv2 paper, the authors recognized that the sizes of anchor boxes are different for each dataset. Therefore, before training the model, they recommend analyzing the data to pick the size of the anchor boxes. To detect pedestrians, as previously, vertical rectangles would be used. To detect apples, square anchor boxes would be used.

How YOLO refines anchor boxes

In practice, YOLOv2 computes each final bounding box's coordinates using the following formulas:

$$b_x = \text{sigmoid}(t_x) + c_x$$
$$b_y = \text{sigmoid}(t_y) + c_y$$
$$b_w = p_w \exp(t_w)$$
$$b_h = p_h \exp(t_h)$$

The terms of the preceding equation can be explained as follows:

- t_x, t_y, t_w, and t_h are the outputs from the last layer.
- b_x, b_y, b_w, and b_h are the position and size of the predicted bounding box, respectively.
- p_w and p_h represent the original size of the anchor box.
- c_x and c_y are the coordinates of the current grid cell (they will be (0,0) for the top-left box, (w - 1,0) for the top-right box, and (0, h - 1) for the bottom-left box).
- *exp* is the exponential function.
- *sigmoid* is the sigmoid function, described in `Chapter 1`, *Computer Vision and Neural Networks*.

While this formula may seem complex, this diagram may help to clarify matters:

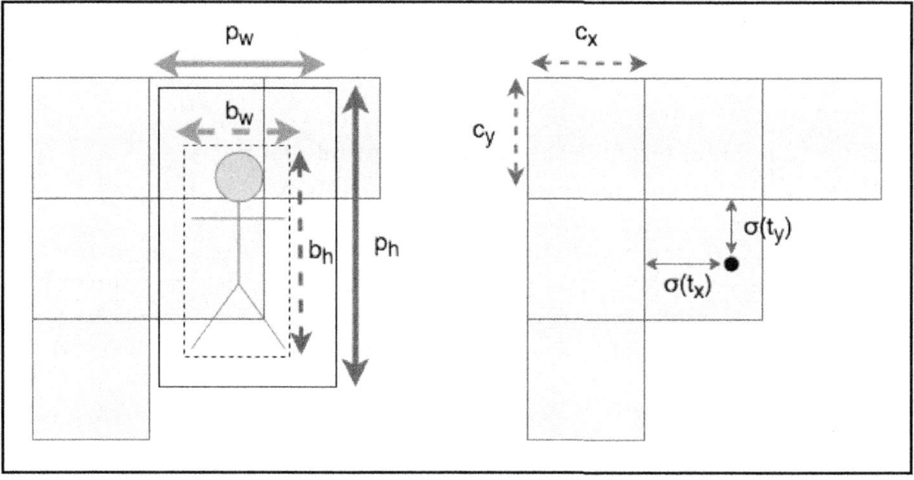

Figure 5.7: How YOLO refines and positions anchor boxes

In the preceding diagram, we see that on the left, the solid line is the anchor box, and the dotted line is the refined bounding box. On the right, the dot is the center of the bounding box.

The output of the neural network, a matrix with raw numbers, needs to be transformed into a list of bounding boxes. A simplified version of the code would look like this:

```
boxes = []
for row in range(grid_height):
    for col in range(grid_width):
        for b in range(num_box):
            tx, ty, tw, th = network_output[row, col, b, :4]
            box_confidence = network_output[row, col, b, 4]
            classes_scores = network_output[row, col, b, 5:]

            bx = sigmoid(tx) + col
            by = sigmoid(ty) + row

            # anchor_boxes is a list of dictionaries containing the size of
each anchor
            bw = anchor_boxes[b]['w'] * np.exp(tw)
            bh = anchors_boxes[b]['h'] * np.exp(th)

            boxes.append((bx, by, bw, bh, box_confidence, classes_scores))
```

This code needs to be run for every inference in order to compute bounding boxes for an image. Before we can display the boxes, we need one more post-processing operation.

Post-processing the boxes

We end up with the coordinates and the size of the predicted bounding boxes, as well as the confidence and the class probabilities. All we have to do now is to multiply the confidence by the class probabilities and threshold them in order to only keep high probabilities:

```
# Confidence is a float, classes is an array of size NUM_CLASSES
final_scores = box_confidence * classes_scores

OBJECT_THRESHOLD = 0.3
# filter will be an array of booleans, True if the number is above
threshold
filter = classes_scores >= OBJECT_THRESHOLD

filtered_scores = class_scores * filter
```

Here is an example of this operation with a simple sample, with a threshold of `0.3` and a box confidence (for this specific box) of `0.5`:

CLASS_LABELS	*dog*	*airplane*	*bird*	*elephant*
classes_scores	0.7	0.8	0.001	0.1
final_scores	0.35	0.4	0.0005	0.05
filtered_scores	0.35	0.4	0	0

Then, if `filtered_scores` contains non-null values, this means we have at least one class above the threshold. We keep the class with the highest score:

```
class_id = np.argmax(filtered_scores)
class_label = CLASS_LABELS[class_id]
```

In our example, `class_label` would be *airplane*.

Once we have applied this filtering to all of the bounding boxes in the grid, we end up with all the information we need to draw the predictions. The following photograph shows what we would obtain by doing so:

Figure 5.8: Example of the raw bounding box output being drawn over the image

Numerous bounding boxes are overlapping. As the plane is covering several grid cells, it has been detected more than once. To correct this, we need one last step in our post-processing pipeline—**non-maximum suppression** (**NMS**).

NMS

The idea of NMS is to remove boxes that overlap the box with the highest probability. We therefore remove boxes that are **non-maximum**. To do so, we sort all the boxes by probability, taking the ones with the highest probability first. Then, for each box, we compute the IoU with all the other boxes.

After computing the IoU between a box and the other boxes, we remove the ones with an IoU above a certain threshold (the threshold is usually around 0.5-0.9).

With pseudo-code, this is what NMS would look like:

```
sorted_boxes = sort_boxes_by_confidence(boxes)
ids_to_suppress = []

for maximum_box in sorted_boxes:
    for idx, box in enumerate(boxes):
        iou = compute_iou(maximum_box, box)
        if iou > iou_threshold:
            ids_to_suppress.append(idx)

processed_boxes = np.delete(boxes, ids_to_suppress)
```

In practice, TensorFlow provides its own implementation of NMS, `tf.image.non_max_suppression(boxes, ...)` (refer to the documentation at `https://www.tensorflow.org/api_docs/python/tf/image/non_max_suppression`), which we recommend using (it is well optimized and offers useful options). Also note that NMS is used in most object detection model post-processing pipelines.

After performing NMS, we obtain a much better result with a single bounding box, as illustrated in the following photograph:

Figure 5.9: Example of the bounding boxes drawn over the image after NMS

YOLO inference summarized

Putting it all together, the YOLO inference comprises several smaller steps. YOLO's architecture is illustrated in the following diagram:

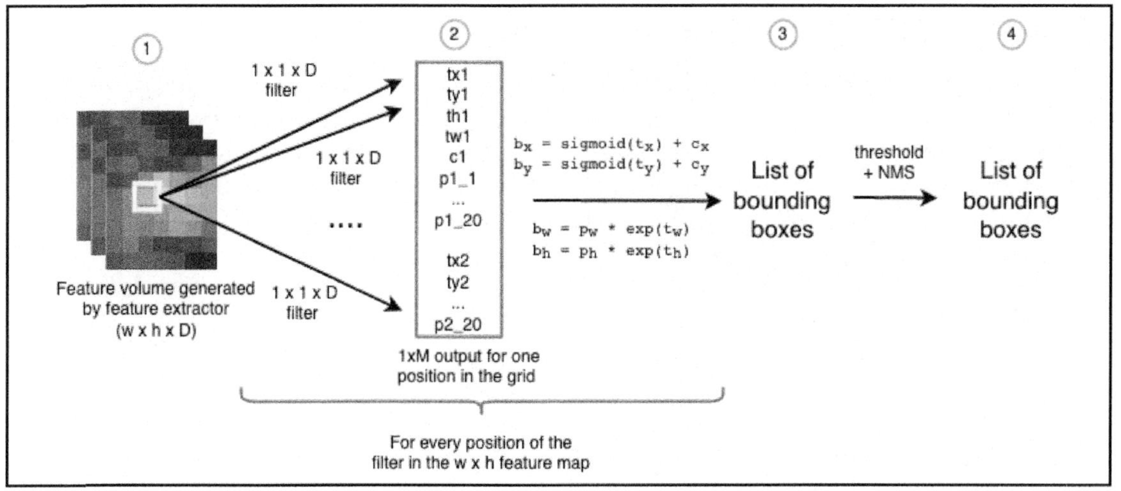

Figure 5.10: YOLO's architecture. In this example, we use two bounding boxes per grid cell

The YOLO inference process can be summarized as follows:

1. Accept an input image and compute a feature volume using a CNN backbone.
2. Use a convolutional layer to compute anchor box corrections, objectness scores, and class probabilities.
3. Using this output, compute the coordinates of the bounding boxes.
4. Filter out the boxes with a low threshold, and post-process the remaining ones using NMS.

At the conclusion of this process, we end up with the final predictions.

Since the whole process is composed of convolutions and filtering operations, the network can accept images of any size and any ratio. Hence, it is very flexible.

Training YOLO

We have outlined the process of inference for YOLO. Using pretrained weights provided online, it is possible to instantiate a model directly and generate predictions. However, you might want to train a model on a specific dataset. In this section, we will go through the training procedure of YOLO.

How the YOLO backbone is trained

As we mentioned earlier, the YOLO model is composed of two main parts—the backbone and the YOLO head. Many architectures can be used for the backbone. Before training the full model, the backbone is trained on a traditional classification task with the aid of ImageNet using the transfer learning technique detailed in `Chapter 4`, *Influential Classification Tools*. While we could train YOLO from scratch, it would take much more time to do so.

Keras makes it very easy to use a pretrained backbone for our network:

```
input_image = Input(shape=(IMAGE_H, IMAGE_W, 3))
true_boxes = Input(shape=(1, 1, 1, TRUE_BOX_BUFFER , 4))

inception = InceptionV3(input_shape=(IMAGE_H, IMAGE_W,3),
weights='imagenet', include_top=False)

features = inception(input_image)
GRID_H, GRID_W =  inception.get_output_shape_at(-1)[1:3]
# print(grid_h, grid_w)
output = Conv2D(BOX * (4 + 1 + CLASS),
                        (1, 1), strides=(1,1),
                        padding='same',
                        name='DetectionLayer',
                        kernel_initializer='lecun_normal')(features)

output = Reshape((GRID_H, GRID_W, BOX, 4 + 1 + CLASS))(output)
```

In our implementation, we will employ the architecture presented in the YOLO paper because it yields the best results. However, if you were to run your model on a mobile, you might want to use a smaller model.

YOLO loss

As the output of the last layer is quite unusual, the corresponding loss will also be. Actually, the YOLO loss is notoriously complex. To explain it, we will break the loss into several parts, each corresponding to one kind of output returned by the last layer. The network predicts multiple kinds of information:

- The bounding box coordinates and size
- The confidence that an object is in the bounding box
- The scores for the classes

The general idea of the loss is that we want it to be high when the error is high. The loss will penalize the incorrect values. However, we only want to do so when it makes sense—if a bounding box contains no objects, we do not want to penalize its coordinates as they will not be used anyway.

The implementation details of neural networks are usually not available in the source paper. Therefore, they will vary from one implementation to another. What we are outlining here is an implementation suggestion, not an absolute reference. We suggest reading the code from existing implementations to understand how the loss is calculated.

Bounding box loss

The first part of the loss helps the network learn the weights to predict the bounding box coordinates and size:

$$\lambda_{\text{coord}} \sum_{i=0}^{S^2} \sum_{j=0}^{B} 1_{ij}^{\text{obj}} \left[(x_i - \hat{x}_i)^2 + (y_i - \hat{y}_i)^2 \right] + \lambda_{\text{coord}} \sum_{i=0}^{S^2} \sum_{j=0}^{B} 1_{ij}^{\text{obj}} \left[\left(\sqrt{w_i} - \sqrt{\hat{w}_i}\right)^2 + \left(\sqrt{h_i} - \sqrt{\hat{h}_i}\right)^2 \right]$$

While this equation may seem scary at first, this part is actually relatively simple. Let's break it down:

- λ (lambda) is the weighting of the loss—it reflects how much importance we want to give to bounding box coordinates during training.
- Σ (capital sigma) means that we sum what is right after them. In this case, we sum for each part of the grid (from i = 0 to $i = S^2$) and for each box in this part of the grid (from 0 to B).
- 1^{obj} (*indicator function* for objects) is a function equal to 1 when the ith part of the grid and the jth bounding box are **responsible** for an object. We will explain what responsible means in the next paragraph.
- x_i, y_i, w_i, and h_i correspond to the bounding box size and coordinates. We take the difference between the predicted value (the output of the network) and the target value (also called the **ground truth**). Here, the predicted value has a hat (^).
- We square the difference to make sure it is positive.
- Notice that we take the square root of w_i and h_i. We do so to make sure errors for small bounding boxes are penalized more heavily than errors for big bounding boxes.

The key part of this loss is the **indicator function**. The coordinates will be correct if, and only if, the box is responsible for detecting an object. For each object in the image, the difficult part is determining which bounding box is responsible for it. For YOLOv2, the anchor box with the highest IoU with the detected object is deemed responsible. The rationale here is to make each anchor box specialize in one type of object.

Object confidence loss

The second part of the loss teaches the network to learn the weights to predict whether a bounding box contains an object:

$$\lambda_{\text{obj}} \sum_{i=0}^{S^2} \sum_{j=0}^{B} 1_{ij}^{\text{obj}} \left(C_{ij} - \hat{C}_{ij}\right)^2 + \lambda_{\text{noobj}} \sum_{i=0}^{S^2} \sum_{j=0}^{B} 1_{ij}^{\text{noobj}} \left(C_{ij} - \hat{C}_{ij}\right)^2$$

We have already covered most of the symbols in this function. The remaining ones are as follows:

- C_{ij}: The confidence that the box, *j*, in the part, *i*, of the grid contains an object (of any kind)
- $\mathbf{1^{noobj}}$ **(indicator function for no object)**: A function equal to 1 when the ith part of the grid and the jth bounding box are *not responsible* for an object

A naive approach to compute 1^{noobj} is $(1 - 1^{obj})$. However, if we do so, it can cause some problems during training. Indeed, we have many bounding boxes on our grid. When determining that one of them is responsible for a specific object, there may have been other suitable candidates for this object. We do not want to penalize the objectness score of those other good candidates that also fit the object. Therefore, 1^{noobj} is defined as follows:

$$1^{noobj} == \begin{cases} 1 & \text{(box not responsible for any object) \& (box not overlapping too much with any object bounding box)} \\ 0 & \text{otherwise} \end{cases}$$

In practice, for each bounding box at position (*i*, *j*), the IoU with regard to each of the ground truth boxes is computed. If the IoU is over a certain threshold (usually 0.6), 1^{noobj} is set to 0. The rationale behind this idea is to avoid punishing boxes that contain objects but are not responsible for said object.

Classification loss

The final part of the loss, the classification loss, ensures that the network learns to predict the proper class for each bounding box:

$$\sum_{i=0}^{S^2} 1_i^{\text{obj}} \sum_{c \in \text{classes}} (p_i(c) - \hat{p}_i(c))^2$$

This loss is very similar to the one presented in `Chapter 1`, *Computer Vision and Neural Networks*. Note that while the loss presented in the YOLO paper is the L2 loss, many implementations use cross-entropy. This part of the loss ensures that correct object classes are predicted.

Full YOLO loss

Full YOLO loss is the sum of the three losses previously detailed. By combining the three terms, the loss penalizes the error for bounding box coordinate refinement, objectness scores, and class prediction. By backpropagating the error, we are able to train the YOLO network to predict correct bounding boxes.

In the book's GitHub repository, readers will find a simplified implementation of the YOLO network. In particular, the implementation contains a heavily commented loss function.

Training techniques

Once the loss has been properly defined, YOLO can be trained using backpropagation. However, to make sure the loss does not diverge and to obtain good performance, we will detail a few training techniques:

- Augmentation (explained in `Chapter 7`, *Training on Complex and Scarce Datasets*) and dropout (explained in `Chapter 3`, *Modern Neural Networks*) are used. Without these two techniques, the network would overfit on the training data and would not be able to generalize much.
- Another technique is **multi-scale training**. Every n batches, the network's input is changed to a different size. This forces the network to learn to predict with accuracy across a variety of input dimensions.

- Like most detection networks, YOLO is pretrained on an image classification task.
- While not mentioned in the paper, the official YOLO implementation uses **burn-in**—the learning rate is reduced at the beginning of training to avoid a loss explosion.

Faster R-CNN – a powerful object detection model

The main benefit of YOLO is its speed. While it can achieve very good results, it is now outperformed by more complex networks. **Faster Region with Convolutional Neural Networks (Faster R-CNN)** is considered state of the art at the time of writing. It is also quite fast, reaching 4-5 FPS on a modern GPU. In this section, we will explore its architecture.

The Faster R-CNN architecture was engineered over several years of research. More precisely, it was built incrementally from two architectures—R-CNN and Fast R-CNN. In this section, we will focus on the latest architecture, Faster R-CNN:

- *Faster R-CNN: towards real-time object detection with region proposal networks (2015)*, Shaoqing Ren, Kaiming He, Ross Girshick, and Jian Sun

This paper draws a lot of knowledge from the two previous designs. Therefore, some of the architecture details can be found in the following papers:

- *Rich feature hierarchies for accurate object detection and semantic segmentation (2013)*, Ross Girshick, Jeff Donahue, Trevor Darrell, and Jitendra Mali
- *Fast R-CNN (2015)*, Ross Girshick

Just as with YOLO architecture, we recommend reading this chapter first and then having a look at the papers to get a deeper understanding. In this chapter, we will use the same notations as in the papers.

Faster R-CNN's general architecture

YOLO is considered a single-shot detector—as its name implies, each pixel of the image is analyzed once. This is the reason for its very high speed. To obtain more accurate results, Faster R-CNN works in two stages:

1. The first stage is to extract a **region of interest** (**RoI**, or RoIs in the plural form). An RoI is an area of the input image that may contain an object. For each image, the first step generates about 2,000 RoIs.
2. The second stage is the **classification step** (sometimes referred to as the **detection step**). We resize each of the 2,000 RoIs to a square to fit the input of a convolutional network. We then use the CNN to classify the RoI.

In R-CNN and Fast R-CNN, regions of interest are generated using a technique called **selective search**. This will not be covered here because it was removed from the Faster R-CNN paper on account of its slowness. Moreover, selective search does not involve any deep learning techniques.

As the two parts of Faster R-CNN are independent, we will cover each one separately. We will then cover the training details of the full model.

Stage 1 – Region proposals

Regions of interest are generated using the **region proposal network** (**RPN**). To generate RoIs, the RPN uses convolutional layers. Therefore, it can be implemented on the GPU and is very fast.

The RPN architecture shares quite a lot of features with YOLO's architecture:

- It also uses anchor boxes—in the Faster R-CNN paper, nine anchor sizes are used (three vertical rectangles, three horizontal rectangles, and three squares).
- It can use any backbone to generate the feature volume.
- It uses a grid, and the size of the grid depends on the size of the feature volume.
- Its last layer outputs numbers that allow the anchor box to be refined into a proper bounding box fitting the object.

However, the architecture is not completely identical to YOLO's. The RPN accepts an image as input and outputs regions of interest. Each region of interest consists of a bounding box and an objectness probability. To generate those numbers, a CNN is used to extract a feature volume. The feature volume is then used to generate the regions, coordinates, and probabilities. The RPN architecture is illustrated in the following diagram:

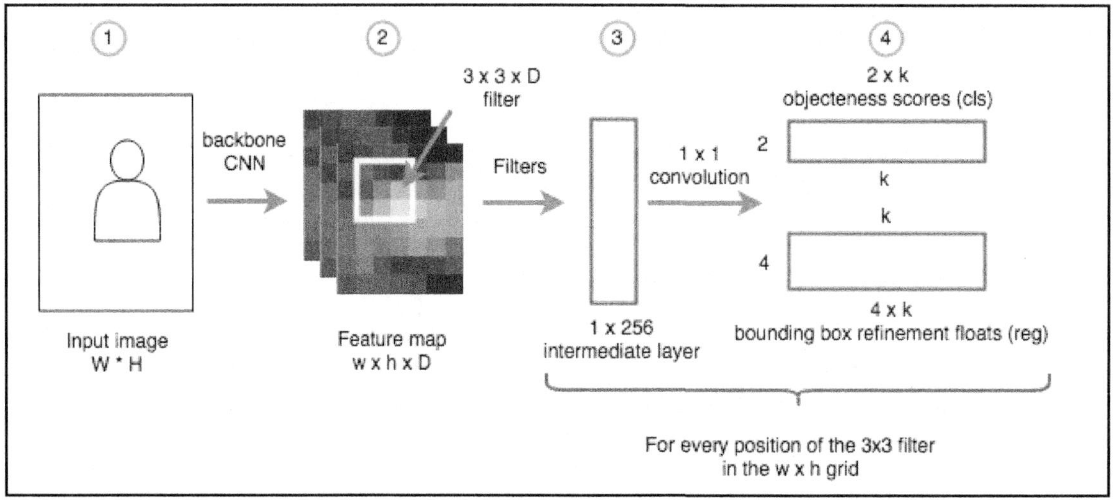

Figure 5.11: RPN architecture summary

The step-by-step process represented in *Figure 5.11* is as follows:

1. The network accepts an image as input and applies several convolutional layers.
2. It outputs a feature volume. A convolutional filter is applied over the feature volume. Its size is *3 × 3 × D*, where *D* is the depth of the feature volume (*D = 512* in our example).
3. At each position in the feature volume, the filter generates an intermediate *1 × D* vector.
4. Two sibling *1 × 1* convolutional layers compute the objectness scores and the bounding box coordinates. There are two objectness scores for each of the *k* bounding boxes. There are also four floats that will be used to refine the coordinates of the anchor boxes.

After post-processing, the final output is a list of RoIs. At this step, no information about the class of the object is generated, only about its location. During the next step, classification, we will classify the objects and refine the bounding boxes.

Stage 2 – Classification

The second part of Faster R-CNN is **classification**. It outputs the final bounding boxes and accepts two inputs—the list of RoIs from the previous step (RPN), and a feature volume computed from the input image.

Since most of the classification stage architecture comes from the previous paper, Fast R-CNN, it is sometimes referred to with the same name. Therefore, Faster R-CNN can be regarded as a combination of RPN and Fast R-CNN.

The classification part can work with any feature volume corresponding to the input image. However, as feature maps have already been computed in the previous region-proposal step, they are simply reused here. This technique has two benefits:

- **Sharing the weights**: If we were to use a different CNN, we would have to store the weights for two backbones—one for the RPN, and one for the classification.
- **Sharing the computation**: For one input image, we only compute one feature volume instead of two. As this operation is the most expensive of the whole network, not having to run it twice allows for a consequent gain in computational performance.

Faster R-CNN architecture

The second stage of Faster R-CNN accepts the feature maps from the first stage, as well as the list of RoIs. For each RoI, convolutional layers are applied to obtain class predictions and **bounding box refinement** information. The operations are represented here:

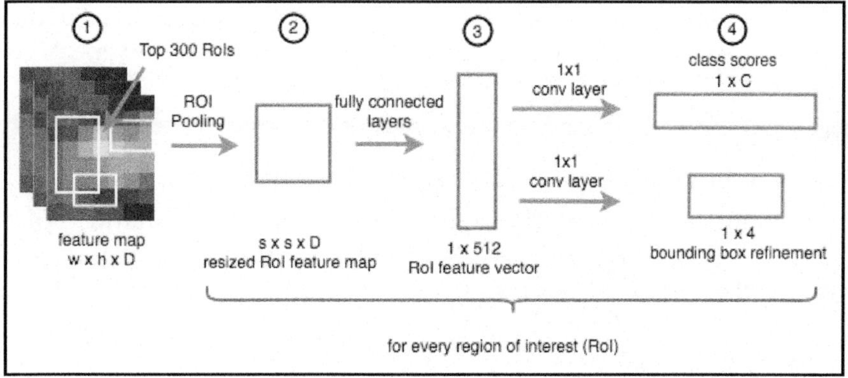

Figure 5.12: Architecture summary of Faster R-CNN

Step by step, the process is as follows:

1. Accept the feature maps and the RoIs from the RPN step. The RoIs generated in the original image coordinate system are converted into the feature map coordinate system. In our example, the stride of the CNN is 16. Therefore, their coordinates are divided by 16.
2. Resize each RoI to make it fit the input of the fully connected layers.
3. Apply the fully connected layer. It is very similar to the final layers of any convolutional network. We obtain a feature vector.
4. Apply two different convolutional layers. One handles the classification (called **cls**) and the other handles the refinement of the RoI (called **rgs**).

The final results are the class scores and bounding box refinement floats that we will be able to post-process to generate the final output of the model.

The size of the feature volume depends on the size of the input and the architecture of the CNN. For instance, for VGG-16, the size of the feature volume is $w \times h \times 512$, where $w = input\_width/16$ and $h = input\_height/16$. We say that VGG-16 has a stride of 16 because one pixel in the feature map equals 16 pixels in the input image.

While convolutional networks can accept inputs of any size (as they use a sliding window over the image), the final fully connected layer (between steps 2 and 3) accepts a feature volume of a fixed size as an input. And since region proposals are of different sizes (a vertical rectangle for a person, a square for an apple...), this makes the final layer impossible to use as is.

To circumvent that, a technique was introduced in Fast R-CNN—**region of interest pooling (RoI pooling)**. This converts a variable-size area of the feature map into a fixed-size area. The resized feature area can then be passed to the final classification layers.

RoI pooling

The goal of the RoI pooling layer is simple—to take a part of the activation map of variable size and convert it into a fixed size. The input activation map sub-window is of size $h \times w$. The target activation map is of size $H \times W$. RoI pooling works by dividing its input into a grid where each cell is of size $h/H \times w/W$.

Let's use an example. If the input is of size $h \times w = 5 \times 4$, and the target activation map is of size $H \times W = 2 \times 2$, then each cell should be of size 2.5×2. Because we can only use integers, we will make some cells of size 3×2 and others of size 2×2. Then, we will take the maximum of each cell:

	A	B	C	D	E	F	G	H	I	J	K
1	0.16	1.00	0.26	0.11	0.14	0.90	0.06	0.15			
2	0.13	0.05	0.58	0.34	0.58	0.13	0.78	0.53			
3	0.89	0.35	0.38	0.65	0.01	0.56	0.97	0.06			
4	0.47	0.97	0.78	0.99	0.82	0.90	0.32	0.89		0.97	0.99
5	0.58	0.13	0.12	0.50	0.99	0.35	0.83	0.39		0.96	0.93
6	0.21	0.59	0.96	0.93	0.08	0.55	0.13	0.89			
7	0.03	0.83	0.63	0.46	0.09	0.03	0.68	0.13			
8	0.82	0.35	0.20	0.48	0.80	0.41	0.46	0.08			

Figure 5.13: Example of RoI pooling with an RoI of size 5 × 4 (from B3 to E7) and an output of size 2 × 2 (from J4 to K5)

An RoI pooling layer is very similar to a max-pooling layer. The difference is that RoI pooling works with inputs of variable size, while max-pooling works with a fixed size only. RoI pooling is sometimes referred to as **RoI max-pooling**.

In the original R-CNN paper, RoI pooling had not yet been introduced. Therefore, each RoI was extracted from the original image, resized, and directly passed to the convolutional network. Since there were around 2,000 RoIs, it was extremely slow. The *Fast* in Fast R-CNN comes from the huge speedup introduced by the RoI pooling layer.

Training Faster R-CNN

Before we explain how to train the network, let's have a look at the full architecture of Faster R-CNN:

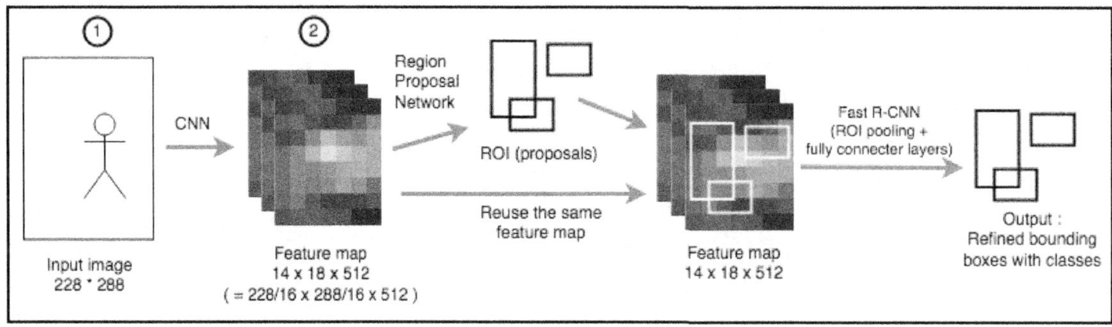

Figure 5.14: Full architecture of Faster R-CNN. Note that it can work with any input size

Because of its unique architecture, Faster R-CNN cannot be trained like a regular CNN. If each of the two parts of the network were trained separately, the feature extractors of each part would not share the same weights. In the next section, we will explain the training of each section and how to make the two sections share the convolutional weights.

Training the RPN

The input of the RPN is an image, and the output is a list of RoIs. As we saw previously, there are $H \times W \times k$ proposals for each image (where H and W represent the size of a feature map and k is the number of anchors). At this step, the class of the object is not yet considered.

It would be difficult to train all the proposals at once—since images are mostly made of background, most of the proposals would be trained to predict *background*. As a consequence, the network would learn to always predict background. Instead, a sampling technique is favored.

Mini-batches of 256 ground truth anchors are built; 128 of them are positive (they contain an object), and the other 128 are negative (they only contain background). If there are fewer than 128 positive samples in the image, all the positive samples available are used and the batch is filled with negative samples.

The RPN loss

The RPN loss is simpler than YOLO's. It is composed of two terms:

$$L(\{p_i\},\{t_i\}) = \frac{1}{N_{cls}}\sum_i L_{cls}(p_i, p_i^*) + \lambda\frac{1}{N_{reg}}\sum_i p_i^* L_{reg}(t_i, t_i^*)$$

The terms in the preceding equation can be explained as follows:

- i is the index of an anchor in a training batch.
- p_i is the probability of the anchor being an object. p_i* is the ground truth—it's 1 if the anchor is "positive"; otherwise, it's 0.
- t_i is the vector representing coordinate refinement; t_i* is the ground truth.
- N_{cls} is the number of ground truth anchors in the training mini-batch.
- N_{reg} is the number of possible anchor locations.
- L_{cls} is the log loss over two classes (object and background).
- λ is a balancing parameter to balance the two parts of the loss.

Finally, the loss is composed of $L_{reg}(t_i, t_i^*) = R(t_i - t_i^*)$, where R is the *smooth* L1 loss function, defined as follows:

$$\text{smooth}_{L_1}(x) = \begin{cases} 0.5x^2 & \text{if } |x| < 1 \\ |x| - 0.5 & \text{otherwise} \end{cases}$$

The $smooth_{L1}$ function was introduced as a replacement for the L2 loss used previously. When the error was too important, the L2 loss would become too large, causing training instability.

Just as with YOLO, the regression loss is used only for anchor boxes that contain an object thanks to the p_i* term. The two parts are divided by N_{cls} and N_{reg}. Those two values are called **normalization terms**—if we were to change the size of mini-batches, the loss would not lose its equilibrium.

Finally, lambda is a balancing parameter. In the paper configuration, N_{cls} ~= *256* and N_{reg} ~= *2,400*. The authors set λ to 10 so that the two terms have the same total weight.

In summary, similar to YOLO, the loss penalizes the following:

- The error in objectness classification with the first term
- The error in bounding box refinement with the second term

However, contrary to YOLO's loss, it does not deal with object classes bceause the RPN only predicts RoIs. Apart from the loss and the way mini-batches are constructed, the RPN is trained like any other network using backpropagation.

Fast R-CNN loss

As stated earlier, the second stage of Faster R-CNN is also referred to as Fast R-CNN. Therefore, its loss is often referenced as the Fast R-CNN loss. While the formulation of the Fast R-CNN loss is different to the RPN loss, it is very similar in essence:

$$L(p, u, t^u, v) = L_{\text{cls}}(p, u) + \lambda[u \geq 1] L_{\text{Loc}}(t^u, v)$$

The terms in the preceding equation can be explained as follows:

- $L_{cls}(p,u)$ is the log loss between the ground truth class, u, and the class probabilities, p.
- $L_{loc}(t^u, v)$ is the same loss as L_{reg} in the RPN loss.
- $\lambda[u \geq 1]$ is equal to 1 when $u \geq 1$ and 0 otherwise.

During Fast R-CNN training, we always use a background class with $id = 0$. Indeed, the RoIs may contain background regions, and it is important to classify them as such. The term $\lambda[u \geq 1]$ avoids penalizing the bounding box error for background boxes. For all the other classes, since u will be above 0, we will penalize the error.

Training regimen

As described earlier, sharing the weights between the two parts of the network allows the model to be faster (as the CNN is only applied once) and lighter. In the Faster R-CNN paper, the recommended training procedure is called **4-step alternating training**. A simplified version of this procedure goes like this:

1. Train the RPN so that it predicts acceptable RoIs.
2. Train the classification part using the output of the trained RPN. At the end of the training, the RPN and the classification part have different convolutional weights since they have been trained separately.
3. Replace the RPN's CNN with the classification's CNN so that they now share convolutional weights. Freeze the shared CNN weights. Train the RPN's last layers again.
4. Train the classification's last layer using the output of the RPN again.

At the end of this process, we obtain a trained network with the two parts sharing the convolutional weights.

TensorFlow Object Detection API

As Faster R-CNN is always improving, we do not provide a reference implementation with this book. Instead, we recommend using the TensorFlow Object Detection API. It offers an implementation of Faster R-CNN that's maintained by contributors and by the TensorFlow team. It offers pretrained models and code to train your own model.

The Object Detection API is not part of the core TensorFlow library, but is available in a separate repository, which was introduced in `Chapter 4`, *Influential Classification Tools*: `https://github.com/tensorflow/models/tree/master/research/object_detection`.

Using a pretrained model

The object detection API comes with several pretrained models trained on the COCO dataset. The models vary in architecture—while they are all based on Faster R-CNN, they use different parameters and backbones. This has an impact on inference speed and performance. A rule of thumb is that the inference time grows with the mean average precision.

Training on a custom dataset

It is also possible to train a model to detect objects that are not in the COCO dataset. To do so, a large amount of data is needed. In general, it is recommended to have at least 1,000 samples per object class. To generate a training set, training images need to be manually annotated by drawing the bounding boxes around them.

Using the Object Detection API does not involve writing Python code. Instead, the architecture is defined using configuration files. We recommend starting from an existing configuration and working from there to obtain good performance. A walk-through is available in this chapter's repository.

Summary

We covered the architecture of two object detection models. The first one, YOLO, is known for its inference speed. We went through the general architecture and how inference works, as well as the training procedure. We also detailed the loss used to train the model. The second one, Faster R-CNN, is known for its state-of-the-art performance. We analyzed the two stages of the network and how to train them. We also described how to use Faster R-CNN through the TensorFlow Object Detection API.

In the next chapter, we will extend object detection further by learning how to segment images into meaningful parts, as well as how to transform and enhance them.

Questions

1. What is the difference between a bounding box, an anchor box, and a ground truth box?
2. What is the role of the feature extractor?
3. What model should be favored, YOLO or Faster R-CNN?
4. What does the use of anchor boxes entail?

Further reading

- *Mastering OpenCV 4* (`https://www.packtpub.com/application-development/mastering-opencv-4-third-edition`), by Roy Shilkrot and David Millán Escrivá, contains practical computer vision projects, including advanced object detection techniques.

- *OpenCV 4 Computer Vision Application Programming Cookbook* (`https://www.packtpub.com/application-development/opencv-4-computer-vision-application-programming-cookbook-fourth-edition`), by David Millán Escrivá and Robert Laganiere, covers classical object descriptors as well as object detection concepts.

6
Enhancing and Segmenting Images

We have just learned how to create neural networks that output predictions that are more complex than just a single class. In this chapter, we will push this concept further and introduce **encoders-decoders**, which are models used to edit or generate full images. We will present how encoder-decoder networks can be applied to a wide range of applications, from image denoising to object and instance segmentation. This chapter comes with several concrete examples, such as the application of encoders-decoders to semantic segmentation for self-driving cars.

The following topics will be covered in this chapter:

- What encoders-decoders are, and how they are trained for pixel-level prediction
- Which novel layers they use to output high-dimensional data (unpooling, transposed, and atrous convolutions)
- How the FCN and U-Net architectures are tackling semantic segmentation
- How the models we have covered so far can be extended to deal with instance segmentation

Technical requirements

Jupyter notebooks illustrating the concepts presented in this chapter can be found in the following Git folder: `github.com/PacktPublishing/Hands-On-Computer-Vision-with-TensorFlow-2/tree/master/Chapter06`.

Later in this chapter, we introduce the `pydensecrf` library to improve segmentation results. As detailed on its GitHub page (refer to the documentation at `https://github.com/lucasb-eyer/pydensecrf#installation`), this Python module can be installed through `pip` (`pip install git+https://github.com/lucasb-eyer/pydensecrf.git`) and requires a recent version of Cython (`pip install -U cython`).

Transforming images with encoders-decoders

As presented in `Chapter 1`, *Computer Vision and Neural Networks*, multiple typical tasks in computer vision require pixel-level results. For example, semantic segmentation methods classify each pixel of an image, and smart editing tools return images with some pixels altered (for example, to remove unwanted elements). In this section, we will present encoders-decoders, and how **convolutional neural networks** (**CNNs**) following this paradigm can be applied to such applications.

Introduction to encoders-decoders

Before tackling complex applications, let's first introduce what encoders-decoders are and what purpose they fulfill.

Encoding and decoding

The encoder-decoder architecture is a very generic framework, with applications in communications, cryptography, electronics, and beyond. According to this framework, the **encoder** is a function that maps input samples into a **latent space**, that is, a hidden structured set of values defined by the encoder. The **decoder** is the complementary function that maps elements from this latent space into a predefined target domain. For example, an encoder can be built to parse media files (with their content represented as elements in its latent space), and it can be paired with a decoder defined, for instance, to output the media contents in a different file format. Well-known examples are the image and audio compression formats we commonly use nowadays. JPEG tools encode our media, compressing them into lighter binary files; they then decode them to recover the pixel values at display time.

In machine learning, encoder-decoder networks have been used for a long time now (for instance, for text translation). An encoder network would take sentences from the source language as input (for instance, French sentences) and learn to project them into a latent space where the meaning of the sentence would be encoded as a feature vector. A decoder network would be trained alongside the encoder to convert the encoded vectors into sentences in the target language (for instance, English).

Vectors from the latent space in encoder-decoder models are commonly called **codes**.

Note that a common property of encoders-decoders is for their latent space to be smaller than the input and target latent spaces, as shown in *Figure 6-1*:

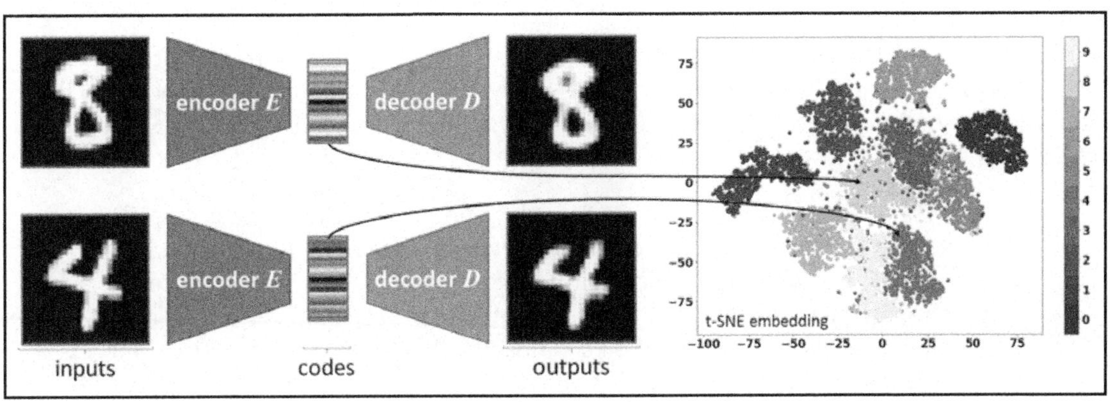

Figure 6-1: Example of an auto-encoder trained on the MNIST dataset (copyright owned by Yann LeCun and Corinna Cortes)

In *Figure 6-1*, the encoder is trained to convert the 28×28 images into vectors (codes) of *32* values here, and the decoder is trained to recover the images. These codes can be plotted with their class labels to highlight similarities/structures in the dataset (the *32*-dimensional vectors are projected on a 2D plane using **t-SNE**, a method developed by Laurens van der Maatens and Geoffrey Hinton and detailed in the notebooks).

Encoders are designed or trained to extract/compress the semantic information contained in the samples (for example, the meaning of a French sentence, without the grammatical particularities of this language). Then, decoders apply their knowledge of the target domain to decompress/complete the information accordingly (for instance, converting the encoded information into a proper English sentence).

Auto-encoding

Auto-encoders (**AEs**) are a special type of encoders-decoders. As shown in *Figure 6-1*, their input and target domains are the same, so their goal is to properly encode and then decode images without impacting their quality, despite their *bottleneck* (their latent space of lower dimensionality). The inputs are reduced to a compressed representation (as feature vectors). If an original input is requested later on, it can be reconstructed from its compressed representation by the decoder.

JPEG tools can thus be called AEs, as their goal is to encode images and then decode them back without losing too much of their quality. The distance between the input and output data is the typical loss to minimize for auto-encoding algorithms. For images, this distance can simply be computed as the cross-entropy loss, or as the L1/L2 loss (Manhattan and Euclidean distances, respectively) between the input images and resulting images (as illustrated in `Chapter 3`, *Modern Neural Networks*).

In machine learning, auto-encoding networks are really convenient to train, not only because their loss is straightforward to express, as we just described, but also because their training does not require any labels. The input images are the targets used to compute the loss.

There is a schism among machine learning experts regarding AEs. Some claim that these models are **unsupervised** since they do not require any additional labels for their training. Others affirm that, unlike purely unsupervised methods (which typically use complex loss functions to discover patterns in unlabeled datasets), AEs have clearly defined targets (that is, their input images). Therefore, it is also common for these models to be called **self-supervised** (that is, their targets can be directly derived from their inputs).

Given the smaller latent space of AEs, their encoding sub-network must learn to properly compress the data, whereas the decoder must learn a proper mapping to decompress it back.

Without the bottleneck condition, this identity mapping would be straightforward for networks with shortcut paths, such as ResNet (refer to `Chapter 4`, *Influential Classification Tools*). They could simply forward the complete input information from encoder to decoder. With a lower-dimensional latent space (bottleneck), they are forced to learn a properly compressed representation.

Purpose

Regarding the more generic encoders-decoders, their applications are numerous. They are used to convert images, to map them from one domain or modality to another. For example, such models are often applied to **depth regression**, that is, the estimation of the distance between the camera and the image content (the depth) for each pixel. This is an important operation for augmented-reality applications, for example, since it allows them to build a 3D representation of the surroundings, and thus to better interact with the environment.

Similarly, encoders-decoders are commonly used for **semantic segmentation** (refer to `Chapter 1`, *Computer Vision and Neural Networks*, for its definition). In this case, the networks are trained not to return the depth, but the estimated class for each pixel (refer to *Figure 6-2-c*). This important application will be detailed in the second part of this chapter. Finally, encoders-decoders are also famous for their more *artistic use cases*, such as transforming doodle art into pseudo-realistic images or estimating the daytime equivalent of pictures taken at night:

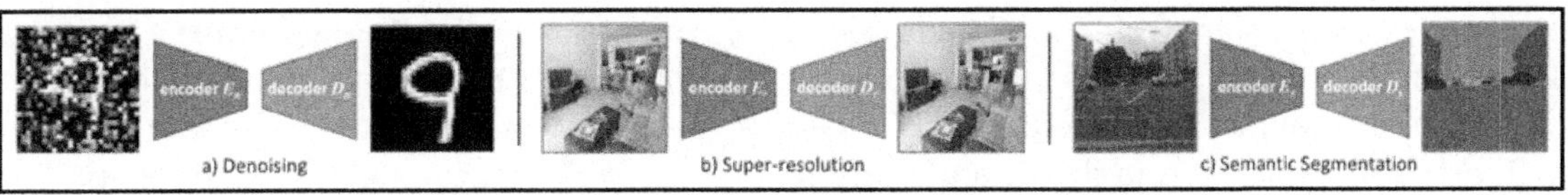

Figure 6-2: Examples of applications for encoders-decoders. These three applications are covered in the Jupyter notebooks for this chapter, with additional explanations and implementation details

The urban scene images and their labels for semantic segmentation in *Figure 6-2*, *Figure 6-10*, and *Figure 6-11* come from the *Cityscapes* dataset (`https://www.cityscapes-dataset.com`). *Cityscapes* is an awesome dataset and a benchmark for recognition algorithms applied to autonomous driving. Marius Cordts et al., the researchers behind this dataset, kindly gave us the authorization to use some of their images to illustrate this book and to demonstrate some algorithms presented later in this chapter (refer to Jupyter notebooks).

Let's now consider AEs. Why should a network be trained to return its input images? The answer lies once again in the bottleneck property of AEs. While the encoding and decoding components are trained as a whole, they are applied separately depending on the use cases.

Because of the bottleneck, the encoder has to compress the data while preserving as much information as possible. Therefore, in case the training dataset has recurring patterns, the network will try to uncover these correlations to improve the encoding. The encoder part of an AE can thus be used to obtain low-dimensional representations of images from the domain it was trained for. The low-dimensional representations they provide are often good at preserving the content similarity between images, for instance. Therefore, they are sometimes used for dataset visualization, to highlight clusters and patterns (refer to *Figure 6-1*).

AEs are not as good as algorithms, such as JPEG for generic image compression. Indeed, AEs are *data-specific*; that is, they can only efficiently compress images from the domain they know (for example, an AE trained on images of natural landscapes would work poorly on portraits since the visual features would be too different). However, unlike traditional compression methods, AEs have a better understanding of the images they were trained for, their recurring features, semantic information, and more).

In some cases, AEs are trained for their decoders, which can be used for **generative tasks**. Indeed, if the latent space has been appropriately structured during training, then any vector randomly picked from this space can be turned into a picture by the decoder! As we will briefly explain later in this chapter and in `Chapter 7`, *Training on Complex and Scarce Datasets*, training a decoder for the generation of new images is actually not that easy, and requires some careful engineering for the resulting images to be realistic (this is especially true for the training of **generative adversarial networks** (**GANs**), as explained in the next chapter).

However, **denoising AEs** are the most common AE instances found in practice. These models have the particularity that their input images undergo a lossy transformation before being passed to the networks. Since these models are still trained to return the original images (before transformation), they will learn to cancel the lossy operation and recover some of the missing information (refer to *Figure 6-2-a*). Typical models are trained to cancel white or Gaussian noise, or to recover missing content (such as occluded/removed image patches). Such AEs are also used for **smart image upscaling**, also called **image super-resolution**. Indeed, these networks can learn to partially remove the artifacts (that is, noise) caused by traditional upscaling algorithms such as bilinear interpolation (refer to *Figure 6-2-b*).

Basic example – image denoising

We will illustrate the usefulness of AEs on a simple example—the denoising of corrupted MNIST images.

Simplistic fully connected AE

To demonstrate how simple, yet efficient, these models can be, we will opt for a shallow, fully connected architecture, which we will implement with Keras:

```
inputs = Input(shape=[img_height * img_width])
# Encoding layers:
enc_1  = Dense(128, activation='relu')(inputs)
code   = Dense(64,  activation='relu')(enc_1)
# Decoding layers:
dec_1  = Dense(64,  activation='relu')(code)
preds  = Dense(128, activation='sigmoid')(dec_1)
autoencoder = Model(inputs, preds)
# Training:
autoencoder.compile(loss='binary_crossentropy')
autoencoder.fit(x_train, x_train) # x_train as inputs and targets
```

We have highlighted here the usual symmetrical architecture of encoders-decoders, with their lower-dimensional bottleneck. To train our AE, we use the images (`x_train`) both as inputs and as targets. Once trained, this simple model can be used to embed datasets, as shown in *Figure 6-1*.

We opted for *sigmoid* as the last activation function, in order to get output values between 0 and 1, like the input values.

Application to image denoising

Training our previous model for image denoising is as simple as creating a noisy copy of the training images and passing it as input to our network instead:

```
x_noisy = x_train + np.random.normal(loc=.0, scale=.5, size=x_train.shape)
autoencoder.fit(x_noisy, x_train)
```

The first two notebooks dedicated to this chapter detail the training process, providing illustrations and additional tips (for instance, to visualize the images predicted during training).

Convolutional encoders-decoders

Like other **neural network** (**NN**)-based systems, encoders-decoders benefited a lot from the introduction of convolutional and pooling layers. **Deep auto-encoders** (**DAEs**) and other architectures soon became widely used for increasingly complex tasks.

In this section, we will first introduce new layers developed for convolutional encoders-decoders. We will then present some significant architectures based on these operations.

Unpooling, transposing, and dilating

As we saw in previous chapters, such as `Chapter 3`, *Modern Neural Networks*, and `Chapter 4`, *Influential Classification Tools*, CNNs are great *feature extractors*. Their convolutional layers convert their input tensors into more and more high-level feature maps, while their pooling layers gradually down-sample the data, leading to compact and semantically rich features. Therefore, CNNs make for performant encoders.

However, how could this process be reversed to decode these low-dimensional features into full images? As we will present in the following paragraphs, the same way convolutions and pooling operations replaced dense layers for the encoding of images, reverse operations—such as **transposed convolution** (also known as **deconvolutions**), **dilated convolutions**, and **unpooling**—were developed to better decode features.

Transposed convolution (deconvolution)

Back in `Chapter 3`, *Modern Neural Networks*, we introduced convolutional layers, the operations they perform, and how their hyperparameters (kernel size k, input depth D, number of kernels N, padding p, and stride s) affect the dimensions of their output (*Figure 6-3* serves as a reminder). For an input tensor of shape (H, W, D), we presented the following equations to evaluate the output shape (H_o, W_o, N):

$$H_o = \frac{H - k + 2p}{s} + 1 \quad , \quad W_o = \frac{W - k + 2p}{s} + 1$$

Now, let's assume that we want to develop a layer to reverse the spatial transformation of convolutions. In other words, given a feature map of shape (H_o, W_o, N) and the same hyperparameters, *k*, *D*, *N*, *p*, and *s*, we would like a *convolution-like* operation to recover a tensor of shape (*H*, *W*, *D*). Isolating *H* and *W* in the previous equations, we thus want an operation upholding the following properties:

$$H = (H_o - 1)s + k - 2p \quad , \quad W = (W_o - 1)s + k - 2p$$

This is how **transposed convolutions** were defined. As we briefly mentioned in `Chapter 4`, *Influential Classification Tools*, this new type of layer was proposed by Zeiler and Fergus, the researchers behind ZFNet, the winning methods at ILSVRC 2013 (*Visualizing and understanding convolutional networks, Springer, 2014*).

With a $k \times k \times D \times N$ stack of kernels, these layers convolve an $H_o \times W_o \times N$ tensor into an $H \times W \times D$ map. To achieve this, the input tensor first undergoes **dilation**. The dilation operation, defined by a rate, *d*, consists of inserting $d - 1$ zeroed rows and columns between each couple of rows and columns (respectively) of the input tensor, as shown in *Figure 6-4*. In a transposed convolution, the dilation rate is set to *s* (the stride used for the standard convolution it is reversing). After this resampling, the tensor is then padded by $p' = k - p - 1$. Both the dilation and padding parameters are defined in this way in order to recover the original shape, (*H*, *W*, *D*). The tensor is then finally convolved with the layer's filters using a stride of $s' = 1$, finally resulting in an $H \times W \times D$ map. Normal and transposed convolutions are compared in *Figures 6-3* and *6-4*.

The following is a normal convolution:

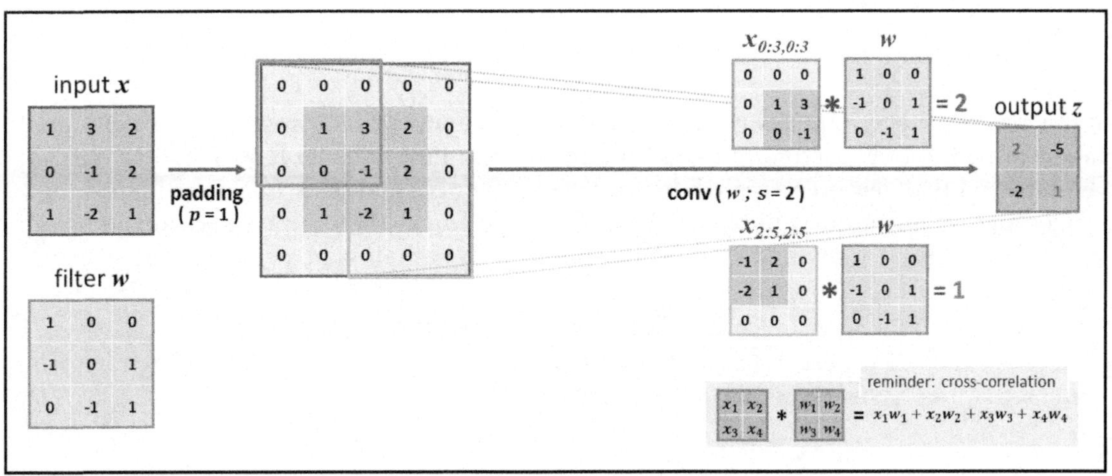

Figure 6-3: Reminder of the operations performed by a convolutional layer (defined here by a 3 x 3 kernel w, padding p = 1, and stride s = 2)

Note that in *Figure 6-3*, the mathematical operation between the patches and the kernel is actually a cross-correlation (refer to `Chapter 3`, *Modern Neural Networks*).

The following is a transposed convolution:

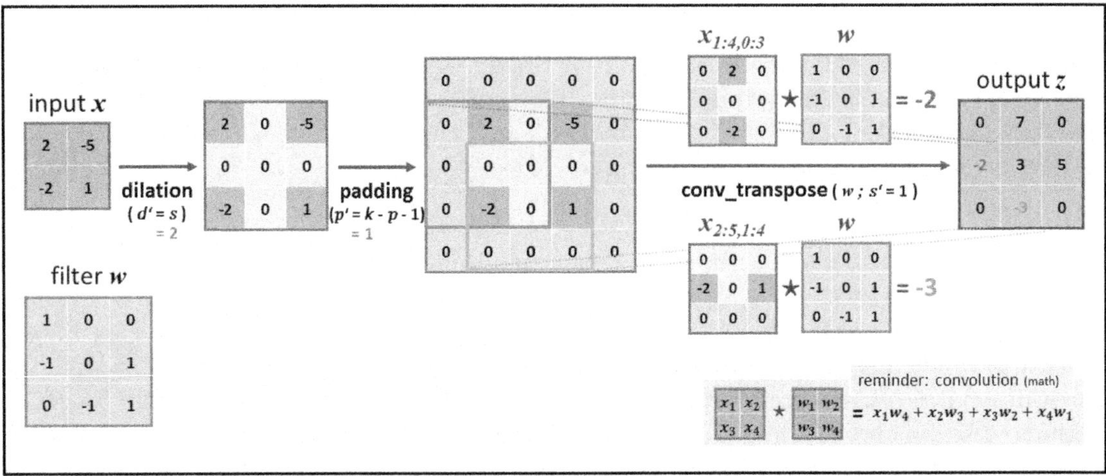

Figure 6-4: Operations performed by a transposed convolution layer to reverse the spatial transformation of a standard convolution (defined here by a 3 × 3 kernel w, padding p = 1, and dilation d = 2, as in Figure 6-3)

Note that this time, in *Figure 6-4*, the operation between the patches and the kernel is mathematical convolution.

If this process seems a bit abstract, it is enough to remember that transposed convolutional layers are commonly used to mirror standard convolutions in order to increase the spatial dimensionality of feature maps while convolving their content with trainable filters. This makes these layers quite suitable for decoder architectures. They can be instantiated using `tf.layers.conv2d_transpose()` (refer to the documentation at `https://www.tensorflow.org/api_docs/python/tf/layers/conv2d_transpose`) and `tf.keras.layers.Conv2DTranspose()` (refer to the documentation at `https://www.tensorflow.org/api_docs/python/tf/keras/layers/Conv2DTranspose`), which have the same signatures as the standard `conv2d` ones.

There is another subtle difference between standard convolutions and transposed ones, which does not have any real impact in practice, but which is still good to know. Going back to `Chapter 3`, *Modern Neural Networks*, we mentioned that convolutional layers in CNNs actually perform cross-correlation. As shown in *Figure 6-4*, transposed convolutional layers actually use mathematical convolution, flipping the indices of the kernels.

Transposed convolutions are also popularly, yet wrongly, called **deconvolutions**. While there is a mathematical operation named *deconvolution*, it performs differently than transposed convolution. Deconvolutions actually fully revert convolutions, returning the original tensors. Transposed convolutions only approximate this process and return tensors with the original shapes. As we can see in *Figures 6-3* and *6-4*, the shapes of the original and final tensors match, but not their values.

Transposed convolutions are also sometimes called **fractionally strided convolutions**. Indeed, the dilation of the input tensors can somehow be seen as the equivalent of using a *fractional* stride for the convolution.

Unpooling

Although strided convolutions are often used in CNN architectures, average-pooling and max-pooling are the most common operations when it comes to reducing the spatial dimensions of images. Therefore, Zeiler and Fergus also proposed a **max-unpooling** operation (often simply referred to as **unpooling**) to pseudo-reverse max-pooling. They used this operation within a network they called a **deconvnet**, to decode and visualize the features of their *convnet* (that is, a CNN). In the paper describing their solution after winning ILSVRC 2013 (in *Visualizing and understanding convolutional networks, Springer, 2014*), they explain that, even though max-pooling is not invertible (that is, we cannot mathematically recover all the non-maximum values the operation discards), it is possible to define an operation approximating its inversion, at least in terms of spatial sampling.

To implement this pseudo-inverse operation, they first modified each max-pooling layer so that it outputs the pooling mask along with the resulting tensor. In other words, this mask indicates the original positions of the selected maxima. The max-unpooling operation takes for inputs the pooled tensor (which may have undergone other shape-preserving operations in-between the operation) and the pooling mask. It uses the latter to scatter the input values into a tensor upscaled to its pre-pooling shape. A picture is worth a thousand words, so *Figure 6-5* may help you to understand the operation:

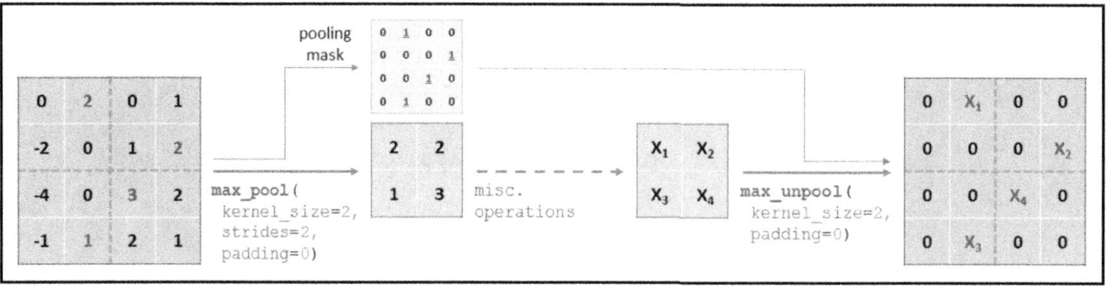

Figure 6-5: Example of a max-unpooling operation, following a max-pooling layer edited to also output its pooling mask

Note that, like pooling layers, unpooling operations are fixed/untrainable operations.

Upsampling and resizing

Similarly, an **average-unpooling** operation was developed to mirror average-pooling. The latter operation takes a pooling region of $k \times k$ elements and averages them into a single value. Therefore, an average-unpooling layer takes each value of a tensor and duplicates it into a $k \times k$ region, as illustrated in *Figure 6-6*:

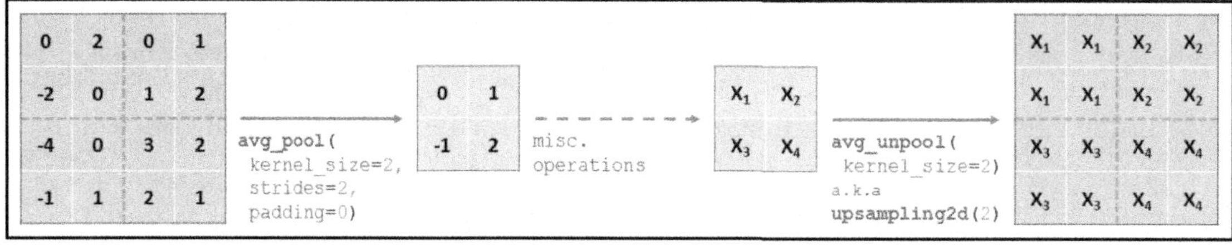

Figure 6-6: Example of an average-unpooling operation (also known as upsampling)

This operation is nowadays used more often than max-unpooling, and is more commonly known as **upsampling**. For instance, this operation can be instantiated through `tf.keras.layers.UpSampling2D()` (refer to the documentation at https://www.tensorflow.org/api_docs/python/tf/keras/layers/UpSampling2D). This method is itself nothing more than a wrapper for `tf.image.resize()` (refer to the documentation at https://www.tensorflow.org/api_docs/python/tf/image/resize) when called with the `method=tf.image.ResizeMethod.NEAREST_NEIGHBOR` argument, used to resize images using nearest-neighbor interpolation (as its name implies). Finally, note that bilinear interpolation is also sometimes used to upscale feature maps without adding any parameters to train, for example, by instantiating `tf.keras.layers.UpSampling2D()` with the `interpolation="bilinear"` argument (instead of the default `"nearest"` value), which is equivalent to calling `tf.image.resize()` with the default `method=tf.image.ResizeMethod.BILINEAR` attribute.

In decoder architecture, each nearest-neighbor or bilinear upscaling is commonly followed by a convolution with stride $s = 1$ and padding `"SAME"` (to preserve the new shape). These combinations of predefined upscaling and convolutional operations mirror the convolutional and pooling layers composing encoders, and allow the decoder to learn its own features to better recover the target signals.

Some researchers, such as Augustus Odena, favor these operations over transposed convolutions, especially for tasks such as image super-resolution. Indeed, transposed convolutions tend to cause some checkerboard artifacts (due to feature overlapping when the kernel size is not a multiple of the stride), impacting the output quality (*Deconvolution and Checkerboard artifacts, Distill, 2016*).

Dilated/atrous convolution

The last operation we will introduce in this chapter is a bit different from the previous ones, as it is not meant to upsample a feature map provided. Instead, it was proposed to artificially increase the receptive field of convolutions without further sacrificing the spatial dimensionality of the data. To achieve this, **dilation** is applied here too (refer to the *Transposed convolutions (deconvolution)* section), though quite differently.

Indeed, **dilated convolutions** are similar to standard convolutions, with an additional hyperparameter, *d*, defining the dilation applied to their kernels. *Figure 6-7* illustrates how this process does artificially increase the layer's receptive field:

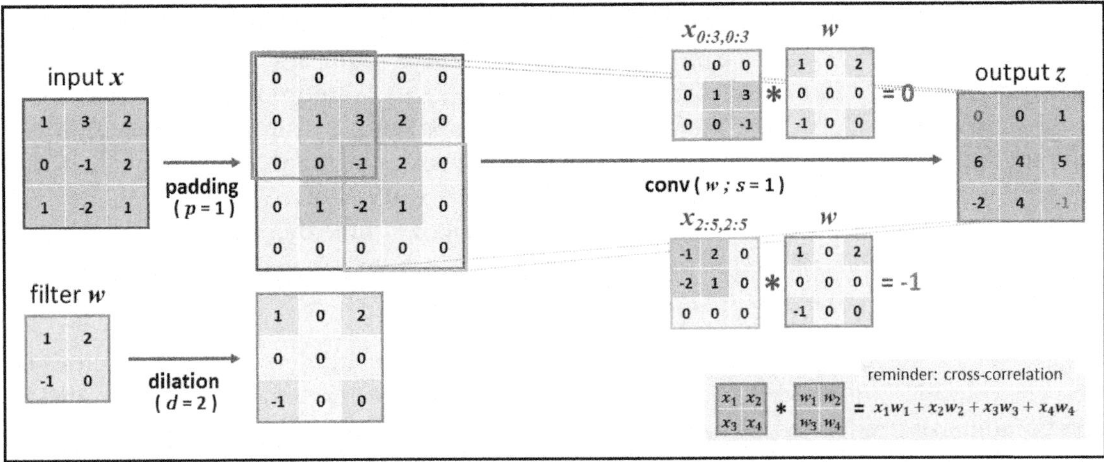

Figure 6-7: Operations performed by a dilated-convolutional layer (defined here by a 2 × 2 kernel w, padding p = 1, stride s = 1, and dilation d = 2)

These layers are also called **atrous convolutions**, from the French expression *à trous* (*with holes*). Indeed, while the kernel dilation increases the receptive field, it does so by carving holes in it.

With such properties, this operation is frequently used in modern encoders-decoders, to map images from one domain to another. In TensorFlow and Keras, instantiating dilated convolutions is just a matter of providing a value above the default 1 for the `dilation_rate` parameter of `tf.layers.conv2d()` and `tf.keras.layers.Conv2D()`.

These various operations developed to preserve or increase the spatiality of feature maps led to multiple CNN architectures for pixel-wise dense prediction and data generation.

Example architectures – FCN and U-Net

Most convolutional encoders-decoders follow the same template as their fully connected counterparts, but leverage the spatial properties of their locally connected layers for higher-quality results. A typical convolutional AE is presented in one of the Jupyter notebooks. In this subsection, we will cover two more advanced architectures derived from this basic template. Both released in 2015, the FCN and U-Net models are still popular, and are commonly used as components for more complex systems (in semantic segmentation, domain adaptation, and others).

Fully convolutional networks

As briefly presented in `Chapter 4`, *Influential Classification Tools*, **fully convolutional networks** (**FCNs**) are based on the VGG-16 architecture, with the final dense layers replaced by 1×1 convolutions. What we did not mention was that these networks are commonly extended with upsampling blocks and used as encoders-decoders. Proposed by Jonathan Long, Evan Shelhamer, and Trevor Darrell from the University of California, Berkeley, the FCN architecture perfectly illustrates the notions developed in the previous subsection:

- How CNNs for feature extraction can be used as efficient encoders
- How their feature maps can then be effectively upsampled and decoded by the operations we just introduced

Indeed, Jonathan Long et al. suggested reusing a pretrained VGG-16 as a feature extractor (refer to `Chapter 4`, *Influential Classification Tools*). With its five convolutional blocks, VGG-16 efficiently transforms images into feature maps, albeit dividing their spatial dimensions by two after each block. To decode the feature maps from the last block (for instance, into semantic masks), the fully connected layers used for classification are replaced by convolutional ones. The final layer is then applied – a transposed convolution to upsample the data back to the input shape (that is, with a stride of $s = 32$, since the spatial dimensions are divided by 32 through VGG).

However, Long et al. quickly noticed that this architecture, named **FCN-32s**, was yielding overly *coarse* results. As explained in their paper (*Fully convolutional networks for semantic segmentation, Proceedings of the IEEE CVPR conference, 2015*), the large stride at the final layer indeed limits the scale of detail. Though the features from the last VGG block contain rich contextual information, too much of their spatial definition is already lost. Therefore, the authors had the idea to fuse the feature maps from the last block with those larger ones from previous blocks.

In FCN-16s, the last layer of FCN-32s is thus replaced by a transposed layer with a stride of $s = 2$ only, so the resulting tensor has the same dimensions as the feature map from the fourth block. Using a skip connection, features from both tensors are merged together (element-wise addition). The result is finally scaled back to the input shape with another transposed convolution with $s = 16$. In FCN-8s, the same procedure is repeated instead with features from the third block, before the final transposed convolution with $s = 8$. For clarity, the complete architecture is presented in *Figure 6-8*, and a Keras implementation is provided in the next example:

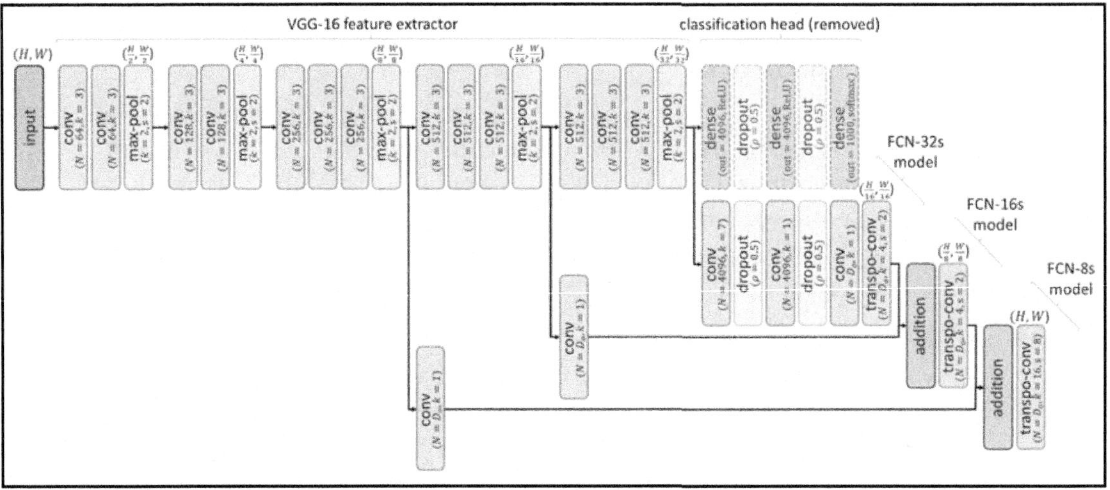

Figure 6-8: FCN-8s architecture. The data dimensions are shown after each block, supposing an $H \times W$ input. D_o represents the desired number of output channels

Figure 6-8 illustrates how VGG-16 serves as a feature extractor/encoder, and how the transposed convolutions are used for decoding. The figure also highlights that FCN-32s and FCN-16s are simpler, lighter architectures, with only one skip connection, or none at all.

With its use of transfer learning and its fusion of multi-scale feature maps, FCN-8s can output images with fine details. Furthermore, because of its fully convolutional nature, it can be applied to encode/decode images of different sizes. Performant and versatile, FCN-8s is still commonly used in many applications, while inspiring multiple other architectures.

U-Net

Among the solutions inspired by FCNs, the U-Net architecture is not only one of the first; it is probably the most popular (proposed by Olaf Ronneberger, Philipp Fischer, and Thomas Brox in a paper entitled *U-Net: Convolutional networks for biomedical image segmentation*, published by Springer).

Also developed for semantic segmentation (applied to medical imaging), it shares multiple properties with FCNs. It is also composed of a multi-block contractive encoder that increases the features' depth while reducing their spatial dimensions, and of an expansive decoder that recovers the image resolution. Moreover, like in FCNs, skip connections are used to connect encoding blocks to their decoding counterparts. The decoding blocks are thus provided with both the contextual information from the preceding block and the location information from the encoding path.

U-Net also differs from FCN in two main ways. Unlike FCN-8s, U-Net is **symmetrical**, going back to the traditional U-shaped encoder-decoder structure (hence the name). Furthermore, the merging with the feature maps from the skip connection is done through **concatenation** (along the channel axis) instead of addition. The U-Net architecture is depicted in *Figure 6-9*. As for the FCN, a Jupyter Notebook is dedicated to its implementation from scratch:

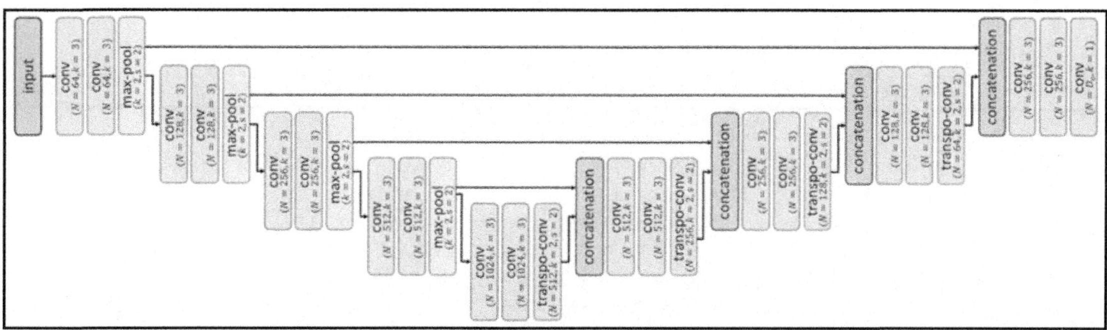

Figure 6-9: U-Net architecture

Note also that while the original decoding blocks have transposed convolutions with $s = 2$ for upsampling, it is common to find implementations using nearest-neighbor scaling instead (refer to the discussion in the previous subsection). Given its popularity, U-Net has known many variations and still inspires numerous architectures (for example, replacing its blocks with residual ones, and densifying the intra-block and extra-block connectivity).

Intermediary example – image super-resolution

Let's briefly apply one of these models to a new problem – image super-resolution (complete implementation and additional tips are found in the related notebook).

FCN implementation

Remembering the architecture we just presented, a simplified version of FCN-8s can be implemented as follows (note that the real model has additional convolutions before each transposed one):

```
inputs = Input(shape=(224, 224, 3))
# Building a pretrained VGG-16 feature extractor as encoder:
vgg16 = VGG16(include_top=False, weights='imagenet', input_tensor=inputs)
# We recover the feature maps returned by each of the 3 final blocks:
f3 = vgg16.get_layer('block3_pool').output # shape: (28, 28, 256)
f4 = vgg16.get_layer('block4_pool').output # shape: (14, 14, 512)
f5 = vgg16.get_layer('block5_pool').output # shape: ( 7, 7, 512)
# We replace the VGG dense layers by convs, adding the "decoding" layers
instead after the conv/pooling blocks:
f3 = Conv2D(filters=out_ch, kernel_size=1, padding='same')(f3)
f4 = Conv2D(filters=out_ch, kernel_size=1, padding='same')(f4)
f5 = Conv2D(filters=out_ch, kernel_size=1, padding='same')(f5)
# We upscale `f5` to a 14x14 map so it can be merged with `f4`:
f5x2 = Conv2DTranspose(filters=out_chh, kernel_size=4,strides=2,
                       padding='same', activation='relu')(f5)
# We merge the 2 feature maps with an element-wise addition:
m1 = add([f4, f5x2])
# We repeat the operation to merge `m1` and `f3` into a 28x28 map:
m1x2 = Conv2DTranspose(filters=out_ch, kernel_size=4, strides=2,
                       padding='same', activation='relu')(m1)
m2 = add([f3, m1x2])
# Finally, we use a transp-conv to recover the original shape:
outputs = Conv2DTranspose(filters=out_ch, kernel_size=16, strides=8,
                          padding='same', activation='sigmoid')(m2)
fcn_8s = Model(inputs, outputs)
```

Reusing the Keras implementation of VGG and the Functional API, an FCN-8s model can be created with minimal effort.

Application to upscaling images

A simple trick to train a network for super-resolution is to use a traditional upscaling method (such as bilinear interpolation) to scale the images to the target dimensions, before feeding them to the model. This way, the network can be trained as a denoising AE, whose task is to clear the upsampling artifacts and to recover lost details:

```
x_noisy = bilinear_upscale(bilinear_downscale(x_train)) # pseudo-code
fcn_8s.fit(x_noisy, x_train)
```

Proper code and complete demonstration on images can be found in the notebooks.

As mentioned earlier, the architectures we just covered are commonly applied to a wide range of tasks, such as depth estimation from color images, next-frame prediction (that is, predicting what the content of the next image could be, taking for input a series of video frames), and image segmentation. In the second part of this chapter, we will develop the latter task, which is essential in many real-life applications.

Understanding semantic segmentation

Semantic segmentation is a more generic term for the task of segmenting images into meaningful parts. It covers both object segmentation and instance segmentation, which were introduced in `Chapter 1`, *Computer Vision and Neural Networks*. Unlike image classification and object detection, covered in the previous chapters, segmentation tasks require the methods to return pixel-level dense predictions, that is, to assign a label to each pixel in the input images.

After explaining in more detail why encoders-decoders are thus great at object segmentation, and how their results can be further refined, we will present some solutions for the more complicated task of instance segmentation.

Object segmentation with encoders-decoders

As we saw in the first part of this chapter, encoding-decoding networks are trained to map data samples from one domain to another (for example, from noisy to noiseless, or from color to depth). Object segmentation can be seen as one such operation – the mapping of images from the color domain to the class domain. Given its value and context, we want to assign one of the target classes to each pixel of a picture, returning a **label map** with the same height and width.

Teaching encoders-decoders to take an image and return a label map still requires some consideration, which we will now discuss.

Overview

In the following paragraphs, we will present how networks such as U-Net are used for object segmentation, and how their outputs can be further processed into refined label maps.

Decoding as label maps

Building encoders-decoders to directly output label maps—where each pixel value represents a class (for instance, `1` for *dog*, and `2` for *cat*)—would yield poor results. As with classifiers, we need a better way to output categorical values.

To classify images among N categories, we learned to build networks with the final layers outputting N logits, representing the predicted per-class scores. We also learned how to convert these scores into probabilities using the **softmax** operation, and how to return the most probable class(es) by picking the highest values (for instance, using **argmax**). The same mechanism can be applied to semantic segmentation, at the pixel level instead of the image level. Instead of outputting a column vector of N logits containing the per-class scores for each full image, our network is built to return an $H \times W \times N$ tensor with scores for each pixel (refer to *Figure 6-10*):

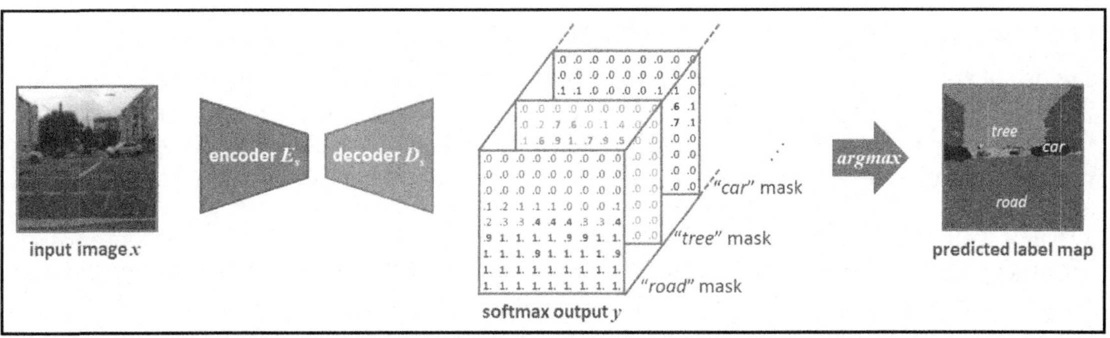

Figure 6-10: Given an input image of dimensions $H \times W$, the network returns an $H \times W \times N$ probability map, with N being the number of classes. Using argmax, the predicted label map can then be obtained

For the architectures we presented in this chapter, obtaining such an output tensor is simply a matter of setting $D_o = N$, that is, setting the number of output channels equal to the number of classes when building the models (refer to *Figures 6-8* and 6-9). They can then be trained as classifiers. The **cross-entropy loss** is used to compare the softmax values with the one-hot-encoded ground truth label maps (the fact that the compared tensors have more dimensions for classification that do not impact the calculations). Also, the $H \times W \times N$ predictions can be similarly transformed into per-pixel labels by selecting the indices of the highest values along the channel axis (that is, `argmax` over the channel axis). For instance, the FCN-8s code presented earlier can be adapted to train a model for object segmentation, as follows:

```
inputs = Input(shape=(224, 224, 3))
out_ch = num_classes = 19 # e.g., for object segmentation over Cityscapes
# [...] building e.g. a FCN-8s architecture, c.f. previous snippet.
outputs = Conv2DTranspose(filters=out_ch, kernel_size=16, strides=8,
                          padding='same', activation=None)(m2)
seg_fcn = Model(inputs, outputs)
seg_fcn.compile(optimizer='adam', loss='sparse_categorical_crossentropy')
# [...] training the network. Then we use it to predict label maps:
label_map = np.argmax(seg_fcn.predict(image), axis=-1)
```

The Git repository contains a complete example of an FCN-8s model built and trained for semantic segmentation, as well as a U-Net model.

Training with segmentation losses and metrics

The use of state-of-the-art architectures, such as FCN-8s and U-Net, is key to building performant systems for semantic segmentation. However, the most advanced models still need a proper loss to converge optimally. While cross-entropy is the default loss to train models both for coarse and dense classification, precautions should be taken for the latter cases.

For image-level and pixel-level classification tasks, **class imbalance** is a common problem. Imagine training models over a dataset of 990 cat pictures and 10 dog pictures. A model that would learn to always output cat would achieve 99% training accuracy, but would not be really useful in practice. For image classification, this can be avoided by adding or removing pictures so that all classes appear in the same proportions. The problem is trickier for pixel-level classification. Some classes may appear in every image but span only a handful of pixels, while other classes may cover most of the images (such as *traffic sign* versus *road* classes for our self-driving car application). The dataset cannot be edited to compensate for such an imbalance.

To prevent the segmentation models from developing a bias toward larger classes, their loss functions should instead be adapted. For instance, it is common practice to weigh the contribution of each class to the cross-entropy loss. As presented in our notebook on semantic segmentation for self-driving cars and in *Figure 6-11*, the less a class appears in training images, the more it should weigh on the loss. This way, the network would be heavily penalized if it starts ignoring smaller classes:

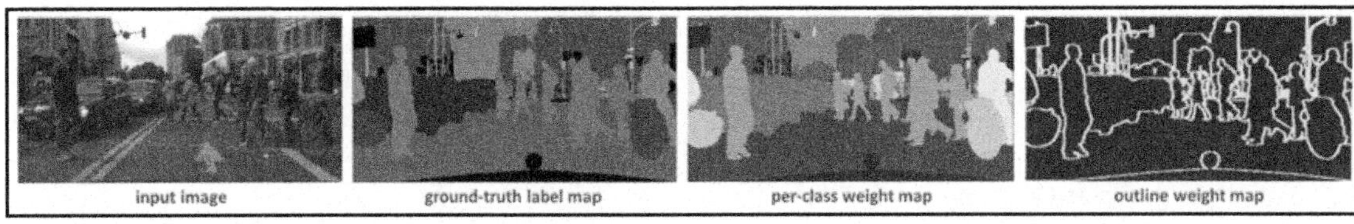

Figure 6-11: Examples of pixel weighing strategies for semantic segmentation (the lighter the pixels, the greater their weight on the loss)

The weight maps are usually computed from the ground truth label maps. It should be noted that, as shown in *Figure 6-11*, the weight applied to each pixel can be set not only according to the class, but also according to the pixel's position relative to other elements, and more.

Another solution is to replace the cross-entropy with another cost function that's not affected by the class proportions. After all, cross-entropy is a surrogate accuracy function, adopted because it is nicely differentiable. However, this function does not really express the actual objective of our models—to properly segment the different classes, whatever their areas. Therefore, several loss functions and metrics that are specific to semantic segmentation have been proposed by researchers to more explicitly capture this objective.

Intersection-over-Union (**IoU**), presented in `Chapter 5`, *Object Detection Models*, is one of these common metrics. The **Sørensen–Dice coefficient** (often simply named the **Dice coefficient**) is another. Like IoU, it measures how well two sets overlap:

$$\text{Dice}(A,B) = \frac{2|A \cap B|}{|A| + |B|}$$

Here, $|A|$ and $|B|$ represent the cardinality of each set (refer to the explanations in the previous chapter), and $|A \cap B|$ represents the number of elements they have in common (cardinality of their intersection). IoU and Dice share several properties, and one can actually help calculate the other:

$$\text{IoU}(A,B) = \frac{\text{Dice}(A,B)}{2 - \text{Dice}(A,B)} \quad ; \quad \text{Dice}(A,B) = \frac{2 \times \text{IoU}(A,B)}{1 + \text{IoU}(A,B)}$$

In semantic segmentation, *Dice* is, therefore, used to measure how well the predicted mask for each class overlaps the ground truth mask. For one class, the numerator then represents the number of correctly classified pixels, and the denominator represents the total number of pixels belonging to this class in both the predicted and ground truth masks. As a metric, the *Dice* coefficient thus does not depend on the relative number of pixels one class takes in images. For multi-class tasks, scientists usually compute the *Dice* coefficient for each class (comparing each pair of predicted and ground truth masks), and then average the results.

From the equation, we can see the *Dice* coefficient is defined between 0 and 1—its value reaches 0 if *A* and *B* do not overlap at all, and it reaches 1 if they do perfectly. Therefore, to use it as a loss function that a network should minimize, we need to reverse this scoring. All in all, for semantic segmentation applied to *N* classes, the *Dice* loss is commonly defined as follows:

$$L_{Dice}(y, y^{true}) = 1 - \frac{1}{N}\sum_{k=0}^{N-1} \text{Dice}(y_k, y_k^{true}) \quad \text{with} \quad \text{Dice}(a,b) = \frac{\epsilon + 2\sum_{i,j}(a \odot b)_{i,j}}{\epsilon + \sum_{i,j} a_{i,j} + \sum_{i,j} b_{i,j}}$$

Let's clarify this equation a bit. If *a* and *b* are two one-hot tensors, then the *Dice* numerator (that is, their intersection) can be approximated by applying the element-wise multiplication between them (refer to `Chapter 1`, *Computer Vision and Neural Networks*), then by summing together all the values in the resulting tensor. The denominator is obtained by summing all the elements, *a* and *b*. Finally, a small value, ϵ (for instance, below *1e-6*), is usually added to the denominator to avoid dividing by zero if the tensors contain nothing, and added to the numerator to smooth the result.

Note that, in practice, unlike the ground truth one-hot tensors, the predictions do not contain binary values. They are composed of the softmax probabilities ranging continuously from 0 to 1. This loss is therefore often named **soft Dice**.

In TensorFlow, this loss can be implemented as follows:

```
def dice_loss(labels, logits, num_classes, eps=1e-6, spatial_axes=[1, 2]):
    # Transform logits in probabilities, and one-hot the ground truth:
    pred_proba = tf.nn.softmax(logits, axis=-1)
    gt_onehot  = tf.one_hot(labels, num_classes, dtype=tf.float32)
    # Compute Dice numerator and denominator:
    num_perclass = 2 * tf.reduce_sum(pred_proba * gt_onehot,
axis=spatial_axes)
    den_perclass = tf.reduce_sum(pred_proba + gt_onehot, axis=spatial_axes)
    # Compute Dice and average over batch and classes:
    dice = tf.reduce_mean((num_perclass + eps) / (den_perclass + eps))
    return 1 - dice
```

Both *Dice* and *IoU* are important tools for segmentation tasks, and their usefulness is further demonstrated in the related Jupyter notebook.

Post-processing with conditional random fields

Labeling every pixel properly is a complex task, and it is common to obtain predicted label maps with poor contours and small incorrect areas. Thankfully, there are some methods that post-process the results, correcting some obvious defects. Among these methods, the **conditional random fields (CRFs)** methods are the most popular because of their overall efficiency.

The theory behind this is beyond the scope of this book, but CRFs are able to improve pixel-level predictions by taking into account the context of each pixel back in the original image. If the color gradient between two neighboring pixels is small (that is, no abrupt change of color), chances are that they belong to the same class. Taking into account this spatial and color-based model, as well as the probability maps provided by the predictors (in our case, the softmax tensors from CNNs), CRF methods return refined label maps, which are better with respect to visual contours.

Several ready-to-use implementations are available, such as `pydensecrf` by Lucas Beyer (`https://github.com/lucasb-eyer/pydensecrf`), a Python wrapper for dense CRFs with Gaussian edge potentials proposed by Philipp Krähenbühl and Vladlen Koltun (refer to *Efficient inference in fully connected CRFs with gaussian edge potentials, Advances in neural information processing systems, 2011*). In the last notebook for this chapter, we explain how to use this framework.

Advanced example – image segmentation for self-driving cars

As suggested at the beginning of this chapter, we will apply this new knowledge to a complex real-life use case—the segmentation of traffic images for self-driving cars.

Task presentation

Like human drivers, self-driving cars need to understand their environment and be aware of the elements around them. Applying semantic segmentation to the video images from a front camera would allow the system to know whether other cars are around, to know whether pedestrians or bikes are crossing the road, to follow traffic lines and signs, and more.

This is, therefore, a critical process, and researchers are putting in lots of effort into refining the models. For that reason, multiple related datasets and benchmarks are available. The *Cityscapes* dataset (`https://www.cityscapes-dataset.com`) we chose for our demonstration is one of the most famous. Shared by Marius Cordts et al. (refer to *The Cityscapes Dataset for Semantic Urban Scene Understanding, Proceedings of the IEEE CVPR Conference*), it contains video sequences from multiple cities, with semantic labels for more than 19 classes (road, car, plant, and so on). A notebook is specifically dedicated to getting started with this benchmark.

Exemplary solution

In the two final Jupyter notebooks for this chapter, FCN and U-Net models are trained to tackle this task, using several of the tricks presented in this section. We demonstrate how to properly weigh each class when computing the loss, we present how to post-process the label maps, and more besides.

As the whole solution is quite long and notebooks are better suited to the present code, we invite you to pursue the reading there, if you're interested in this use case. This way, we can dedicate the rest of this chapter to another fascinating problem—instance segmentation.

The more difficult case of instance segmentation

With models trained for object segmentation, the *softmax* output represents for each pixel the probability that it belongs to one of *N* classes. However, it does not express whether two pixels or blobs of pixels belong to the same instance of a class. For example, given the predicted label map shown in *Figure 6-10*, we have no way of counting the number of *tree* or *building* instances.

In the following subsection, we will present two different ways of achieving instance segmentation by extending solutions for two related tasks that we've tackled already—object segmentation and object detection.

From object segmentation to instance segmentation

First, we will present some tools that we can use to obtain instance masks from the segmentation models we just covered. The U-Net authors popularized the idea of tuning encoders-decoders so that their output can be used for instance segmentation. This idea was pushed further by Alexander Buslaev, Victor Durnov, and Selim Seferbekov, who famously won Kaggle's 2018 Data Science Bowl (`https://www.kaggle.com/c/data-science-bowl-2018`), a sponsored competition to advance instance segmentation for medical applications.

Respecting boundaries

If elements captured by a semantic mask are well-separated/non-overlapping, splitting the masks to distinguish each instance is not too complicated a task. Plenty of algorithms are available to estimate the contours of distinct blobs in binary matrices and/or to provide a separate mask for each blob. For multi-class instance segmentation, this process can just be repeated for each class mask returned by object segmentation methods, splitting them further into instances.

But precise semantic masks should first be obtained, or elements too close to each other may be returned as a single blob. So, how can we ensure that segmentation models put enough attention into generating masks with precise contours, at least for non-overlapping elements? We know the answer already—the only way to teach networks to do something specific is to adapt their training loss accordingly.

U-Net was developed for biomedical applications, to segment neuronal structures in microscope images. To teach their network to separate nearby cells properly, the authors decided to weight their loss function to more heavily penalize misclassified pixels at the boundaries of several instances. Also illustrated in *Figure 6-11*, this strategy is quite similar to the per-class loss weighting we presented in the previous subsection, although here, the weighting is specifically computed for each pixel. The U-Net authors present a formula to compute these weight maps based on the ground truth class mask. For each pixel and for each class, this formula takes into account the pixel's distance to the two nearest class instances. The smaller the two distances, the higher the weight. The weight maps can be precomputed and stored along the ground truth masks to be used together during training.

Note that this per-pixel weighting can be combined with the per-class weighting in multi-class scenarios. The idea to penalize the networks more heavily for certain regions of the images can also be adapted to other applications (for example, to better segment critical parts of manufactured objects).

We mentioned the winners of Kaggle's 2018 Data Science Bowl, who put a noteworthy spin on this idea. For each class, their custom U-Net was outputting two masks: the usual mask predicting the per-pixel class probability, and a second mask capturing the class boundaries. The ground truth boundary masks were precomputed based on the class masks. After proper training, the information from the two predicted masks can be used to obtain well-separated elements for each class.

Post-processing into instance masks

As discussed earlier in the previous section, once precise masks are obtained, non-overlapping instances can be identified from them by applying proper algorithms. This post-processing is usually done using **morphological functions**, such as **mask erosion** and **dilation**.

Watershed transforms are another common family of algorithms that further segment the class masks into instances. These algorithms take a one-channel tensor and consider it as a topographic surface, where each value represents an elevation. Using various methods that we won't go into, they then extract the ridges' tops, representing the instance boundaries. Several implementations of these transforms are available, some of which are CNN-based, such as the *Deep watershed transform for instance segmentation* (*Proceedings of the IEEE CVPR conference, 2017*), by Min Bai and Raquel Urtasun from the University of Toronto. Inspired by the FCN architecture, their network takes for input both the predicted semantic mask and the original RGB image, and returns an energy map that can be used to identify the ridges. Thanks to the RGB information, this solution can even separate overlapping instances with good accuracy.

From object detection to instance segmentation – Mask R-CNN

A second way of addressing instance segmentation is from the angle of object detection. In `Chapter 5`, *Object Detection Models*, we presented solutions to return the bounding boxes for object instances appearing in images. In the following paragraphs, we will demonstrate how these results can be turned into more refined instance masks. More precisely, we will present **Mask R-CNN**, a network extending **Faster R-CNN**.

Applying semantic segmentation to bounding boxes

When we introduced object detection in `Chapter 1`, *Computer Vision and Neural Networks*, we explained that this process is often used as a preliminary step, providing image patches containing a single instance for further analysis. With this in mind, instance segmentation becomes a matter of two steps:

1. Using an object detection model to return bounding boxes for each instance of target classes
2. Feeding each patch to a semantic segmentation model to obtain the instance mask

If the predicted bounding boxes are accurate (each capturing a whole, single element), then the task of the segmentation network is straightforward—to classify which pixels in the corresponding patch belong to the captured class, and which pixels are part of the background/belong to another class.

This way of solving instance segmentation is advantageous, as we already have all the necessary tools to implement it (object detection and semantic segmentation models)!

Building an instance segmentation model with Faster-RCNN

While we could simply use a pretrained detection network followed by a pretrained segmentation network, the whole pipeline would certainly work better if the two networks were stitched together and trained in an end-to-end manner. Backpropagating the segmentation loss through the common layers would better ensure that the features extracted are meaningful both for the detection and the segmentation tasks. This is pretty much the original idea behind *Mask R-CNN* by Kaiming He et al. from **Facebook AI Research** (**FAIR**) in 2017 (*Mask R-CNN, Proceedings of the IEEE CVPR conference*).

If the name rings a bell, Kaiming He was also among the main authors of ResNet and Faster R-CNN.

Mask R-CNN is mostly based on Faster R-CNN. Like Faster R-CNN, Mask R-CNN is composed of a region-proposal network, followed by two branches predicting the class and the box offset for each proposed region (refer to `Chapter 5`, *Object Detection Models*). However, the authors extended this model with a *third parallel branch*, outputting a binary mask for the element in each region (as shown in *Figure 6-12*). Note that this additional branch is only composed of a couple of standard and transposed convolutions. As the authors highlighted in their paper, this parallel processing follows the spirit of Faster R-CNN, and contrasts with other instance segmentation methods, which are usually sequential:

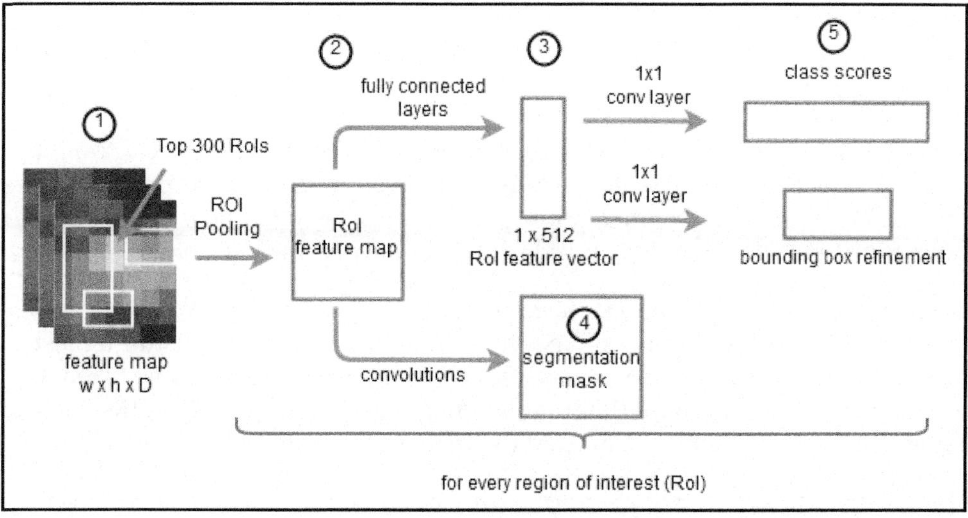

Figure 6-12: Mask R-CNN architecture, based on Faster R-CNN

Thanks to this parallelism, He et al. could decouple the classification and segmentation. While the segmentation branch is defined to output *N* binary masks (one for each class, like any usual semantic segmentation model), only the mask corresponding to the class predicted by the other branch will be considered for the final prediction and for the training loss. In other words, only the mask of the instance class contributes to the cross-entropy loss applied to the segmentation branch. As explained by the authors, this lets the segmentation branch predict label maps without competition among the classes, thereby simplifying its task.

Another famous contribution of the Mask R-CNN authors is the **RoI align layer**, replacing the **RoI pooling** of Faster R-CNN. The difference between the two is actually quite subtle, but provides a non-negligible accuracy boost. RoI pooling causes quantization, for instance, by discretizing the coordinates of the subwindow cells (refer to `Chapter 5`, *Object Detection Models,* and *Figure 5-13*). While this does not really impact the predictions of the classification branch (it's robust to such small misalignments), this would affect the quality of the pixel-level prediction of the segmentation branch. To avoid this, He et al. simply *removed the discretization* and *used bilinear interpolation* instead to obtain the cells' content.

Mask R-CNN distinguished itself at the COCO 2017 challenges, and is widely used nowadays. Multiple implementations can be found online, for instance, in the folder of the `tensorflow/models` repository dedicated to object detection and instance segmentation (`https://github.com/tensorflow/models/tree/master/research/object_detection`).

Summary

In this chapter, we covered several paradigms for pixel-precise applications. We introduced encoders-decoders and some specific architectures and applied them to multiple tasks from image denoising to semantic segmentation. We also demonstrated how different solutions can be combined to tackle more advanced problems, such as instance segmentation.

As we tackle more and more complex tasks, new challenges arise. For example, in semantic segmentation, precisely annotating images to train models is a time-consuming task. Available datasets are thus usually scarce, and specific measures should be taken to avoid overfitting. Furthermore, because the training images and their ground truths are heavier, well-engineered data pipelines are needed for efficient training.

In the following chapter, we will, therefore, provide in-depth details of how TensorFlow can be used to effectively augment and serve training batches.

Questions

1. What is the particularity of AEs?
2. Which classification architecture are FCNs based on?
3. How can a semantic segmentation model be trained so that it does not ignore small classes?

Further reading

Mask R-CNN (`http://openaccess.thecvf.com/content_iccv_2017/html/He_Mask_R-CNN_ICCV_2017_paper.html`) by Kaiming He, Georgia Gkioxari, Piotr Dollar, and Ross Girshick: This nicely written conference paper mentioned in the chapter presents Mask R-CNN, providing additional illustrations and details that may help you to understand this model.

Section 3: Advanced Concepts and New Frontiers of Computer Vision

This final section addresses several contemporary challenges in our domain and provides essential techniques for those who want to apply computer vision to novel use cases. First, TensorFlow tools that are designed to process large amounts of data in an efficient manner are presented. Tackling the opposite scenario, where data is too scarce, you will also be introduced to domain adaptation, as well as image generation with computer graphics, GANs, and VAEs. To learn how to extract information from videos, a chapter is dedicated to recurrent neural networks, their theory, and some illustrated applications. Finally, the book ends with a discussion about the challenges related to on-device computer vision, teaching you how to deploy your solutions on mobile phones and in web browsers.

The following chapters will be covered in this section:

- `Chapter 7`, *Training on Complex and Scarce Datasets*
- `Chapter 8`, *Video and Recurrent Neural Networks*
- `Chapter 9`, *Optimizing Models and Deploying on Mobile Devices*

7
Training on Complex and Scarce Datasets

moData is the lifeblood of deep learning applications. As such, training data should be able to flow unobstructed into networks, and it should contain all the meaningful information that is essential to prepare the methods for their tasks. Oftentimes, however, datasets can have complex structures or be stored on heterogeneous devices, complicating the process of efficiently feeding their content to the models. In other cases, relevant training images or annotations can be unavailable, depriving models of the information they need to learn.

Thankfully, for the former cases, TensorFlow provides a rich framework to set up optimized data pipelines—`tf.data`. For the latter cases, researchers have been proposing multiple alternatives when relevant training data is scarce—data augmentation, generation of synthetic datasets, domain adaptation, and more. These alternatives will also give us the opportunity to elaborate on generative models, such as **variational autoencoders** (**VAEs**) and **generative adversarial networks** (**GANs**).

The following topics will thus be covered in this chapter:

- How to build efficient input pipelines with `tf.data`, extracting and processing samples of all kinds
- How to augment and render images to compensate for training data scarcity
- What domain adaptation methods are, and how they can help train more robust models
- How to create novel images with generative models such as VAEs and GANs

Technical requirements

Once again, several Jupyter notebooks and related source files to illustrate the chapter can be found in the Git repository dedicated to this book: `https://github.com/PacktPublishing/Hands-On-Computer-Vision-with-TensorFlow-2/tree/master/Chapter07`.

Some additional Python packages are required for the notebook, demonstrating how to render synthetic images from 3D models, such as `vispy` (`http://vispy.org`) and `plyfile` (`https://github.com/dranjan/python-plyfile`). Installation instructions are provided in the notebook itself.

Efficient data serving

Well-defined input pipelines cannot only greatly reduce the time needed to train models, but also help to better preprocess the training samples to guide the networks toward more performant configurations. In this section, we will demonstrate how to build such optimized pipelines, diving into the TensorFlow `tf.data` API.

Introducing the TensorFlow Data API

While `tf.data` has already appeared multiple times in the Jupyter notebooks, we have yet to properly introduce this API and its multiple facets.

Intuition behind the TensorFlow Data API

Before covering `tf.data`, we will provide some context to justify its relevance to the training of deep learning models.

Feeding fast and data-hungry models

Neural networks (**NNs**) are *data-hungry* models. The larger the datasets they can iterate on during training, the more accurate and robust these neural networks will become. As we have already noticed in our experiments, training a network is thus a heavy task, which can take hours, if not days.

As GPU/TPU hardware architectures are becoming more and more performant, the time needed to feed forward and backpropagate for each training iteration keeps decreasing (for those who can afford these devices). The speed is such nowadays that NNs tend to *consume* training batches faster than typical input pipelines can *produce* them. This is especially true in computer vision. Image datasets are commonly too heavy to be entirely preprocessed, and reading/decoding image files on the fly can cause significant delays (especially when repeated millions of times per training).

Inspiration from lazy structures

More generally, with the rise of *big data* some years ago, plenty of literature, frameworks, best practices, and more have appeared, offering new solutions to the processing and serving of huge amounts of data for all kinds of applications. The `tf.data` API was built by TensorFlow developers with those frameworks and practices in mind, in order to provide *a clear and efficient framework to feed data to neural networks*. More precisely, the goal of this API is to define input pipelines that are able to *deliver data for the next step before the current step has finished* (refer to the official API guide, `https://www.tensorflow.org/guide/performance/datasets`).

As explained in several online presentations by Derek Murray, one of the Google experts working on TensorFlow (one of his presentations was video recorded and is available at `https://www.youtube.com/watch?v=uIcqeP7MFH0`), pipelines built with the `tf.data` API are comparable to *lazy lists* in functional languages. They can iterate over huge or infinite datasets batch by batch in a call-by-need fashion (*infinite*, for instance, when new data samples are generated on the fly). They provide operations such as `map()`, `reduce()`, `filter()`, and `repeat()` to process data and control its flow. They can be compared to Python generators, but with a more advanced interface and, more importantly, with a C++ backbone for computational performance. Though you could manually implement a multithreaded Python generator to process and serve batches in parallel with the main training loop, `tf.data` does all this out of the box (and most probably in a more optimized manner).

Structure of TensorFlow data pipelines

As indicated in the previous paragraphs, data scientists have already developed extensive know-how regarding the processing and pipelining of large datasets, and the structure of `tf.data` pipelines directly follows these best practices.

Extract, Transform, Load

The API guide also makes the parallel between data pipelines for training and **Extract, Transform, Load** (**ETL**) processes. ETL is a common paradigm for data processing in computer science. In computer vision, ETL pipelines in charge of feeding models with training data usually look like this:

Figure 7-1: A typical ETL pipeline to provide data for the training of computer vision models

The **extraction** step consists of selecting data sources and extracting their content. These sources may be listed explicitly by a document (for instance, a CSV file containing the filenames for all the images), or implicitly (for instance, with all the dataset's images already stored in a specific folder). Sources may be *stored on different devices* (local or remote), and it is also the task of the extractor to list these different sources and extract their content. For example, it is common in computer vision to have datasets so big that they have to be stored on multiple hard drives. To train NNs in a supervised manner, we also need to extract the annotations/ground truths along the images (for instance, class labels contained in CSV files, and ground truth segmentation masks stored in another folder).

The fetched data samples should then be *transformed*. One of the most common transformations is the parsing of extracted data samples into a common format. For instance, this means parsing the bytes read from image files into a matrix representation (for instance, to decode JPEG or PNG bytes into image tensors). Other heavy transformations can be applied in this step, such as *cropping/scaling* images to the same dimensions, or *augmenting* them with various random operations. Again, the same applies to annotations for supervised learning. They should also be parsed, for instance, into tensors that could later be handed to loss functions.

Once ready, the data is *loaded* into the target structure. For the training of machine learning methods, this means sending the batch samples into the device in charge of running the model, such as the selected GPU(s). The processed dataset can also be cached/saved somewhere for later use.

This ETL process can already be observed, for instance, in the Jupyter notebook setting up the *Cityscapes* input pipeline in `Chapter 6`, *Enhancing and Segmenting Images*. The input pipeline was iterating over the input/ground truth filenames provided, and parsing and augmenting their content, before passing the results as batches to our training processes.

API interface

`tf.data.Dataset` is the central class provided by the `tf.data` API (refer to the documentation at `https://www.tensorflow.org/api_docs/python/tf/data/Dataset`). Instances of this class (which are simply called **datasets**) represent data sources, following the lazy list paradigm we just presented.

Datasets can be initialized in a multitude of ways, depending on how their content is initially stored (in files, NumPy arrays, tensors, and others). For example, a dataset can be based on a list of image files, as follows:

```
dataset = tf.data.Dataset.list_files("/path/to/dataset/*.png")
```

Datasets also have numerous methods they can apply to themselves in order to provide a transformed dataset. For example, the following function returns a new dataset instance with the file's contents properly transformed (that is, parsed) into homogeneously resized image tensors:

```
def parse_fn(filename):
    img_bytes = tf.io.read_file(filename)
    img = tf.io.decode_png(img_bytes, channels=3)
    img = tf.image.resize(img, [64, 64])
    return img  # or for instance, `{'image': img}` if we want to name this
input
dataset = dataset.map(map_func=parse_fn)
```

The function passed to `.map()` will be applied to every sample in the dataset when iterating. Indeed, once all the necessary transformations are applied, datasets can be used as any lazy lists/generators, as follows:

```
print(dataset.output_types)   # > "tf.uint8"
print(dataset.output_shapes) # > "(64, 64, 3)"
for image in dataset:
     # do something with the image
```

All the data samples are already returned as `Tensor`, and can easily be loaded into the device(s) in charge of the training. To make things even more straightforward, `tf.estimator.Estimator` and `tf.keras.Model` instances can directly receive a `tf.data.Dataset` object as input for their training (for estimators, the dataset operations have to be wrapped into a function returning the dataset) as follows:

```
keras_model.fit(dataset, ...)     # to train a Keras model on the data
def input_fn():
    # ... build dataset
    return dataset
tf_estimator.train(input_fn, ...) # ... or to train a TF estimator
```

With estimators and models tightly integrating the `tf.data` API, TensorFlow 2 has made data preprocessing and data loading both modular and clear.

Setting up input pipelines

Keeping in mind the ETL procedure, we will develop some of the most common and important methods provided by `tf.data`, at least for computer vision applications. For an exhaustive list, we invite our readers to refer to the documentation (`https://www.tensorflow.org/api_docs/python/tf/data`).

Extracting (from tensors, text files, TFRecord files, and more)

Datasets are usually built for specific needs (companies gathering images to train smarter algorithms, researchers setting up benchmarks, and so on), so it is rare to find two datasets with the same structure and format. Thankfully for us, TensorFlow developers are well aware of this and have provided plenty of tools to list and extract data.

From NumPy and TensorFlow data

First of all, if data samples were already somehow loaded by the program (for instance, as NumPy or TensorFlow structures), they can be passed directly to `tf.data` using the `.from_tensors()` or `.from_tensor_slices()` static methods.

Both accept nested array/tensor structures, but the latter will slice the data into samples along the first axis as follows:

```
x, y = np.array([1, 2, 3, 4]), np.array([5, 6, 7, 8])
d = tf.data.Dataset.from_tensors((x,y))
print(d.output_shapes) # > (TensorShape([4]), TensorShape([4]))
d_sliced = tf.data.Dataset.from_tensor_slices((x,y))
print(d_sliced.output_shapes) # > (TensorShape([]), TensorShape([]))
```

As we can observe, the second dataset, `d_sliced`, ends up containing four pairs of samples, each containing only one value.

From files

As seen in a previous example, datasets can iterate over files using the `.list_files()` static method. This method creates a dataset of string tensors, each containing the path of one of the listed files. Each file can then be opened using, for instance, `tf.io.read_file()` (`tf.io` contains file-related operations).

The `tf.data` API also provides some specific datasets to iterate over binary or text files. `tf.data.TextLineDataset()` can be used to read documents line by line (useful for some public datasets that are listing their image files and/or labels in text files); `tf.data.experimental.CsvDataset()` can parse CSV files and return their content line by line too.

`tf.data.experimental` does not ensure the same backward compatibility as other modules. By the time this book reaches our readers, methods may have been moved to `tf.data.Dataset` or simply removed (for methods that are temporary solutions to some TensorFlow limitations). We invite our readers to check the documentation.

From other inputs (generator, SQL database, range, and others)

Although we will not list them all, it is good to keep in mind that `tf.data.Dataset` can be defined from a wide range of input sources. For example, datasets simply iterating over numbers can be initialized with the `.range()` static method. Datasets can also be built upon Python generators with `.from_generator()`. Finally, even if elements are stored in a SQL database, TensorFlow provides some (experimental) tools to query it, including the following:

```
dataset = tf.data.experimental.SqlDataset(
    "sqlite", "/path/to/my_db.sqlite3",
    "SELECT img_filename, label FROM images", (tf.string, tf.int32))
```

For more specific dataset instantiators, we invite our readers to check the `tf.data` documentation.

Transforming the samples (parsing, augmenting, and more)

The second step of ETL pipelines is **transform**. Transformations can be split into two types—those that affect data samples individually, and those that affect a dataset as a whole. In the following paragraphs, we will cover the former transformations and explain how our samples can be preprocessed.

Parsing images and labels

In the `parse_fn()` method we wrote in the previous subsection for `dataset.map()`, `tf.io.read_file()` was called to read the file corresponding to each filename listed by the dataset, and then `tf.io.decode_png()` converted the bytes into an image tensor.

`tf.io` also contains `decode_jpeg()`, `decode_gif()`, and more. It also provides the more generic `decode_image()`, which can infer which image format to use (refer to the documentation at `https://www.tensorflow.org/api_docs/python/tf/io`).

Furthermore, numerous methods can be applied to parsing computer vision labels. Obviously, if the labels are also images (for instance, for image segmentation or edition), the methods we just listed can be reused all the same. If the labels are stored in text files, `TextLineDataset` or `FixedLengthRecordDataset` (refer to the documentation at `https://www.tensorflow.org/api_docs/python/tf/data`) can be used to iterate over them, and modules such as `tf.strings` can help parse the lines/records. For example, let's imagine we have a training dataset with a text file listing the filename of an image and its class identifier on each line, separated by a comma. Each pair of images/labels could be parsed this way:

```
def parse_fn(line):
    img_filename, img_label = tf.strings.split(line, sep=',')
    img = tf.io.decode_image(tf.io.read_file(img_filename))[0]
    return {'image': img, 'label': tf.strings.to_number(img_label)}
dataset = tf.data.TextLineDataset('/path/to/file.txt').map(parse_fn)
```

As we can observe, TensorFlow provides multiple helper functions to process and convert strings, to read binary files, to decode PNG or JPEG bytes into images, and so on. With these functions, pipelines to handle heterogeneous data can be set up with minimal effort.

Parsing TFRecord files

While listing all the image files and then iterating to open and parse them is a straightforward pipeline solution, it can be suboptimal. Loading and parsing image files one by one is resource-consuming. Storing a large number of images together into a binary file would make the read-from-disk operations (or streaming operations for remote files) much more efficient. Therefore, TensorFlow users are often advised to use the TFRecord file format, based on Google's Protocol Buffers, a language-neutral, platform-neutral extensible mechanism for serializing structured data (refer to the documentation at `https://developers.google.com/protocol-buffers`).

TFRecord files are binary files aggregating data samples (such as images, labels, and metadata). A TFRecord file contains serialized `tf.train.Example` instances, which are basically dictionaries naming each data element (called **features** according to this API) composing the sample (for example, `{'img': image_sample1, 'label': label_sample1, ...}`). Each element/feature that a sample contains is an instance of `tf.train.Feature` or of its subclasses. These objects store the data content as lists of bytes, of floats, or of integers (refer to the documentation at `https://www.tensorflow.org//api_docs/python/tf/train`).

Because it was developed specifically for TensorFlow, this file format is very well supported by `tf.data`. In order to use TFRecord files as data source for input pipelines, TensorFlow users can pass the files to `tf.data.TFRecordDataset(filenames)` (refer to the documentation at `https://www.tensorflow.org/api_docs/python/tf/data/TFRecordDataset`), which can iterate over the serialized `tf.train.Example` elements they contain. To parse their content, the following should be done:

```
dataset = tf.data.TFRecordDataset(['file1.tfrecords','file2.tfrecords'])
# Dictionary describing the features/tf.trainExample structure:
feat_dic = {'img': tf.io.FixedLenFeature([], tf.string), # image's bytes
            'label': tf.io.FixedLenFeature([1], tf.int64)} # class label
def parse_fn(example_proto): # Parse a serialized tf.train.Example
    sample = tf.parse_single_example(example_proto, feat_dic)
    return tf.io.decode_image(sample['img])[0], sample['label']
dataset = dataset.map(parse_fn)
```

`tf.io.FixedLenFeature(shape, dtype, default_value)` lets the pipeline know what kind of data to expect out of the serialized sample, which can then be parsed with a single command.

In one of the Jupyter notebooks, we cover TFRecord in more detail, explaining step by step how data can be preprocessed and stored as TFRecord files, and how these files can then be used as a data source for `tf.data` pipelines.

Editing samples

The `.map()` method is central to `tf.data` pipelines. Besides parsing samples, it is also applied to edit them further. For example, in computer vision, it is common for some applications to crop/resize input images to the same dimensions (for instance, applying `tf.image.resize()`) or to one-hot target labels (`tf.one_hot()`).

As we will detail later in this chapter, it is also recommended to wrap the optional augmentations for training data into a function passed to `.map()`.

Transforming the datasets (shuffling, zipping, parallelizing, and more)

The API also provides numerous functions to transform one dataset into another, to adapt its structure, or to merge it with other data sources.

Structuring datasets

In data science and machine learning, operations such as filtering data, shuffling samples, and stacking samples into batches are extremely common. The `tf.data` API offers simple solutions to most of those (refer to the documentation at `https://www.tensorflow.org/api_docs/python/tf/data/Dataset`). For example, some of the most frequently used datasets' methods are as follows:

- `.batch(batch_size, ...)`, which returns a new dataset, with the data samples batched accordingly (`tf.data.experimental.unbatch()` does the opposite). Note that if `.map()` is called after `.batch()`, the mapping function will therefore receive batched data as input.

- `.repeat(count=None)`, which repeats the data `count` times (infinitely if `count = None`).
- `.shuffle(buffer_size, seed, ...)`, which shuffles elements after filling a buffer accordingly (for instance, if `buffer_size = 10`, the dataset will virtually divide the dataset into subsets of 10 elements, and randomly permute the elements in each, before returning them one by one). The larger the buffer size is, the more stochastic the shuffling becomes, but also the heavier the process is.
- `.filter(predicate)`, which keeps/removes elements depending on the Boolean output of the `predicate` function provided. For example, if we wanted to filter a dataset to remove elements stored online, we could use this method as follows:

```
url_regex = "(?i)([a-z][a-z0-9]*)://([^ /]+)(/[^ ]*)?|([^ @]+)@([^
@]+)"
def is_not_url(filename): #NB: the regex isn't 100% sure/covering
all cases
    return ~(tf.strings.regex_full_match(filename, url_regex))
dataset = dataset.filter(is_not_url)
```

- `.take(count)`, which returns a dataset containing the first `count` elements at most.
- `.skip(count)`, which returns a dataset without the first `count` elements. Both methods can be used to split a dataset, for instance, into training and validation sets as follows:

```
num_training_samples, num_epochs = 10000, 100
dataset_train = dataset.take(num_training_samples)
dataset_train = dataset_train.repeat(num_epochs)
dataset_val   = dataset.skip(num_training_samples)
```

Many other methods are available to structure data or to control its flow, usually inspired by other data processing frameworks (such as `.unique()`, `.reduce()`, and `.group_by_reducer()`).

Merging datasets

Some methods can also be used to merge datasets together. The two most straightforward ones are `.concatenate(dataset)` and the static `.zip(datasets)` (refer to the documentation at `https://www.tensorflow.org/api_docs/python/tf/data/Dataset`). The former *concatenates* the samples of the dataset provided with those of the current one, while the latter *combines* the dataset's elements into tuples (similar to Python's `zip()`) as follows:

```
d1 = tf.data.Dataset.range(3)
d2 = tf.data.Dataset.from_tensor_slices([[4, 5], [6, 7], [8, 9]])
d = tf.data.Dataset.zip((d1, d2))
# d will return [0, [4, 5]], [1, [6, 7]], and [2, [8, 9]]
```

Another method often used to merge data from different sources is `.interleave(map_func, cycle_length, block_length, ...)` (refer to the documentation at `https://www.tensorflow.org/api_docs/python/tf/data/Dataset#interleave`). This applies the `map_func` function to the elements of the datasets and *interleaves* the results. Let's now go back to the example presented in the *Parsing images and labels* section, with image files and classes listed in a text file. If we have several such text files and want to combine all their images into a single dataset, `.interleave()` could be applied as follows:

```
filenames = ['/path/to/file1.txt', '/path/to/file2.txt', ...]
d = tf.data.Dataset.from_tensor_slices(filenames)
d = d.interleave(lambda f: tf.data.TextLineDataset(f).map(parse_fn),
                 cycle_length=2, block_length=5)
```

The `cycle_length` parameter fixes the number of elements processed concurrently. In our preceding example, `cycle_length = 2` means that the function will concurrently iterate over the lines of the first two files, before iterating over the lines of the third and fourth files, and so on. The `block_length` parameter controls the number of consecutive samples returned per element. Here, `block_length = 5` means that the method will yield a maximum of `5` consecutive lines from one file before iterating over another.

With all these methods and much more available, complex pipelines for data extraction and transformation can be set up with minimal effort, as already illustrated in some previous notebooks (for instance, for the *CIFAR* and *Cityscapes* datasets).

Loading

Another advantage of `tf.data` is that all its operations are registered in the TensorFlow operational graph, and the extracted and processed samples are returned as `Tensor` instances. Therefore, we do not have much to do regarding the final step of ETL, that is, the *loading*. As with any other TensorFlow operation or tensor, the library will take care of loading them into the target devices—unless we want to choose them ourselves (for instance, wrapping the creation of datasets with `tf.device()`). When we start iterating over a `tf.data` dataset, generated samples can be directly passed to the models.

Optimizing and monitoring input pipelines

While this API simplifies the setting up of efficient input pipelines, some best practices should be followed to fully harness its power. After sharing some recommendations from TensorFlow creators, we will also present how to monitor and reuse pipelines.

Following best practices for optimization

The API provides several methods and options to optimize the data processing and flow, which we will now cover in detail.

Parallelizing and prefetching

By default, most of the dataset methods are processing samples one by one, with no parallelism. However, this behavior can be easily changed, for example, to take advantage of multiple CPU cores. For instance, the `.interleave()` and `.map()` methods both have a `num_parallel_calls` parameter to specify the number of threads they can create (refer to the documentation at `https://www.tensorflow.org/api_docs/python/tf/data/Dataset`). **Parallelizing** the extraction and transformation of images can greatly decrease the time needed to generate training batches, so it is important to always properly set `num_parallel_calls` (for instance, to the number of CPU cores the processing machine has).

TensorFlow also provides `tf.data.experimental.parallel_interleave()` (refer to the documentation at https://www.tensorflow.org/versions/r2.0/api_docs/python/tf/data/experimental/parallel_interleave), a parallelized version of `.interleave()` with some additional options. For instance, it has a `sloppy` parameter, which, if set to `True`, allows each thread to return its output as soon as it is ready. On the one hand, this means that the data will no longer be returned in a deterministic order, but, on the other hand, this can further improve the pipeline performance.

Another performance-related feature of `tf.data` is the possibility to *prefetch* data samples. When applied through the dataset's `.prefetch(buffer_size)` method, this feature allows the input pipelines to start preparing the next samples while the current ones are being consumed, instead of waiting for the next dataset call. Concretely, this allows TensorFlow to start preparing the next training batch(es) on the CPU(s), while the current batch is being used by the model running on the GPU(s), for instance.

Prefetching basically enables the *parallelization of the data preparation and training operations* in a *producer-consumer* fashion. Enabling parallel calls and prefetching can thus be done with minor changes, while greatly reducing the training time, as follows:

```
dataset = tf.data.TextLineDataset('/path/to/file.txt')
dataset = dataset.map(parse_fn, num_threads).batch(batch_size).prefetch(1)
```

Inspired by TensorFlow's official guide (https://www.tensorflow.org/guide/performance/datasets), *Figure 7-2* illustrates the performance gain these best practices can bring:

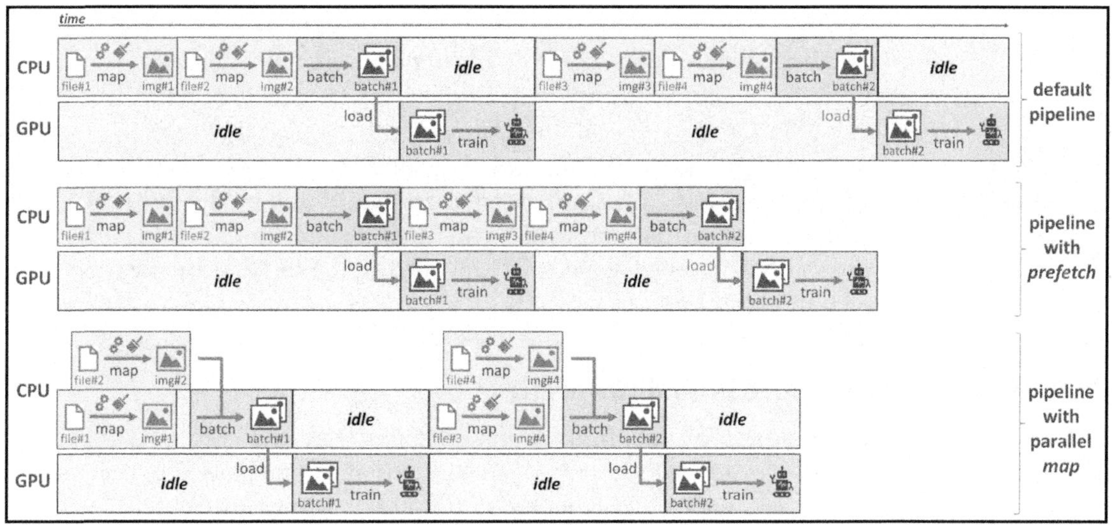

Figure 7-2: Visual representation of the performance gain obtained from parallelizing and prefetching

By combining these different optimizations, CPU/GPU idle time can be reduced further. The performance gain in terms of preprocessing time can become really significant, as demonstrated in one of the Jupyter notebooks for this chapter.

Fusing operations

It is also useful to know that `tf.data` offers functions that combine some key operations for greater performance or more reliable results.

For example, `tf.data.experimental.shuffle_and_repeat(buffer_size, count, seed)` fuses together the shuffling and repeating operations, making it easy to have datasets shuffled differently at each epoch (refer to the documentation at `https://www.tensorflow.org/versions/r2.0/api_docs/python/tf/data/experimental/shuffle_and_repeat`).

Back to optimization matters, `tf.data.experimental.map_and_batch(map_func, batch_size, num_parallel_batches, ...)` (refer to the documentation at `https://www.tensorflow.org/versions/r2.0/api_docs/python/tf/data/experimental/map_and_batch`) applies the `map_func` function and then batches the results together. By fusing these two operations, this solution prevents some computational overheads and should thus be preferred.

`map_and_batch()` is meant to disappear, as TensorFlow 2 is implementing several tools to automatically optimize the `tf.data` operations, for instance, grouping multiple `.map()` calls together, vectorizing the `.map()` operations and fusing them directly with `.batch()`, fusing `.map()` and `.filter()`, and more. Once this automatic optimization has been fully implemented and validated by the TensorFlow community, there will be no further need for `map_and_batch()` (once again, this may already be the case by the time you reach this chapter).

Passing options to ensure global properties

In TensorFlow 2, it is also possible to configure datasets by *setting global options,* which will affect all their operations. `tf.data.Options` is a structure that can be passed to datasets through their `.with_options(options)` method and that has several attributes to parametrize the datasets (refer to the documentation at `https://www.tensorflow.org/api_docs/python/tf/data/Options`).

For instance, if the `.experimental_autotune` Boolean attribute is set to `True`, TensorFlow will automatically tune the values of `num_parallel_calls` for all the dataset's operations, according to the capacity of the target machine(s).

The attribute currently named `.experimental_optimization` contains a set of *sub-options* related to the automatic optimization of the dataset's operations (refer to the previous information box). For example, its own `.map_and_batch_fusion` attribute can be set to `True` to let TensorFlow automatically fuse the `.map()` and `.batch()` calls; `.map_parallelization` can be set to `True` to let TensorFlow automatically parallelize some of the mapping functions, and so on, as follows:

```
options = tf.data.Options()
options.experimental_optimization.map_and_batch_fusion = True
dataset = dataset.with_options(options)
```

Plenty of other options are available (and more may come). We invite our readers to have a look at the documentation, especially if the performance of their input pipelines is a key matter.

Monitoring and reusing datasets

We presented multiple tools to optimize `tf.data` pipelines, but how can we make sure they positively affect the performance? Are there other tools to figure out which operations may be slowing down the data flow? In the following paragraphs, we will answer these questions by demonstrating how input pipelines can be monitored, as well as how they can be cached and restored for later use.

Aggregating performance statistics

One of the novelties of TensorFlow 2 is the possibility to aggregate some statistics regarding `tf.data` pipelines, such as their latency (for the whole process and/or for each operation) or the number of bytes produced by each of their elements.

TensorFlow can be notified to gather these metric values for a dataset *through its global options* (refer to previous paragraphs). The `tf.data.Options` instances have a `.experimental_stats` field from the `tf.data.experimental.StatsOption` class (refer to the documentation at https://www.tensorflow.org/versions/r2.0/api_docs/python/tf/data/experimental/StatsOptions). This class defines several options related to the aforementioned dataset metrics (for instance, setting `.latency_all_edges` to `True` to measure the latency). It also has a `.aggregator` attribute, which can receive an instance of `tf.data.experimental.StatsAggregator` (refer to the documentation at https://www.tensorflow.org/versions/r2.0/api_docs/python/tf/data/experimental/StatsAggregator). As its name implies, this object will be attached to the dataset and aggregate the requested statistics, providing summaries that can be logged and visualized in TensorBoard, as shown in the following code sample.

At the time of writing this book, these features are still highly experimental and are not fully implemented yet. For example, there is no easy way to log the summaries containing the aggregated statistics. Given how important monitoring tools are, we still covered these features, believing they should soon be fully available.

Dataset statistics can, therefore, be aggregated and saved (for instance, for TensorBoard) as follows:

```
# Use utility function to tell TF to gather latency stats for this dataset:
dataset = dataset.apply(tf.data.experimental.latency_stats("data_latency"))
# Link stats aggregator to dataset through the global options:
stats_aggregator = tf.data.experimental.StatsAggregator()
options = tf.data.Options()
options.experimental_stats.aggregator = stats_aggregator
dataset = dataset.with_options(options)
```

```
# Later, aggregated stats can be obtained as summary, for instance, to log
them:
summary_writer = tf.summary.create_file_writer('/path/to/summaries/folder')
with summary_writer.as_default():
    stats_summary = stats_aggregator.get_summary()
    # ... log summary with `summary_writer` for Tensorboard (TF2 support
coming soon)
```

Note that it is possible to obtain statistics not only for the input pipeline as a whole, but also for each of its inner operations.

Caching and reusing datasets

Finally, TensorFlow offers several functions to *cache* generated samples or to save `tf.data` pipeline states.

Samples can be cached by calling the dataset's `.cache(filename)` method. If cached, data will not have to undergo the same transformations when iterated over again (that is, for the next epochs). Note that the content of the cached data will not be the same depending on when the method is applied. Take the following example:

```
dataset = tf.data.TextLineDataset('/path/to/file.txt')
dataset_v1 = dataset.cache('cached_textlines.temp').map(parse_fn)
dataset_v2 = dataset.map(parse_fn).cache('cached_images.temp')
```

The first dataset will cache the samples returned by `TextLineDataset`, that is, the text lines (the cached data is stored in the specified file, `cached_textlines.temp`). The transformation done by `parse_fn` (for instance, opening and decoding the corresponding image file for each text line) will have to be repeated for each epoch. On the other hand, the second dataset is caching the samples returned by `parse_fn`, that is, the images. While this may save precious computational time for the next epochs, this also means caching all the resulting images, which may be memory inefficient. Therefore, caching should be carefully thought through.

Finally, it is also possible to *save the state of a dataset*, for instance, so that if the training is somehow stopped, it can be resumed without re-iterating over the precedent input batches. As mentioned in the documentation, this feature can have a positive impact on models being trained on a small number of different batches (and thus with a risk of overfitting). For estimators, one solution to save the iterator state of a dataset is to set up the following hook—`tf.data.experimental.CheckpointInputPipelineHook` (refer to the documentation at https://www.tensorflow.org/api_docs/python/tf/data/experimental/CheckpointInputPipelineHook).

Aware of how important a configurable and optimized data flow is to machine learning applications, TensorFlow developers are continuously providing new features to refine the `tf.data` API. As covered in this past section and illustrated in the related Jupyter Notebook, taking advantage of these features—even the experimental ones—can greatly reduce implementation overheads and training time.

How to deal with data scarcity

Being able to efficiently extract and transform data for the training of complex applications is primordial, but this is assuming that *enough data* is available for such tasks in the first place. After all, NNs are *data-hungry* methods and even though we are in the big data era, large enough datasets are still tenuous to gather and even more difficult to annotate. It can take several minutes to annotate a single image (for instance, to create the ground truth label map for semantic segmentation models), and some annotations may have to be validated/corrected by experts (for instance, when labeling medical pictures). In some cases, images themselves may not be easily available. For instance, it would be too time- and money-consuming to take pictures of every manufactured object and their components when building automation models for industrial plants.

Data scarcity is, therefore, a common problem in computer vision, and much effort has been expended trying to train robust models despite the lack of training images or rigorous annotations. In this section, we will cover several solutions proposed over the years, and we will demonstrate their benefits and limitations in relation to various tasks.

Augmenting datasets

We have been mentioning this first approach since `Chapter 4`, *Influential Classification Tools,* and we have already put it into use for some applications in previous notebooks. This is finally the opportunity for us to properly present what **data augmentation** is and how to apply it with TensorFlow 2.

Overview

As indicated before, *augmenting* datasets means applying random transformations to their content in order to obtain different-looking versions for each. We will present the benefits of this procedure, as well as some related best practices.

Why augment datasets?

Data augmentation is probably the most common and simple method to deal with overly small training sets. It can virtually multiply their number of images by providing different looking versions of each. These various versions are obtained by applying a combination of random transformations, such as scale jittering, random flipping, rotation, and color shift. Data augmentation can incidentally help *prevent overfitting*, which would usually happen when training a large model on a small set of images.

But even when enough training images are available, this procedure should still be considered. Indeed, data augmentation has other benefits. Even large datasets can suffer from *biases*, and data augmentation can compensate for some of them. We will illustrate this concept with an example. Let's imagine we want to build a classifier for brush versus pen pictures. However, the pictures for each class were gathered by two different teams that did not agree on a precise acquisition protocol beforehand (for instance, which camera model or lighting conditions to opt for). As a result, the *brush* training images are clearly darker and noisier than the *pen* ones. Since NNs are trained to use any visual cues to predict correctly, the models learning on such a dataset may end up relying on these obvious lighting/noise differences to classify the objects, instead of purely focusing on the object representations (such as their shape and texture). Once in production, these models will fare poorly, no longer being able to rely on these biases. This example is illustrated in *Figure 7-3*:

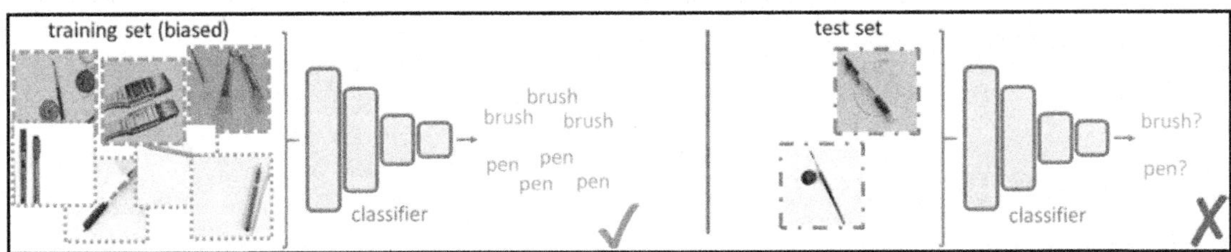

Figure 7-3: Example of a classifier trained on a biased dataset, unable to apply its knowledge to the target data

Randomly adding some noise to the pictures or randomly adjusting their brightness would prevent the networks from relying on these cues. These augmentations would thus partially compensate for the dataset's biases, and make these visual differences too unpredictable to be used by the networks (that is, preventing models from overfitting biased datasets).

Augmentations can also be used to improve the dataset's coverage. Training datasets cannot cover all image variations (otherwise we would not have to build machine learning models to deal with new different images). If, for example, all the images of a dataset were shot under the same light, then the recognition models trained on them would fare really poorly with images taken under different lighting conditions. These models were basically not taught that *lighting conditions is a thing* and that they should learn to ignore it and focus on the actual image content. Therefore, randomly editing the brightness of the training images before passing them to the networks would educate them on this visual property. By better preparing them for the variability of target images, data augmentation helps us to train more robust solutions.

Considerations

Data augmentation can take multiple forms, and several options should be considered when performing this procedure. First of all, data augmentation can be done either offline or online. Offline augmentation means transforming all the images before the training even starts, and saving the various versions for later use. Online means applying the transformations when generating each new batch inside the training input pipelines.

Since augmentation operations can be computationally heavy, applying them beforehand and storing the results can be advantageous in terms of latency for the input pipelines. However, this implies having enough memory space to store the augmented dataset, often limiting the number of different versions generated. By randomly transforming the images on the fly, online solutions can provide different looking versions for every epoch. While computationally more expensive, this means presenting more variation to the networks. The choice between offline and online augmentation is thus conditioned by the memory/processing capacity of the available devices, and by the desired variability.

The variability is itself conditioned by the choice of transformations to be applied. For example, if only random horizontal and vertical flipping operations are applied, then this means a maximum of four different versions per image. Depending on the size of the original dataset, you could consider applying the transformations offline and storing the four-times-larger dataset. On the other hand, if operations such as random cropping and random color shift are considered, then the number of possible variations can become almost infinite.

When setting up data augmentation, the first thing to do, therefore, is to shortlist the relevant transformations (and their parameters when applicable). The list of possible operations is huge, but not all make sense with regard to the target data and use cases. For instance, vertical flipping should only be considered if the content of images can be naturally found upside down (such as close-up images of larger systems or birdview/satellite images). Vertically flipping images of urban scenes (such as the *Cityscapes* images) would not help the models at all, since they would (hopefully) never be confronted with such upside down images.

Similarly, you should be careful to properly parameterize some transformations such as cropping or brightness adjustment. If an image becomes so dark/bright that its content cannot be identified anymore, or if the key elements are cropped out, then the models won't learn anything from training on this edited picture (it may even confuse them if too many images are inappropriately augmented). Therefore, it is important to shortlist and parametrize transformations that add meaningful variations to the dataset (with respect to the target use cases) while preserving its semantic content.

Figure 7-4 provides some examples of what invalid and valid augmentations can be for an autonomous driving application:

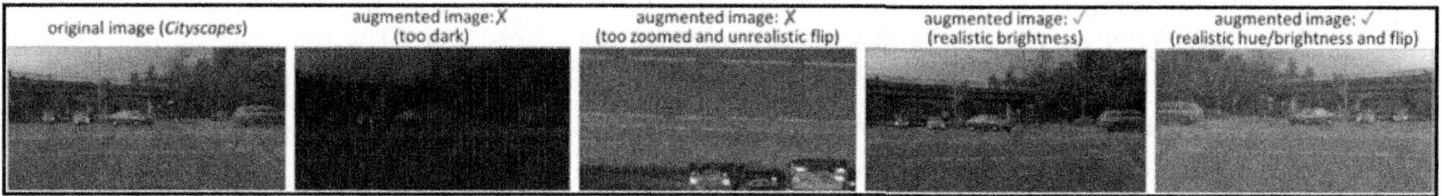

Figure 7-4: Valid/invalid augmentations for an autonomous driving application

It is also important to keep in mind that data augmentation cannot fully compensate for data scarcity. If we want a model to be able to recognize cats, but only have training images of Persian cats, no straightforward image transformations will help our model identify other cat breeds (for instance, Sphynx cats).

Some advanced data augmentation solutions include applying computer graphics or encoder-decoder methods to alter images. For example, computer graphics algorithms could be used to add fake sun blares or motion blur, and CNNs could be trained to transform daytime images into nighttime ones. We will develop some of these techniques later in this chapter.

Finally, you should not forget to transform the labels accordingly, when applicable. This especially concerns detection and segmentation labels, when geometrical transformations are performed. If an image is resized or rotated, its related label map or bounding boxes should undergo the same operation(s) to stay aligned (refer to the *Cityscapes* experiments in `Chapter 6`, *Enhancing and Segmenting Images*).

Augmenting images with TensorFlow

Having clarified *why* and *when* images should be augmented, it is time to properly explain *how*. We will introduce some useful tools provided by TensorFlow to transform images, sharing a number of concrete examples.

TensorFlow Image module

Python offers a huge variety of frameworks to manipulate and transform images. Besides the generic ones such as *OpenCV* (`https://opencv.org`) and *Python Imaging Library* (PIL—`http://effbot.org/zone/pil-index.htm`), some packages specialize in providing data augmentation methods for machine learning systems. Among those, `imgaug` by Alexander Jung (`https://github.com/aleju/imgaug`) and `Augmentor` by Marcus D. Bloice (`https://github.com/mdbloice/Augmentor`) are probably the most widely used, both offering a wide range of operations and a neat interface. Even Keras provides functions to preprocess and augment image datasets. `ImageDataGenerator` (`https://keras.io/preprocessing/image`) can be used to instantiate an image batch generator covering data augmentation (such as image rotation, zoom, or channel shifting).

However, TensorFlow has its own module for image processing that can seamlessly integrate `tf.data` pipelines—`tf.image` (refer to the documentation at `https://www.tensorflow.org/api_docs/python/tf/image`). This module contains all sorts of functions. Some of them implement common image-related metrics (for instance, `tf.image.psnr()` and `tf.image.ssim()`), and others can be used to convert images from one format to another (for instance, `tf.image.rgb_to_grayscale()`). But before all else, `tf.image` implements multiple image transformations. Most of these functions come in pairs—one function implementing a fixed version of the operation (such as `tf.image.central_crop()`, `tf.image.flip_left_right()` and `tf.image.adjust_jpeg_quality()`) and the other a randomized version (such as `tf.image.random_crop()`, `tf.image.random_flip_left_right()`, and `tf.image.random_jpeg_quality()`). The randomized functions usually take for arguments a range of values from which the attributes of the transformation are randomly sampled (such as `min_jpeg_quality` and `max_jpeg_quality` for `tf.image.random_jpeg_quality()` parameters).

Directly applicable to image tensors (single or batched), the `tf.image` functions are recommended within `tf.data` pipelines for online augmentation (grouping the operations into a function passed to `.map()`).

Example – augmenting images for our autonomous driving application

In the previous chapter, we introduced some state-of-the-art models for semantic segmentation and applied them to urban scenes in order to guide self-driving cars. In the related Jupyter notebooks, we provided an `_augmentation_fn(img, gt_img)` function passed to `dataset.map()` to augment the pictures and their ground truth label maps. Though we did not provide detailed explanations back then, this augmentation function illustrates well how `tf.image` can augment complex data.

For example, it offers a simple solution to the problem of transforming both the input images and their dense labels. Imagine we want some of the samples to be randomly horizontally flipped. If we call `tf.image.random_flip_left_right()` once for the input image and once for the ground truth label map, there is only a half chance that both images will undergo the same transformation.

One solution to ensure that the same set of geometrical transformations are applied to the image pairs is the following:

```
img_dim, img_ch = tf.shape(img)[-3:-1], tf.shape(img)[-1]
# Stack/concatenate the image pairs along the channel axis:
stacked_imgs = tf.concat([img, tf.cast(gt_img, img.dtype)], -1)
# Apply the random operations, for instance, horizontal flipping:
stacked_imgs = tf.image.random_flip_left_right(stacked_imgs)
# ... or random cropping (for instance, keeping from 80 to 100% of the
images):
rand_factor = tf.random.uniform([], minval=0.8, maxval=1.)
crop_shape = tf.cast(tf.cast(img_dim, tf.float32) * rand_factor, tf.int32)
crop_shape = tf.concat([crop_shape, tf.shape(stacked_imgs)[-1]], axis=0)
stacked_imgs = tf.image.random_crop(stacked_imgs, crop_shape)
# [...] (apply additional geometrical transformations)
# Unstack to recover the 2 augmented tensors:
img = stacked_imgs[..., :img_ch]
gt_img = tf.cast(stacked_imgs[..., img_ch:], gt_img.dtype)
# Apply other transformations in the pixel domain, for instance:
img = tf.image.random_brightness(image, max_delta=0.15)
```

Since most `tf.image` geometrical functions do not have any limitations regarding the number of channels the images can have, concatenating images along the channel axis beforehand is a simple trick to ensure that they undergo the same geometrical operations.

The preceding example also illustrates how some operations can be further randomized by sampling some parameters from random distributions. `tf.image.random_crop(images, size)` returns crops of a fixed size, extracted from random positions in the images. Picking a size factor with `tf.random.uniform()`, we obtain crops that are not only randomly positioned in the original images, but also randomly dimensioned.

Finally, this example is also a reminder that *not* all transformations should be applied to both the input images and their label maps. Trying to adjust the brightness or saturation of label maps would not make sense (and would, in some cases, raise an exception).

We will conclude this subsection on data augmentation by emphasizing that this procedure should always be considered. Even when training on large datasets, augmenting their images can only make the models more robust—as long as the random transformations are selected and applied with care.

Rendering synthetic datasets

However, what if we have no images to train on, at all? A common solution in computer vision is the use of *synthetic datasets*. In the following subsection, we will explain what synthetic images are, how they can be generated, and what their limitations are.

Overview

Let's first clarify what is meant by *synthetic images*, and why they are so often used in computer vision.

Rise of 3D databases

As mentioned in the introduction of this section on data scarcity, the complete lack of training images is not that uncommon a situation, especially in industry. Gathering hundreds of images for each new element to recognize is costly, and sometimes completely impractical (for instance, when the target objects are not produced yet or are only available at some remote location).

However, for industrial applications and others, it is increasingly common to have access to 3D models of the target objects or scenes (such as 3D **computer-aided design** (**CAD**) blueprints or 3D scenes captured with depth sensors). Large datasets of 3D models have even multiplied on the web. With the coincidental development of computer graphics, this led more and more experts to use such 3D databases to *render* synthetic images on which to train their recognition models.

Benefits of synthetic data

Synthetic images are thus images generated by computer graphics libraries from 3D models. Thanks to the lucrative entertainment industry, computer graphics have indeed come a long way, and rendering engines can nowadays generate highly realistic images from 3D models (such as for video games, 3D animated movies, and special effects). It did not take long for scientists to see the potential for computer vision.

Given some detailed 3D models of the target objects/scenes, it is possible with modern 3D engines to render huge datasets of pseudo-realistic images. With proper scripting, you can, for instance, render images of target objects from every angle, at various distances, with different lighting conditions or backgrounds, and so on. Using various rendering methods, it is even possible to simulate different types of cameras and sensors (for instance, depth sensors such as the *Microsoft Kinect* or *Occipital Structure* sensors).

Having full control over the scene/image content, you can also easily obtain all kinds of ground truth labels for each synthetic image (such as precise 3D positions of the rendered models or object masks). For example, targeting driving scenarios, a team of researchers from the Universitat Autònoma de Barcelona built virtual replicas of city environments and used them to render multiple datasets of urban scenes, named *SYNTHIA* (`http://synthia-dataset.net`). This dataset is similar to *Cityscapes* (`https://www.cityscapes-dataset.com`), though larger.

Another team from the Technical University of Darmstadt and Intel Labs successfully demonstrated self-driving models trained on images taken from the realistic looking video game *Grand Theft Auto V (GTA 5)* (`https://download.visinf.tu-darmstadt.de/data/from_games`).

These three datasets are presented in *Figure 7-5*:

Figure 7-5: Samples from the *Cityscapes*, *SYNTHIA*, and *Playing for Data* datasets (links to the datasets are provided in the section). Images and their class labels are superposed

Besides the generation of static datasets, 3D models and game engines can also be used to create *interactive simulation environments*. After all, *simulation-based learning* is commonly used to teach humans complex skills, for instance, when it would be too dangerous or complicated to learn in real conditions (for instance, simulating zero gravity environments to teach astronauts how to perform some tasks once in space, and building game-based platforms to help surgeons learning on virtual patients). If it works for humans, why not machines? Companies and research labs have been developing a multitude of simulation frameworks covering various applications (robotics, autonomous driving, surveillance, and so on).

In these virtual environments, people can train and test their models. At each time step, the models receive some visual inputs from the environments, which they can use to take further action, affecting the simulation, and so on (this kind of interactive training is actually central to *reinforcement learning* as mentioned in `Chapter 1`, *Computer Vision and Neural Networks*).

Synthetic datasets and virtual environments are used to compensate for the lack of real training data or to avoid the consequences of directly applying immature solutions to complex or dangerous situations.

Generating synthetic images from 3D models

Computer graphics is a vast and fascinating domain by itself. In the following paragraphs, we will simply point out some useful tools and ready-to-use frameworks for those in need of rendering data for their applications.

Rendering from 3D models

Generating images from 3D models is a complex, multi-step process. Most 3D models are represented by a *mesh*, a set of small *faces* (usually triangles) delimited by *vertices* (that is, points in the 3D space) representing the model's surface. Some models also contain some *texture or color information*, indicating which color each vertex or small surface should be. Finally, models can be placed into a larger 3D scene (translated/rotated). Given a virtual camera defined by its **intrinsic parameters** (such as its focal length and principal point) and its own pose in the 3D scene, the task is to render what the camera sees of the scene. This procedure is presented in a simplified manner in the following *Figure 7-6*:

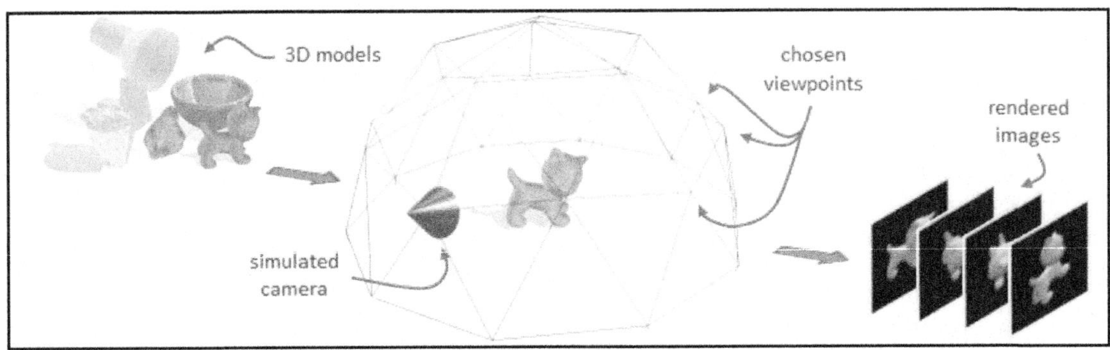

Figure 7-6: Simplistic representation of a 3D rendering pipeline (3D models are from the LineMOD dataset—http://campar.in.tum.de/Main/StefanHinterstoisser)

Converting a 3D scene into a 2D image thus implies multiple transformations, projecting the faces of each model from 3D coordinates relative to the object to coordinates relative to the whole scene (world coordinates), then, relative to the camera (camera coordinates), and finally to 2D coordinates relative to the image space (image coordinates). All these projections can be expressed as direct *matrix multiplications*, but constitute (alas) only a small part of the rendering process. Surface colors should also be properly interpolated, *visibility* should be respected (elements occluded by others should not be drawn), realistic light effects should be applied (for instance, illumination, reflection, and refraction), and so on.

Operations are numerous and computationally heavy. Thankfully for us, GPUs were originally built to efficiently perform them, and frameworks such as *OpenGL* (`https://www.opengl.org`) have been developed to help interface with the GPUs for computer graphics (for instance, to load vertices/faces in the GPUs as *buffers*, or to define programs named *shaders* to specify how to project and color scenes) and streamline some of the process.

Most of the modern computer languages offer libraries built on top of *OpenGL*, such as `PyOpenGL` (`http://pyopengl.sourceforge.net`) or the object-oriented `vispy` (`http://vispy.org`) for Python. Applications such as *Blender* (`https://www.blender.org`) provide graphical interfaces to also build and render 3D scenes. While it requires some effort to master all these tools, they are extremely versatile and can be immensely helpful to render any kind of synthetic data.

However, it is good to keep in mind that, as we previously mentioned, labs and companies have been sharing many higher-level frameworks to render synthetic datasets specifically for machine learning applications. For example, Michael Gschwandtner and Roland Kwitt from the University of Salzburg developed *BlenSor* (`https://www.blensor.org`), a Blender-based application to simulate all kinds of sensors (*BlenSor: blender sensor simulation toolbox*, Springer, 2011); more recently, Simon Brodeur and a group of researchers from various backgrounds shared the *HoME-Platform*, simulating a variety of indoor environments for intelligent systems (*HoME: A household multimodal environment*, ArXiv, 2017).

When manually setting up a complete rendering pipeline or using a specific simulation system, in both cases, the end goal is to render a large amount of training data with ground truths and enough variation (viewpoints, lighting conditions, textures, and more).

To better illustrate these notions, a complete notebook is dedicated to rendering synthetic datasets from 3D models, briefly covering concepts such as *3D meshes*, *shaders*, and *view matrices*. A simple renderer is implemented using `vispy`.

Post-processing synthetic images

While 3D models of target objects are often available in industrial contexts, it is rare to have a 3D representation of the environments they will be found in (for instance, a 3D model of the industrial plant). The 3D objects/scenes then appear isolated, with no proper background. But, like any other visual content, if models are not trained to deal with background/clutter, they won't be able to perform properly once confronted with real images. Therefore, it is common for researchers to post-process synthetic images, for instance, to merge them with relevant background pictures (replacing the blank background with pixel values from images of related environments).

While some augmentation operations could be taken care of by the rendering pipeline (such as brightness changes or motion blur), other 2D transformations are still commonly applied to synthetic data during training. This additional post-processing is once again done to reduce the risk of overfitting and to increase the robustness of the models.

In May 2019, **TensorFlow Graphics** was released. This module provides a computer graphics pipeline to generate images from 3D models. Because this rendering pipeline is composed of novel differentiable operations, it can be tightly combined with—or integrated into—NNs (these graphics operations are differentiable, so the training loss can be backpropagated through them, like any other NN layer). With more and more features being added to TensorFlow Graphics (such as 3D visualization add-ons for TensorBoard and additional rendering options), it will certainly become a central component of solutions dealing with 3D applications or applications relying on synthetic training data. More information, as well as detailed tutorials, can be found in the related GitHub repository (`https://github.com/tensorflow/graphics`).

Problem – realism gap

Though rendering synthetic images has enabled a variety of computer vision applications, it is, however, not the perfect remedy for data scarcity (or at least not yet). While computer graphics frameworks can nowadays render hyper-realistic images, they *need detailed 3D models* for that (with precise surfaces and high-quality texture information). Gathering the data to build such models is as *expensive* as—if not more than—directly building a dataset of real images for the target objects.

Because 3D models sometimes have simplified geometries or lack texture-related information, realistic synthetic datasets are not that common. This **realism gap** between the rendered training data and the real target images *harms the performance* of the models. The visual cues they have learned to rely on while training on synthetic data may not appear in real images (which may have differently saturated colors, more complex textures or surfaces, and so on).

Even when the 3D models are properly depicting the original objects, it often happens that the appearance of these objects changes over time (for instance, from wear and tear).

Currently, a lot of effort is being devoted to tackling the realism gap for computer vision. While some experts are working on building more realistic 3D databases or developing more advanced simulation tools, others are coming up with new machine learning models that are able to transfer the knowledge they acquired from synthetic environments to real situations. The latter approach will be the topic of this chapter's final subsection.

Leveraging domain adaptation and generative models (VAEs and GANs)

Domain adaptation methods were briefly mentioned in `Chapter 4`, *Influential Classification Tools*, among transfer learning strategies. Their goal is to transpose the knowledge acquired by models from one *source domain* (that is, one data distribution) to another *target domain*. Resulting models should be able to properly recognize samples from the new distribution, even if they were not directly trained on it. This fits scenarios when training samples from the target domain are unavailable, but other related datasets are considered as training substitutes.

Suppose we want to train a model to classify household tools in real scenes, but we only have access to uncluttered product pictures provided by the manufacturers. Without domain adaptation, models trained on these advertising pictures will not perform properly on target images with actual clutter, poor lighting, and other discrepancies.

Training recognition models on synthetic data so that they can be applied to real images has also become a common application for domain adaptation methods. Indeed, synthetic images and real pictures of the same semantic content can be considered as two different data distributions, that is, two domains with different levels of detail, noise, and so on.

In this section, we will consider the following two different flavors of approaches:

- Domain adaptation methods that aim to train models so that they perform indifferently on the source and target domains
- Methods for adapting the training images to make them more similar to the target images

Training models to be robust to domain changes

A first approach to domain adaptation is to encourage the models to focus on robust features, which can be found in both the source and target domains. Multiple solutions following this approach have been proposed, contingent on the availability of target data during training.

Supervised domain adaptation

Sometimes, you may be lucky enough to have access to some pictures from the target domain and relevant annotations, besides a larger source dataset (for instance, of synthetic images). This is typically the case in industry, where companies have to find a compromise between the high cost of gathering enough target images to train recognition models, and the performance drop they would experience if models are taught on synthetic data only.

Thankfully, multiple studies have demonstrated that adding even a small number of target samples to training sets can boost the final performance of the algorithms. The following two main reasons are usually put forward:

- Even if scarce, this provides the models with some information on the target domain. To minimize their training loss over all samples, the networks will have to learn how to process this handful of added images (this can even be accentuated by weighing the loss more for these images).
- Since source and target distributions are, by definition, different, mixed datasets display *greater visual variability*. As previously explained, models will have to learn more robust features, which can be beneficial once applied to target images only (for example, models become better prepared to deal with varied data, and thus better prepared for whatever the target image distribution is).

A direct parallel can also be made with the transfer learning methods we explored in `Chapter 4`, *Influential Classification Tools* (training models first on a large source dataset, and then fine-tuning them on the smaller target training set). As mentioned then, the closer the source data is to the target domain, the more efficient such a training scheme becomes—and the other way around (in a Jupyter Notebook, we highlight these limitations, training our segmentation model for self-driving cars on synthetic images too far removed from the target distribution).

Unsupervised domain adaptation

When preparing training datasets, gathering images is often not the main problem. But properly annotating these images is, as it is a tedious and therefore costly procedure. Plenty of domain adaptation methods are thus targeting these scenarios when only source images, their corresponding annotations, and target images are available. With no ground truth, these target samples cannot be directly used to train the models in the usual *supervised* manner. Instead, researchers have been exploring *unsupervised* schemes to take advantage of the visual information these images still provide of the target domain.

For example, works such as *Learning Transferable Features with Deep Adaptation Networks*, by Mingsheng Long et al. (from Tsinghua University, China) are adding constraints to some layers of the models, so that the feature maps they generate have the same distribution, whichever domain the input images belong to. The training scheme proposed by this flavor of approach can be oversimplified as the following:

1. For several iterations, train the model on source batches in a supervised manner.
2. Once in a while, feed the training set to the model and compute the distribution (for instance, mean and variance) of the feature maps generated by the layers we want to adapt.
3. Similarly, feed the set of target images to the model and compute the distribution of the resulting feature maps.
4. Optimize each layer to reduce the distance between the two distributions.
5. Repeat the whole process until you achieve convergence.

Without the need for target labels, these solutions force the networks to learn features that can transfer to both domains while the networks are trained on the source data (the constraints are usually added to the last convolutional layers in charge of feature extraction, as the first ones are often generic enough already).

Other methods are taking into account an implicit label always available in these training scenarios—the domain each image belongs to (that is, *source* or *target*). This information can be used to train a supervised binary classifier—given an image or feature volume, its task is to predict whether it comes from the source or target domain. This secondary model can be trained along with the main one, to guide it toward extracting features that could belong to any of the two domains.

For example, in their **Domain-Adversarial Neural Networks** (**DANN**) paper (published in JMLR, 2016), Hana Ajakan, Yaroslav Ganin, et al. (from Skoltech) proposed adding a secondary head to the models to train (right after their feature extraction layers) whose task is to identify the domain of the input data (binary classification). The training then proceeds as follows (once again, we simplify):

1. Generate a batch of source images and their task-related ground truths to train the main network on it (normal feed-forwarding and backpropagation through the main branch).
2. Generate a batch mixing source and target images with their domain labels and feed it forward through the feature extractor and the secondary branch, which tries to predict the correct domain for each input (*source* or *target*).

3. Backpropagate the domain classification loss normally through the layers of the secondary branch, but then *reverse the gradient* before backpropagating through the feature extractor.
4. Repeat the whole process until convergence, that is, until the main network can perform its task as expected, whereas the domain classification branch can no longer properly predict the domains.

This training procedure is illustrated in *Figure 7-7*:

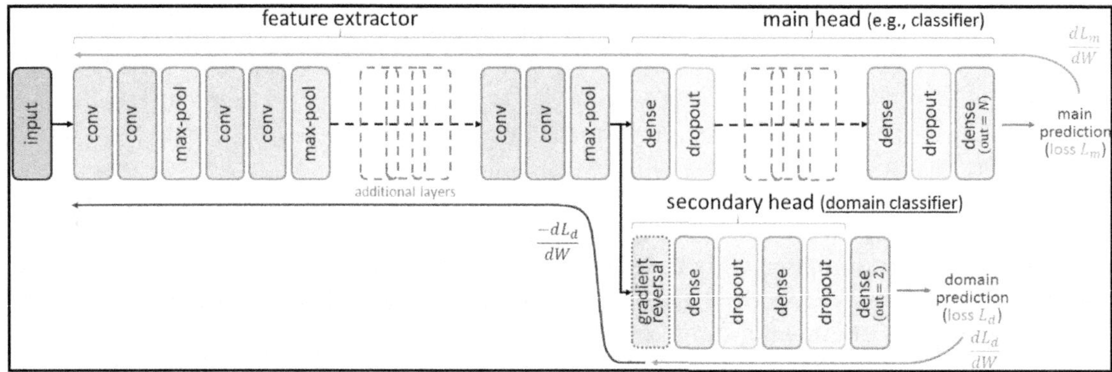

Figure 7-7: DANN concept applied to the training of a classifier

With proper control of the data flow or weighting of the main loss, the three steps can be executed at once in a single iteration. This is demonstrated in the Jupyter Notebook we dedicate to this method.

This scheme got a lot of attention for its cleverness. By *reversing* the gradient from the domain classification loss (that is, multiplying it by *-1*) before propagating it through the feature extractor, its layers will *learn to maximize this loss*, not to *minimize* it. This method is called **adversarial** because the secondary head will keep trying to properly predict the domains, while the upstream feature extractor will learn to *confuse* it. Concretely, this leads the feature extractor to learn features that *cannot* be used to *discriminate* the domains of the input images but are useful to the network's main task (since the normal training of the main head is done in parallel). After training, the domain classification head can simply be discarded.

Note that with TensorFlow 2, it is quite straightforward to manipulate the gradients of specific operations. This can be done by applying the `@tf.custom_gradient` decorator (refer to the documentation at `https://www.tensorflow.org/api_docs/python/tf/custom_gradient`) to functions and by providing the custom gradient operations. Doing so, we can implement the following operation for *DANN*, to be called after the feature extractor and before the domain classification layers in order to reverse the gradient at that point during backpropagation:

```
# This decorator specifies the method has a custom gradient. Along with its
normal output, the method should return the function to compute its
gradient:
@tf.custom_gradient
def reverse_gradient(x): # Flip the gradient's sign.
    y = tf.identity(x) # the value of the tensor itself isn't changed
    return y, lambda dy: tf.math.negative(dy) # output + gradient method
```

Since *DANN*, a multitude of other domain adaptation methods have been released (for instance, *ADDA* and *CyCaDa*), following similar adversarial schemes.

In some cases, annotations for the target images are available, but not with the desired *density* (for instance, with only image-level class labels when the target task is pixel-level semantic segmentation). **Auto-labeling methods** have been proposed for such scenarios. For example, guided by the sparse labels, the models trained on source data are used to predict the denser labels of the target training images. Then, these source labels are added to the training set to refine the models. This process is repeated iteratively until the target labels look correct enough and the models trained on the mixed data have converged.

Domain randomization

Finally, it may happen that *no target data is available* at all for training (no image, no annotation). The performance of the models then relies entirely on the relevance of the source dataset (for instance, how realistic looking and relevant to the task the rendered synthetic images are).

Pushing the concept of data augmentation for synthetic images to the extreme, *domain randomization* can also be considered. Mostly explored by industrial experts, the idea is to train models on large data variations (as described in *Domain randomization for transferring deep neural networks from simulation to the real world*, IEEE, 2017). For example, if we only have access to 3D models of the objects we want the networks to recognize, but we do not know in what kind of scenes these objects may appear, we could use a 3D simulation engine to generate images with a significant number of *random* backgrounds, lights, scene layouts, and so on. The claim is that with enough variability in the simulation, real data may appear just as another variation to the models. As long as the target domain somehow overlaps the randomized training one, the networks would not be completely clueless after training.

Obviously, we cannot expect such NNs to perform as well as any trained on target samples, but domain randomization is a fair solution to desperate situations.

Generating larger or more realistic datasets with VAEs and GANs

The second main type of domain adaptation methods we will cover in this chapter will give us the opportunity to introduce what many call the most interesting development in machine learning these past years—generative models, and, more precisely *VAEs* and *GANs*. Highly popular since they were proposed, these models have been incorporated into a large variety of solutions. Therefore, we will confine ourselves here to a generic introduction, before presenting how these models are applied to dataset generation and domain adaptation.

Discriminative versus generative models

So far, most of the models we have been studying are **discriminative**. Given an input, x, they learn the proper parameters, W, in order to return/discriminate the correct label, y, out of those considered (for instance, x may be an input image and y may be the image class label). A discriminative model can be interpreted as a *function* $f(x ; W) = y$. They can also be interpreted as models trying to learn the *conditional probability distribution*, $p(y|x)$ (meaning *the probability of y given x*; for instance, given a specific picture x, what is the probability that its label is y = "*cat picture*"?).

There is a second category of models we have yet to introduce—*generative* models. Given some samples, x, drawn from an unknown probability distribution, $p(x)$, generative models are trying to *model this distribution*. For example, given some images, x, representing cats, a generative model will attempt to infer the data distribution (what makes these cat pictures, out of all possible pixel combinations) in order to generate new cat images that could belong to the same set as x.

In other words, a discriminative model learns to recognize a picture based on specific features (for instance, it is probably a cat picture because it depicts something with whiskers, paws, and a tail). A generative model learns to sample new images from the input domain, reproducing its typical features (for instance, here is a plausible new cat picture, obtained by generating and combining typical cat features).

As functions, generative CNNs need an input they can process into a new picture. Oftentimes, they are *conditioned by a noise vector*, that is, a tensor, z, sampled from a random distribution (such as $z \sim \mathcal{N}(0, 1)$, meaning z is randomly sampled from a normal distribution of mean $\mu = 0$ and standard deviation $\sigma = 1$). For each random input they receive, the models provide a new image from the distribution they learned to model. When available, generative networks can also be conditioned by the labels, y. In such cases, they have to model the conditional distribution, $p(x|y)$ (for instance, considering the label y = "*cat*", what is the probability of sampling the specific image x)?

According to the majority of experts, generative models hold the key to the next stage of machine learning. To be able to generate a large and varied amount of new data despite their limited number of parameters, networks have to distill the dataset to uncover its structure and key features. They have to *understand* the data.

VAEs

While auto-encoders can also learn some aspects of a data distribution, their goal is only to reconstruct encoded samples, that is, to *discriminate* the original image out of all possible pixel combinations, based on the encoded features. Standard auto-encoders are not meant to *generate* new samples. If we randomly sample a *code* vector from their latent space, chances are high that we will obtain a gibberish image out of their decoder. This is because their latent space is unconstrained and typically *not continuous* (that is, there are usually large regions in the latent space that are not corresponding to any valid image).

Variational auto-encoders (**VAEs**) are particular auto-encoders designed to have continuous latent space, and they are therefore used as generative models. Instead of directly extracting the code corresponding to an image, x, the encoder of a VAE is tasked to provide a simplified estimation of the distribution in the latent space that the image belongs to.

Typically, the encoder is built to return two vectors, respectively representing the mean, $\mu \in \mathbb{R}^n$, and the standard deviation, $\sigma \in \mathbb{R}^n$, of a multivariate normal distribution (for an n-dimensional latent space). Figuratively speaking, the mean represents the *most likely* position of the image in the latent space, and the standard deviation controls the size of the circular area, around that position, where the image *could also be*. From this distribution defined by the encoder, a random code, z, is picked and passed to the decoder. The decoder's task is then to recover image x based on z. Since z can slightly vary for the same image, the decoder has to learn to deal with these variations to return the input image.

To illustrate the differences between them, auto-encoders and VAEs are depicted side by side in *Figure 7-8*:

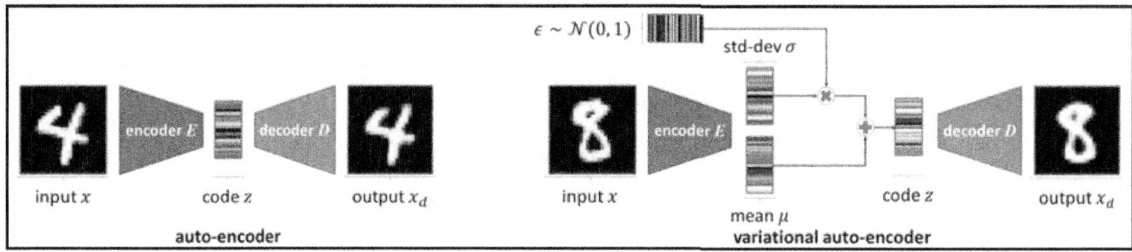

Figure 7-8: Comparison of standard auto-encoders and variational ones

Gradients cannot flow back through random sampling operations. To be able to backpropagate the loss through the encoder despite the sampling of z, a **reparameterization trick** is used. Instead of directly sampling $z \sim \mathcal{N}(\mu, \sigma^2)$, this operation is approximated by $z = \mu + \epsilon\sigma$, with $\epsilon \sim \mathcal{N}(0,1)$. This way, z can be obtained through a derivable operation, considering ϵ as a random vector passed as an additional input to the model.

During training, a loss—usually the **mean-squared error** (**MSE**)—measures how similar the output image is to the input one, as we do for standard auto-encoders. However, another loss is added to VAE models, to make sure the distribution estimated by their encoder is well-defined. Without this constraint, the VAEs could otherwise end up behaving like normal auto-encoders, returning σ null and μ as the images' code. This second loss is based on the **Kullback–Leibler divergence** (named after its creators and usually contracted to *KL divergence*). The KL divergence measures the difference between two probability distributions. It is adapted into a loss, to ensure that the distributions defined by the encoder are close enough to the standard normal distribution, $\mathcal{N}(0,1)$:

$$\mathcal{L}_{KL}\left(\mathcal{N}(\mu,\sigma),\mathcal{N}(0,1)\right) = \frac{1}{2}\left(\sigma^2 + \mu^2 - \log(\sigma^2) - 1\right)$$

With this reparameterization trick and KL divergence, auto-encoders become powerful generative models. Once the models are trained, their encoders can be discarded, and their decoders can be directly used to generate new images, given random vectors, $z \sim \mathcal{N}(0,1)$, as inputs. For example, *Figure 7-9* shows a grid of results for a simple convolutional VAE with a latent space of dimension $n = 2$, trained to generate MNIST-like images (additional details and source code are available as a Jupyter Notebook):

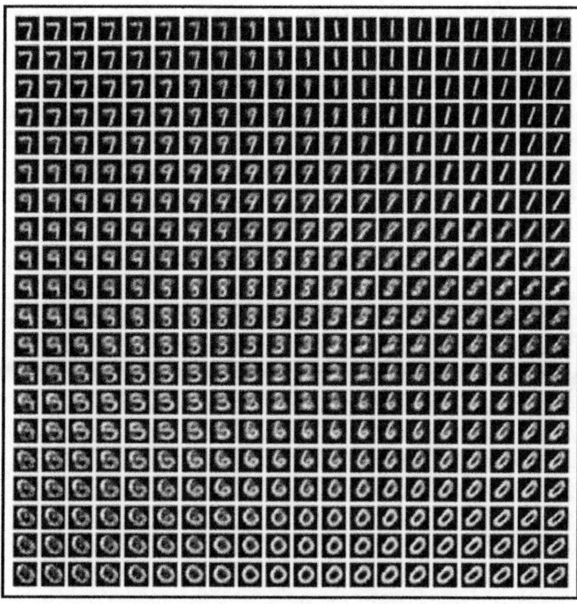

Figure 7-9: Grid of images generated by a simple VAE trained to create MNIST-like results

To generate this grid, the different vectors, *z*, are not randomly picked, but are sampled to homogeneously cover part of the 2D latent space, hence the grid figure that shows the output images for *z* varying from (*-1.5, -1.5*) to (*1.5, 1.5*). We can thus observe the continuity of the latent space, with the content of the resulting images varying from one digit to another.

GANs

First proposed in 2014 by Ian Goodfellow et al. from the University of Montreal, GANs are certainly the most popular solution for generative tasks.

As their name indicates, GANs use an adversarial scheme so they can be trained in an unsupervised manner (this scheme inspired the *DANN* method introduced earlier in this chapter). Having only a number of images, *x*, we want to train a *generator* network to model *p*(*x*), that is, to create new valid images. We thus have no proper ground truth data to directly compare the new images with (since they are *new*). Not able to use a typical loss function, we pit the generator against another network—the **discriminator**.

The discriminator's task is to evaluate whether an image comes from the original dataset (*real* image) or if it was generated by the other network (*fake* image). Like the domain discriminating head in *DANN*, the discriminator is trained in a supervised manner as a binary classifier using the implicit image labels (*real* versus *fake*). Playing against the discriminator, the generator tries to fool it, generating new images conditioned by noise vectors, *z*, so the discriminator believes they are *real* images (that is, sampled from *p(x)*).

When the discriminator predicts the binary class of generated images, its results are backpropagated all the way into the generator. The generator thus learns purely from the *discriminator's feedback*. For example, if the discriminator learns to check whether an image contains whiskers to label it as *real* (if we want to create cat images), then the generator will receive this feedback from backpropagation and learn to draw whiskers (even though only the discriminator was fed with actual cat images!). *Figure 7-10* illustrates the concept of GANs with the generation of handwritten digit images:

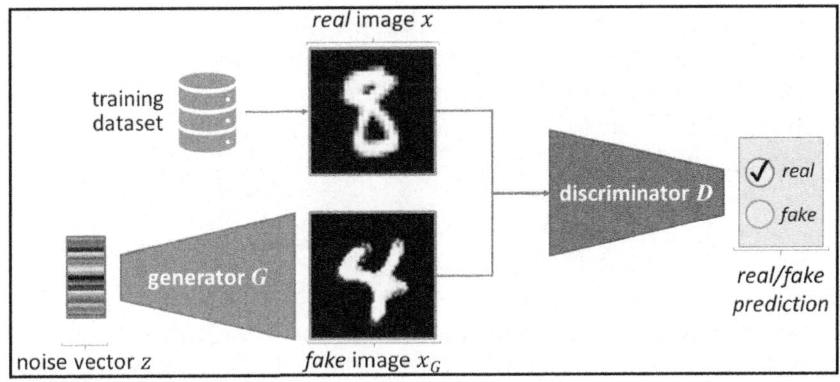

Figure 7-10: GAN representation

GANs were inspired by *game theory*, and their training can be interpreted as a *two-player zero-sum minimax game*. Each phase of the game (that is, each training iteration) takes place as follows:

1. The generator, *G*, receives *N* noise vectors, *z*, and outputs as many images, x_G.
2. These *N fake* images are mixed with *N real* images, *x*, picked from the training set.
3. The discriminator, *D*, is trained on this mixed batch, trying to estimate which images are *real* and which are *fake*.
4. The generator, *G*, is trained on another batch of *N* noise vectors, trying to generate images so that *D* assumes they are real.

Therefore, at each iteration, the discriminator, *D* (parameterized by P_D), tries to maximize the game reward, *V(G, D)*, while the generator, *G* (parameterized by P_G), tries to minimize it:

$$\min_G \max_D V(G, D) = \min_G \max_D \mathbb{E}_x \left[\log D(x, P_D)\right] + \mathbb{E}_z \left[1 - \log D\big(G(z, P_G), P_D\big)\right]$$

Note that this equation assumes that the label *real* is 1 and the label *fake* is 0. The first term of *V(G, D)* represents the averaged log probability estimated by the discriminator, *D*, that the images, *x*, are *real* (*D* should return 1 for each). Its second term represents the averaged log probability estimated by *D* that the generator's outputs are *fake* (*D* should return 0 for each). Therefore, this reward, *V(G, D)*, is used to train the discriminator, *D*, as a classification metric that *D* has to maximize (although in practice, people rather train the network to minimize -*V(G, D)*, out of habit for decreasing losses).

Theoretically, *V(G, D)* should also be used to train the generator, *G*, as a value to minimize this time. However, the gradient of its second term would *vanish* toward 0 if *D* becomes too confident (and the derivative of the first term with respect to P_G is always null, since P_G does not play any role in it). This vanishing gradient can be avoided with a small mathematical change, using instead the following loss to train *G*:

$$\mathcal{L}(G) = -\mathbb{E}_z\left[\log D\big(G(z, P_G), P_D\big)\right]$$

According to game theory, the outcome of this *minimax game* is an *equilibrium* between *G* and *D* (called **Nash equilibrium**, after the mathematician John Forbes Nash Jr, who defined it). Though hard to achieve in practice with GANs, the training should end with *D* unable to differentiate *real* from *fake* (that is, $D(x) = {}^1/_2$ and $D(G(z)) = {}^1/_2$ for all samples) and with *G* modeling the target distribution, *p(x)*.

Though difficult to train, GANs can lead to highly realistic results and are therefore commonly used to generate new data samples (GANs can be applied to any data modality: image, video, speech, text, and more.)

While VAEs are easier to train, GANs usually return crisper results. Using the MSE to evaluate the generated images, VAE results can be slightly blurry, as the models tend to return averaged images to minimize this loss. Generators in GANs cannot cheat this way, as the discriminators would easily spot blurry images as *fake*. Both VAEs and GANs can be used to generate larger training datasets for image-level recognition (for instance, preparing one GAN to create new *dog* images and another to create new *cat* images, to train a *dog* versus *cat* classifier on a larger dataset).

Both VAEs and GANs are implemented in the Jupyter Notebooks provided.

Augmenting datasets with conditional GANs

Another great advantage GANs have is that they can be conditioned by any kind of data. **Conditional GANs (cGANs)** can be trained to model the *conditional distribution, p(x|y)*, that is, to generate images conditioned by a set of input values, *y* (refer to the introduction to generative models). The conditional input, *y*, can be an image, a categorical or continuous label, a noise vector, and more, or any combination of those.

In conditional GANs, the discriminator is edited to receive both an image, x (real or fake), and its corresponding conditional variable, y, as a paired input (that is, $D(x, y)$). Though its output is still a value between *0* and *1* measuring how *real* the input seems, its task is slightly changed. To be considered as *real*, an image should not only look as if drawn from the training dataset; it should also correspond to its paired variable.

Imagine, for instance, that we want to train a generator, G, to create images of handwritten digits. Such a generator would be much more useful if, instead of outputting images of random digits, it could be conditioned to output images of requested ones (that is, *draw an image whose* $y = 3$, with y the categorical digit label). If the discriminator is not given y, the generator would learn to generate realistic images, but with no certainty that these images would be depicting the desired digits (for instance, we could receive from G a realistic image of a *5* instead of a *3*). Giving the conditioning information to D, this network would immediately spot a fake image that does not correspond to its y, forcing G to effectively model $p(x \mid y)$.

The *Pix2Pix* model by Phillip Isola and others from Berkeley AI Research is a famous image-to-image conditional GAN (that is, with y being an image), demonstrated on several tasks, such as converting hand-drawn sketches into pictures, semantic labels into actual pictures, and more (*Image-to-image translation with conditional adversarial networks*, IEEE, 2017). While *Pix2Pix* works best in supervised contexts, when the target images were made available to add an MSE loss to the GAN objective, more recent solutions removed this constraint. This is, for instance, the case of *CycleGAN*, by Jun-Yan Zhu et al. from Berkeley AI Research (published by IEEE in 2017, in collaboration with the *Pix2Pix* authors) or *PixelDA* by Konstantinos Bousmalis and colleagues from Google Brain (*Unsupervised pixel-level domain adaptation with generative adversarial networks*, IEEE, 2017).

Like other recent conditional GANs, *PixelDA* can be used as a domain adaptation method, to map training images from the source domain to the target domain. For example, the *PixelDA* generator can be applied to generating realistic-looking versions of synthetic images, learning from a small set of unlabeled real images. It can thus be used to augment synthetic datasets so that the models trained on them do not suffer as much from the realism gap.

Though mostly known for their artistic applications (GAN-generated portraits are already being exhibited in many art galleries), generative models are powerful tools that, in the long term, could become central to the understanding of complex datasets. But nowadays, they are already being used by companies to train more robust recognition models despite scarce training data.

Summary

Although the exponential increase in computational power and the availability of larger datasets have led to the deep learning era, this certainly does not mean that best practices in data science should be ignored or that relevant datasets will be easily available for all applications.

In this chapter, we took a deep dive into the `tf.data` API, learning how to optimize the data flow. We then covered different, yet compatible, solutions to tackle the problem of data scarcity: data augmentation, synthetic data generation, and domain adaptation. The latter solution gave us the opportunity to present VAEs and GANs, which are powerful generative models.

The importance of well-defined input pipelines will be highlighted in the next chapter, as we will apply NNs to data of higher dimensionality: image sequences and videos.

Questions

1. Given a tensor, `a = [1, 2, 3]`, and another tensor, `b = [4, 5, 6]`, how do you build a `tf.data` pipeline that would output each value separately, from `1` to `6`?
2. According to the documentation of `tf.data.Options`, how do you make sure that a dataset always returns samples in the same order, run after run?
3. Which domain adaptation methods that we introduced can be used when no target annotations are available for training?
4. What role does the discriminator play in GANs?

Further reading

- *Learn OpenGL* (`https://www.packtpub.com/game-development/learn-opengl`), by Frahaan Hussain: For readers interested in computer graphics and eager to learn how to use OpenCV, this book is a nice place to start.
- *Hands-On Artificial Intelligence for Beginners* (`https://www.packtpub.com/big-data-and-business-intelligence/hands-artificial-intelligence-beginners`), by Patrick D. Smith: Though written for TensorFlow 1, this book dedicates a complete chapter to generative networks.

8
Video and Recurrent Neural Networks

So far in this book, we have only considered still images. However, in this chapter, we will introduce the techniques that are applied to video analysis. From self-driving cars to video streaming websites, computer vision techniques have been developed to enable sequences of images to be processed.

We will introduce a new type of neural network—**recurrent neural networks** (**RNNs**), which are designed specifically for sequential inputs such as video. As a practical application, we will combine them with **convolutional neural networks** (**CNNs**) to detect actions included in short video clips.

The following topics will be covered in this chapter:

- Introduction to RNNs
- Inner workings of long short-term memory networks
- Applications of computer vision models to videos

Technical requirements

Commented code in the form of Jupyter notebooks is available in this book's GitHub repository at `https://github.com/PacktPublishing/Hands-On-Computer-Vision-with-TensorFlow-2/tree/master/Chapter08`.

Introducing RNNs

RNNs are a type of neural network that are suited for *sequential* (or *recurrent*) data. Examples of sequential data include sentences (sequences of words), time series (sequences of stock prices, for instance), or videos (sequences of frames). They qualify as recurrent data as each time step is related to the previous ones.

While RNNs were originally developed for time series analysis and natural language processing tasks, they are now applied to various computer vision tasks.

We will first introduce the basic concepts behind RNNs, before trying to get a general understanding of how they work. We will then describe how their weights can be learned.

Basic formalism

To introduce RNNs, we will use the example of video recognition. A video is composed of *N* frames. The naive method to classify a video would be to apply a CNN to each frame, and then take the average of the outputs.

While this would provide decent results, it does not reflect the fact that some parts of the video are more important than others. Moreover, the important parts do not always take more frames than the meaningless ones. The risk of averaging the output would be to lose important information.

To circumvent this problem, an RNN is applied to all the frames of the video, one after the other, from the first one to the last one. The main attribute of RNNs is adequately combining features from all the frames in order to generate meaningful results.

We do not apply the RNN directly to the raw pixels of the frame. As described later in the chapter, we first use a CNN to generate a feature volume (a stack of feature maps). The concept of feature volume was detailed in `Chapter 3`, *Modern Neural Networks*. As a reminder, a feature volume is the output of a CNN and usually represents the input with a smaller dimensionality.

To do so, RNNs introduce a new concept called the **state**. State can be pictured as the memory of the RNN. In practice, *state* is a float matrix. The *state* starts as a zero matrix and is updated with each frame of the video. At the end of the process, the final state is used to generate the output of the RNN.

The main component of an RNN is the **RNN cell**, which we will apply to every frame. A cell receives as inputs both the *current frame* and the *previous state*. For a video composed of *N* frames, an unfolded representation of a simple recurrent network is depicted in *Figure 8-1*:

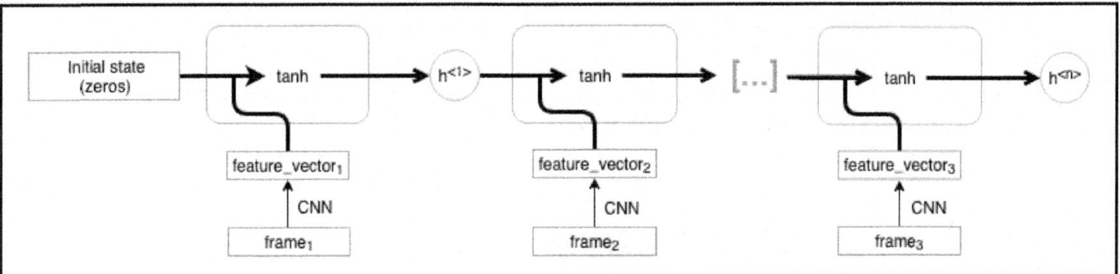

Figure 8-1: Basic RNN cell

In detail, we start with a null state ($h^{<0>}$). As a first step, the cell combines the current state ($h^{<0>}$) with the current frame ($frame_1$) to generate a new state ($h^{<1>}$). Then, the same process is applied to the next frames. At the end of this process, we end up with the final state ($h^{<n>}$).

Note the vocabulary here—*RNN* refers to the component that accepts an image and returns a final output. An *RNN cell* refers to the sub-component that combines a frame as well as a current state, and returns the next state.

In practice, the cell combines the current state and the frame to generate a new state. This combination happens according to the following formula:

$$h^{<t>} = \tanh(W_{rec}h^{<t-1>} + W_{input}x^{<t>} + b)$$

In the formula, the following applies:

- b is the bias.
- W_{rec} is the recurrent weight matrix, and W_{input} is the weight matrix.
- $x^{<t>}$ is the input.
- $h^{<t-1>}$ is the current state, and $h^{<t>}$ is the new state.

The hidden state is not used as is. A weight matrix, *V*, is used to compute the final prediction:

$$\hat{y}^{<t>} = \text{softmax}(Vh^{<t>})$$

Throughout this chapter, we will make use of chevrons (< >) to denote temporal information. Other sources may use different conventions. Note, however, that the *y* with a hat ($\hat{y}$) commonly represents the prediction of a neural network, while *y* represents the ground truth.

When applied to videos, RNNs can be used to classify the whole video or every single frame. In the former case, for instance, when predicting whether a video is violent, only the final prediction, $\hat{y}^{<t>}$, will be used. In the latter case, for instance, to detect which frames may contain nudity, predictions for each time step will be used.

General understanding of RNNs

Before we detail how the network learns the weights of W_{input}, W_{rec}, and *V*, let's try to get a broad understanding of how a basic RNN works. The general idea is that W_{input} will influence the results if some of the features from the input make it into the hidden state, and W_{rec} will influence the results if some features stay in the hidden state.

Let's use specific examples—classifying a violent video and a dance video.

As a gunshot can be quite sudden, it would represent only a few frames among all the frames of the video. Ideally, the network will learn W_{input}, so that when $x^{<t>}$ contains the information of a gunshot, the concept of *violent video* would be added to the state. Moreover, W_{rec} (defined in the previous equation) must be learned in a way that prevents the concept of *violent* from disappearing from the state. This way, even if the gunshot appears only in the first few frames, the video would still be classified as violent (see *Figure 8-2*).

However, to classify dance videos, we would adopt another behavior. Ideally, the network would learn W_{input} so that, for example, when $x^{<t>}$ contains people who appear to be dancing, the concept of *dance* would only be lightly incremented in the state (see *Figure 8-2*):

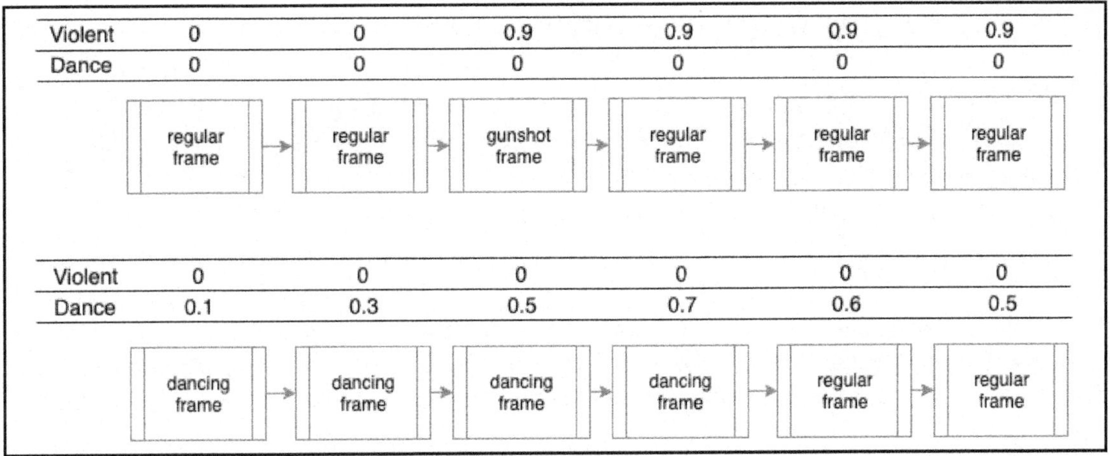

Figure 8-2: Simplified representation of how the hidden state should evolve, depending on the video content

Indeed, if the input is a sport video, we would not want a single frame mistakenly classified as *dancing people* to change our state to *dancing*. As a dancing video is mostly made of frames containing dancing people, by incrementing the state little by little, we would avoid misclassification.

Moreover, W_{rec} must be learned in order to make *dance* gradually disappear from the state. This way, if the introduction of the video is about dance, but the whole video is not, it would not be classified as such.

Learning RNN weights

In practice, the state of the network is much more complex than a vector containing a weight for each class, as in the previous example. The weights of W_{input}, W_{rec}, and V cannot be engineered by hand. Thankfully, they can be learned through **backpropagation**. This technique was detailed in `Chapter 1`, *Computer Vision and Neural Networks*. The general idea is to learn the weights by correcting them based on the errors that the network makes.

Backpropagation through time

For RNNs, however, we not only backpropagate the error through the depth of the network, but also through time. First of all, we compute the total loss by summing the individual loss (L) over all the time steps:

$$L^{<t>}(y, \hat{y}) = \sum_t L\left(y^{<t>}, \hat{y}^{<t>}\right)$$

This means that we can compute the gradient for each time step separately. To greatly simplify the calculations, we will assume that *tanh* = *identity* (that is, we assume that there is no activation function). For instance, at $t = 4$, we will compute the gradient by applying the chain rule:

$$\frac{\partial L^{<4>}}{\partial W_{rec}} = \frac{\partial L^{<4>}}{\partial \hat{y}^{<4>}} \frac{\partial \hat{y}^{<4>}}{\partial h^{<4>}} \frac{\boldsymbol{\partial h^{<4>}}}{\boldsymbol{\partial W_{rec}}}$$

Here, we stumble upon a complexity—the third term (in bold) on the right-hand side of the equation cannot be easily derived. Indeed, to take the derivative of $h^{<4>}$ with respect to W_{rec}, all other terms must not depend on W_{rec}. However, $h^{<4>}$ also depends on $h^{<3>}$. And $h^{<3>}$ depends on W_{rec}, since $h^{<3>} = tanh\,(W_{rec}\,h^{<2>} + W_{input}\,x^{<3>} + b)$, and so on and so forth until we reach $h^{<0>}$, which is entirely composed of zeros.

To properly derive this term, we apply the total derivative formula on this partial derivative:

$$\frac{\partial h^{<4>}}{\partial W_{rec}} \rightarrow \frac{\partial h^{<4>}}{\partial W_{rec}} + \frac{\partial h^{<4>}}{\partial h^{<3>}} \frac{\partial h^{<3>}}{\partial W_{rec}} + \frac{\partial h^{<4>}}{\partial h^{<3>}} \frac{\partial h^{<3>}}{\partial h^{<2>}} \frac{\partial h^{<2>}}{\partial W_{rec}}$$

It might seem weird that a term is equal to itself plus other (non-null) terms. However, since we are taking the total derivative of a partial derivative, we need to take into account all the terms in order to generate the gradient.

By noticing that all the other terms are remaining constant, we obtain the following equations:

$$\frac{\partial h^{<n+1>}}{\partial h^{<n>}} = W \quad \text{and} \quad \frac{\partial h^{<t>}}{\partial W_{rec}} = h^{<t>}$$

Therefore, the partial derivative presented before can be expressed as follows:

$$\frac{\partial h^{<4>}}{\partial W_{rec}} = h^{<3>} + h^{<2>} W_{rec} + h^{(1)} (W_{rec})^2$$

In conclusion, we notice that the gradient will depend on all the previous states as well as W_{rec}. This concept is called **backpropagation through time** (**BPTT**). Since the latest state depends on all the states before it, it only makes sense to consider them to compute the error. As we sum the gradient of each time step to compute the total gradient, and since, for each time step, we have to go back to the first time step to compute the gradient, a large amount of computation is implied. For this reason, RNNs are notoriously slow to train.

Moreover, we can generalize the previous formula to show that $\frac{\partial L^{<t>}}{\partial W_{rec}}$ depends on W_{rec} to the power of (t-2). This is very problematic when t is large. Indeed, if the terms of W_{rec} are below one, with the high exponent, they become very small. Worse, if the terms are above one, the gradient tends toward infinity. These phenomena are called **gradient vanishing** and **gradient explosion**, respectively (they were previously described in `Chapter 4`, *Influential Classification Tools*). Thankfully, workarounds exist to avoid this problem.

Truncated backpropagation

To circumvent the long training time, it is possible to compute the gradient every k_1 time step instead of every step. This divides the number of gradient operations by k_1, making the training of the network faster.

Instead of backpropagating throughout all the time steps, we can also limit the propagation to k_2 steps in the past. This effectively limits the gradient vanishing, since the gradient will depend on W^{k_2} at most. This also limits the computations that are necessary to compute the gradient. However, the network will be less likely to learn long-term temporal relations.

The combination of those two techniques is called **truncated backpropagation**, with its two parameters commonly referred to as k_1 and k_2. They must be tuned to ensure a good trade-off between training speed and model performance.

This technique—while powerful—remains a workaround for a fundamental RNN problem. In the next section, we will introduce a change of architecture that can be used to solve this issue in its entirety.

Long short-term memory cells

As we saw previously, regular RNNs suffer from gradient explosion. As such, it can sometimes be hard to teach them long-term relations in sequences of data. Moreover, they store information in a single-state matrix. For instance, if a gunshot happens at the very beginning of a very long video, it will be unlikely that the hidden state of the RNNs will not be overridden by noise by the time it reaches the end of the video. The video might not be classified as violent.

To circumvent those two problems, Sepp Hochreiter and Jürgen Schmidhuber proposed, in their paper (*Long Short-Term Memory, Neural Computation*, 1997), a variant of the basic RNN—the **Long Short-Term Memory** (**LSTM**) cell. This has improved markedly over the years, with many variants being introduced. In this section, we will give an overview of its inner workings, and we will show why gradient vanishing is less of an issue.

LSTM general principles

Before we detail the mathematics behind the LSTM cell, let's try to get a general understanding of how it works. To do so, we will use the example of a live classification system that is applied to the Olympic Games. The system has to detect, for every frame, which sport is being played during a long video from the Olympics.

If the network sees people standing in line, can it infer what sport it is? Is it soccer players singing the anthem, or is it athletes preparing to run a 100-meter race? Without information about what happened in the frames just prior to this, the prediction will not be accurate. The basic RNN architecture we presented earlier would be able to store this information in the hidden state. However, if the sports are alternating one after the other, it would be much harder. Indeed, the state is used to generate the current predictions. The basic RNN is unable to store information that it will not use immediately.

The LSTM architecture solves this by storing a memory matrix, which is called the **cell state** and is referred to as $C^{<t>}$. At every time step, $C^{<t>}$ contains information about the current state. But this information will not be used directly to generate the output. Instead, it will be filtered by a *gate*.

Note that the LSTM's cell state is different from the simple RNN's state, as outlined by the following equations. The LSTM's cell state is filtered before being transformed into the final state.

Gates are the core idea of LSTM's cell. A gate is a matrix that will be multiplied term by term to another element in the LSTM. If all the values of the gate are *0*, none of the information from the other element will pass through. On the other hand, if the gate values are all around *1*, all the information of the other element will pass through.

As a reminder, an example of term-by-term multiplication (also called **element-wise multiplication** or the **Hadamard product**) can be depicted as follows:

$$\begin{bmatrix} a & b \\ c & d \end{bmatrix} \odot \begin{bmatrix} e & f \\ g & h \end{bmatrix} = \begin{bmatrix} a*e & b*f \\ c*g & d*h \end{bmatrix}$$

At each time step, three gate matrices are computed using the current input and the previous output:

- **The input gate**: Applied to the input to decide which information gets through. In our example, if the video is showing members of the audience, we would not want to use this input to generate predictions. The gate would be mostly zeros.
- **The forget gate**: Applied to the cell state to decide which information to forget. In our example, if the video is showing presenters talking, we would want to forget about the current sport, as we are probably going to see a new sport next.
- **The output gate**: This will be multiplied by the cell state to decide which information to output. We might want to keep in the cell state the fact that the previous sport was soccer, but this information will not be useful for the current frame. Outputting this information would perturb the upcoming time steps. By setting the gate around zero, we would effectively keep this information for later.

In the next section, we will cover how the gates and the candidate state are computed and demonstrate why LSTMs suffer less from gradient vanishing.

LSTM inner workings

First, let's detail how the gates are computed:

$$\begin{aligned} i^{<t>} &= \sigma\left(W_i \cdot \left[h^{<t-1>}, x^{<t>}\right] + b_i\right) \\ f^{<t>} &= \sigma\left(W_f \cdot \left[h^{<t-1>}, x^{<t>}\right] + b_f\right) \\ o^{<t>} &= \sigma\left(W_o \cdot \left[h^{<t-1>}, x^{<t>}\right] + b_o\right) \end{aligned}$$

As detailed in the previous equations, the three gates are computed using the same principle—by multiplying a weight matrix (W) by the previous output ($h^{<t-1>}$) and the current input ($x^{<t>}$). Notice that the activation function is the sigmoid (σ). As a consequence, the gate values are always between *0* and *1*.

The candidate state ($\tilde{C}^{<t>}$) is computed in a similar fashion. However, the activation function used is a hyperbolic tangent instead of the sigmoid:

$$\tilde{C}^{<t>} = \tanh\left(W_C \cdot \left[h^{<t-1>}, x_t\right] + b_C\right) \quad (1)$$

Notice that this formula is exactly the same as the one used to compute $h^{<t>}$ in the basic RNN architecture. However, $h^{<t>}$ was the *hidden state* while, in this case, we are computing the **candidate cell state**. To compute the new cell state, we combine the previous one with the candidate cell state. Both states are gated by the forget and input gates, respectively:

$$C^{<t>} = f^{<t>} \odot C^{<t-1>} + i^{<t>} \odot \tilde{C}^{<t>} \quad (2)$$

Finally, the LSTM hidden state (output) will be computed from the cell state as follows:

$$h^{<t>} = o^{<t>} \odot \tanh\left(C^{<t>}\right) \quad (3)$$

The simplified representation of the LSTM cell is depicted in *Figure 8-3*:

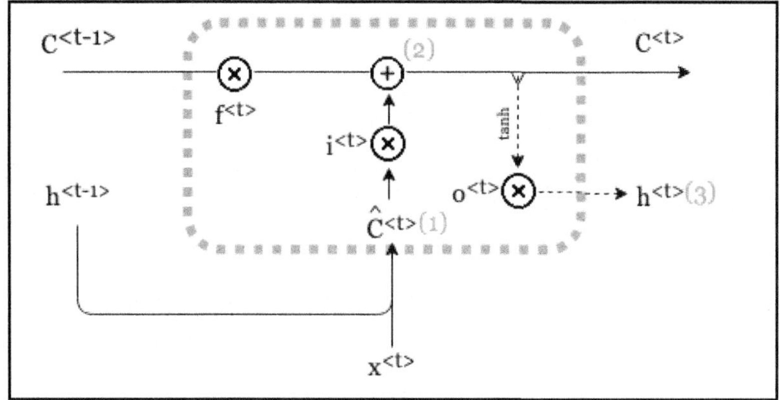

Figure 8-3: Simplified representation of the LSTM cell. Gate computation is omitted

LSTM weights are also computed using backpropagation through time. Due to the numerous information paths in LSTM cells, gradient computation is even more complex. However, we can observe that if the terms of the forget gate, $f^{<t>}$, are close to *1*, information can be passed from one cell state to the other, as shown in the following equation:

$$\frac{\partial C^{<t>}}{\partial C^{<t-1>}} = f^{<t>}$$

For this reason, by initializing the forget gate bias to a vector of ones, we can ensure that the information backpropagates through numerous time steps. As such, LSTMs suffer less from gradient vanishing.

This concludes our introduction to RNNs; we can now begin with the hands-on classification of a video.

Classifying videos

From television to web streaming, the video format is getting more and more popular. Since the inception of computer vision, researchers have attempted to apply computer vision to more than one image at a time. While limited by computing power at first, they more recently have developed powerful techniques for video analysis. In this section, we will introduce video-related tasks and detail one of them—video classification.

Applying computer vision to video

At 30 frames per second, processing every frame of a video implies analyzing $30 \times 60 = 180$ frames per minute. This problem was faced really early in computer vision, before the rise of deep learning. Techniques were then devised to analyze videos efficiently.

The most obvious technique is **sampling**. We can analyze only one or two frames per second instead of all the frames. While more efficient, we may lose information if an important scene appears very briefly, such as in the case of a gunshot, which was mentioned earlier.

A more advanced technique is **scene extraction**. This is particularly popular for analyzing movies. An algorithm detects when the video is changing from one scene to another. For instance, if the camera goes from a close-up view to a wide view, we would analyze a frame from each framing. Even if the close-up is really short and the wide view occurs over many frames, we would extract only one frame from each shot. *Scene extraction* can be done by using fast and efficient algorithms. They process the pixels of images and evaluate the variation between two consecutive frames. A large variation indicates a scene change.

In addition, all the image-related tasks described in `Chapter 1`, *Computer Vision and Neural Networks*, also apply to video. For instance, super-resolution, segmentation, and style transfer are commonly targeted at video. However, the temporal aspect of a video creates new applications in the form of the following video-specific tasks:

- **Action detection**: A variant of video classification, the goal here is to classify what actions a person is accomplishing. Actions range from running to playing soccer, but can also be as precise as the kind of dance being performed, or the musical instrument being played.
- **Next-frame prediction**: Given *N* consecutive frames, this predicts how frame *N+1* is going to look.
- **Ultra slow motion**: This is also called **frame interpolation**. The model has to generate intermediate frames to make slow motion look less jerky.
- **Object tracking**: This was executed historically using classical computer vision techniques such as descriptors. However, deep learning is now applied to track objects in videos.

Of these video-specific tasks, we will focus on action detection. In the next section, we will introduce an action video dataset and cover how to apply an LSTM cell to videos.

Classifying videos with an LSTM

We will make use of the *UCF101* dataset (`https://www.crcv.ucf.edu/data/UCF101.php`), which was put together by K. Soomro et al. (refer to *UCF101: A Dataset of 101 Human Actions Classes From Videos in The Wild*, CRCV-TR-12-01, 2012). Here are a few examples from the dataset:

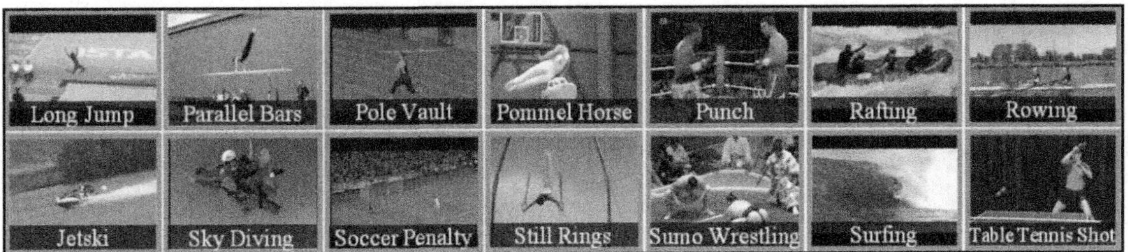

Figure 8-4: Example images from the UCF101 dataset

The dataset is composed of 13,320 segments of video. Each segment contains a person performing one of 101 possible actions.

To classify the video, we will use a two-step process. Indeed, a recurrent network is not fed the raw pixel images. While it could technically be fed with full images, CNN feature extractors are used beforehand in order to reduce the dimensionality, and to reduce the computations done by LSTMs. Therefore, our network architecture can be represented by *Figure 8-5*:

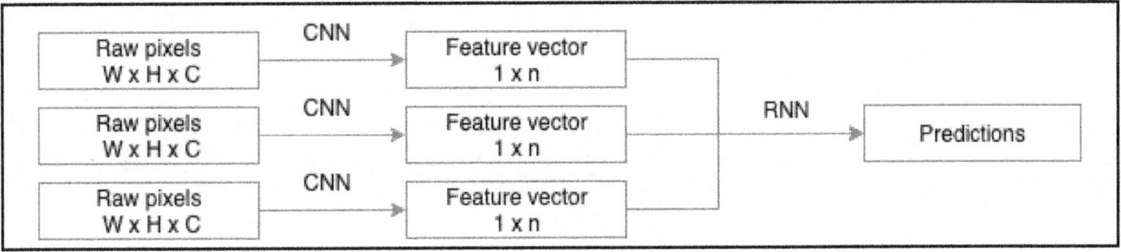

Figure 8-5: Combination of a CNN and an RNN to categorize videos. In this simplified example, the sequence length is 3

As stated earlier, backpropagating errors through RNNs is difficult. While we could train the CNN from scratch, it would take a tremendous amount of time for sub-par results. Therefore, we use a pretrained network, applying the transfer learning technique that was introduced in `Chapter 4`, *Influential Classification Tools*.

For the same reason, it is also common practice not to fine-tune the CNN and to keep its weights untouched, as this does not bring any performance improvement. Since the CNN will stay unchanged throughout all the epochs of training, a specific frame will always return the same feature vector. This allows us to *cache* the feature vectors. As the CNN step is the most time-consuming, caching the results means computing the feature vector only once instead of at each epoch, saving us a tremendous amount of training time.

Therefore, we will classify the videos in two steps. First, we will extract the features and cache them. Once this is done, we will train the LSTM on extracted features.

Extracting features from videos

To generate feature vectors, we will use a pretrained inception network trained on the ImageNet dataset to categorize images in different categories.

We will remove the last layer (the fully connected layer) and only keep the feature vector that is generated after a max-pooling operation.

Another option would be to keep the output of the layer just before average-pooling, that is, the higher-dimensional feature maps. However, in our example, we will not need spatial information—whether the action takes place in the middle of the frame or in the corner, the predictions will be the same. Therefore, we will use the output of the two-dimensional max-pooling layer. This will make the training faster, since the input of the LSTM will be 64 times smaller (*64 = 8* x *8* = the size of a feature map for an input image of size *299* x *299*).

TensorFlow allows us to access a pretrained model with a single line, as described in `Chapter 4`, *Influential Classification Tools*:

```
inception_v3 = tf.keras.applications.InceptionV3(include_top=False,
weights='imagenet')
```

We add the max-pooling operation to transform the *8* x *8* x *2,048* feature map into a *1* x *2,048* vector:

```
x = inception_v3.output
pooling_output = tf.keras.layers.GlobalAveragePooling2D()(x)

feature_extraction_model = tf.keras.Model(inception_v3.input,
pooling_output)
```

We will use the `tf.data` API to load the frames from the video. An initial problem arises—all the videos have different lengths. Here is the distribution of the number of frames:

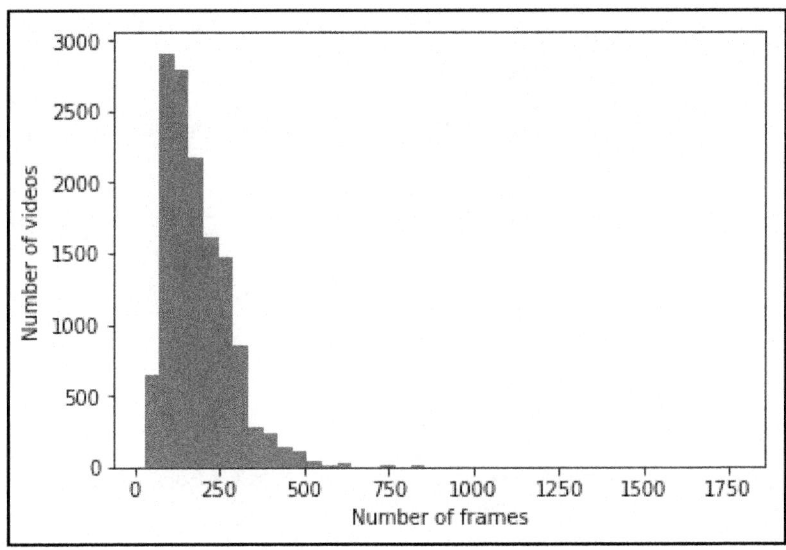

Figure 8-6: Distribution of the number of frames per video in the UCF101 dataset

It is always good practice to run a quick analysis on data before using it. Manually reviewing it and plotting the distributions can save a lot of experimenting time.

With TensorFlow, as with most deep learning frameworks, all examples in a batch must be of the same length. The most common solution to fit this requirement is *padding*—we fill the first temporal time steps with actual data and the last ones with zeros.

In our case, we will not use all the frames from the video. At 25 frames per second, most of the frames look alike. By using only a subset of the frames, we will reduce the size of our input, and therefore speed up the training process. To select this subset, we can use any of the following options:

- Extract *N* frames per second.
- Sample *N* frames out of all the frames.
- Segment the videos in scenes and extract *N* frames per scene, as shown in the following diagram:

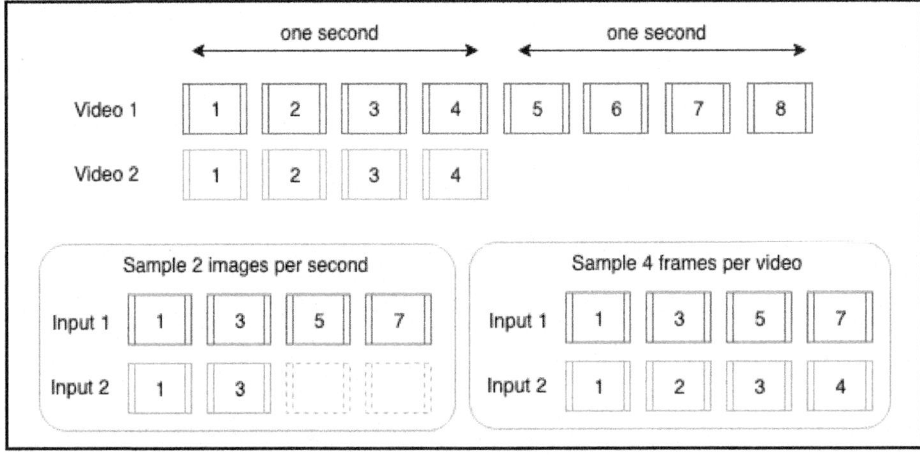

Figure 8-7: Comparison of two sampling techniques. Dotted rectangles indicate zero padding

Due to the large variation in video length, extracting *N* frames per second would also result in a large variation in input length. Although this could be solved with padding, we would end up with some inputs mostly composed of zeros—this could lead to poor training performance. We will, therefore, sample *N* images per video.

We will use the TensorFlow dataset API to feed the input to our feature extraction network:

```
dataset = tf.data.Dataset.from_generator(frame_generator,
            output_types=(tf.float32, tf.string),
            output_shapes=((299, 299, 3), ()))
```

In the previous code, we specify the input type and the input shape. Our generator will return images of shape *299* x *299* with three channels, as well as a string representing the filename. The filename will be used to group the frames by video later on.

The role of `frame_generator` is to select the frames that will be processed by the network. We use the OpenCV library to read from the video file. For each video, we will sample an image every *N* frames, where *N* equals `num_frames / SEQUENCE_LENGTH` and `SEQUENCE_LENGTH` is the size of the input sequence of the LSTM. A simplified version of this generator looks like this:

```
def frame_generator():
    video_paths = tf.io.gfile.glob(VIDEOS_PATH)
    for video_path in video_paths:
        capture = cv2.VideoCapture(video_path)
        num_frames = int(cap.get(cv2.CAP_PROP_FRAME_COUNT))
        sample_every_frame = max(1, num_frames // SEQUENCE_LENGTH)
        current_frame = 0

        label = os.path.basename(os.path.dirname(video_path))
        while True:
            success, frame = capture.read()
            if not success:
                break

            if current_frame % sample_every_frame == 0:
                img = preprocess_frame(frame)
                yield img, video_path

            current_frame += 1
```

We iterate over the frames of the video, processing only a subset. At the end of the video, the OpenCV library will return `success` as `False` and the loop will terminate.

Note that just like in any Python generator, instead of using the `return` keyword, we use the `yield` keyword. This allows us to start returning frames before the end of the loop. This way, the network can start training without waiting for all the frames to be preprocessed.

Finally, we iterate over the dataset to generate video features:

```
dataset = dataset.batch(16).prefetch(tf.data.experimental.AUTOTUNE)
current_path = None
all_features = []

for img, batch_paths in tqdm.tqdm(dataset):
    batch_features = feature_extraction_model(img)
```

```
for features, path in zip(batch_features.numpy(), batch_paths.numpy()):
    if path != current_path and current_path is not None:
        output_path = current_path.decode().replace('.avi', '')
        np.save(output_path, all_features)
        all_features = []
    current_path = path
    all_features.append(features)
```

In the previous code, note that we iterate over the batch output and compare video filenames. We do so because the batch size is not necessarily the same as *N* (the number of frames we sample per video). Therefore, a batch may contain frames from multiple consecutive sequences:

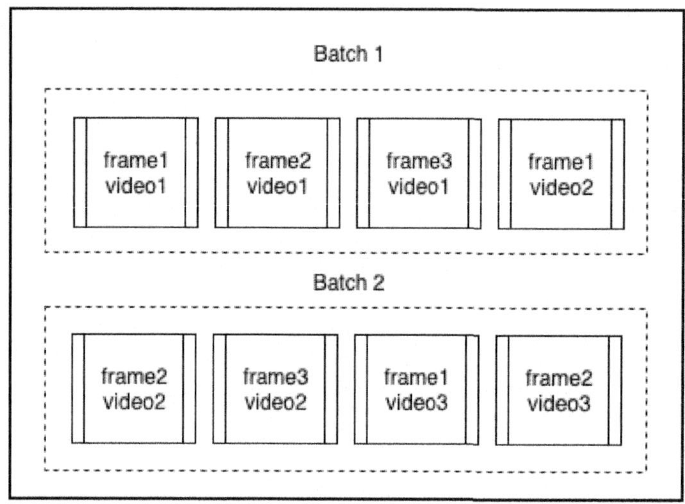

Figure 8-8: Representation of the input for a batch size of four and three sampled frames per video

We read the output of the network, and when we reach a different filename, we save the video features to file. Note that this technique will only work if the frames are in the correct order. If the dataset is shuffled, it would no longer work. Video features are saved at the same location as the video, but with a different extension (`.npy` instead of `.avi`).

This step iterates over the 13,320 videos of the dataset and generates features for every single one of them. Sampling 40 frames per video takes about one hour on a modern GPU.

Training the LSTM

Now that the video features are generated, we can use them to train an LSTM. This step is very similar to the training steps described earlier in the book—we define a model and an input pipeline, and launch the training.

Defining the model

Our model is a simple sequential model, defined using Keras layers:

```
model = tf.keras.Sequential([
    tf.keras.layers.Masking(mask_value=0.),
    tf.keras.layers.LSTM(512, dropout=0.5, recurrent_dropout=0.5),
    tf.keras.layers.Dense(256, activation='relu'),
    tf.keras.layers.Dropout(0.5),
    tf.keras.layers.Dense(len(LABELS), activation='softmax')
])
```

We apply a dropout, a concept introduced in `Chapter 3`, *Modern Neural Networks*. The `dropout` parameter of the LSTM controls how much dropout is applied to the input weight matrix. The `recurrent_dropout` parameter controls how much dropout is applied to the previous state. Similar to a mask, `recurrent_dropout` randomly ignores part of the previous state activations in order to avoid overfitting.

The very first layer of our model is a `Masking` layer. As we padded our image sequences with empty frames in order to batch them, our LSTM cell would needlessly iterate over those added frames. Adding the `Masking` layer ensures the LSTM layer stops at the actual end of the sequence, before it encounters a zero matrix.

The model will categorize videos in 101 categories, such as *kayaking*, *rafting*, or *fencing*. However, it will only predict a vector representing the predictions. We need a way to convert those 101 categories into vector form. We will use a technique called **one-hot encoding**, described in `Chapter 1`, *Computer Vision and Neural Networks*. Since we have 101 different labels, we will return a vector of size 101. For *kayaking*, the vector will be full of zeros except for the first item, which is set to *1*. For *rafting*, it will be *0* except for the second element, which is set to *1*, and so on for the other categories.

Loading the data

We will load the `.npy` files that are produced when generating frame features using a generator. The code ensures that all the input sequences have the same length, padding them with zeros if necessary:

```
def make_generator(file_list):
    def generator():
        np.random.shuffle(file_list)
        for path in file_list:
            full_path = os.path.join(BASE_PATH, path)
            full_path = full_path.replace('.avi', '.npy')

            label = os.path.basename(os.path.dirname(path))
            features = np.load(full_path)

            padded_sequence = np.zeros((SEQUENCE_LENGTH, 2048))
            padded_sequence[0:len(features)] = np.array(features)

            transformed_label = encoder.transform([label])
            yield padded_sequence, transformed_label[0]
    return generator
```

In the previous code, we defined a Python **closure function**—a function that returns another function. This technique allows us to create `train_dataset`, returning training data, and `validation_dataset`, returning validation data with just one generator function:

```
train_dataset = tf.data.Dataset.from_generator(make_generator(train_list),
                 output_types=(tf.float32, tf.int16),
                 output_shapes=((SEQUENCE_LENGTH, 2048), (len(LABELS))))
train_dataset = train_dataset.batch(16)
train_dataset = train_dataset.prefetch(tf.data.experimental.AUTOTUNE)

valid_dataset = tf.data.Dataset.from_generator(make_generator(test_list),
                 output_types=(tf.float32, tf.int16),
                 output_shapes=((SEQUENCE_LENGTH, 2048), (len(LABELS))))
valid_dataset = valid_dataset.batch(16)
valid_dataset = valid_dataset.prefetch(tf.data.experimental.AUTOTUNE)
```

We also batch and prefetch the data according to the best practices that were described in `Chapter 7`, *Training on Complex and Scarce Datasets*.

Training the model

The training procedure is very similar to those previously described in the book, and we invite the readers to refer to the notebook attached to this chapter. Using the model described previously, we reach a precision level of 72% on the validation set.

This result can be compared to the state-of-the-art precision level of 94%, which is obtained when using more advanced techniques. Our simple model could be enhanced by improving frame sampling, using data augmentation, using a different sequence length, or by optimizing the size of the layers.

Summary

We expanded our knowledge of neural networks by describing the general principles of RNNs. After covering the inner workings of the basic RNN, we extended backpropagation to apply it to recurrent networks. As presented in this chapter, BPTT suffers from gradient vanishing when applied to RNNs. This can be worked around by using truncated backpropagation, or by using a different type of architecture—LSTM networks.

We applied those theoretical principles to a practical problem—action recognition in videos. By combining CNNs and LSTMs, we successfully trained a network to classify videos in 101 categories, introducing video-specific techniques such as frame sampling and padding.

In the next chapter, we will broaden our knowledge of neural network applications by covering new platforms—mobile devices and web browsers.

Questions

1. What are the main advantages of LSTMs over the simple RNN architecture?
2. What is the CNN used for when it is applied before the LSTM?
3. What is gradient vanishing and why does it occur? Why is it a problem?
4. What are some of the workarounds for gradient vanishing?

Further reading

- *RNNs with Python Quick Start Guide* (`https://www.packtpub.com/big-data-and-business-intelligence/recurrent-neural-networks-python-quick-start-guide`), by Simeon Kostadinov: This book details RNN architectures, and applies them to examples using TensorFlow 1.
- *A Critical Review of RNNs for Sequence Learning* (`https://arxiv.org/abs/1506.00019`), by Zachary C. Lipton et al.: This survey reviews and synthesizes three decades of RNN architectures.
- *Empirical Evaluation of Gated RNNs on Sequence Modeling* (`https://arxiv.org/abs/1412.3555`), by Junyoung Chung et al.: This paper compares the performance of different RNN architectures.

9 Optimizing Models and Deploying on Mobile Devices

Computer vision applications are various and multifaceted. While most of the training steps take place on a server or a computer, deep learning models are used on a variety of frontend devices, such as mobile phones, self-driving cars, and **Internet-of-Things** (**IoT**) devices. With limited computing power, performance optimization becomes paramount.

In this chapter, we will introduce techniques to limit your model size and improve inference speed while maintaining good prediction quality. As a practical example, we will create a simple mobile application to recognize facial expressions on iOS and Android devices, as well as in the browser.

The following topics will be covered in this chapter:

- How to reduce model size and boost speed without impacting accuracy
- Analyzing model computational performance in depth
- Running models on mobile phones (iOS and Android)
- Introducing TensorFlow.js to run models in the browser

Technical requirements

The code for this chapter is available from `https://github.com/PacktPublishing/Hands-On-Computer-Vision-with-TensorFlow-2/tree/master/Chapter09`.

When developing applications for mobile phones, you will need knowledge of **Swift** (for iOS) or **Java** (for Android). For computer vision in the browser, you will require knowledge of **JavaScript**. The examples in this chapter are simple and thoroughly explained, making it easy to understand for developers who are more familiar with Python.

Moreover, to run the example iOS app, you will need a compatible device as well as a Mac computer with Xcode installed. To run the Android app, you will need an Android device.

Optimizing computational and disk footprints

When using a computer vision model, some characteristics are crucial. Optimizing a model for *speed* may allow it to run in real time, opening up many new uses. Improving a model's *accuracy* by even a few percent may make the difference between a toy model and a real-life application.

Another important characteristic is *size*, which impacts how much storage the model will use and how long it will take to download it. For some platforms, such as mobile phones or web browsers, the size of the model matters to the end user.

In this section, we will describe techniques to improve the model inference speed and how to reduce its size.

Measuring inference speed

Inference describes the process of using a deep learning model to get predictions. It is measured in images per second or seconds per image. Models must run between 5 and 30 images per second to be considered real-time processing. Before we can improve inference speed, we need to measure it properly.

If a model can process i images per second, we can always run N inference pipelines simultaneously to boost performance—the model will then be able to process $N \times i$ images per second. While parallelism benefits many applications, it would not work for real-time applications.

In a real-time context, such as with a self-driving car, no matter how many images can be processed in parallel, what matters is **latency**—how long it takes to compute predictions for a single image. Therefore, for real-time applications, we only measure the latency of a model—how much time it takes to *process a single image.*

For non-real-time applications, you can run as many inference processes in parallel as necessary. For instance, for a video, you can analyze N chunks of video in parallel and concatenate the predictions at the end of the process. The only impact will be in terms of financial cost, as you will need more hardware to process the frames in parallel.

Measuring latency

As stated, to measure how fast a model performs, we want to compute the time it takes to process a *single image*. However, to minimize measuring error, we will actually measure the processing time for several images. We will then divide the time obtained by the number of images.

We are not measuring the computing time over a single image for several reasons. First, we want to remove measurement error. When running the inference for the first time, the machine could be busy, the GPU might not be initialized yet, or many other technicalities could be causing the slowdown. Running several times allows us to minimize this error.

The second reason is TensorFlow's and CUDA's warmup. When running an operation for the first time, deep learning frameworks are usually slower—they have to initialize variables, allocate memory, move data around, and so on. Moreover, when running repetitive operations, they usually automatically optimize for it.

For all those reasons, it is recommended to measure inference time with multiple images to simulate a real environment.

When measuring inference time, it is also very important to include data loading, data preprocessing, and post-processing times, as these can be significant.

Using tracing tools to understand computational performance

While measuring the total inference time of a model informs you of the feasibility of an application, you might sometimes need a more detailed performance report. To do so, TensorFlow offers several tools. In this section, we will discuss the **trace tool**, which is part of the TensorFlow summary package.

In `Chapter 7`, *Training on Complex and Scarce Datasets*, we described how to analyze the performance of input pipelines. Refer to this chapter to monitor preprocessing and data ingestion performance.

To use it, call `trace_on` and set `profiler` to `True`. You can then run TensorFlow or Keras operations and export the trace to a folder:

```
logdir = './logs/model'
writer = tf.summary.create_file_writer(logdir)

tf.summary.trace_on(profiler=True)
model.predict(train_images)
with writer.as_default():
  tf.summary.trace_export('trace-model', profiler_outdir=logdir)
```

Omitting the call to `create_file_writer` and `with writer.as_default()` will still create a trace of the operations. However, the model graph representation will not be written to disk.

Once the model starts running with tracing enabled, we can point TensorBoard to this folder by executing the following command in the command line:

```
$ tensorboard --logdir logs
```

After opening TensorBoard in the browser and clicking on the **Profile** tab, we can then review the operations:

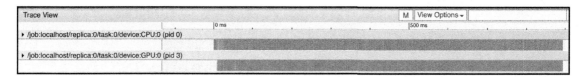

Figure 9-1: Trace of the operations for a simple fully connected model over multiple batches of data

As seen in the preceding timeline, the model is composed of many small operations. By clicking on an operation, we can obtain its name and its duration. For instance, here are the details for a dense matrix multiplication (a fully-connected layer):

Title	dense/MatMul:MatMul#id=0#
User Friendly Category	other
Start	17,582,000 ns
Wall Duration	16,000 ns

Figure 9-2: The details of a matrix multiplication operation

TensorFlow traces can end up taking a large amount of disk space. For this reason, we recommend running the operations you want to trace on a few batches of data only.

On the TPU, a dedicated **Capture Profile** button is available in TensorBoard. The TPU name, IP, and the trace recording time need to be specified.

In practice, the tracing tool is used on much larger models to determine the following:

- Which layers are taking the most computing time.
- Why a model is taking more time than usual after a modification to the architecture.
- Whether TensorFlow is always computing numbers or is waiting on data. This can happen if preprocessing takes too long or if there is a lot of back and forth between CPUs.

We encourage you to trace the models you are using to get a better understanding of the computational performance.

Improving model inference speed

Now that we know how to properly measure a model inference speed, we can use several approaches to improve it. Some involve changing the hardware used, while others imply changing the model architecture itself.

Optimizing for hardware

As we saw previously, the hardware used for inference is crucial for speed. From the slowest option to the fastest, it is recommended to use the following:

- **CPU**: While slower, it is often the cheapest option.
- **GPU**: Faster but more expensive. Many smartphones have integrated GPUs that can be used for real-time applications.
- **Specialized hardware**: For instance, Google's *TPU* (for servers), Apple's *Neural Engine* (on mobile), or *NVIDIA Jetson* (for portable hardware). They are chips made specifically for running deep learning operations.

If speed is crucial for your application, it is important to use the fastest hardware available and to adapt your code.

Optimizing on CPUs

Modern Intel CPUs can compute matrix operations more quickly through special instructions. This is done using the **Math Kernel Library for Deep Neural Networks (MKL-DNN)**. Out-of-the-box TensorFlow does not exploit those instructions. Using them requires either compiling TensorFlow with the right options or installing a special build of TensorFlow called `tensorflow-mkl`.

Information on how to build TensorFlow with MKL-DNN is available at `https://www.tensorflow.org/`. Note that the toolkit currently only works on Linux.

Optimizing on GPUs

To run models on NVIDIA GPUs, two libraries are mandatory—`CUDA` and `cuDNN`. TensorFlow natively exploits the speed-up offered by those libraries.

To properly run operations on the GPU, the `tensorflow-gpu` package must be installed. Moreover, the CUDA version of `tensorflow-gpu` must match the one installed on the computer.

Some modern GPUs offer **Floating Point 16 (FP16)** instructions. The idea is to use reduced precision floats (16 bits instead of the 32 bits commonly used) in order to speed up inference while not impacting the output quality by much. Not all GPUs are compatible with FP16.

Optimizing on specialized hardware

Since every chip is different, the techniques ensuring faster inference vary from one manufacturer to another. The steps necessary for running a model are well documented by the manufacturer.

A rule of thumb is to not use exotic operations. If one of the layers is running operations that include conditions or branching, it is likely that the chip will not support it. The operations will have to run on the CPU, making the whole process slower. It is therefore recommended to *only use standard operations*—convolution, pooling, and fully connected layers.

Optimizing input

The inference speed of a computer vision model is directly proportional to the size of the input image. Moreover, dividing the dimensions of an image by two means four times fewer pixels for the model to process. Therefore, using *smaller images improves inference speed.*

When using smaller images, the model has less information and fewer details to work with. This often has an impact on the quality of the results. It is necessary to experiment with image size to find a good *trade-off between speed and accuracy*.

Optimizing post-processing

As we saw previously in the book, most models require post-processing operations. If implemented using the wrong tools, post-processing can take a lot of time. While most post-processing happens on the CPU, it is sometimes possible to run some operations on the GPU.

Using tracing tools, we can analyze the time taken by post-processing to optimize it. **Non-Maximum Suppression** (**NMS**) is an operation that can take a lot of time if not implemented correctly (refer to `Chapter 5`, *Object Detection Models*):

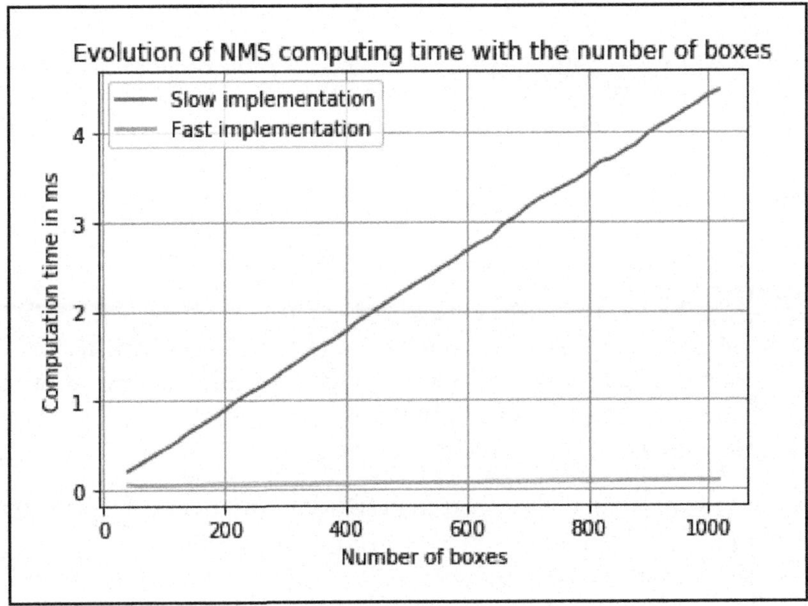

Figure 9-3: Evolution of NMS computing time with the number of boxes

Notice in the preceding diagram that the slow implementation takes linear computing time, while the fast implementation is almost constant. Though four milliseconds may seem quite low, keep in mind that some models can return an even larger number of boxes, resulting in a post-processing time.

When the model is still too slow

Once the model has been optimized for speed, it can sometimes still be too slow for real-time applications. There are a few techniques to work around the slowness while maintaining a real-time feeling for the user.

Interpolating and tracking

Object detection models are notoriously computationally-intensive. Running on every frame of a video is sometimes impractical. A common technique is to use the model every few frames only. In-between frames, linear interpolation is used to follow the tracked object.

While this technique does not work for real-time applications, another one that is commonly used is **object tracking.** Once an object is detected with a deep learning model, a more simple model is used to follow the boundaries of the object.

Object tracking can work on almost any kind of object as long as it is well distinguishable from its background and its shape does not change excessively. There are many object tracking algorithms (some of them are available through OpenCV's tracker module, documented here `https://docs.opencv.org/master/d9/df8/group__tracking.html`); many of them are available for mobile applications.

Model distillation

When none of the other techniques work, one last option is **model distillation**. The general idea is to train a small model to learn the output of a bigger model. Instead of training the small model to learn the raw labels (we could use the data for this), we train it to learn the output of the bigger model.

Let's see an example—we trained a very large network to predict an animal's breed from a picture. The output is as follows:

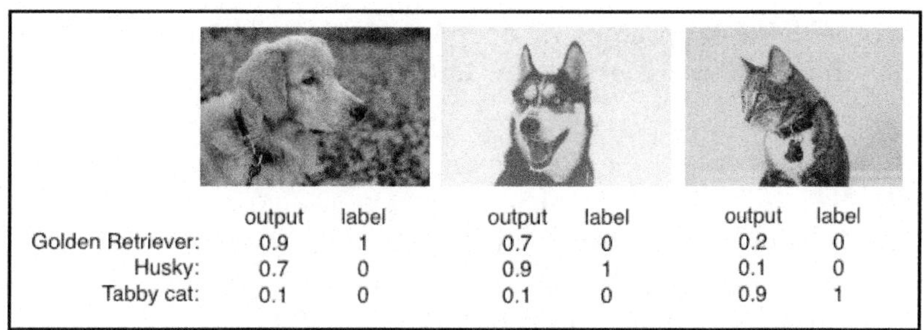

	output	label	output	label	output	label
Golden Retriever:	0.9	1	0.7	0	0.2	0
Husky:	0.7	0	0.9	1	0.1	0
Tabby cat:	0.1	0	0.1	0	0.9	1

Figure 9-4: Examples of predictions made by our network

Because our model is too large to run on mobile, we decided to train a smaller model. Instead of training it with the labels we have, we decided to distill the knowledge of the larger network. To do so, we will use the output of the larger network as targets.

For the first picture, instead of training the new model with a target of *[1, 0, 0]*, we will use the output of the larger network, a target of *[0.9, 0.7, 0.1]*. This new target is called a **soft target**. This way, the smaller network will be taught that, while the animal in the first picture is not a husky, it does look similar to one according to more advanced models, as the picture has a score of *0.7* for the *husky* class.

The larger network managed to directly learn from the original labels (*[1, 0, 0]* in our example) because it has more computing and memory power. During training, it was able to deduce that breeds of dogs look like one another but belong to different classes. A smaller model would not have the capacity to learn such abstract relations in the data by itself, but it can be guided by the other network. Following the aforementioned procedure, the inferred knowledge from the first model will be passed to the new one, hence the name **knowledge distillation**.

Reducing model size

When using a deep learning model in the browser or on mobile, the model needs to be downloaded on the device. It needs to be as lightweight as possible for the following reasons:

- Users are often using their phone on a cellular connection that is sometimes metered.
- The connection can also be slow.
- Models can be frequently updated.
- Disk space on portable devices is sometimes limited.

With hundreds of millions of parameters, deep learning models are notoriously disk space-consuming. Thankfully, there are techniques to reduce their size.

Quantization

The most common technique is to reduce the precision of the parameters. Instead of storing them as 32-bit floats, we can store them as 16- or 8-bit floats. There have been experiments for using binary parameters, taking only 1 bit to store.

Quantization is often done at the end of training, when converting the model for use on the device. This conversion impacts the accuracy of the model. Because of this, it is very important to evaluate the model after quantization.

Among all the compression techniques, quantization is often the one with the highest impact on size and the least impact on performance. It is also very easy to implement.

Channel pruning and weight sparsification

Other techniques exist but can be harder to implement. There is no straightforward way to apply them because they rely mostly on trial and error.

The first one, **channel pruning**, consists of removing some convolutional filters or some channels. Convolutional layers usually have between 16 and 512 different filters. At the end of the training phase, it often appears that some of them are not useful. We can remove them to avoid storing weights that will not help the model performance.

The second one is called **weight sparsification**. Instead of storing weights for the whole matrix, we can store only the ones that are deemed important or not close to zero.

For instance, instead of storing a weight vector such as *[0.1, 0.9, 0.05, 0.01, 0.7, 0.001]*, we could keep weights that are not close to zero. The result is a list of tuples in the form *(position, value)*. In our example, it would be *[(1, 0.9), (4, 0.7)]*. If many of the vector's values are close to zero, we could expect a large reduction in stored weights.

On-device machine learning

Due to their high computational requirements, deep learning algorithms are most commonly run on powerful servers. They are computers specifically designed for this task. For latency, privacy, or cost reasons, it is sometimes more interesting to run inference on customers' devices: smartphones, connected objects, cars, or microcomputers.

What all those devices have in common are lower computational power and low power requirements. Because they are at the end of the data life cycle, on-device machine learning is also referred to as **edge computing** or **machine learning on the edge**.

With regular machine learning, the computation usually happens in the data center. For instance, when you upload a photo to Facebook, a deep learning model is run in Facebook's data center to detect your friends' faces and help you tag them.

With on-device machine learning, the inference happens on your device. A common example is Snapchat face filters—the model that detects your face position is run directly on the device. However, model training still happens in data centers—the device uses a trained model fetched from the server:

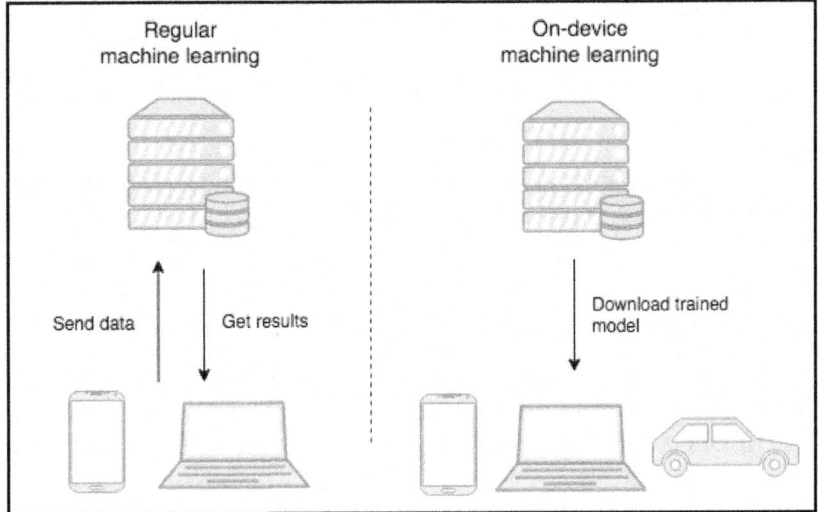

Figure 9-5: Diagram comparing on-device machine learning with conventional machine learning

Most on-device machine learning happens for inference. The training of models is still mostly done on dedicated servers.

Considerations of on-device machine learning

The use of **on-device machine learning (on-device ML)** is usually motivated by a combination of reasons, but also has its limitations.

Benefits of on-device ML

The following paragraphs list the main benefits of running machine learning algorithms directly on users' devices.

Latency

The most common motivation is **latency**. Because sending data to a server for processing takes time, real-time applications make it impossible to use conventional machine learning. The most striking illustration is self-driving cars. To react quickly to its environment, the car must have the lowest latency possible. Therefore, it is crucial to run the model in the car. Moreover, some devices are used in places where internet access is simply not available.

Privacy

As consumers care more and more about their privacy, companies are devising techniques to run deep learning models while respecting this demand.

Let's use a large-scale example from Apple. When browsing through photos on an iOS device, you may notice that it is possible to search for objects or things—`cat`, `bottle`, `car` will return the corresponding images. This is the case even if the pictures are not sent to the cloud. For Apple, it was important to make that feature available while respecting the privacy of its users. Sending pictures for processing without the users' consent would have been impossible.

Therefore, Apple decided to use on-device ML. Every night, when the phone is charging, a computer vision model is run on the iPhone to detect objects in the image and make this feature available.

Cost

On top of respecting user privacy, this feature also reduces costs for Apple because the company does not have to pay the bill for servers to process the hundreds of millions of images that their customers produce.

On a much smaller scale, it is now possible to run some deep learning models in the browser. This is especially useful for demos—by running the models on the user's computer, you can avoid paying for a costly GPU-enabled server to run inference at scale. Moreover, there will not be any overloading issues because the more users that access the page, the more computing power that is available.

Limitations of on-device ML

While it has many benefits, this concept also has a number of limitations. First of all, the limited computing power of devices means that some of the most powerful models cannot be considered.

Also, many on-device deep learning frameworks are not compatible with the most innovative or the most complex layers. For instance, TensorFlow Lite is not compatible with custom LSTM layers, making it hard to port advanced recurrent neural networks on mobile using this framework.

Finally, making models available on devices implies sharing the weights and the architecture with users. While encryption and obfuscation methods exist, it increases the risk of reverse engineering or model theft.

Practical on-device computer vision

Before discussing the practical application of on-device computer vision, we will have a look at the general considerations for running deep learning models on mobile devices.

On-device computer vision particularities

When running computer vision models on mobile devices, the focus switches from raw performance metrics to user experience. On mobile phones, this means minimizing battery and disk usage: we don't want to drain the phone's battery in minutes or fill up all the available space on the device. When running on mobile, it is recommended to use smaller models. As they contain fewer parameters, they use less disk space. Moreover, as they require fewer operations, this leads to reduced battery usage.

Another particularity of mobile phones is orientation. In training datasets, most pictures are provided with the correct orientation. While we sometimes change this orientation during data augmentation, the images are rarely upside down or completely sideways. However, there are many ways to hold a mobile phone. For this reason, we must monitor the device's orientation to make sure that we are feeding the model with images that are correctly oriented.

Generating a SavedModel

As we mentioned earlier, on-device machine learning is typically used for inference. Therefore, a prerequisite is to have a *trained model*. Hopefully, this book will have given you a good idea of how to implement and prepare your network. We now need to convert the model to an intermediate file format. It will then be converted by a library for mobile use.

In TensorFlow 2, the intermediate format of choice is **SavedModel**. A SavedModel contains the model architecture (the graph) and the weights.

Most TensorFlow objects can be exported as a SavedModel. For instance, the following code exports a trained Keras model:

```
tf.saved_model.save(model, export_dir='./saved_model')
```

Generating a frozen graph

Before introducing the **SavedModel** API, TensorFlow mainly used the **frozen graphs** format. In practice, a SavedModel is a wrapper around a frozen graph. The former includes more metadata and can include the preprocessing function needed to serve the model. While SavedModel is gaining in popularity, some libraries still require frozen models.

To convert a SavedModel to a frozen graph, the following code can be used:

```
from tensorflow.python.tools import freeze_graph

output_node_names = ['dense/Softmax']
input_saved_model_dir = './saved_model_dir'
input_binary = False
input_saver_def_path = False
restore_op_name = None
filename_tensor_name = None
clear_devices = True
input_meta_graph = False
checkpoint_path = None
input_graph_filename = None
saved_model_tags = tag_constants.SERVING

freeze_graph.freeze_graph(input_graph_filename, input_saver_def_path,
                          input_binary, checkpoint_path, output_node_names,
                          restore_op_name, filename_tensor_name,
                          'frozen_model.pb', clear_devices, "", "", "",
                          input_meta_graph, input_saved_model_dir,
                          saved_model_tags)
```

On top of specifying the input and output, we also need to specify `output_node_names`. Indeed, it is not always clear what the inference output of a model is. For instance, image detection models have several outputs—the box coordinates, the scores, and the classes. We need to specify which one(s) to use.

Note that many arguments are `False` or `None` because this function can accept many different formats, and SavedModel is only one of them.

Importance of preprocessing

As explained in `Chapter 3`, *Modern Neural Networks,* input images have to be **preprocessed**. The most common preprocessing method is to divide each channel by *127.5* (*127.5* = *255*/*2* = middle value of an image pixel) and subtract 1. This way, we represent images with values between -1 and 1:

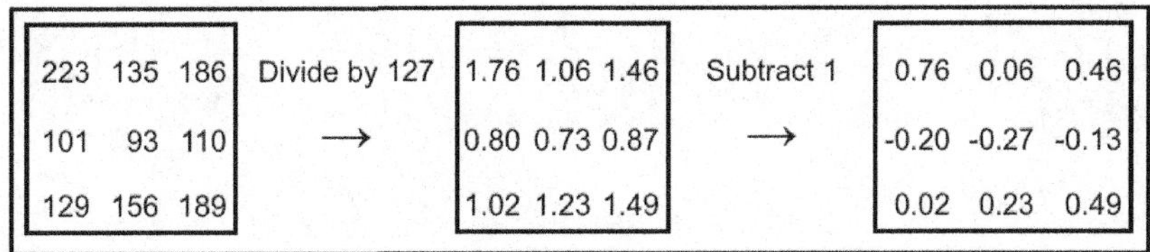

Figure 9-6: Example of preprocessing for a *3 x 3* image with a single channel

However, there are many ways to represent images, depending on the following:

- The order of the channels: RGB or BGR
- Whether the image is between *0* and *1*, *-1* and *1*, or *0* and *255*
- The order of the dimensions: *[W, H, C]* or *[C, W, H]*
- The orientation of the image

When porting a model, it is paramount to use the *exact same preprocessing* on a device as during training. Failing to do so will lead the model to infer poorly, sometimes even to fail completely, as the input data will be too different compared with the training data.

All mobile deep learning frameworks provide some options to specify preprocessing settings. It is up to you to set the correct parameters.

Now that we have obtained a **SavedModel** and that we know the importance of pre-processing, we are ready to use our model on different devices.

Example app – recognizing facial expressions

To directly apply the notions presented in this chapter, we will develop an app making use of a lightweight computer vision model, and we will deploy it to various platforms.

We will build an app that classifies facial expressions. When pointed to a person's face, it will output the expression of that person—happy, sad, surprised, disgusted, angry, or neutral. We will train our model on the **Facial Expression Recognition** (**FER**) dataset available at `https://www.kaggle.com/c/challenges-in-representation-learning-facial-expression-recognition-challenge`, put together by Pierre-Luc Carrier and Aaron Courville. It is composed of 28,709 grayscale images of 48×48 in size:

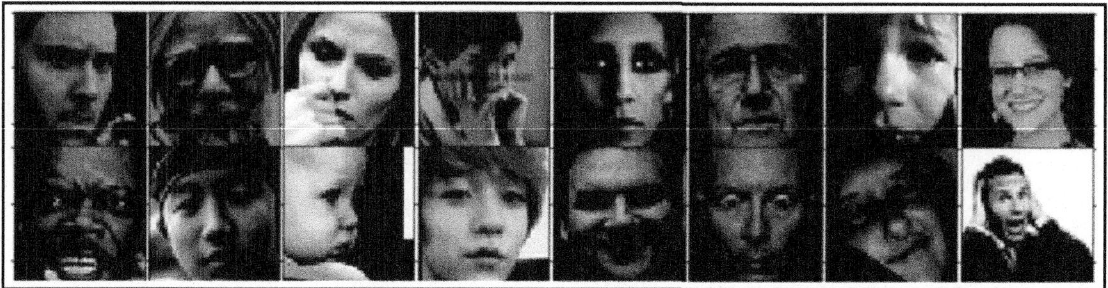

Figure 9-7: Images sampled from the FER dataset

Inside the app, the naive approach would be to capture images with the camera and then feed them directly to our trained model. However, this would yield poor results as objects in the environment would impair the quality of the prediction. We need to crop the face of the user before feeding it to the user:

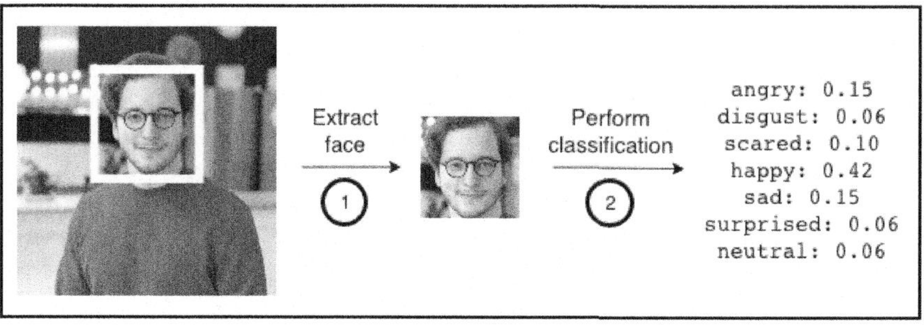

Figure 9-8: Two-step flow of our facial expression classification app

While we could build our own model for the first step (face detection), it is much more convenient to use out-of-the-box APIs. They are available natively on iOS and through libraries on Android and in the browser. The second step, expression classification, will be performed using our custom model.

Introducing MobileNet

The architecture we will use for classification is named **MobileNet**. It is a convolutional model designed to run on mobile. Introduced in 2017, in the paper *MobileNets: Efficient Convolutional Neural Networks for Mobile Vision Applications*, by Andrew G Howard et al., it uses a special kind of convolution to reduce the number of parameters as well as the computations necessary to generate predictions.

MobileNet uses **depthwise separable** convolutions. In practice, this means that the architecture is composed of an alternation of two types of convolutions:

1. **Pointwise convolutions**: These are just like regular convolutions, but with a 1×1 kernel. The purpose of pointwise convolutions is to combine the different channels of the input. Applied to an RGB image, they will compute a weighted sum of all channels.
2. **Depthwise convolutions**: These are like regular convolutions, but do not combine channels. The role of depthwise convolutions is to filter the content of the input (detect lines or patterns). Applied to an RGB image, they will compute a feature map for each channel.

When combined, these two types of convolutions perform similarly to regular convolutions. However, due to the small size of their kernels, they require fewer parameters and computational power, making this architecture suited for mobile devices.

Deploying models on-device

To illustrate on-device machine learning, we will port a model to iOS and Android devices, as well as for web browsers. We will also describe the other types of devices available.

Running on iOS devices using Core ML

With the release of its latest devices, Apple is putting the emphasis on machine learning. They designed a custom chip—the **neural engine**. This can achieve fast deep learning operations while maintaining a low power usage. To fully benefit from this chip, developers must use a set of official APIs called **Core ML** (refer to the documentation at `https://developer.apple.com/documentation/coreml`).

To use an existing model with Core ML, developers need to convert it to the `.mlmodel` format. Thankfully, Apple provides Python tools to convert from Keras or TensorFlow.

In addition to speed and energy efficiency, one of the strengths of Core ML is its integration with other iOS APIs. Powerful native methods exist for augmented reality, face detection, object tracking, and much more.

While TensorFlow Lite supports iOS, as of now, we still recommend using Core ML. This allows faster inference time and broader feature compatibility.

Converting from TensorFlow or Keras

To convert our model from Keras or TensorFlow, another tool is needed—`tf-coreml` (`https://github.com/tf-coreml/tf-coreml`).

At the time of writing, `tf-coreml` is not compatible with TensorFlow 2. We have provided a modified version while the library's developers are updating it. Refer to the chapter's notebook for the latest installation instructions.

We can then convert our model to `.mlmodel`:

```
import tfcoreml as tf_converter

tf_converter.convert('frozen_model.pb',
                     'mobilenet.mlmodel',
                     class_labels=EMOTIONS,
                     image_input_names=['input_0:0'],
                     output_feature_names=[output_node_name + ':0'],
                     red_bias=-1,
                     green_bias=-1,
                     blue_bias=-1,
                     image_scale=1/127.5,
                     is_bgr=False)
```

A few arguments are important:

- `class_labels`: The list of labels. Without this, we would end up with class IDs instead of readable text.
- `input_names`: The name of the input layer.
- `image_input_names`: This is used to specify to the Core ML framework that our input is an image. This will be useful later on because the library will handle all preprocessing for us.
- `output_feature_names`: As with the frozen model conversion, we need to specify the outputs we will target in our model. In this case, they are not operations but outputs. Therefore, `:0` must be appended to the name.
- `image_scale`: The scale used for preprocessing.
- `bias`: The bias of the preprocessing for each color.
- `is_bgr`: Must be `True` if channels are in the BGR order, or `False` if RGB.

As stated earlier, `scale`, `bias`, and `is_bgr` must match the ones used during training.

After converting the model to a `.mlmodel` file, it can be opened in Xcode:

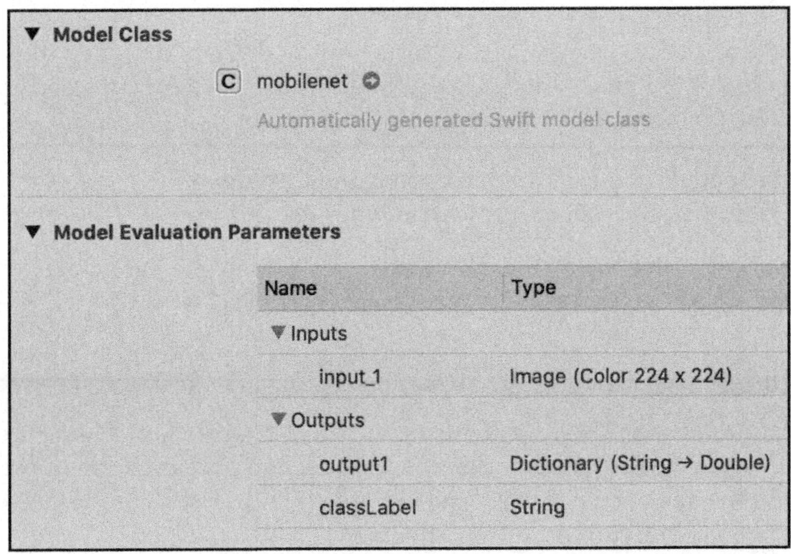

Figure 9-9: Screenshot of Xcode showing the details of a model

Note that the input is recognized as an `Image` since we specified `image_input_names`. Thanks to this, Core ML will be able to handle the preprocessing of the image for us.

Loading the model

The full app is available in the chapter repository. A Mac computer and an iOS device are necessary to build and run it. Let's briefly detail the steps to get predictions from the model. Note that the following code is written in Swift. It has a similar syntax to Python:

```
private lazy var model: VNCoreMLModel = try! VNCoreMLModel(for:
mobilenet().model)

private lazy var classificationRequest: VNCoreMLRequest = {
    let request = VNCoreMLRequest(model: model, completionHandler: { [weak
self] request, error in
        self?.processClassifications(for: request, error: error)
    })
    request.imageCropAndScaleOption = .centerCrop
    return request
}()
```

The code consists of three main steps:

1. Loading the model. All the information about it is available in the `.mlmodel` file.
2. Setting a custom callback. In our case, after the image is classified, we will call `processClassifications`.
3. Setting `imageCropAndScaleOption`. Our model was designed to accept square images, but the input often has a different ratio. Therefore, we configure Core ML to crop the center of the image by setting it to `centerCrop`.

We also load the model used for face detection using the native `VNDetectFaceRectanglesRequest` and `VNSequenceRequestHandler` functions:

```
private let faceDetectionRequest = VNDetectFaceRectanglesRequest()
private let faceDetectionHandler = VNSequenceRequestHandler()
```

Using the model

As an input, we access `pixelBuffer`, which contains the pixel of the video feed from the camera of the device. We run our face detection model and obtain `faceObservations`. This will contain the detection results. If the variable is empty, it means that no face was detected and we do not go further in the function:

```
try faceDetectionHandler.perform([faceDetectionRequest], on: pixelBuffer,
orientation: exifOrientation)

guard let faceObservations = faceDetectionRequest.results as?
[VNFaceObservation], faceObservations.isEmpty == false else {
```

```
        return
    }
```

Then, for each `faceObservation` in `faceObservations`, we classify the area containing the face:

```
let classificationHandler = VNImageRequestHandler(cvPixelBuffer:
pixelBuffer, orientation: .right, options: [:])

let box = faceObservation.boundingBox
let region = CGRect(x: box.minY, y: 1 - box.maxX, width: box.height,
height:box.width)
self.classificationRequest.regionOfInterest = region

try classificationHandler.perform([self.classificationRequest])
```

To do so, we specify `regionOfInterest` of the request. This notifies the Core ML framework that the input is this specific area of the image. This is very convenient as we do not have to crop and resize the image—the framework handles this for us. Finally, we call the `classificationHandler.perform` native method.

Note that we had to change the coordinate system. The face coordinates are returned with an origin at the top left of the image, while `regionOfInterest` must be specified with an origin in the bottom left.

Once the predictions are generated, our custom callback, `processClassifications`, will be called with the results. We will then be able to display the results to the user. This part is covered in the full application available in the book's GitHub repository.

Running on Android using TensorFlow Lite

TensorFlow Lite is a mobile framework that allows you to run TensorFlow models on mobile and embedded devices. It supports Android, iOS, and Raspberry Pi. Unlike Core ML on iOS devices, it is not a native library but an external dependency that must be added to your app.

While Core ML was optimized for iOS device hardware, TensorFlow Lite performance may vary from device to device. On some Android devices, it can use the GPU to improve inference speed.

To use TensorFlow Lite for our example application, we will first convert our model to the library's format using the TensorFlow Lite converter.

Converting the model from TensorFlow or Keras

TensorFlow integrates a function to transform a SavedModel model to the TF Lite format. To do so, we first create a TensorFlow Lite converter object:

```
# From a Keras model
converter = tf.lite.TFLiteConverter.from_keras_model(model)
## Or from a SavedModel
converter = tf.lite.TFLiteConverter('./saved_model')
```

Then, the model is saved to disk:

```
tflite_model = converter.convert()
open("result.tflite", "wb").write(tflite_model)
```

You will notice that the TensorFlow Lite function offers fewer options than the Apple Core ML equivalent. Indeed, TensorFlow Lite does not handle preprocessing and resizing of the images automatically. This has to be handled by the developer in the Android app.

Loading the model

After converting the model to the `.tflite` format, we can add it to the assets folder of our Android application. We can then load the model using a helper function, `loadModelFile`:

```
tfliteModel = loadModelFile(activity);
```

Because our model is in the assets folder of our app, we need to pass the current activity. If you are not familiar with Android app development, you can think of an activity as a specific screen of an app.

We can then create `Interpreter`. In TensorFlow Lite, the interpreter is necessary to run a model and return predictions. In our example, we pass the default `Options` constructor. The `Options` constructor could be used to change the number of threads or the precision of the model:

```
Interpreter.Options tfliteOptions = new Interpreter.Options();
tflite = new Interpreter(tfliteModel, tfliteOptions);
```

Finally, we will create `ByteBuffer`. This is a data structure that contains the input image data:

```
imgData =
    ByteBuffer.allocateDirect(
        DIM_BATCH_SIZE
```

```
            * getImageSizeX()
            * getImageSizeY()
            * DIM_PIXEL_SIZE
            * getNumBytesPerChannel());
```

`ByteBuffer` is an array that will contain the pixels of the image. Its size depends on the following:

- The batch size—in our case, 1.
- The dimensions of the input image.
- The number of channels (`DIM_PIXEL_SIZE`)—3 for RGB, 1 for grayscale.
- Finally, the number of bytes per channel. As *1 byte = 8 bits*, a 32-bits input will require 4 bytes. If using quantization, an 8-bits input will require 1 byte.

To process predictions, we will later fill this `imgData` buffer and pass it to the interpreter. Our facial expression detection model is ready to be used. Before we can start using our full pipeline, we only need to instantiate the face detector:

```
faceDetector = new FaceDetector.Builder(this.getContext())
        .setMode(FaceDetector.FAST_MODE)
        .setTrackingEnabled(false)
        .setLandmarkType(FaceDetector.NO_LANDMARKS)
        .build();
```

Note that this `FaceDetector` class comes from the Google Vision framework and has nothing to do with TensorFlow Lite.

Using the model

For our example app, we will work with bitmap images. You can see bitmaps as a matrix of raw pixels. They are compatible with most of the image libraries on Android. We obtain this bitmap from the view that displays the video feed from the camera, called `textureView`:

```
Bitmap bitmap = textureView.getBitmap(previewSize.getHeight() / 4,
previewSize.getWidth() / 4)
```

We do not capture the bitmap at full resolution. Instead, we divide its dimensions by `4` (this number was picked by trial and error). Choosing a size that's too large would result in very slow face detection, reducing the inference time of our pipeline.

We then proceed to create `vision.Frame` from the bitmap. This step is necessary to pass the image to `faceDetector`:

```
Frame frame = new Frame.Builder().setBitmap(bitmap).build();
faces = faceDetector.detect(frame);
```

Then, for each `face` in `faces`, we can crop the face of the user in the bitmap. Provided in the GitHub repository, the `cropFaceInBitmap` helper function does precisely this—it accepts the coordinates of the face and crops the corresponding area in the bitmap:

```
Bitmap faceBitmap = cropFaceInBitmap(face, bitmap);
Bitmap resized = Bitmap.createScaledBitmap(faceBitmap,
classifier.getImageSizeX(), classifier.getImageSizeY(), true)
```

After resizing the bitmap to fit the input of our model, we fill `imgData`, `ByteBuffer`, which `Interpreter` accepts:

```
imgData.rewind();
resized.getPixels(intValues, 0, resized.getWidth(), 0, 0,
resized.getWidth(), resized.getHeight());

int pixel = 0;
for (int i = 0; i < getImageSizeX(); ++i) {
  for (int j = 0; j < getImageSizeY(); ++j) {
    final int val = intValues[pixel++];
    addPixelValue(val);
  }
}
```

As you can see, we iterate over the bitmap's pixels to add them to `imgData`. To do so, we use `addPixelValue`. This function handles the preprocessing of each pixel. It will be different depending on the characteristics of the model. In our case, the model is using a grayscale image. We must therefore convert each pixel from color to grayscale:

```
protected void addPixelValue(int pixelValue) {
  float mean =  (((pixelValue >> 16) & 0xFF) + ((pixelValue >> 8) & 0xFF) +
(pixelValue & 0xFF)) / 3.0f;
  imgData.putFloat(mean / 127.5f - 1.0f);
}
```

In this function, we are using bit-wise operations to compute the mean of the three colors of each pixel. We then divide it by `127.5` and subtract `1` as this is the preprocessing step of our model.

At the end of this process, `imgData` contains the input information in the correct format. Finally, we can run the inference:

```
float[][] labelProbArray = new float[1][getNumLabels()];
tflite.run(imgData, labelProbArray);
```

The predictions will be inside `labelProbArray`. We can then process and display them.

Running in the browser using TensorFlow.js

With web browsers packing more and more features every year, it was only a matter of time before they could run deep learning models. Running models in the browser has many advantages:

- The user does not have anything to install.
- The computing is done on the user's machine (mobile or computer).
- The model can sometimes make use of the device's GPU.

The library to run in the browser is called TensorFlow.js (refer to the documentation at `https://github.com/tensorflow/tfjs`). We will implement our face expression classification application using it.

While TensorFlow cannot take advantage of non-NVIDIA GPUs, TensorFlow.js can use GPUs on almost any device. GPU support in the browser was first implemented to display graphical animations through WebGL (a computer graphics API for web applications, based on OpenGL). Since it involves matrix calculus, it was then repurposed to run deep learning operations.

Converting the model to the TensorFlow.js format

To use TensorFlow.js, the model must first be converted to the correct format using `tfjs-converter`. It can convert Keras models, frozen models, and SavedModels. Installation instructions are provided in the GitHub repository.

Then, converting a model is very similar to the process done for TensorFlow Lite. Instead of being done in Python, it is done from the command line:

```
$ tensorflowjs_converter ./saved_model --input_format=tf_saved_model my-tfjs --output_format tfjs_graph_model
```

Similar to TensorFlow Lite, we need to specify the names of the output nodes.

The output is composed of multiple files:

- `optimized_model.pb`: Contains the model graph
- `weights_manifest.json`: Contains information about the list of weights
- `group1-shard1of5`, `group1-shard2of5`, ..., `group1-shard5of5`: Contains the weights of the model split into multiple files

The model is split into multiple files because parallel downloads are usually faster.

Using the model

In our JavaScript app, after importing TensorFlow.js, we can load our model. Note that the following code is in JavaScript. It has a similar syntax to Python:

```
import * as tf from '@tensorflow/tfjs';
const model = await tf.loadModel(MOBILENET_MODEL_PATH);
```

We will also use a library called `face-api.js` to extract faces:

```
import * as faceapi from 'face-api.js';
await faceapi.loadTinyFaceDetectorModel(DETECTION_MODEL_PATH)
```

Once both models are loaded, we can start processing images from the user:

```
const video = document.getElementById('video');
const detection = await faceapi.detectSingleFace(video, new
faceapi.TinyFaceDetectorOptions())

if (detection) {
 const faceCanvases = await faceapi.extractFaces(video, [detection])
 const values = await predict(faceCanvases[0])
}
```

Here, we grab a frame from the `video` element displaying the webcam of the user. The `face-api.js` library will attempt to detect a face in this frame. If it detects a frame, the part of the image containing the frame is extracted and fed to our model.

The `predict` function handles the preprocessing of the image and the classification. This is what it looks like:

```
async function predict(imgElement) {
  let img = await tf.browser.fromPixels(imgElement, 3).toFloat();

  const logits = tf.tidy(() => {
    // tf.fromPixels() returns a Tensor from an image element.
    img = tf.image.resizeBilinear(img, [IMAGE_SIZE, IMAGE_SIZE]);
```

```
    img = img.mean(2);
    const offset = tf.scalar(127.5);
    // Normalize the image from [0, 255] to [-1, 1].
    const normalized = img.sub(offset).div(offset);
    const batched = normalized.reshape([1, IMAGE_SIZE, IMAGE_SIZE, 1]);

    return mobilenet.predict(batched);
  });

  return logits
}
```

We first resize the image using `resizeBilinear` and convert it from color to grayscale using `mean`. We then preprocess the pixels, normalizing them between `-1` and `1`. Finally, we run the data through `model.predict` to get predictions. At the end of this pipeline, we end up with predictions that we can display to the user.

Note the use of `tf.tidy`. This is very important because TensorFlow.js creates intermediate tensors that might never be removed from memory. Wrapping our operations inside `tf.tidy` automatically purges intermediate elements from memory.

Over the last few years, technology improvements have made new applications in the browser possible—image classification, text generation, style transfer, and pose estimation are now available to anyone without needing to install anything.

Running on other devices

We have covered the conversion of models to run in the browser, and on iOS and Android devices. TensorFlow Lite can also run on the Raspberry Pi, a pocket-sized computer running Linux.

Moreover, devices designed specifically to run deep learning models started to emerge over the years. Here are a few examples:

- **NVIDIA Jetson TX2**: The size of a palm; it is often used for robotics applications.
- **Google Edge TPU**: A chip designed by Google for IoT applications. It is the size of a nail, and is available with a developer kit.
- **Intel Neural Compute Stick**: The size of a USB flash drive; it can be connected to any computer (including the Raspberry Pi) to improve its machine learning capabilities.

These devices all focus on maximizing computing power while minimizing power consumption. With each generation getting more powerful, the on-device ML field is moving extremely quickly, opening new applications every year.

Summary

In this chapter, we covered several topics on performance. First, we learned how to properly measure the inference speed of a model, and then we went through techniques to reduce inference time: choosing the right hardware and the right libraries, optimizing input size, and optimizing post-processing. We covered techniques to make a slower model appear, to the user, as if it were processing in real time, and to reduce the model size.

Then, we introduced on-device ML, along with its benefits and limitations. We learned how to convert TensorFlow and Keras models to a format that's compatible with on-device deep learning frameworks. With examples on iOS and Android, and in the browser, we covered a wide range of devices. We also introduced some existing embedded devices.

Throughout this book, we have presented TensorFlow 2 in detail, applying it to multiple computer vision tasks. We have covered a variety of state-of-the-art solutions, providing both a theoretical background and some practical implementations. With this last chapter tackling their deployment, it is now up to you to harness the power of TensorFlow 2 and to develop computer vision applications for the use cases of your choice!

Questions

1. When measuring a model's inference speed, should you measure with a single image or multiple ones?
2. Is a model with *float32* weights smaller or larger than one with *float16* weights?
3. On iOS devices, should Core ML or TensorFlow Lite be favored? What about Android devices?
4. What are the benefits and limitations of running a model in the browser?
5. What is the most important requirement for embedded devices running deep learning algorithms?

Migrating from TensorFlow 1 to TensorFlow 2

Since TensorFlow 2 has only been released very recently, most of the projects that are available online are still built for TensorFlow 1. While this first version was already packed with useful features, such as AutoGraph and the Keras API, it is recommended that you migrate to the latest version of TensorFlow so as to avoid any technical debt. Thankfully, TensorFlow 2 comes with an automatic migration tool that is able to convert most projects to its latest version. It requires little effort and outputs functional code. However, migrating to idiomatic TensorFlow 2 code requires some diligence and knowledge of both versions. In this section, we will introduce the migration tool and compare TensorFlow 1 concepts with their TensorFlow 2 counterparts.

Automatic migration

After installing TensorFlow 2, the migration tool is available from the command line. To convert a project directory, run the following command:

```
$ tf_upgrade_v2 --intree ./project_directory --outtree
./project_directory_updated
```

Here is a sample of the command's logs on an example project:

```
INFO line 1111:10: Renamed 'tf.placeholder' to 'tf.compat.v1.placeholder'
 INFO line 1112:10: Renamed 'tf.layers.dense' to
'tf.compat.v1.layers.dense'
 TensorFlow 2.0 Upgrade Script
 -----------------------------
 Converted 21 files
 Detected 1 issues that require attention
 --------------------------------------------------------------------
 --------------------------------------------------------------------
 File: project_directory/test_tf_converter.py
 --------------------------------------------------------------------
 project_directory/test_tf_converter.py:806:10: WARNING:
tf.image.resize_bilinear called with align_corners argument requires manual
check: align_corners is not supported by tf.image.resize, the new default
transformation is close to what v1 provided. If you require exactly the
same transformation as before, use compat.v1.image.resize_bilinear.
  Make sure to read the detailed log 'report.txt'
```

The conversion tool details all the changes it made to the files. In the rare case when it detects a code line that requires manual attention, it outputs a warning with instructions to update.

Most of the outdated calls are moved to `tf.compat.v1`. Indeed, despite the deprecation of many concepts, TensorFlow 2 still provides access to the old API through this module. However, be aware that calls to `tf.contrib` will cause the conversion tool to fail and generate an error:

```
ERROR: Using member tf.contrib.copy_graph.copy_op_to_graph in deprecated
module tf.contrib. tf.contrib.copy_graph.copy_op_to_graph cannot be
converted automatically. tf.contrib will not be distributed with TensorFlow
2.0, please consider an alternative in non-contrib TensorFlow, a community-
maintained repository, or fork the required code.
```

Migrating TensorFlow 1 code

If the tool runs without any error, the code can be used as is. However, the `tf.compat.v1` module used by the migration tool is deemed to be deprecated. Calling this module already outputs deprecation warnings, and its content will not be further updated by the community. For this reason, it is recommended that you refactor the code in order to make it more idiomatic. In the following sections, we will introduce TensorFlow 1 concepts and explain how to migrate them to TensorFlow 2. In the following examples, `tf1` will be used instead of `tf` to denote the use of TensorFlow 1.13.

Sessions

Since TensorFlow 1 does not use eager execution by default, the results of the operations are not directly available. For instance, when summing two constants, the output object is an operation:

```
import tensorflow as tf1 # TensorFlow 1.13

a = tf1.constant([1,2,3])
b = tf1.constant([1,2,3])
c = a + b
print(c) # Prints <tf.Tensor 'add:0' shape=(3,) dtype=int32
```

To compute a result, you need to manually create `tf1.Session`. A session takes care of the following:

- Managing the memory
- Running operations on CPU or GPU
- Running on several machines if necessary

The most common way of using a session is through the `with` statement in Python. As with other unmanaged resources, the `with` statement guarantees that the session is properly closed after we use it. If the session is not closed, it may keep using memory. Sessions in TensorFlow 1 are, therefore, typically instantiated and used as follows:

```
with tf1.Session() as sess:
 result = sess.run(c)
print(result) # Prints array([2, 4, 6], dtype=int32)
```

You can also explicitly close a session, but it is not recommended:

```
sess = tf1.Session()
result = sess.run(c)
sess.close()
```

In TensorFlow 2, session management happens behind the scenes. As the new version uses eager execution, there is no need for this superfluous code to compute results. Calls to `tf1.Session()` can, therefore, be removed.

Placeholders

In the previous example, we computed the sum of two vectors. However, we defined the value of those vectors when creating the graph. If we wanted to use variables instead, we could have used `tf1.placeholder`:

```
a = tf1.placeholder(dtype=tf.int32, shape=(None,))
b = tf1.placeholder(dtype=tf.int32, shape=(None,))
c = a + b

with tf1.Session() as sess:
  result = sess.run(c, feed_dict={
      a: [1, 2, 3],
      b: [1, 1, 1]
    })
```

In TensorFlow 1, placeholders are mostly used to provide input data. Their type and shape have to be defined. In our example, the shape is `(None, )` because we may want to run the operation on vectors of any size. When running the graph, we have to provide specific values for our placeholders. This is why we use the `feed_dict` argument in `sess.run`, passing the content of variables as a dictionary, with the placeholders as keys. Failing to provide a value for all placeholders would cause an exception.

Before TensorFlow 2, placeholders were used to provide input data, as well as layers' parameters. The former use case can be replaced with `tf.keras.Input`, while the latter can be addressed using `tf.keras.layers.Layer` parameters.

Variable management

In TensorFlow 1, variables were created globally. Each variable had a unique name and the best practice in terms of creating them was to use `tf1.get_variable()`:

```
weights = tf1.get_variable(name='W', initializer=[3])
```

Here, we created a global variable named `W`. Deleting the Python `weights` variable (using the Python `del weights` command, for instance) would have no effect on TensorFlow memory. In fact, if we try to create the same variable again, we would end up with an error:

```
Variable W already exists, disallowed. Did you mean to set reuse=True or
reuse=tf.AUTO_REUSE in VarScope?
```

While `tf1.get_variable()` allows you to reuse variables, its default behavior is to throw an error if a variable with the chosen name already exists, preventing you from mistakenly overriding variables. To avoid this error, we can update our call to `tf1.variable_scope(...)` and employ the `reuse` argument:

```
with tf1.variable_scope("conv1", reuse=True):
    weights = tf1.get_variable(name='W', initializer=[3])
```

The `variable_scope` context manager was used to manage variable creation. On top of handling variable reuse, it was useful to group variables together by appending a prefix to their name. In the previous example, the variable would be named `conv1/W`.

In this case, setting reuse to `True` means that if TensorFlow encounters a variable called `conv1/W`, it will not throw an error as it did before. Instead, it will reuse the existing variable, including its content. However, if you try calling the preceding code and the variable named `conv1/W` does not exist, you will encounter the following error:

```
Variable conv1/W does not exist
```

Indeed, `reuse=True` can only be specified when reusing an existing variable. If you want to create a variable if it does not exist, and reuse it when it does exist, you can pass `reuse=tf.AUTO_REUSE`.

In TensorFlow 2, the behavior is different. While variable scope still exists to make naming and debugging easier, variables are no longer global. They are handled at the Python level. As long as you can access the Python reference (the `weights` variable, in our example), you can modify the variable. To delete the variable, you need to delete its reference, for instance, by running the following command:

```
del weights
```

Previously, variables could be accessed and modified globally, and could potentially be overridden by other pieces of code. The deprecation of global variables makes TensorFlow code more readable and less prone to errors.

Layers and models

TensorFlow models were originally defined using `tf1.layers`. As this module has been deprecated in TensorFlow 2, the replacement of choice is `tf.keras.layers`. To train a model using TensorFlow 1, a *train operation* has to be defined using an optimizer and a loss. For instance, if `y` is the output of a fully connected layer, we would define the training operation using the following command:

```
cross_entropy =
tf.reduce_mean(tf.nn.softmax_cross_entropy_with_logits_v2(labels=output,
logits=y))
train_step = tf.train.AdamOptimizer(1e-3).minimize(cross_entropy)
```

Every time we call this operation, a batch of images will be fed to the network and a single step of backpropagation will happen. We then run a loop to compute multiple training steps:

```
num_steps = 10**7

with tf1.Session() as sess:
    sess.run(tf1.global_variables_initializer())

    for i in range(num_steps):
        batch_x, batch_y = next(batch_generator)
        sess.run(train_step, feed_dict={x: batch_x, y: batch_y})
```

When opening the session, a call to `tf1.global_variables_initializer()` is necessary so that layers are initialized with the correct weights. A failure to do so would throw an exception. In TensorFlow 2, the initialization of variables is handled automatically.

Other concepts

We detailed the most common TensorFlow 1 concepts that were deprecated in the new version. Many smaller modules and paradigms were also redesigned in TensorFlow 2. When migrating a project, we recommend having a thorough look at the documentation of both versions. To ensure that a migration went well and the TensorFlow 2 version works as expected, we recommend that you log both inference metrics (such as latency, accuracy, or average precision) and training metrics (such as the number of iterations before convergence), and compare their values between the old and new versions.

As it is open source and backed by an active community, TensorFlow is constantly evolving—integrating new features, optimizing others, improving the developer experience, and more. While this may sometimes require some additional effort, upgrading to the latest version as soon as possible will provide you with the best environment to develop more performant recognition applications.

References

This section lists the scientific papers and other web resources mentioned in this book.

Chapter 1: Computer Vision and Neural Networks

- Angeli, A., Filliat, D., Doncieux, S., Meyer, J.-A., 2008. *A Fast and Incremental Method for Loop-Closure Detection Using Bags of Visual Words. IEEE Transactions on Robotics 1027–1037.*
- Bradski, G., Kaehler, A., 2000. OpenCV. *Dr. Dobb's Journal of Software Tools 3.*
- Cortes, C., Vapnik, V., 1995. *Support-Vector Networks. Machine Learning 20, 273–297.*
- Drucker, H., Burges, C.J., Kaufman, L., Smola, A.J., Vapnik, V., 1997. *Support Vector Regression Machines. In: Advances in Neural Information Processing Systems, pp. 155–161.*
- Krizhevsky, A., Sutskever, I., Hinton, G.E., 2012. *ImageNet Classification with Deep Convolutional Neural Networks. In: Advances in Neural Information Processing Systems, pp. 1097–1105.*

- Lawrence, S., Giles, C.L., Tsoi, A.C., Back, A.D., 1997. *Face Recognition: A Convolutional Neural-Network Approach. IEEE Transactions on Neural Networks 8, 98–113.*
- LeCun, Y., Boser, B.E., Denker, J.S., Henderson, D., Howard, R.E., Hubbard, W.E., Jackel, L.D., 1990. *Handwritten Digit Recognition with a Back-Propagation Network. In: Advances in Neural Information Processing Systems, pp. 396–404.*
- LeCun, Y., Cortes, C., Burges, C., 2010. *MNIST Handwritten Digit Database. AT&T Labs [Online].* Available at `http://yann.lecun.com/exdb/mnist` 2, 18.
- Lowe, D.G., 2004. *Distinctive Image Features from Scale-Invariant Keypoints. International Journal of Computer Vision 60, 91–110.*
- Minsky, M., 1961. *Steps Toward Artificial Intelligence. Proceedings of the IRE 49, 8–30.*
- Minsky, M., Papert, S.A., 2017. *Perceptrons: An Introduction to Computational Geometry. MIT press.*
- Moravec, H., 1984. *Locomotion, Vision, and Intelligence.*
- Papert, S.A., 1966. *The Summer Vision Project.*
- Plaut, D.C., et al., 1986. *Experiments on Learning by Back Propagation.*
- Rosenblatt, F., 1958. *The Perceptron: A Probabilistic Model for Information Storage and Organization in the Brain. Psychological Review 65, 386.*
- Turk, M., Pentland, A., 1991. *Eigenfaces for Recognition. Journal of Cognitive Neuroscience 3, 71–86.*
- Wold, S., Esbensen, K., Geladi, P., 1987. *Principal Component Analysis. Chemometrics and Intelligent Laboratory Systems 2, 37–52.*

Chapter 2: TensorFlow Basics and Training a Model

- Abadi, M., Agarwal, A., Barham, P., Brevdo, E., Chen, Z., Citro, C., Corrado, G.S., Davis, A., Dean, et al. *TensorFlow: Large-Scale Machine Learning on Heterogeneous Distributed Systems 19.*
- *API Documentation [WWW Document], n.d. TensorFlow.* URL: `https://www.tensorflow.org/api_docs/` (accessed December 14, 2018).
- Chollet, F., 2018. TensorFlow is the platform of choice for deep learning in the research community. There are deep learning framework mentions on arXiv over the past three months, *pic.twitter.com/v6ZEi63hzP. @fchollet.*
- Goldsborough, P., 2016. *A Tour of TensorFlow. arXiv:1610.01178 [cs].*

Chapter 3: Modern Neural Networks

- Abadi, M., Barham, P., Chen, J., Chen, Z., Davis, A., Dean, J., Devin, M., Ghemawat, S., Irving, G., Isard, M., et al., 2016. *Tensorflow: A System for Large-Scale Machine Learning. In: OSDI, pp. 265–283.*
- *API Documentation, URL:* `https://www.tensorflow.org/api_docs/` (accessed December 14, 2018).
- Bottou, L., 2010. *Large-Scale Machine Learning with Stochastic Gradient Descent. In: Proceedings of COMPSTAT'2010. Springer, pp. 177–186.*
- Bottou, L., Curtis, F.E., Nocedal, J., 2018. *Optimization Methods for Large-Scale Machine Learning. SIAM Review 60, 223–311.*
- Dozat, T., 2016. *Incorporating Nesterov Momentum into Adam.*
- Duchi, J., Hazan, E., Singer, Y., 2011. *Adaptive Subgradient Methods for Online Learning and Stochastic Optimization. Journal of Machine Learning Research 12, 2121–2159.*
- Gardner, W.A., 1984. *Learning Characteristics of Stochastic Gradient Descent Algorithms: A General Study, Analysis, and Critique. Signal Processing 6, 113–133.*
- Girosi, F., Jones, M., Poggio, T., 1995. *Regularization Theory and Neural Networks Architectures. Neural Computation 7, 219–269.*
- Ioffe, S., Szegedy, C., 2015. *Batch Normalization: Accelerating Deep Network Training by Reducing Internal Covariate Shift. arXiv preprint arXiv:1502.03167.*
- Karpathy, A., n.d. *Stanford University CS231n: Convolutional Neural Networks for Visual Recognition [WWW Document].* URL: `http://cs231n.stanford.edu/` (accessed December 14, 2018).
- Kingma, D.P., Ba, J., 2014. *Adam: A Method for Stochastic Optimization. arXiv preprint arXiv:1412.6980.*
- Krizhevsky, A., Sutskever, I., Hinton, G.E., 2012. *ImageNet Classification with Deep Convolutional Neural Networks. In: Advances in Neural Information Processing Systems, pp. 1097–1105.*
- Lawrence, S., Giles, C.L., Tsoi, A.C., Back, A.D., 1997. *Face Recognition: A Convolutional Neural Network Approach. IEEE Transactions on Neural Networks 8, 98–113.*
- Le and Borji – 2017 – *What are the Receptive, Effective Receptive, and P.pdf, n.d.*
- Le, H., Borji, A., 2017. *What are the Receptive, Effective Receptive, and Projective Fields of Neurons in Convolutional Neural Networks? arXiv:1705.07049 [cs].*
- LeCun, Y., Cortes, C., Burges, C., 2010. *MNIST Handwritten Digit Database. AT&T Labs [Online].* Available at `http://yann.lecun.com/exdb/mnist` 2.

- LeCun, Y., et al., 2015. LeNet-5, *Convolutional Neural Networks*. URL: `http://yann.lecun.com/exdb/lenet` 20.
- Lenail, A., *n.d. NN SVG [WWW Document]*. URL: `http://alexlenail.me/NN-SVG/` (accessed December 14, 2018).
- Luo, W., Li, Y., Urtasun, R., Zemel, R., n.d. *Understanding the Effective Receptive Field in Deep Convolutional Neural Networks 9.*
- Nesterov, Y., 1998. *Introductory Lectures on Convex Programming Volume I: Basic Course. Lecture notes.*
- Perkins, E.S., Davson, H., n.d. *Human Eye | Definition, Structure, & Function [WWW Document]. Encyclopedia Britannica.* URL: `https://www.britannica.com/science/human-eye` (accessed December 14, 2018).
- Perone, C.S., n.d. *The effective receptive field on CNNs | Terra Incognita. Terra Incognita.*
- Polyak, B.T., 1964. *Some methods of speeding up the convergence of iteration methods. USSR Computational Mathematics and Mathematical Physics 4, 1–17.*
- Raj, D., 2018. *A Short Note on Gradient Descent Optimization Algorithms. Medium.*
- Simard, P.Y., Steinkraus, D., Platt, J.C., 2003. *Best Practices for Convolutional Neural Networks Applied to Visual Document Analysis. In: Null, p. 958.*
- Srivastava, N., Hinton, G., Krizhevsky, A., Sutskever, I., Salakhutdinov, R., 2014. *Dropout: A Simple Way to Prevent Neural Networks from Overfitting. The Journal of Machine Learning Research 15, 1929–1958.*
- Sutskever, I., Martens, J., Dahl, G., Hinton, G., 2013. *On the importance of initialization and momentum in deep learning. In: International Conference on Machine Learning, pp. 1139–1147.*
- Tieleman, T., Hinton, G., 2012. *Lecture 6.5-rmsprop: Divide the gradient by a running average of its recent magnitude. COURSERA: Neural Networks for Machine Learning 4, 26–31.*
- Walia, A.S., 2017. *Types of Optimization Algorithms Used in Neural Networks and Ways to Optimize Gradient Descent [WWW Document]. Towards Data Science.* URL: `https://towardsdatascience.com/types-of-optimization-algorithms-used-in-neural-networks-and-ways-to-optimize-gradient-95ae5d39529f` (accessed December 14, 2018).
- Zeiler, M.D., 2012. *ADADELTA: An Adaptive Learning Rate Method. arXiv preprint arXiv:1212.5701.*
- Zhang, T., 2004. *Solving large-scale linear prediction problems using stochastic gradient descent algorithms. In: Proceedings of the Twenty-first International Conference on Machine Learning, p. 116.*

Chapter 4: Influential Classification Tools

- *API Documentation [WWW Document], n.d. TensorFlow.* URL: `https://www.tensorflow.org/api_docs/` (accessed December 14, 2018).
- Goodfellow, I., Bengio, Y., Courville, A., 2016. *Deep Learning. MIT Press.*
- He, K., Zhang, X., Ren, S., Sun, J., 2015. *Deep Residual Learning for Image Recognition. arXiv:1512.03385 [cs].*
- Howard, A.G., Zhu, M., Chen, B., Kalenichenko, D., Wang, W., Weyand, T., Andreetto, M., Adam, H., 2017. *MobileNets: Efficient Convolutional Neural Networks for Mobile Vision Applications. arXiv:1704.04861 [cs].*
- Huang, G., Liu, Z., van der Maaten, L., Weinberger, K.Q., 2016. *Densely Connected Convolutional Networks. arXiv:1608.06993 [cs].*
- Karpathy, A., n.d. *Stanford University CS231n: Convolutional Neural Networks for Visual Recognition [WWW Document].* URL: `http://cs231n.stanford.edu/` (accessed December 14, 2018).
- Karpathy, A. *What I learned from competing against a ConvNet on ImageNet [WWW Document], n.d.* URL: `http://karpathy.github.io/2014/09/02/what-i-learned-from-competing-against-a-convnet-on-imagenet/` (accessed January 4, 2019).
- Lin, M., Chen, Q., Yan, S., 2013. *Network In Network. arXiv:1312.4400 [cs].*
- Pan, S.J., Yang, Q., 2010. *A Survey on Transfer Learning. IEEE Transactions on Knowledge and Data Engineering 22, 1345–1359.*
- Russakovsky, O., Deng, J., Su, H., Krause, J., Satheesh, S., Ma, S., Huang, Z., Karpathy, A., Khosla, A., Bernstein, M., Berg, A.C., Fei-Fei, L., 2014. *ImageNet Large-Scale Visual Recognition Challenge. arXiv:1409.0575 [cs].*
- Sarkar, D. (DJ), 2018. *A Comprehensive Hands-on Guide to Transfer Learning with Real-World Applications in Deep Learning [WWW Document]. Towards Data Science.* URL: `https://towardsdatascience.com/a-comprehensive-hands-on-guide-to-transfer-learning-with-real-world-applications-in-deep-learning-212bf3b2f27a` (accessed January 15, 2019).
- shu-yusa, 2018. *Using Inception-v3 from TensorFlow Hub for Transfer Learning. Medium.*
- *Simonyan, K., Zisserman, A., 2014. Very Deep Convolutional Networks for Large-Scale Image Recognition. arXiv:1409.1556 [cs].*
- Srivastava, R.K., Greff, K., Schmidhuber, J., 2015. *Highway Networks. arXiv:1505.00387 [cs].*
- Szegedy, C., Ioffe, S., Vanhoucke, V., Alemi, A., 2016. *Inception-v4, Inception-ResNet and the Impact of Residual Connections on Learning. arXiv:1602.07261 [cs].*

- Szegedy, C., Liu, W., Jia, Y., Sermanet, P., Reed, S., Anguelov, D., Erhan, D., Vanhoucke, V., Rabinovich, A., 2014. *Going Deeper with Convolutions. arXiv:1409.4842 [cs].*
- Szegedy, C., Vanhoucke, V., Ioffe, S., Shlens, J., Wojna, Z., 2015. *Rethinking the Inception Architecture for Computer Vision. arXiv:1512.00567 [cs].*
- Thrun, S., Pratt, L., 1998. *Learning to Learn.*
- Zeiler, Matthew D., Fergus, R., 2014. *Visualizing and Understanding Convolutional Networks.* In: Fleet, D., Pajdla, T., Schiele, B., Tuytelaars, T. (Eds.), *Computer Vision – ECCV 2014. Springer International Publishing, Cham, pp. 818–833.*
- Zeiler, Matthew D, Fergus, R., 2014. *Visualizing and Understanding Convolutional Networks. In: European Conference on Computer Vision, pp. 818–833.*

Chapter 5: Object Detection Models

- Everingham, M., Eslami, S.M.A., Van Gool, L., Williams, C.K.I., Winn, J., Zisserman, A., 2015. *The Pascal Visual Object Classes Challenge: A Retrospective. International Journal of Computer Vision 111, 98–136.*
- Girshick, R., 2015. *Fast R-CNN. arXiv:1504.08083 [cs].*
- Girshick, R., Donahue, J., Darrell, T., Malik, J., 2013. *Rich feature hierarchies for accurate object detection and semantic segmentation. arXiv:1311.2524 [cs].*
- Redmon, J., Divvala, S., Girshick, R., Farhadi, A., 2015. *You Only Look Once: Unified, Real-Time Object Detection. arXiv:1506.02640 [cs].*
- Redmon, J., Farhadi, A., 2016. YOLO9000: *Better, Faster, Stronger. arXiv:1612.08242 [cs].*
- Redmon, J., Farhadi, A., 2018. YOLOv3: *An Incremental Improvement. arXiv:1804.02767 [cs].*
- Ren, S., He, K., Girshick, R., Sun, J., 2015. *Faster R-CNN: Towards Real-Time Object Detection with Region Proposal Networks. arXiv:1506.01497 [cs].*

Chapter 6: Enhancing and Segmenting Images

- Bai, M., Urtasun, R., 2016. *Deep Watershed Transform for Instance Segmentation. arXiv:1611.08303 [cs].*
- Beyer, L., 2019. *Python wrapper to Philipp Krähenbühl's dense (fully connected) CRFs with gaussian edge potentials: lucasb-eyer/pydensecrf.*
- *Building Autoencoders in Keras [WWW Document]*, n.d. URL: `https://blog.keras.io/building-autoencoders-in-keras.html` (accessed January 18, 2019).

- Cordts, M., Omran, M., Ramos, S., Rehfeld, T., Enzweiler, M., Benenson, R., Franke, U., Roth, S., Schiele, B., 2016. *The Cityscapes Dataset for Semantic Urban Scene Understanding. In: 2016 IEEE Conference on Computer Vision and Pattern Recognition (CVPR). Presented at the 2016 IEEE Conference on Computer Vision and Pattern Recognition (CVPR), IEEE, Las Vegas, NV, USA, pp. 3213–3223.*
- Dice, L.R., 1945. *Measures of the Amount of Ecologic Association Between Species. Ecology 26, 297–302.*
- Drozdzal, M., Vorontsov, E., Chartrand, G., Kadoury, S., Pal, C., 2016. *The Importance of Skip Connections in Biomedical Image Segmentation. arXiv:1608.04117 [cs].*
- Dumoulin, V., Visin, F., 2016. *A Guide to Convolution Arithmetic for Deep Learning. arXiv:1603.07285 [cs, stat].*
- Guan, S., Khan, A., Sikdar, S., Chitnis, P.V., n.d. *Fully Dense UNet for 2D Sparse Photoacoustic Tomography Artifact Removal 8.*
- He, K., Gkioxari, G., Dollár, P., Girshick, R., 2017. *Mask R-CNN. arXiv:1703.06870 [cs].*
- *Kaggle. 2018 Data Science Bowl [WWW Document]*, n.d. URL: `https://kaggle.com/c/data-science-bowl-2018` (accessed February 8, 2019).
- Krähenbühl, P., Koltun, V., n.d. *Efficient Inference in Fully Connected CRFs with Gaussian Edge Potentials 9.*
- Lan, T., Li, Y., Murugi, J.K., Ding, Y., Qin, Z., 2018. *RUN: Residual U-Net for Computer-Aided Detection of Pulmonary Nodules without Candidate Selection. arXiv:1805.11856 [cs].*
- Li, X., Chen, H., Qi, X., Dou, Q., Fu, C.-W., Heng, P.A., 2017. *H-DenseUNet: Hybrid Densely Connected UNet for Liver and Tumor Segmentation from CT Volumes. arXiv:1709.07330 [cs].*
- Lin, T.-Y., Goyal, P., Girshick, R., He, K., Dollár, P., 2017. *Focal Loss for Dense Object Detection. arXiv:1708.02002 [cs].*
- Milletari, F., Navab, N., Ahmadi, S.-A., 2016. *V-Net: Fully Convolutional Neural Networks for Volumetric Medical Image Segmentation. In: 2016 Fourth International Conference on 3D Vision (3DV). Presented at the 2016 Fourth International Conference on 3D Vision (3DV), IEEE, Stanford, CA, USA, pp. 565–571.*
- Noh, H., Hong, S., Han, B., 2015. *Learning Deconvolution Network for Semantic Segmentation.* In: 2015 *IEEE International Conference on Computer Vision (ICCV). Presented at the 2015 ICCV, IEEE, Santiago, Chile, pp. 1520–1528.*
- Odena, A., Dumoulin, V., Olah, C., 2016. *Deconvolution and Checkerboard Artifacts. Distill 1, e3.*

- Ronneberger, O., Fischer, P., Brox, T., 2015. *U-Net: Convolutional Networks for Biomedical Image Segmentation. arXiv:1505.04597 [cs].*
- Shelhamer, E., Long, J., Darrell, T., 2017. *Fully Convolutional Networks for Semantic Segmentation. IEEE Transactions on Pattern Analysis and Machine Intelligence 39, 640–651.*
- Sørensen, T., 1948. *A method of establishing groups of equal amplitude in plant sociology based on similarity of species and its application to analyses of the vegetation on Danish commons. Biol. Skr. 5, 1–34.*
- *Unsupervised Feature Learning and Deep Learning Tutorial [WWW Document]*, n.d. URL: `http://ufldl.stanford.edu/tutorial/unsupervised/Autoencoders/` (accessed January 17, 2019).
- Zeiler, M.D., Fergus, R., 2013. *Visualizing and Understanding Convolutional Networks. arXiv:1311.2901 [cs].*
- Zhang, Z., Liu, Q., Wang, Y., 2018. *Road Extraction by Deep Residual U-Net. IEEE Geoscience and Remote Sensing Letters 15, 749–753.*

Chapter 7: Training on Complex and Scarce Datasets

- Bousmalis, K., Silberman, N., Dohan, D., Erhan, D., Krishnan, D., 2017a. *Unsupervised Pixel-Level Domain Adaptation with Generative Adversarial Networks. In: 2017 IEEE Conference on Computer Vision and Pattern Recognition (CVPR). Presented at the 2017 IEEE Conference on Computer Vision and Pattern Recognition (CVPR), IEEE, Honolulu, HI, pp. 95–104.*
- Bousmalis, K., Silberman, N., Dohan, D., Erhan, D., Krishnan, D., 2017b. *Unsupervised Pixel-Level Domain Adaptation with Generative Adversarial Networks. In: Proceedings of the IEEE Conference on Computer Vision and Pattern Recognition, pp. 3722–3731.*
- Brodeur, S., Perez, E., Anand, A., Golemo, F., Celotti, L., Strub, F., Rouat, J., Larochelle, H., Courville, A., 2017. *HoME: a Household Multimodal Environment. arXiv:1711.11017 [cs, eess].*
- Chang, A.X., Funkhouser, T., Guibas, L., Hanrahan, P., Huang, Q., Li, Z., Savarese, S., Savva, M., Song, S., Su, H., Xiao, J., Yi, L., Yu, F., 2015. ShapeNet: *An Information-Rich 3D Model Repository (No. arXiv:1512.03012 [cs.GR]). Stanford University – Princeton University – Toyota Technological Institute at Chicago.*

- Chen, Y., Li, W., Sakaridis, C., Dai, D., Van Gool, L., 2018. *Domain Adaptive Faster R-CNN for Object Detection in the Wild. In: 2018 IEEE/CVF Conference on Computer Vision and Pattern Recognition. Presented at the 2018 IEEE/CVF Conference on Computer Vision and Pattern Recognition (CVPR), IEEE, Salt Lake City, UT, USA, pp. 3339–3348.*
- Cordts, M., Omran, M., Ramos, S., Rehfeld, T., Enzweiler, M., Benenson, R., Franke, U., Roth, S., Schiele, B., 2016. *The Cityscapes Dataset for Semantic Urban Scene Understanding. In: Proceedings of the IEEE Conference on Computer Vision and Pattern Recognition, pp. 3213–3223.*
- Ganin, Y., Ustinova, E., Ajakan, H., Germain, P., Larochelle, H., Laviolette, F., Marchand, M., Lempitsky, V., 2017. *Domain-Adversarial Training of Neural Networks. In: Csurka, G. (Ed.), Domain Adaptation in Computer Vision Applications. Springer International Publishing, Cham, pp. 189–209.*
- Goodfellow, I., Pouget-Abadie, J., Mirza, M., Xu, B., Warde-Farley, D., Ozair, S., Courville, A., Bengio, Y., 2014. *Generative Adversarial Nets. In: Advances in Neural Information Processing Systems, pp. 2672–2680.*
- Gschwandtner, M., Kwitt, R., Uhl, A., Pree, W., 2011. *BlenSor: Blender Sensor Simulation Toolbox. In: International Symposium on Visual Computing, pp. 199–208.*
- Hernandez-Juarez, D., Schneider, L., Espinosa, A., Vázquez, D., López, A.M., Franke, U., Pollefeys, M., Moure, J.C., 2017. *Slanted Stixels: Representing San Francisco's Steepest Streets. arXiv:1707.05397 [cs].*
- Hoffman, J., Tzeng, E., Park, T., Zhu, J.-Y., Isola, P., Saenko, K., Efros, A.A., Darrell, T., 2017. *CyCADA: Cycle-Consistent Adversarial Domain Adaptation. arXiv:1711.03213 [cs].*
- Isola, P., Zhu, J.-Y., Zhou, T., Efros, A.A., 2017. *Image-to-Image Translation with Conditional Adversarial Networks. In: Proceedings of the IEEE Conference on Computer Vision and Pattern Recognition, pp. 1125–1134.*
- Kingma, D.P., Welling, M., 2013. *Auto-encoding Variational Bayes. arXiv preprint arXiv:1312.6114.*
- Long, M., Cao, Y., Wang, J., Jordan, M.I., n.d. *Learning Transferable Features with Deep Adaptation Networks 9.*
- Planche, B., Wu, Z., Ma, K., Sun, S., Kluckner, S., Lehmann, O., Chen, T., Hutter, A., Zakharov, S., Kosch, H., et al., 2017. *Depthsynth: Real-Time Realistic Synthetic Data Generation from CAD Models for 2.5D Recognition. In: 2017 International Conference on 3D Vision (3DV), pp.* 1–10.
- Planche, B., Zakharov, S., Wu, Z., Hutter, A., Kosch, H., Ilic, S., 2018. *Seeing Beyond Appearance—Mapping Real Images into Geometrical Domains for Unsupervised CAD-based Recognition. arXiv preprint arXiv:1810.04158.*

- *Protocol Buffers [WWW Document], n.d. Google Developers.* URL: `https://developers.google.com/protocol-buffers/` (accessed February 23, 2019).
- Radford, A., Metz, L., Chintala, S., 2015. *Unsupervised Representation Learning with Deep Convolutional Generative Adversarial Networks. arXiv:1511.06434 [cs].*
- Richter, S.R., Vineet, V., Roth, S., Koltun, V., 2016. *Playing for Data: Ground Truth from Computer Games. In: European Conference on Computer Vision, pp. 102–118.*
- Ros, G., Sellart, L., Materzynska, J., Vazquez, D., Lopez, A.M., 2016. *The SYNTHIA Dataset: A Large Collection of Synthetic Images for Semantic Segmentation of Urban Scenes. In: 2016 IEEE Conference on Computer Vision and Pattern Recognition (CVPR). Presented at the 2016 IEEE Conference on Computer Vision and Pattern Recognition (CVPR), IEEE, Las Vegas, NV, USA, pp. 3234–3243.*
- Rozantsev, A., Lepetit, V., Fua, P., 2015. *On Rendering Synthetic Images for Training an Object Detector. Computer Vision and Image Understanding 137, 24–37.*
- Tremblay, J., Prakash, A., Acuna, D., Brophy, M., Jampani, V., Anil, C., To, T., Cameracci, E., Boochoon, S., Birchfield, S., 2018. *Training Deep Networks with Synthetic Data: Bridging the Reality Gap by Domain Randomization. In: 2018 IEEE/CVF Conference on Computer Vision and Pattern Recognition Workshops (CVPRW). Presented at the 2018 IEEE/CVF CVPRW, IEEE, Salt Lake City, UT, pp. 1082–10828.*
- Tzeng, E., Hoffman, J., Saenko, K., Darrell, T., 2017. *Adversarial Discriminative Domain Adaptation. In: 2017 IEEE Conference on Computer Vision and Pattern Recognition (CVPR). Presented at the 2017 IEEE CVPR, IEEE, Honolulu, HI, pp. 2962–2971.*
- Zhu, J.-Y., Park, T., Isola, P., Efros, A.A., 2017. *Unpaired Image-to-Image Translation Using Cycle-Consistent Adversarial Networks. In: Proceedings of the IEEE International Conference on Computer Vision, pp. 2223–2232.*

Chapter 8: Video and Recurrent Neural Networks

- Britz, D., 2015. *Recurrent Neural Networks Tutorial, Part 3 – Backpropagation Through Time and Vanishing Gradients. WildML.*
- Brown, C., 2019. *repo for learning neural nets and related material: go2carter/nn-learn.*
- *Chung, J., Gulcehre, C., Cho, K., Bengio, Y., 2014. Empirical Evaluation of Gated Recurrent Neural Networks on Sequence Modeling. arXiv:1412.3555 [cs].*
- Hochreiter, S., Schmidhuber, J., 1997. *Long Short-Term Memory. Neural Computation 9, 1735–1780.*

- Lipton, Z.C., Berkowitz, J., Elkan, C., 2015. *A Critical Review of Recurrent Neural Networks for Sequence Learning. arXiv:1506.00019 [cs].*
- Soomro, K., Zamir, A.R., Shah, M., 2012. *UCF101: A Dataset of 101 Human Actions Classes From Videos in The Wild. arXiv:1212.0402 [cs].*

Chapter 9: Optimizing Models and Deploying on Mobile Devices

- Goodfellow, I.J., Erhan, D., Carrier, P.L., Courville, A., Mirza, M., Hamner, B., Cukierski, W., Tang, Y., Thaler, D., Lee, D.-H., Zhou, Y., Ramaiah, C., Feng, F., Li, R., Wang, X., Athanasakis, D., Shawe-Taylor, J., Milakov, M., Park, J., Ionescu, R., Popescu, M., Grozea, C., Bergstra, J., Xie, J., Romaszko, L., Xu, B., Chuang, Z., Bengio, Y., 2013. *Challenges in Representation Learning: A Report on Three Machine Learning Contests. arXiv:1307.0414 [cs, stat].*
- Hinton, G., Vinyals, O., Dean, J., 2015. *Distilling the Knowledge in a Neural Network. arXiv:1503.02531 [cs, stat].*
- Hoff, T., n.d. *The Technology Behind Apple Photos and the Future of Deep Learning and Privacy – High Scalability.*
- *Tencent, n.d. Tencent/PocketFlow: An Automatic Model Compression (AutoMC) Framework for Developing Smaller and Faster AI Applications.*

Assessments

Answers

The answers to the assessment questions found at the end of each chapter are shared in the following sections.

Chapter 1

1. **Which of the following tasks does not belong to computer vision: a web search of images similar to a query, a 3D scene reconstruction from image sequences, or the animation of a video character?**

   The *latter,* which instead belongs to the domain of **computer graphics.** Note, however, that increasingly, computer vision algorithms are helping artists to generate or animate content more efficiently (such as the *motion capture* methods, for instance, which record actors performing some actions and transfer the motions to virtual characters).

2. **Which activation function did the original perceptrons use?**

   The `step` function.

3. **Suppose we want to train a method to detect whether a handwritten digit is a 4. How should we adapt the network implemented in the chapter for this task?**

   In the chapter, we trained a classification network to identify pictures of digits from `0` to `9`. Therefore, the network had to predict the proper class among 10, hence, an output vector of 10 values (one for each class score/probability).

   In this question, we define a different classification task. We want the network to identify whether an image contains a *4* or *not a 4*. This is a **binary classification**, and the network should, therefore, be edited to *output only two values*.

Chapter 2

1. **What is Keras compared to TensorFlow? What is its purpose?**

   Keras was designed as a wrapper around other deep learning libraries to make development easier. TensorFlow is now fully integrated with Keras through `tf.keras`. It is best practice to use this module to create models in TensorFlow 2.

2. **Why does TensorFlow use graphs? How can they be created manually?**

   TensorFlow relies on graphs to ensure model performance and portability. In TensorFlow 2, the best way to create graphs manually is to employ the `tf.function` decorator.

3. **What is the difference between eager execution mode and lazy execution mode?**

   In lazy execution mode, no computation is performed until the user specifically asks for a result. In eager execution mode, every operation is run when it is defined. While the former can be faster thanks to graph optimizations, the latter is easier to use and easier to debug. In TensorFlow 2, lazy execution mode has been deprecated in favor of eager execution mode.

4. **How do you log information in TensorBoard, and how do you display it?**

   To log information in TensorBoard, you can use the `tf.keras.callbacks.TensorBoard` callback and pass it to the `.fit` method when training a model. To log information manually, you can use the `tf.summary` module. To display information, launch the following command:

   ```
   $ tensorboard --logdir ./model_logs
   ```

   Here, `model_logs` is the directory where TensorBoard logs are stored. This command will output a URL. Navigate to this URL to monitor training.

5. **What are the main differences between TensorFlow 1 and 2?**

   TensorFlow 2 focuses on simplicity by removing graph management from the hands of the user. It also uses eager execution by default, making models easier to debug. Nevertheless, it still maintains its performance thanks to AutoGraph and `tf.function`. It also integrates deeply with Keras, making model creation easier than ever.

Chapter 3

1. **Why does the output of a convolutional layer have a smaller width and height than the input, unless it is padded?**

   The spatial dimensions of the output of a convolutional layer represent the number of valid positions the kernels could take when sliding over the input tensors, vertically and horizontally. Since kernels span over $k \times k$ pixels (if square), the number of positions they can take over the input image without being partially out of it can only be equal to (if $k = 1$), or less than, the image dimensions.

   This is expressed by the equations presented in the chapter, to compute the output dimensions based on the layer's hyper parameters.

2. **What would be the output of a max-pooling layer with a receptive field of (2, 2) and a stride of 2 on the input matrix in Figure 3-6?**

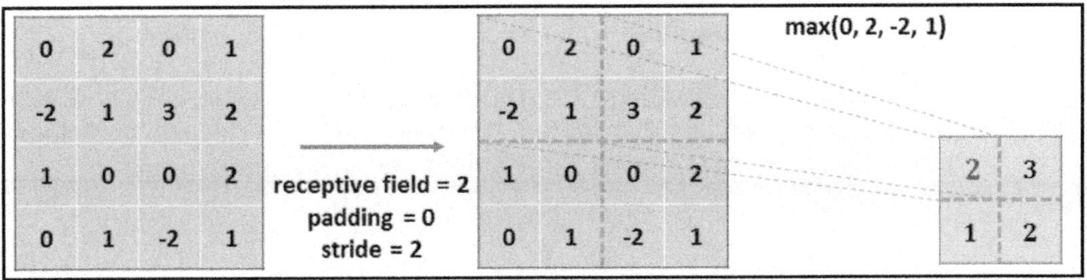

3. **How could LeNet-5 be implemented using the Keras Functional API in a non-object-oriented manner ?**

    The code is as follows:

    ```
    from tensorflow.keras import Model
    from tensorflow.keras.layers import Inputs, Conv2D,
    MaxPooling2D, Flatten, Dense

    # "Layer" representing the network's inputs:
    inputs = Input(shape=input_shape)
    # First block (conv + max-pool):
    conv1 = Conv2D(6, kernel_size=5, padding='same',
    activation='relu')(inputs)
    max_pool1 = MaxPooling2D(pool_size=(2, 2))(conv1)
    # 2nd block:
    conv2 = Conv2D(16, kernel_size=5, activation='relu')(max_pool1)
    max_pool2 = MaxPooling2D(pool_size=(2, 2))(conv2)
    # Dense layers:
    flatten = Flatten()(max_pool2)
    dense1 = Dense(120, activation='relu')(flatten)
    dense2 = Dense(84, activation='relu')(dense1)
    dense3 = Dense(num_classes, activation='softmax')(dense2)

    lenet5_model = Model(inputs=inputs, outputs=dense3)
    ```

4. **How does L1/L2 regularization affect the networks?**

    L1 regularization forces the layers to which it is applied to bring toward zero the values of the parameters linked to less important features; that is, to ignore less meaningful features (such as features tied to dataset noise).

    L2 regularization compels the layers to keep their variables low, and, hence, more homogeneously distributed. It prevents the network from developing a small set of parameters with large values that overly influence its predictions.

Chapter 4

1. **Which TensorFlow Hub module can be used to instantiate an Inception classifier for ImageNet?**

    The model at `https://tfhub.dev/google/tf2-preview/inception_v3/classification/2` can be directly used to classify ImageNet-like images, as this classification model was pretrained over this dataset.

2. **How can the first three residual macro-blocks of a ResNet-50 model from Keras Applications be frozen?**

   The code is as follows:

```
freeze_num = 3
# Looking at `resnet50.summary()`, we could observe that the
1st layer of the 4th macro-block is named "res5[...]":
break_layer_name = 'res{}'.format(freeze_num + 2)
for layer in resnet50_finetune.layers:
   if break_layer_name in layer.name:
        break
    if isinstance(layer, tf.keras.layers.Conv2D):
        # If the layer is a convolution, and isn't after
        # the 1st layer not to train:
        layer.trainable = False
```

3. **When is transfer learning discouraged?**

   Transfer learning may not be beneficial when the *domains* are too dissimilar and the target data has a structure that is completely different to the source data structure. As mentioned in the chapter, while CNNs can be applied to images, text, and audio files, transferring weights trained for one modality to another is not encouraged.

Chapter 5

1. **What is the difference between a bounding box, an anchor box, and a ground truth box?**

   A **bounding box** is the smallest rectangle enclosing an object. An **anchor box** is a bounding box with a specific size. For each position in the image grid, there are usually several anchor boxes with different aspect ratios—square, vertical rectangle, and horizontal rectangle. By refining the size and the position of the anchor box, the object detection model generates predictions. A **ground truth box** is a bounding box corresponding to a specific object in the training set. If a model is trained perfectly, it generates predictions that are very close to ground truth boxes.

2. **What is the role of the feature extractor?**

   A feature extractor is a CNN that converts an image into a feature volume. The feature volume is usually smaller in dimension than the input image and contains meaningful features that can be passed to the remainder of the network in order to generate predictions.

3. **Which of the following models should you choose: YOLO or Faster R-CNN?**

   If speed is the priority, you should pick YOLO as it is the fastest architecture. If accuracy is paramount, you should choose Faster R-CNN as it generates the best predictions.

4. **When are anchor boxes used?**

   Before anchor boxes, box prediction dimensions were generated using the output of the network. As object sizes vary (a person usually fits in a vertical rectangle, while a car fits in a horizontal rectangle), anchor boxes were introduced. Using this technique, each anchor box is able to specialize for one object ratio, leading to more precise predictions.

Chapter 6

1. **What is the particularity of autoencoders?**

   Autoencoders are encoders-decoders whose **inputs and targets are the same**. Their goal is to properly encode and then decode images without impacting their quality, despite their *bottleneck* (that is, their latent space of lower dimensionality).

2. **Which classification architecture are fully convolutional networks (FCNs) based on?**

   FCNs use **VGG-16** as the feature extractor.

3. **How can a semantic segmentation model be trained so that it does not ignore small classes?**

   Per-class weighing can be applied to the cross-entropy loss, thereby penalizing more heavy pixels from smaller classes that are misclassified. Losses that are not affected by the classes' proportions can also be used instead, such as **Dice**.

Chapter 7

1. **Given an** `a = [1, 2, 3]` **tensor and a** `b = [4, 5, 6]` **tensor, how can a** `tf.data` **pipeline that would output each value separately, from** `1` **to** `6`**, be built?**

   The code is as follows:

   ```
   dataset_a = tf.data.Dataset.from_tensor_slices(a)
   dataset_b = tf.data.Dataset.from_tensor_slices(b)
   dataset_ab = dataset_a.concatenate(dataset_b)
   for element in dataset_ab:
       print(element) # will print 1, then 2, ... until 6
   ```

2. **According to the documentation of** `tf.data.Options`**, how can you ensure that a dataset always returns samples in the same order, run after run?**

   The `.experimental_deterministic` attribute of `tf.data.Options` should be set to `True` before being passed to the dataset.

3. **Which domain adaptation methods that we introduced can be used when no target annotations are available for training?**

   Unsupervised domain adaptation methods should be considered, such as *Learning Transferable Features with Deep Adaptation Networks*, by Mingsheng Long et al. (from Tsinghua University, China), or **Domain-Adversarial Neural Networks** (**DANN**), by Yaroslav Ganin et al. (from Skoltech).

4. **What role does the discriminator play in GANs?**

   It plays against the generator, trying to distinguish fake images from real images. The discriminator can be considered as a **trainable loss function** to guide the generator—the generator tries to minimize how *correct* the discriminator is, with both networks becoming better and better at their task as the training proceeds.

Chapter 8

1. **What are the main advantages of LSTMs over the simple RNN architecture?**

   LSTMs suffer less from gradient vanishing and are more capable of storing long-term relationships in recurrent data. While they require more computing power, this usually leads to better predictions.

2. **How is a CNN used when it is applied before the LSTM?**

   The CNN acts as a feature extractor and reduces the dimensionality of the input data. By applying a pretrained CNN, we extract meaningful features from the input images. The LSTM trains faster since those features have a much smaller dimensionality than the input image.

3. **What is vanishing gradient and why does it occur? Why is it a problem?**

   When backpropagating the error in RNNs, we need to go back through the time steps as well. If there are many time steps, the information slowly fades away due to the way in which the gradient is computed. It is a problem since it makes it harder for the network to learn how to generate good predictions.

4. **What are some of the workarounds for the vanishing gradient problem?**

   One workaround is to use truncated backpropagation, which is a technique described in the chapter. Another option is to use LSTMs instead of simple RNNs, as they suffer less from gradient vanishing.

Chapter 9

1. **When measuring a model's inference speed, should you measure with single or multiple images?**

   Multiple images should be used to avoid measure bias.

2. **Is a model with `float32` weights larger or smaller than one with `float16` weights?**

   `Float16` weights use about half the space of `float32` weights. On compatible devices, they can also be faster.

3. **On iOS devices, should you use Core ML or TensorFlow Lite? What about Android devices?**

    On iOS devices, we recommend using Core ML where possible as it is available natively and is tightly integrated with the hardware. On Android devices, TensorFlow Lite should be used as there is no alternative.

4. **What are the benefits and limitations of running a model in the browser?**

    It does not require any installation on the user side and does not require computing power on the server side, making the application almost infinitely scalable.

5. **What is the most important requirement for embedded devices running deep learning algorithms?**

    On top of computing power, the most important requirement is power consumption, since most embedded devices run on batteries.

Other Books You May Enjoy

If you enjoyed this book, you may be interested in these other books by Packt:

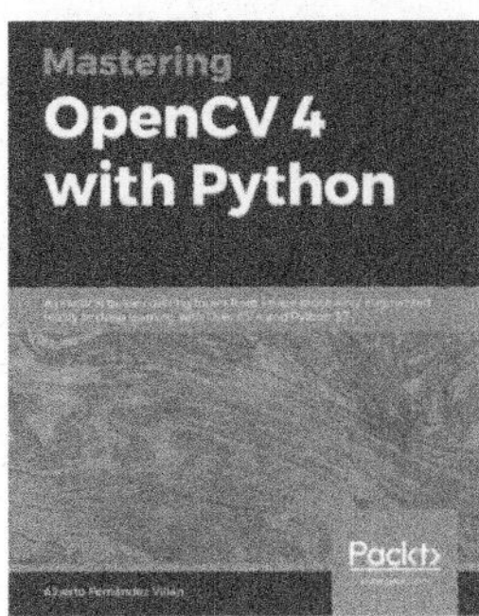

Mastering OpenCV 4 with Python
Alberto Fernández Villán

ISBN: 9781789344912

- Handle files and images, and explore various image processing techniques
- Explore image transformations, including translation, resizing, and cropping
- Gain insights into building histograms
- Brush up on contour detection, filtering, and drawing
- Work with Augmented Reality to build marker-based and markerless applications
- Work with the main machine learning algorithms in OpenCV
- Explore the deep learning Python libraries and OpenCV deep learning capabilities
- Create computer vision and deep learning web applications

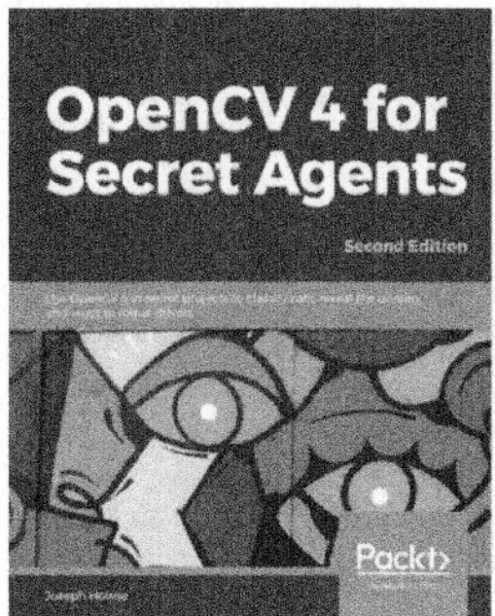

OpenCV 4 for Secret Agents - Second Edition
Joseph Howse

ISBN: 9781789345360

- Detect motion and recognize gestures to control a smartphone game
- Detect car headlights and estimate their distance
- Detect and recognize human and cat faces to trigger an alarm
- Amplify motion in a real-time video to show heartbeats and breaths
- Make a physics simulation that detects shapes in a real-world drawing
- Build OpenCV 4 projects in Python 3 for desktops and Raspberry Pi
- Develop OpenCV 4 Android applications in Android Studio and Unity

Leave a review - let other readers know what you think

Please share your thoughts on this book with others by leaving a review on the site that you bought it from. If you purchased the book from Amazon, please leave us an honest review on this book's Amazon page. This is vital so that other potential readers can see and use your unbiased opinion to make purchasing decisions, we can understand what our customers think about our products, and our authors can see your feedback on the title that they have worked with Packt to create. It will only take a few minutes of your time, but is valuable to other potential customers, our authors, and Packt. Thank you!

Index

3

3D databases
  rise 243, 244

4

4-step alternating training 182

A

action recognition 18
adaptive moment estimation (Adam) 105
adversarial 252
AlexNet 28
anchor boxes 162, 163
argmax
  using 204
Artificial Intelligence (AI) 21
artificial neural networks (ANNs)
  about 29
  deep learning 27
  rebranding 27
atrous convolution 198
auto-encoders (AEs) 188
auto-labeling methods 253
average precision (AP) 156
average-pooling layers 89

B

backbone model 160
backpropagation 45, 267
backpropagation through time (BPTT) 269
batch normalization
  about 111, 112
  Keras methods 112
  reference 112
  TensorFlow methods 112
binary cross-entropy (BCE) 42
Blender
  reference 247
BlenSor
  reference 247
bottleneck features 144
bottlenecks 128
boundaries
  respecting 210, 211
bounding box 152
bounding box precision 153

C

C++ 53
candidate cell state 272
cardinality 156
cell state 270
central fovea 95
chain rule 44
channel pruning 294
characteristic images 22
characteristic vectors 22
Cityscapes
  reference 244
class imbalance 206
class precision 153
classification 177
closure function 282
cloud computing 28
cls 178
CNN architectures
  about 118
  depth, increasing of feature maps 121
  fully connected layers, replacing with convolutions 122
  large convolutions, replacing with multiple smaller ones 120
  residual network (ResNet) 134

standardizing 120
VGG 118
CNN operations
about 80
convolutional layers 80
fully connected layers 92
pooling layers 89
codes 187
Common Objects in Context (COCO) 156
computer graphics 245
computer vision model
Keras, using 54
computer vision
about 12, 13
applications 13
applying, to videos 273
content recognition 13
content-aware image edition 19, 20
history 20
local features, hand-crafting 21, 22
machine learning, adding 23, 24
perception task, underestimating 21
scene reconstruction 20
tasks 13
video analysis 17
computer-aided design (CAD) 244
concrete function 67
Conditional GANs (cGANs) 260
conditional random fields (CRFs)
about 208
post-processing with 208
content recognition
about 13
instance segmentation 16
object classification 13, 14
object detection 15
object identification 14
object localization 15
object segmentation 16
pose estimation 17
content-aware image edition 19, 20
ConvNets 77
convolution operation 81
convolutional encoders-decoders
about 192
atrous convolution 197, 198
dilated convolution 197, 198
dilating 192
example architectures 199
fully convolutional networks (FCNs) 199, 200
resizing 196, 197
transposed convolution (deconvolution) 192, 194
transposing 192
U-Net architecture 201
unpooling 192, 195, 196
upsampling 196, 197
convolutional layers
about 80
concept 80, 81
hyperparameters 83, 84
properties 82, 83
TensorFlow/Keras methods 85, 86, 88
convolutional neural networks (CNNs)
about 25, 77, 79, 80, 117, 186, 263
discovering 77
effective receptive field (ERF) 93
for multidimensional data 78
implementing 96
with TensorFlow 95
Core ML
about 302
used, for running model on iOS devices 302
cross-entropy loss
using 205
cross-validation 106
CUDA 53
custom Estimator
training 70

D

data augmentation
about 237
considerations 239, 240
need for 238, 239
overview 237
with scale jittering 121, 122
data scarcity
dealing with 237
data

loading 282
preparing 54, 55
serving 220
datasets
about 223
augmenting, with conditional GANs 260, 261
caching 236, 237
generating, with GANs 254
generating, with VAEs 254
merging 230
monitoring 235
performance statistics, aggregating 235, 236
reusing 235, 236, 237
structuring 228, 229
transforming 228
decoder 186
deconvnet 195
deconvolution 134, 192, 195
deep auto-encoders (DAEs) 192
deep learning models
examples 311
deep learning
about 24, 27
era 28
failures 24
internet, using 26
of artificial neural networks 27
perceptron, falling 25
perceptron, rising 25
too heavy to scale 25
deep-n-wide models 69
denoising auto-encoders 190
dense 55
densely connected 92
DenseNet models 138
depth regression 189
depthwise convolutions 301
depthwise separable 301
Dice coefficient 207
dilated convolutions 192, 198
dilation 193
directed acyclic graph (DAC) 59
discriminative models
versus generative models 254, 255
discriminator 258
domain adaptation
about 143
leveraging 249
domain randomization 253, 254
Domain-Adversarial Neural Networks (DANN) 251
domains 143
dropout
about 110, 111
Keras methods 111
TensorFlow methods 111

E

eager execution 60
early stopping 106
edge computing 295
effective receptive field (ERF)
about 93, 94, 95, 120
formula 95
element-wise multiplication 271
encoder 186
encoders-decoders
about 186, 187
auto-encoding 188
images, transforming with 186
purpose 189, 190
semantic segmentation, objecting with 204
epoch 46
Estimated Time of Arrival (ETA) 57
Estimator API
about 53
using 69
exploding gradient 130
Extract, Transform, and Load (ETL) 222
extraction 222

F

Facebook AI Research (FAIR) 213
Facial Expression Recognition (FER)
about 300, 301
URL 300
false negatives (FN) 154
false positives (FP) 154
Faster R-CNN, TensorFlow object detection API
pre-trained model 183
training, on custom dataset 183

Faster R-CNN
about 158, 212
architecture 175, 177, 178
classification 177
loss 182
regimen, training 182
Region Proposal Network (RPN) 175, 176
ROI pooling 178, 179
TensorFlow object detection API 183
training 180
Faster Region with Convolutional Neural Networks (Faster R-CNN)
about 174
instance segmentation model, building from 213, 214
FCN-32s 199
feature extractor 160
feature maps 83
feature volume 83
features
about 21
extracting, from videos 276, 277, 278, 279, 280
filters 82
Floating Point 16 (FP16) 290
floating window 153
fractionally strided convolutions 195
frame interpolation 274
frames per second (FPS) 157
frozen graphs
using 298
full YOLO loss 173
fully connected (FC) layers
about 55, 78, 92, 122, 127
TensorFlow/Keras methods 93
usage, in CNNs 92, 93
fully connected networks
issues 78
lack of spatial reasoning 78
number of parameters 78
fully convolutional networks (FCNs) 122, 199, 200
functional API 98

G

generative adversarial networks (GANs) 219, 258, 259, 260
generative models
leveraging 249
versus discriminative models 254, 255
generative tasks 190
global minimum 102
Google Cloud
reference 75
GoogLeNet 124
GoogLeNet architecture, contributions
1 x 1 convolutions, using as bottlenecks 128, 129
details, capturing with Inception modules 127, 128
pooling, instead of fully-connecting 129
vanishing gradient, fighting with intermediary losses 129
GoogLeNet architecture
about 125, 126
bottlenecks, popularizing 127
implementing, in Keras 130
implementing, in TensorFlow 130
inception module, with Keras Functional API 130, 131, 132
Keras model 133
larger blocks, popularizing 127
motivation 124, 125
overview 124
TensorFlow Hub 132, 133
TensorFlow model 132, 133
gradient descent
about 43
single hyperparameter, for heterogeneous parameters 102
suboptimal local minima 101, 102
trade-off, training 100
gradient explosion 269
gradient tape
used, for backpropagating error 63, 64
gradient vanishing 269
graph 59
graph optimizer 61
graphics processing unit (GPU) 26
ground truth 171

H

Hadamard product 271
hyperbolic tangent 31

I

identity mapping 137
image classification 13
image denoising
  application 191
  example 191
  fully-connected auto-encoder 191
image descriptors 152
image feature vector 133
image segmentation, for self-driving cars
  about 209
  exemplary solution 210
  task presentation 209
image super-resolution
  about 190
  application, for upscaling images 203
  example 202
  FCN, implementing 202
ImageNet Large Scale Visual Recognition Challenge (ILSVRC)
  about 28, 118
  reference 28
images
  augmenting, for autonomous driving application 242, 243
  augmenting, with TensorFlow 241
  parsing 226, 227
  TensorFlow Image module 241
  transforming, with encoders-decoders 186
Inception network 124
indicator function 172
inference 160, 286
input 30
input function
  using 70
input pipelines
  extracting, from files 225
  extracting, from inputs 225
  extracting, from NumPy data 224
  extracting, from tensors 224
  extracting, from text files 224
  extracting, from TFRecord files 224
  monitoring 231
  operations, fusing 233
  optimizing 231
  optimizing, best practices 231
  options, passing to ensure global properties 234
  parallelizing 231, 233
  prefetching 231
  setting up 224
instance masks
  post-processing 211, 212
instance segmentation model
  building, from Faster-RCNN 213, 214
instance segmentation
  about 16
  difficulties 210
instance tracking 18
Intersection-over-Union (IoU) 207
intrinsic parameters 246

J

Jaccard index 156

K

Keras API
  reference 123
Keras callbacks 65, 66
Keras model
  reference 133
Keras
  about 53, 54, 58
  Functional API 65
  implementing 97, 98
  layers 64
  model, converting from 302, 303, 306
  models 64
  Sequential API 65
  using, for computer vision model 54
  working with 52
kernels 82
knowledge distillation 293
Kullback–Leibler divergence 257

L

L1 regularization
  principles 106
L2 loss 42
label map
  about 204
  decoding 204, 205
labels
  parsing 226, 227
latency 286, 296
latent space 186
layering, neurons
  implementation, in Python 35, 36
  mathematical model 34, 35
lazy execution 60
learning rate 45
learning rate decay 101
least absolute shrinkage and selection operator (LASSO) regularizer 107
LeNet-5 architecture 96, 97
loading 231
local features 22
logits 97
Long Short-Term Memory (LSTM)
  about 270
  inner workings 271, 272, 273
  principles 270
  training 281
  videos, classifying with 276

M

machine learning 23, 24
Mask R-CNN 212
Math Kernel Library for Deep Neural Networks (MKL-DNN) 290
max-pooling layers 89
max-unpooling 195
mean Average Precision (mAP) 156
mean-absolute error (MAE) 43
mean-square error (MSE) 43, 257
MobileNet 301
MobileNet, convolutions
  depthwise convolutions 301
  pointwise convolutions 301
  types 301
model averaging 122
model distillation 292, 293
model inference speed, improving approaches
  input, optimizing 291
  optimizing, for hardware 289
  optimizing, on CPUs 290
  Optimizing, on GPUs 290
  optimizing, on specialized hardware 290
  post-processing, optimizing 291, 292
model inference speed
  improving 289
  latency, measuring 287
  measuring 286
  tracing tools, using to computational performance 287, 288, 289
model size, reducing techniques
  about 293
  channel pruning 294
  quantization 294
  weight sparsification 294
model surgery, transfer learning with TensorFlow and Keras
  grafting layers 148
  layers, removing 147
model, speeding techniques
  about 292
  interpolating 292
  model distillation 292, 293
  tracking 292
model
  about 53
  arguments 56
  building 55, 56
  converting, from Keras 302, 303, 306
  converting, from TensorFlow 302, 303, 306
  converting, to TensorFlow.js format 309, 310
  defining 281
  layer 55
  loading 304, 306, 307
  optimizing 286
  performance 57
  running 73
  running, on devices 311
  running, on Google Cloud 75

running, on local machine 74
running, on remote machine 74
training 56, 283
training, to be robust to domain changes 249
using 304, 307, 308, 309, 310, 311
models on-device
deploying 301
modern network optimizers
about 100
gradient descent challenges 100
Modified National Institute of Standards and Technology (MNIST)
about 37, 54
reusing 99
momentum 102
morphological functions
using 211
motion continuity 18
motion estimation 19

N

Nadam 105
Nash equilibrium 260
Nesterov accelerated gradient (NAG) 104
Network in Network (NIN) 127
neural engine 302
neural network (NN)
about 192
applying, to classification 36
building 29
implementing 38, 40
learning strategies 40
loss, back-propagating 43, 44, 46
loss, evaluating 42
neurons, imitating 29
overfitting 49
task, setting up 37, 38
teaching time 42
teaching, to classify 46, 48
training 40
training considerations 49
underfitting 49
working with 29
neurons
biological inspiration 29
imitating 29
implementation 32
layering 33
mathematical model 30, 31, 32
Non-Maximum Suppression (NMS) 167, 168, 291
normalization terms 181

O

object classification 13, 14
object detection models, performance
average precision 156
average precision threshold 156, 157
evaluating 153
mean average precision 156
precision 154
precision-recall curve 154, 155
recall 154
object detection
about 15, 151, 152
algorithm 157
application 152
history 152, 153
to instance segmentation 212
object identification 14
object localization 15, 152
object segmentation
about 16
to instance segmentation 210
object tracking
used 292
on-device computer vision
considerations 297
frozen graph, generating 298, 299
particularities 297
preprocessing, requisites 299
SavedModel, generating 298
on-device machine learning, benefits
about 296
cost 296
latency 296
privacy 296
on-device machine learning
about 294, 295
consideration 295
limitations 297

one-hot encoding 281
OpenCL 27
OpenCV
  reference 23
  URL 241
OpenGL
  URL 246
operation 59
optimization algorithms
  about 102
  Ada family 104, 105
  momentum algorithms 102, 103, 104
  reference link 105
overfitting 49

P

parallelizing 231
PASCAL Visual Object Classes (Pascal VOC) 156
perception 21
perceptron 25
pointwise convolutions 301
pooling layers
  about 89
  concept 89, 90
  hyperparameters 89, 90
  TensorFlow/Keras methods 90, 91, 92
pose estimation 17
pre-made Estimators
  availability 69
precision 154
precision-recall curve 154, 155
Principal Component Analysis (PCA) 22
priors 163
PyOpenGL
  reference 247
Python decorator 62
Python Imaging Library
  URL 241
PyTorch
  reference 98

Q

quantization 294

R

realism gap
  about 248
  issues 248
recall 153, 154
receptive field (RF) 79, 94
rectified linear activation units (ReLUs) 28, 32, 118
recurrent neural networks (RNNs)
  about 263, 264, 266, 267
  formalism 264, 265
Region of Interest (RoI) 175
region of interest pooling (RoI pooling) 178
Regions with Convolutional Neural Networks (R-CNN) 151
regularization 105
regularization methods
  batch normalization 111
  dropout 110
  early stopping 106
  Keras, implementing 107, 108, 109
  L1 regularization 106
  L2 regularization 106
  methods 105
  TensorFlow, implementing 107, 108, 109
reinforcement learning 41
reparameterization trick 256
residual network (ResNet) 134
residual path 138
ResNet architecture, contributions
  going, ultra-deep 138
  residual function, estimating instead of mapping 137
ResNet architecture
  about 136, 137
  contributions 137
  implementing, in Keras 138
  implementing, in TensorFlow 138
  Keras model 140
  motivation 135
  overview 135
  residual blocks, with Keras Functional API 139
  TensorFlow Hub 139
  TensorFlow model 139
rgs 178

ridge regularization 107
RMSprop 105
RNN cell 265
RNN weights
  backpropagation through time (BPTT) 268, 269
  learning 267
  truncated propagation 269
RoI Align layer 214
RoI max-pooling 179
ROI pooling layer 178, 179
RPN loss 181, 182
RPN
  training 180

S

samples
  editing 228
  transforming 226
sampling 273
SavedModel 298
Scale Invariant Feature Transform (SIFT) 22
scale jittering
  about 121
  data augmentation with 121
scene extraction 274
scene reconstruction 20
scikit-learn 57
segmentation losses
  training with 206, 207, 208
segmentation metrics
  training with 206, 207, 208
selective search 175
selective training, transfer learning with TensorFlow and Keras
  layers, freezing 149
  pre-trained parameters, restoring 148, 149
self-supervised learning 188
semantic segmentation
  about 189, 203
  applying, to bounding boxes 212
  objecting, with encoders-decoders 204
shortcut 138
sigmoid function 31
skip 138
smart image upscaling 190
soft Dice 208
soft target 293
softmax
  using 204
spatial information 79
state 264
step function 31
stochastic gradient descent (SGD) 46, 99
strategies, neural network
  reinforcement learning 41
  supervised learning 40
  unsupervised learning 41
subnetworks 125
suboptimal local minima 101
supervised domain adaptation 250
supervised learning 40
Support vector machines (SVMs) 23
synthetic data
  benefits 244, 245
synthetic datasets
  rendering 243
synthetic images
  about 244
  generating, from 3D models 245
  post-processing 247
  rendering, from 3D models 246, 247
SYNTHIA
  URL 244
Sørensen–Dice coefficient 207

T

t-SNE
  using 187
tensor 58
Tensor object
  rank 59
  shape 59
  type 59
Tensor Processing Unit (TPU) 68
TensorBoard 71, 72
TensorFlow 1 code
  concepts 318
  layers 317
  migrating 314
  model 317

placeholders 315
sessions 314
variable management 316, 317
TensorFlow 1.x
automatic migration 313
migrating from 313
TensorFlow 2
about 58
graphs, creating in 61
variables 67, 68
working with 52
TensorFlow Addons 70, 72
TensorFlow AutoGraph 62, 63
TensorFlow Data API
about 220
data-hungry methods 220, 221
inspiration, from lazy structures 221
intuitions 220
TensorFlow Data pipelines
API interface 223, 224
Extract, Transform, and Load (ETL) 222, 223
structure 221
TensorFlow Data Validation 72
TensorFlow ecosystem
about 70
model, running 73
TensorBoard 71
TensorFlow Addons 72
TensorFlow Extended 72
TensorFlow Lite 73
TensorFlow.js 73
TensorFlow Extended (TFX) 70, 72
TensorFlow Graphics 248
TensorFlow Lite
about 73
used, for running model on Android 305
TensorFlow Model Analysis 73
TensorFlow Serving 73
TensorFlow Transform 72
TensorFlow.js format
model, converting to 309, 310
TensorFlow.js
about 73
used, for running model in browser 309
TensorFlow
about 52
architecture 52, 53
distribute strategies 68
graph 59, 60
implementing 97, 98
lazy execution, versus eager execution 60, 61
model, converting from 302, 303, 306
reference 85, 111
tf.function
about 62, 63
working with 66, 67
TFRecord files
parsing 227, 228
Theano 53
threshold of confidence 154
trace tool
using, to computational performance 287
training 160
training process
refining 99
transfer learning, with Keras
model surgery 147
selective training 148
transfer learning, with TensorFlow
model surgery 147
selective training 148
transfer learning
about 141
CNN knowledge, transferring 144
human inspiration 141
leveraging 140
motivation 142, 143
overview 141
use-cases 144
with Keras 146
with TensorFlow 146
transposed convolution 134, 192
true positives (TP) 154
truncated propagation 269

U

U-Net architecture 201
underfitting 49
unpooling 134, 192, 195

unsupervised domain adaptation 250, 251, 252, 253
unsupervised learning 41, 188
upsampling 197
use-cases, transfer learning
  dissimilar task, with abundant training data 146
  dissimilar task, with limited training data 146
  similar task, with abundant training data 145
  similar task, with limited training data 145

V

vanishing gradient 130
variables
  in TensorFlow 2 67, 68
variational autoencoders (VAEs) 219, 255, 256, 257, 258
VGG architecture
  about 119
  implementing, in Keras 123
  implementing, in TensorFlow 123
  Keras model 123, 124
  motivation 118, 119
  overview 118
  TensorFlow model 123
VGG-16 120
VGG-19 120
video analysis
  about 17
  action recognition 18
  instance tracking 18
  motion estimation 19
videos
  classifying 273
  classifying, with LSTM 274, 276
  computer vision, applying to 273
  features, extracting from 276, 277, 278, 279, 280
vispy
  reference 247
Visual Geometry Group (VGG) architecture 118

W

watershed transforms 212
weight sparsification 294

Y

You Only Look Once (YOLO)
  about 151, 157, 158
  anchor boxes 162, 163
  anchor boxes, refining 164, 165
  backbone 160, 161
  backbone, training 170
  box loss, bounding 171
  boxes, post-processing 165, 166, 167
  classification loss 173
  concepts 158, 159
  inferring with 160
  layers output 161, 162
  limitations 158
  loss 170, 171
  NMS 167, 168
  object confidence loss 172
  strengths 158
  summarizing 168, 169
  training 169
  training techniques 173

Z

ZFNet architecture 134

Printed in Great Britain
by Amazon

36765325R00209